Inherit the Holy Mountain

Inherit the Holy Mountain

Religion and the Rise of
American Environmentalism

MARK R. STOLL

OXFORD
UNIVERSITY PRESS

OXFORD
UNIVERSITY PRESS

Oxford University Press is a department of the University of
Oxford. It furthers the University's objective of excellence in research,
scholarship, and education by publishing worldwide.

Oxford New York
Auckland Cape Town Dar es Salaam Hong Kong Karachi
Kuala Lumpur Madrid Melbourne Mexico City Nairobi
New Delhi Shanghai Taipei Toronto

With offices in
Argentina Austria Brazil Chile Czech Republic France Greece
Guatemala Hungary Italy Japan Poland Portugal Singapore
South Korea Switzerland Thailand Turkey Ukraine Vietnam

Oxford is a registered trademark of Oxford University Press
in the UK and certain other countries.

Published in the United States of America by
Oxford University Press
198 Madison Avenue, New York, NY 10016

Library of Congress Cataloging-in-Publication Data
Stoll, Mark, 1954–
Inherit the holy mountain : religion and the rise of American environmentalism / Mark R. Stoll.
    pages cm
Includes bibliographical references and index.
ISBN 978–0–19–023086–9 (cloth : alk. paper)
1. Nature—Religious aspects—Christianity.   2. Environmental protection—Religious
aspects—Christianity.   3. Environmentalism—United States—Religious aspects—History.
4. Environmental protection—United States—Public opinion—History.   I. Title.
BR115.N3S76 2015
261.8′80973—dc23
2014037389

9 8 7 6 5 4 3 2 1
Printed in the United States of America
on acid-free paper

For Alex and Erin

But he that putteth his trust in me shall possess the land, and shall inherit my holy mountain.

—ISAIAH 57:13

These achievements are more glorious than the proudest triumphs of war, but, thus far, they give but faint hope that we shall yet make full atonement for our spendthrift waste of the bounties of nature.

—GEORGE PERKINS MARSH

The foregoing generations beheld God and nature face to face; we, through their eyes. Why should not we also enjoy an original relation to the universe?

—RALPH WALDO EMERSON

Underlying the beauty of the spectacle [of life] there is meaning and significance. It is the elusiveness of that meaning that haunts us, that sends us again and again into the natural world where the key to the riddle is hidden.

—RACHEL CARSON

Original sin, the true original sin, is the blind destruction for the sake of greed of this natural paradise which lies all around us.

—EDWARD ABBEY

The drive toward perpetual expansion—or personal freedom—is basic to the human spirit. But to sustain it we need the most delicate, knowing stewardship of the living world that can be devised.

—EDWARD O. WILSON

The way we eat represents our most profound engagement with the natural world. . . . How and what we eat determines to a great extent the use we make of the world—and what is to become of it.

—MICHAEL POLLAN

Contents

List of Figures

Acknowledgments

FOR A PROJECT so long in the making, thanking everyone who helped along the way is a happy but daunting undertaking. I must first thank Laurence Moore, who read the sprawling first draft and made very helpful comments. Other people who read portions of the manuscript at various stages and offered their thoughts are John Opie, Aliza Wong, Julianne Warren, Donald Worster, and John McNeill. Linda Lear and David Lowenthal responded to my interpretations of Rachel Carson and George Perkins Marsh. Two anonymous reviewers gave valuable comments.

At the kind invitation of many people, I publicly presented material that went into the book: Alberto Vieira in Madeira in 1999; Bill Forbes at the Society of American Foresters meeting in Portland, Oregon, in 1999; Christian Pfister in Bern, Switzerland, in 2001; Franz-Josef Brüggemeier in Freiburg, Germany, in 2001; Verena Winiwarter at the Institut für interdisziplinäre Forschung und Fortbildung, Vienna, Austria, in 2001; Philip Scranton at Rutgers University in 2002; Nicolaas Rupke at the University of Göttingen in 2002, who invited me back in 2003 for a summer of research; Donald Worster at the University of Kansas in 2003; Carolyn Merchant at the University of California, Berkeley, in 2003; Wybren Verstegen at the Free University of Amsterdam in 2003; Christopher Hamlin at the University of Notre Dame in 2004; and Sandro Dutra e Silva at State University of Goiás, Brazil, in 2014.

I am very grateful to great-granddaughter Joan Burroughs (and to Julianne Warren) for the personal tour of John Burroughs's writing cabin, Slabsides. Special thanks go to Tim Maguire, chief of interpretation and visitor services at the Marsh-Billings-Rockefeller National Historical Park, who opened up the Marsh home for me and gave me a tour. Kathleen McGwinn of the Marquette County (Wisconsin) Historical Society and the Montello Historic Preservation Society gave me valuable local information about John Muir's youth. Kathleen also led a delightful tour of sites associated with Muir for a field trip of the American Society for Environmental History meeting in 2012. Dwight Pogue, professor of art at Smith College, took me to the top of Mount Holyoke to see the Oxbow.

I have discussed the issues in this book with many people over the years. In addition to those I have named, a very incomplete list of people to whom I owe my thanks includes Eugene Cittadino, Fritz Davis, Greg Dehler, Brian Donahue, Thomas Dunlap, Sterling Evans, Susan Flader, Bonnie Gisel, Dianne Glave, Marc Hall, Mark Harvey, Donald Hughes, Belden Lane, Barry Lopez, Geneviève Massard-Guildbaud, Martin Melosi, Char Miller, Jean-François Mouhot, David Quammen, the late Hal Rothman, Lisa Sedaris, Adam Sowards, Jay Taylor, Jim Warren, Aaron Yoshinobu, and Greg Zuschlag.

Of my intellectual debts, I would like to single out three in particular. The idea of the unintended consequences of religious belief was first introduced to me at Rice University by Thomas Haskell, who assigned Max Weber's *The Protestant Ethic and the Spirit of Capitalism* to his American intellectual history class in fall 1974, my *semestris mirabilis*. The late William Goetzmann set me on the path that led to this book back in 1987 in his research seminar at the University of Texas at Austin and guided me on through my dissertation. Don Worster has also been a valuable friend and supporter since I attended his memorable NEH Summer Seminar in 1993.

Texas Tech University, the College of Arts and Sciences, and the History Department have given me generous support for both conference travel and research. Department chairs Allen Kuethe, Bruce Daniels, George Iber, Randy McBee, and Sean Cunningham have found funding when it did not seem possible.

I have kept the untiring staff of the interlibrary loan department of the Texas Tech University Library very busy for years, and they have tracked down many rather obscure works. I am also grateful for the archival assistance of Jennifer Callaway, Denver Public Library; Linda Eade, Yosemite Research Library; Laurie A. Hilsinger, Alumni Affairs and Development, Cornell University; Danielle Kovacs, W.E.B. Du Bois Library, University of Massachusetts, Amherst; Linda McLean, Olana State Historic Site; Martin D. Meeker and Linda Norton, Regional Oral History Office, Bancroft Library, University of California, Berkeley; Cheryl Oakes, Forest History Society; Rebecca Philpott, Grey Towers National Historic Site; Richard Thomas, Connecticut Science Center, Hartford; Florence M. Turcotte,

George A. Smathers Libraries, University of Florida; and Hilary Dorsch Wong, Cornell University Library.

Thanks, too, to my editor Cynthia Read at Oxford University Press and her excellent team of Glenn Ramirez and Alyssa Bender.

Earlier versions of some sections of some chapters appeared in previous publications and appear by permission: "'Sagacious' Bernard Palissy: Pinchot, Marsh, and the Connecticut Origins of Conservation," *Environmental History* 16 (January 2011): 4–37; "Rachel Carson: The Presbyterian Genesis of a Nature Writer," and "Edward Osborne Wilson: The Gospel According to Sociobiology," both in *Eminent Lives in Twentieth-Century Science and Religion*, ed. Nicolaas Rupke, 2nd rev. and much exp. ed. (New York: Peter Lang, 2009); "Milton in Yosemite: *Paradise Lost* and the National Parks Idea," *Environmental History* 13 (April 2008): 237–274; and "Green *versus* Green: Religions, Ethics, and the Bookchin-Foreman Dispute," *Environmental History* 6 (July 2001): 412–27. A portion of Chapter 8 is based on "Religion and African American Environmental Activism," from *"To Love the Wind and the Rain": Essays in African American Environmental History*, edited by Dianne D. Glave and Mark Stoll, © 2006. Used by permission of the University of Pittsburgh Press.

My biggest debt is also my most personal. My wife, Lyn, enthusiastically supported and encouraged the project all along, gave valuable advice, came along on far-flung research trips, read the manuscript from beginning to end, and helped in many ways to make this book a success. To her I owe far more than I can tell.

Inherit the Holy Mountain

Introduction

THIS WHOLE PROJECT started nearly thirty years ago. In 1987 in a graduate seminar taught by William Goetzmann at the University of Texas, I wrote a research paper about the continuities between John Muir's deeply religious upbringing and his environmental activism, rather than the complete break between them that most biographers asserted. Intrigued by those connections, I went on to write a dissertation on Protestant roots of American environmentalism, which would be the basis for my book, *Protestantism, Capitalism, and Nature in America*, published in 1997. While I was writing the book, I noticed correlations between people's origins in specific denominations and certain attitudes toward nature and the environment. I began an investigation of those patterns that has produced two decades' worth of conference papers, articles, essays, and now the book you are holding.

A lot has happened while I was thinking about this. In 1987, Ronald Reagan was president. His notorious former Secretary of the Interior James G. Watt was fresh in everyone's memory and, as a Pentecostal, was Exhibit A for the popular belief that Christians and Christianity bore a hostile or imperial attitude toward the natural world. Such was the thesis of a powerful essay that Lynn White Jr. published in the journal *Science* in 1967, "The Historical Roots of Our Ecologic Crisis," claiming that Christianity had caused the environmental crisis. White's thesis is still today in the back of a lot of people's minds when they think about religion and the environment.

Changes were afoot, though. Mainstream Protestant denominations (an already inaccurate appellation) had issued statements about the Christian duty to be stewards of the environment and to care for creation. Pope John Paul II would issue the first papal environmental message, "Peace with God the Creator, Peace with All Creation," in 1990. By 1995 Robert Booth Fowler could publish on *The Greening of Protestant Thought*. Recently some have turned the tables and asked if environmentalism itself were not a quasi-religion, as Thomas Dunlap did in *Faith in Nature: Environmentalism as Religious Quest* of 2004.

This was all well and good, but the example of John Muir alerted me to the significance of religious upbringing, not adult beliefs, of the leading figures in the history of American environmentalism. After all, while church doctrine did clearly influence people's understanding of God's relationship to creation and nature's relationship to society, the churches had never stood in the vanguard of conservation or environmentalism. Furthermore, environmentalism was too diverse and complex to be reduced to some sort of virtual religion. Yet the evidence convinced me that there must be some close relationship between religion and environmentalism. A high proportion of leading figures in environmental history had religious childhoods. A surprisingly large contingent had ministers or preachers as close relatives or had even considered the ministry themselves. Curiously, few (and after 1900, hardly any) were churchgoers as adults. Lastly, Calvinism obviously played some kind of major role. Especially before the 1960s, a very large majority of the figures of the standard histories of environmentalism grew up in just two denominations, Congregationalism and Presbyterianism, both in the Calvinist tradition.

Why should this be so? How did those denominations foster so many figures in conservation and environmentalism? Conversely, how did the presence of so many from those churches affect the character and history of those movements? These questions gave me pause. I am a lapsed Presbyterian environmentalist myself. One would think this would give me some keen insight into what was going on here, but really, I could only shake my head. I grew up in conservative states. From experience I knew that Presbyterian churches were no schools for environmentalism. Yet there was something about being raised Presbyterian, something that stayed behind after creed and dogma fell away, that made excellent environmental leaders. There is an "inner Presbyterian" that has an enduring moral map and an urgent need to right the wrongs of the world. It does not take much asking around to find that deep immersion in a religious culture creates an "inner Baptist" or "inner Catholic" and so forth.

To answer this question, I would have to figure out what it means to grow up Congregationalist or Presbyterian, not to mention Baptist or Catholic or Jewish. There is not much scholarly literature on how denominational cultures of childhood and youth survive into adulthood, aside from a handful of books like Philip Greven's *The Protestant Temperament*. To add to the challenge, biographical information for figures both historical and contemporary often omits details about religion. For some—artist Albert Bierstadt, for example—no religious information seems to have survived. A handful of others—such as environmental author Bill McKibben, whose forebears were Baptist missionaries, who was baptized Presbyterian in California and raised in the United Church in Canada and the United Church of Christ in Massachusetts, and who teaches Methodist Sunday School in Vermont—had religious biographies too complex to make easy sense of.

To form a good picture of each religious tradition's general environmental consequences, I needed to identify and compare a substantial number of individuals with known religious background and a significant body or work or activism related to nature and environment. Reading and researching about denominational culture and history for every major denomination, plus long tedious digging for information about the religious backgrounds of scores of people (not to mention interruptions for various other projects) combined to make this a very long project indeed.

The subject matter itself produced a sprawling, almost incoherent narrative. I started by looking at every important figure in the standard histories of the movement. I realized that many threads come together in the concept of *nature*, each with its own significance for uncovering patterns of thought and action about nature and the environment: theology of course, and conservation and environmentalism, but also politics, landscape art, sport, agriculture, agrarianism, natural science, literature, and music. I drew examples from as many different strands as possible, and for each denomination they harmonized nicely into a distinctive design.

Regarding individuals and denominations, choices had to be made. Gender imbalance inheres in the nature of environmental history, but I balanced examples as well as I could. The reader will immediately notice that I have not discussed some religious traditions, in part because I only have a finite time on this earth, but mostly because I could identify no significant body of environmental thought or activism that came out of them. Still, I accumulated a vast amount of information. The book you read has been trimmed and cut into shape. Lots of interesting people and connections are piled on the cutting-room floor.

I compiled my early research into a sort of taxonomy by correlating each denomination or religious tradition with typical environmental attitudes. I was faced with the question of how best to illustrate each mode of thinking about nature. Why, literally, of course—with an illustration! Paintings and photographs are pure cultural productions. They reflect as perfectly as anything can the way their creators see the world. Artists include and exclude, exaggerate and diminish, foreground and background, all the while telegraphing messages with each brushstroke or darkroom technique. Landscape art is not merely a landscape. How is nature portrayed? Are there any people or their works in it? How prominent are they, and what is their relationship to the landscape? How are light and the elements depicted? Do they imply something about a divine presence? And so on. I have chosen representative paintings by figures of each religious background in every chapter. A big segment of my argument is art-historical.

So far, so good. And then surprises started piling up. A huge proportion of the leaders of environmentalism during its mid-twentieth-century heyday were raised Presbyterian. That was curious, but it became clear early on. I dug back into the nineteenth century and was startled to find that virtually every single person associated with the early movements for parks and forest conservation was no further than one generation away from a Congregational church in a small New England town. I had expected *some* New Englanders, of course, but not everyone. The standard literature had led me to believe that Emerson and Transcendentalism had played a big role, but amazingly, hardly any of these Congregationalists said so much as one word about Emerson. A chapter that I had expected would write itself at first baffled me, and then led me into unexplored territory. What was motivating them, then? My discovery of the centrality to them of the New England town fundamentally changed my understanding of conservation and early environmentalism.

I would find that Emerson was quite important, of course, but later, and among people less directly involved with creating parks and forests and advocating conservation. Also, I realized that there were many Emersons. There was the Emerson of *Nature,* crossing the commons at twilight and feeling a perfect exhilaration as the currents of Universal Being flow through him. There was the Emerson of "Self-Reliance," telling young people to ignore convention and follow their genius. Emerson had a gift for writing glittering oracular enigmatic essays in which listeners and readers discovered their own meanings. Artists, authors, and poets loved him. The spiritually minded loved him. That is, if they came from a Reformed or New England background. Emerson did not appeal equally across confessional and sectional boundaries.

The biggest surprise in writing the book came when I began to examine the conservation movement during its glory days in the Progressive Era between 1900 and 1920. Of all federal officials associated with conservation, almost none was raised Congregationalist. Congregationalists had nearly vanished from conservation by then. Progressive conservationists were nearly all raised Presbyterian. The almost complete unanimity astonished me. Presbyterians dominated federal conservation for several decades and then vanished as completely as Congregationalists, only to reemerge in the environmental movement after World War II. This handoff from Congregationalists to Presbyterians, and then gradually since 1960 from Presbyterians to non-Presbyterians, has been difficult to understand and explain.

Since Congregationalists and Presbyterians of course had no monopoly on conservation or environmentalism, I wondered what sort of environmentalists came from other groups. A substantial body of work relating to nature in some way came out of denominations originally from New England that Puritans marginalized and persecuted. Mostly Baptist, these figures have remained by and large on the political sidelines and thought more in individualistic than social terms. Thoreau belongs in this group.

As Presbyterian leadership faded away after the 1960s, writers and activists from groups that had earlier stayed pretty much in the background, especially African-American Baptists, Catholics, and Jews, came forward to take their place. The transition changed the character and priorities of environmentalism to a greater focus on human health and justice. Presbyterians, though, had given the movement a moral and political center that no one has replaced. I think it is no accident that a more fragmented environmentalism has lost relevance and power.

The final surprise, reserved for the concluding chapter, is the thoroughly areligious character of the wilderness movement, whose leaders have been "everybody else"—that is, they were raised in a hodgepodge of denominations that otherwise contributed little to American environmental thought and activism. The conclusion explores the implications of this fact. The book ends with a meditation on what the current religious scene implies for the future of American environmentalism, if the experience of the past is any guide.

Inherit the Holy Mountain overlays American environmental history on American religious history. A summary of what might be called the standard narratives of each field follows to help readers get their bearings.

The standard narrative of American religious history begins with colonial settlement, which took place in the midst of religious turmoil in Europe. Martin Luther sparked the Reformation in 1517. Soon western Europe split between Roman Catholicism and Protestantism. A generation later, John Calvin led a more militant and purist movement, Reformed Protestantism. Reformed sway was strongest in Switzerland, the Rhineland, parts of France, the Netherlands, England, and Scotland. Spanish and French colonists first brought Catholicism to North America in the sixteenth century. In 1607 the English founded Virginia, the first of the southern slave colonies, where Anglicanism (later known as Episcopalianism) predominated. Calvinist Puritans (later called Congregationalists) founded Massachusetts and Connecticut in New England, where some Baptists and Quakers found homes around the margins. Dutch Calvinists settled New York, and Quakers founded Pennsylvania. A sprinkling of Protestant refugees from France, called Huguenots, settled all along the coast.

In the eighteenth century, Calvinist Presbyterians from Scotland and northern Ireland immigrated to Pennsylvania and spread north and south into the valleys of the Appalachians. In the 1730s and 1740s, a burst of revivalism in New England, the Great Awakening, prompted Jonathan Edwards to write his great theological works. It also gave Baptists a boost. Baptist missionaries went to the South, where they found enthusiastic converts before the Revolution, joined by Methodists right after. In the new nation, Baptists and Methodists rapidly became the two largest Protestant denominations nationwide.

In the nineteenth century the open American religious scene encouraged new religious movements, many of which sprang up in another national explosion of revivalism, the Second Great Awakening: Unitarians, Campbellites (Churches of Christ and Disciples of Christ), Mormons, and Seventh-Day Adventists. They were later joined by the charismatics—the Holiness people (who usually do not speak in tongues) and Pentecostals (who do). Immigration undermined Protestant hegemony. German Catholic and Lutheran immigration began in the 1840s, which along with Irish Catholic immigration made the Catholic Church the nation's largest single denomination. Massive Catholic immigration continued between

1880 and the 1920s, and started again in the 1980s. Immigration also brought waves of German and eastern European Jews.

In the 1920s, Protestants divided into liberal Modernist and conservative Fundamentalist camps. Liberals dominated the national scene until the 1960s, when they began to fade away. Conservative evangelicals and charismatics, whose movements had been quietly growing, suddenly surged to prominence. Young liberal Protestants left church, often to become "spiritual but not religious" and adopt whatever practices from world religions that seemed most appealing. The denominations in which they grew up began to shrink in absolute numbers. In the late 1970s, conservatives declared what they termed a culture war and opposed most liberal initiatives (including environmentalism), along with homosexuality and abortion, in the name of family and traditional values. At present, the conservative Protestant tide appears to be receding, leaving behind an unsettled American religious scene.[1]

The standard narrative of environmental history begins with the retreat of Indians before European colonists and their diseases. Indians had tended and shaped the landscape, and when they died or left, pioneers often marveled at the Edenic abundance they found. Abundant cheap land and rich virgin soil encouraged wasteful farming practices and outside of New England and some German communities, few took good care of the land. In the nineteenth century, the Industrial Revolution transformed watersheds for waterpower, destroyed forests for fuel and building materials, and generally treated natural resources as if they were inexhaustible. As coal replaced renewable wood as fuel, sooty smoke darkened city air. Waters grew appallingly polluted. Wildlife species retreated and occasionally, like the Carolina parakeet and passenger pigeon, went extinct.

Alarmed, some far-sighted individuals advocated preserving nature from the onslaught in parks for the benefit of the people, including Yosemite in California in 1864, the first park preserved for its natural beauty. Yellowstone, the first national park, followed in 1872. John Muir, founder of the Sierra Club, became the well-loved champion of Yosemite and the national parks. George Perkins Marsh, author of *Man and Nature* in 1864, and many others advocated sustainable use of forests and resources. Another movement promoted scientific agricultural advances to make farmers more efficient and prosperous. Congress established forest reserves in the late nineteenth century, which President Theodore Roosevelt and Chief Forester Gifford Pinchot put under the Forest Service in 1905. Pinchot also promoted the newly coined term and concept of "conservation." Muir and Pinchot found themselves on opposite sides in the battle against a dam and reservoir in Hetch Hetchy in Yosemite National Park, which Muir bitterly and unsuccessfully opposed. Congress created the National Parks Service in 1916 to administer the growing hodgepodge of national parks. Hunters, fishermen, and their advocates successfully achieved game preserves and game laws, and the bison was saved from extinction. In the 1930s the Dust Bowl, one of the great environmental disasters in history, created widespread support for government conservation. In 1935 the Wilderness Society was founded to preserve wilderness, and in 1964, after years of lobbying, Congress passed the Wilderness Act establishing a system of wilderness areas.

Unprecedented prosperity after World War II created new problems. Rampant development seemed to threaten America's scenic beauty. David Brower, director of the Sierra Club, led successful campaigns to stop federal dams in Dinosaur National Monument and the Grand Canyon. The public grew anxious about increasing pollution and overuse of dangerous chemicals. Rachel Carson's pesticide exposé *Silent Spring* shocked the nation in 1962 and led to the rise of a new environmental movement. A slew of federal legislation in the next dozen years regulated chemicals, cleaned air and water, protected endangered species, established the Environmental Protection Agency, and regulated chemical-free organic food. The dramatic success of the first Earth Day in 1970 showed how widespread support for environmentalism had become. Discovery of toxic wastes in neighborhoods like Love Canal in the late 1970s started the environmental justice movement, which opposed the siting of hazardous materials in poor or minority neighborhoods. The antienvironmentalist, procorporate Reagan administration fought the environmental movement to a standstill in the 1980s, and it has achieved little since, despite urgent crises from global warming to depletion of ocean species.

Inherit the Holy Mountain merges the narratives of American religious and environmental history. The book begins with Calvinism, early America's dominant theology, which shaped fundamental American ideas about nature in religion, aesthetics, and natural science. It goes on to show how Calvinist New England Puritans developed and implemented an ethic and program for an orderly and moral society. To preserve the New England town and offer it as a model for the growing nation, Congregationalists developed a program of agricultural improvement, parks, and forest conservation. The liberal branch of the Puritan tradition—Unitarianism and its offshoot Transcendentalism—spread ideas of nature as a spiritual resource and teacher to an influential generation of Modernist artists and architects, who in turn inspired the architects and designers of national parks. In the Progressive Era, Presbyterians took the stage and implemented conservation and parks at the federal level. Their vast legacy included the National Forests and National Parks systems. Presbyterians mostly vanished from national government by 1946. In postwar America they fundamentally shaped the environmental movement. Various New England religious outsiders, including Thoreau and the Baptists, at the same time contributed much toward individualist environmentalism and very little toward environmental solutions from a community, social, or political standpoint. As Presbyterian environmental activists and thinkers died off, African Americans, Catholics, and Jews emerged to become the leading voices of the movement and take it in new directions. The book concludes with a brief look at those wings of the environmental movement with no discernible correlation with a denominational or religious ethic and considers the implications of the current religious scene for a future environmentalism.

Inherit the Holy Mountain uses religion as a wholly new tool for dissecting American environmental history. Historians have invoked a long list of factors to explain the motivations behind conservation and environmentalism: nationalism; monumentalism; Transcendentalism; democratic ideals; growing appreciation for wilderness; nostalgia for the disappearing frontier; alarm at disappearing game; antimodernism; fear of urban pollution, corruption, disorder, immigrants, and class conflict; automobiles and leisure time; and masculine ideals of conquest and domination. All of these factors, and more, played their roles.[2] Yet as this book shows, a religious perspective gives the history and development of environmentalism a trajectory, unity, and power. Rather unexpectedly, even to the author, religion turns out to provide extraordinary insights into the environmental movement's past—and future.

Calvinism and Nature: Environmentalism's Foundations

The Making of a Landscape Masterpiece

The "fierce and terrible" winter of 1836 only deepened Thomas Cole's gloom and discouragement.[1] For a year and a half, first in New York City and now in the scenic village of Catskill on the Hudson River, Cole had been working on a series of five large paintings that he called *The Course of Empire*. These unprecedented and ambitious pictures, he told his patron Luman Reed, would surely "establish a lasting reputation" for him as an artist.[2] However, Cole was stymied. He had quickly finished the first two of the series only to struggle for a whole year with the grand central painting, *The Consummation of Empire*. The design of the fourth presented him with several serious difficulties as well. As he stared at the large blank canvas in his rented second-floor studio on John Alexander Thomson's Cedar Grove estate, Cole also worried about the upcoming annual April exhibition of the National Academy of Design. As one of the academy's founders and a member of its governing council, he keenly felt the need to show new work.[3] Moreover, he needed the money that the sale of a painting would bring. In desperation, Cole wrote to Reed to propose that he paint the fifth of the series, *Desolation*, and exhibit that. Absolutely not, Reed replied. He felt it would ruin the "grand effect" of unveiling the full series at one time and suggested that Cole instead paint something in his "accustomed manner," perhaps an Arcadian scene.[4]

It was nearly March and Cole knew he would never be able to work out a new Arcadian scene in the remaining time. Indeed, he would have a hard time finishing a respectable picture of any sort to hang among other "dashing landscapes" at the exhibition. He had just enough time

to complete a landscape view, which anyway always sold better than alle-
gories and histories. The frozen Hudson kept ships from bringing him
a new frame from his New York suppliers, and he had no time to stretch
canvas on it in any case. Cole had to use the only unpainted canvas at
hand, a six-foot, four-inch-wide canvas covered with a rejected chalk sketch
for *The Consummation of Empire,* quite a large size for a landscape at the
time. Fortunately, Cole wrote Reed, he had a very promising subject in
mind that he had been thinking about for years.[5] He pulled out "the finest
scene I have in my sketchbook"—the famous view from Mount Holyoke
near Northampton, Massachusetts, which he probably sketched on a trip
to Boston in 1833. More importantly, this painting would be no simple
landscape painting. It "would tell a tale," he wrote Reed.[6] Fired with new
hope and enthusiasm, Cole set to work.

Ironically, Cole's last-minute landscape painting was the masterpiece
that established his lasting reputation, rather than *The Course of Empire,*
which he completed in a burst of activity later that year. On April 27, 1836,
the National Academy exhibition opened its doors and admitted a stream
of visitors to see the 236 pictures on display, among them Thomas Cole's
View from Mount Holyoke, Northampton, Massachusetts, after a Thunderstorm,
better known as *The Oxbow* (Figure 1.1; see color insert). First reviews were
positive, but not glowing. The editor of *The Knickerbocker Magazine* commented, "This is really a fine landscape, although at first it does not appear
so. It wants to be studied."[7] With study and with time, *The Oxbow* has
become Cole's best-known painting and in the twentieth century helped
revive his faded fame. Art historians single it out as the first painting of the
first American art movement, the "Hudson River School."[8] About a foot
wider than Cole's largest American landscapes up until then, *The Oxbow*
was the first painting of such size to depict American landscape. Repeated
public exhibitions in 1838, 1848 (Cole's influential memorial exhibition),
and 1862 kept it in the public eye and inspired imitators.[9] Ambitious artists for the rest of the century painted their own huge, gloriously gran-
diose American nature landscapes with splendid views, dramatic skies,
and diminished human presence. Cole's *The Oxbow* launched the great
landscape tradition in American art, strong and vibrant after close to two
centuries through the popular work of painters Frederick Church, Albert
Bierstadt, Thomas Moran, Georgia O'Keeffe, photographer Ansel Adams,
and countless minor and amateur artists.

The tale that Cole wanted the painting to tell is not as obvious as the work's
significance as a landmark of art history. He wrote no program specifically

for it, nor did he explain it in any detail in his surviving letters. Yet from the wild mountains and storm clouds of one corner to the bountiful fields and warm sunshine of the other Cole embedded symbols and aesthetic concepts that narrate a tale of the moral meaning of landscape. They speak eloquently as well of the vital place of nature and landscape in the Reformed Protestant tradition in which Cole was raised. The scene that *The Oxbow* looks out on, near Northampton, lay at the geographic center of a Puritan culture region stretching from New Haven, Connecticut, up the Connecticut River Valley to Vermont, where soon the conservation movement would be born. Cole's masterwork hints even at that story. His religious and moral purposes reflected Calvinist and Puritan ideals that, still vigorous in 1836, were fostering an art aesthetic, a landscape ideal, a scientific worldview, and moral and practical notions about land and landscape that would inspire and galvanize the American conservation and environmental movements. This multilayered, complex landscape painting (although at first it does not appear so) captures on canvas the hugely influential and fertile Reformed nature tradition near its exact geographical center.

The Oxbow's Tale

The Oxbow itself invites viewers to read it as a tale. Its official title, *View . . . after a Thunderstorm,* implies a narrative or sequence of events. The strong diagonal that figures in the design of many of Cole's early paintings sweeps from bottom right to upper left, directing the eye and lending dynamic tension to the scene.[10] Stormy violence in the wilderness on the left side contrasts with peaceful prosperity of settled farms on the right. The thunderstorm is moving to the left with a following wind. A snapped tree trunk and a broken limb in the foreground suggests its recent power and fury, while its branches frame a lightning bolt from the heart of the black storm. Tugged by the breeze, an upright, furled umbrella above a folding camp-chair at lower right gives evidence of recent rain. Dark retreating clouds allow sunlight to shine on now peaceful fields near the calm river and illumine the distant wooded hills. Cole never painted a sunnier, happier landscape than the right half of *The Oxbow.* The harvest stands in sheaves upon the fields. Sheep and cattle graze nearby. Mists rise from the forests and plumes of smoke from snug hearths. A few sails mark where boats have returned to the water, and a ferry crosses the river.

According to Ellwood C. Parry III and other modern critics, Cole intended *The Oxbow*'s tale to contribute to the then-contentious debate over whether American scenery had any validity as a subject for fine art.[11] Boston critics in particular emphatically preferred the ideal to the real and an Italian landscape with "associations" with history and literature to an American landscape either wild or settled without them.[12] True enough—yet surely Cole intended something more. *The Oxbow* was Cole's first painting after the publication of his famous "Essay on American Scenery" and very likely constituted an energetic illustration of its points. Cole had read the essay in May 1835 before the American Lyceum Society in New York. It was a manifesto that would lay the foundation for the entire American landscape tradition. In early 1836, as he stared glumly at the blank canvas of *The Consummation of Empire,* the mail brought the January issue of *The American Monthly Magazine* with his "Essay on American Scenery" on the first page. It was fresh on his mind as he began to plan out a landscape scene a foot larger than any he had ever painted. "Essay on American Scenery" accords so well with the design and details of *The Oxbow* that it forms an excellent starting point for interpretating the painting.

The essay praised American scenery, often in comparison with English, Swiss, or Italian examples, and asserted its potential to exemplify the aesthetic categories of the day: the sublime and the beautiful, the picturesque, and associations, all of which appear in *The Oxbow.* Horizontal and diagonal lines separate three themes of "the loveliness of the verdant fields, the sublimity of lofty mountains, [and] the varied loveliness of the sky."[13] The diagonal divides the picture into two almost unrelated scenes that illustrate the principles of the sublime and the beautiful. The left side represents the American Sublime, what Cole's essay called "wild and uncultivated scenery" and "the stern sublimity of the wild." English critics had long defined "sublime" as a wild scene evoking awe and terror and named seventeenth-century Italian landscape painter Salvator Rosa as the genre's master.[14] In *The Oxbow*'s sublime half the primal forest reigns, uncontrollable forces of nature rage, and trees snap in the fury of the storm. Cole noted that such a scene had no European counterpart because "the most distinctive, and perhaps the most impressive, characteristic of American scenery is its wildness."[15] In this section Cole was in his element. From his very first landscape, he excelled in the Salvatorean idiom, with its dead and broken trees, retiring storms, and insignificant or absent human figures.

The right side of *The Oxbow* depicts the Beautiful—that is, a soft, often pastoral or Arcadian view inspiring pleasure, which English critics identified with the style of the seventeenth-century painter Claude Lorrain.

Here Cole presented a sunlit, prosperous, productive landscape, which, unlike the sublime left half, had no counterpart in his other paintings. In this portion Cole included numerous details that rewarded the study that *The Knickerbocker* had recommended—the ferry, the boats, shocks drying in the fields, houses with smoke issuing from chimneys, and small animals and figures. Very unusually, in the foreground stands an artist (Cole himself), with a paintbrush in his hand and an oil sketch on an easel, who turns his head to smile over his shoulder at the viewer. The artist's furled umbrella, folding chair, and case appear at right. A mood of cheer and optimism pervades.

Cole paired the beauty of the landscape with the beauty of the sky. "American Scenery" also urged artists to paint the sky: "Look at the heavens when the thunder shower has passed and the sun stoops behind the western mountains," Cole wrote; "—there the low purple clouds hang in festoons around the steeps—in the higher heaven are crimson bands interwoven with feathers of gold, fit for the wings of angels—and still above is spread that interminable field of ether, whose color is too beautiful to have a name."[16]

The presence of the artist indicates the picturesqueness of the view. According to late eighteenth-century English theorists, the "picturesque" mediated between the sublime and the beautiful. The picturesque valued irregularity, pleasant variety, asymmetry, and interesting textures. The works of Lorrain or another seventeenth-century artist, Gaspard Poussin, were thought to exemplify the picturesque. "We have many a spot," Cole insisted, ". . . as picturesque as the solitudes of Vaucluse [in France]."[17] The artist looks back at the viewer as if to say that the view from Mount Holyoke across the gently flowing Connecticut to the distant forested mountains easily bested the scenery of Vaucluse.

The right side also illustrates Cole's insistence that the American landscape had associations as worthy as the literary and historical associations of any scene in Europe. "The cultivated must not be forgotten," wrote Cole, "for it is still more important to man in his social capacity—necessarily bringing him in contact with the cultured; it encompasses our homes, and . . . its quieter spirit steals tenderly into our bosoms mingled with a thousand domestic affections and heart-touching associations—human hands have wrought, and human deeds hallowed all around."[18] The peaceful pastoral scene called forth connections in the imagination to the work of Puritan colonists and their offspring in building a moral, orderly, prosperous society in harmony with God and nature.

The sublime wilderness on the left had associations unlike any scene in civilized Europe. To Cole, the associations of wild nature were superior to those of humanized landscapes because they suggested the divine and not the human. Cole was a deeply religious man, and the tale he wanted *The Oxbow* to tell must surely have been a religious one. He had made his reputation as a painter of landscapes but in his own mind he was first and foremost a religious painter. Cole disparaged his landscape paintings as mere money-makers that allowed him to follow his true calling as a painter of moral and religious subjects, which also dominated his poetry, essays, stories, and letters. He hoped his landscape art would encourage an appreciation for natural beauty among American "dollar-godded utilitarians," as he called them in a letter to Reed, destroying nature for profit, and lead to preservation of picturesque landscape for its spiritual value.[19] "It was Cole's aim to give, in all his landscapes, that spiritual meaning which he himself drew from nature," his pastor, friend, and biographer Louis Legrand Noble remarked, "and to teach, when the subject admitted of it, a strong moral lesson."[20]

Cole dreamed of the day he could stop painting landscapes and paint just religious pictures. "It is not riches that I aspire to," he wrote his patron Daniel Wadsworth in 1828; "—I flatter myself I have a nobler object in view, it is the attainment of excellence in my art—. . . And I still look forward with hope to the time when I shall be able to produce paintings that shall affect the mind of the beholder like the works of a great poet—that shall elevate the imagination and produce a happy moral effect."[21] *The Course of Empire* illustrated the moral lessons of "the mutation of earthly things" and the vanity of the works of man,[22] themes that Cole depicted again in two pairs of paintings, *The Departure* and *The Return* of 1837 and *Past* and *Present* of 1838. In 1844, at the height of his fame, Cole wrote to Wadsworth about his ideas for future paintings: "They are subjects of a moral or religious nature & on such I think it the duty of the artist to turn—for his mission if I may so term it—is a great & serious one—his works ought not be mere dead imitations of things—without the power to impress a Sentiment or enforce a moral or religious truth."[23] His close friend and champion William Cullen Bryant noted that Cole "reverenc[ed] his profession as the instrument of good to mankind."[24] Many of Cole's major landscape compositions illustrated Biblical passages: *Christ Crowned with Thorns and Mocked* (1825), *Landscape, Composition, St. John in the Wilderness* (1827), *Subsiding of the Waters of the Deluge* (1829), *Hagar in the Wilderness* (1829), *Elijah at the Mouth of the Cave* (1830), *Dead Abel* (1831–32), *The*

Angel Appearing to the Shepherds (1834), *Angels Ministering to Christ in the Wilderness* (1843, which hung over Cole's mantle until his widow's death in 1884), and *The Good Shepherd* (1847, Cole's last completed painting). In 1827 and 1828 Cole portrayed two scenes from Puritan poet John Milton's *Paradise Lost, The Garden of Eden* and *Expulsion from the Garden of Eden;* and in 1845 he painted passages from Milton's *L'Allegro* and *Il Penseroso.* He painted two religious allegorical series that as mass-market etchings were his most popular works: the four-part *Voyage of Life* of 1840 and the five-part *The Cross and the World,* unfinished at Cole's untimely death in 1848. Fittingly, perhaps, Bryant pronounced the completed second painting of *The Cross and the World* "Miltonic."[25]

In *The Oxbow,* allusions abound to passages in both the Bible and religious literature. They suggest as well the Reformed themes of God's presence in nature, the desirability of godly use of nature's abundance, and the dangers of destructive avarice. Cole began "American Scenery" with a lament for those who could not see nature's beauty, since they were cut off from God: "For those whose days are all consumed in the low pursuits of avarice, or the gaudy frivolities of fashion, unobservant of nature's loveliness, are unconscious of the harmony of creation."[26] The blind destructiveness of his countrymen appalled Cole: "The beauty of such landscapes are quickly passing away—the ravages of the axe are daily increasing—the most noble scenes are made desolate, and oftentimes with a wantonness and barbarism scarcely credible in a civilized nation."[27] A lover of poetry and a published poet himself, Cole illustrated the point with lines about these "Short lived, short sighted" people taken from "Living Without God in the World" by Charles Lamb.[28] Cole fervently affirmed the world's purpose:

It *has not* been in vain—the good, the enlightened of all ages and nations, have found pleasure and consolation in the beauty of the rural earth. Prophets of old retired into the solitudes of nature to wait the inspiration of heaven. It was on Mount Horeb that Elijah witnessed the mighty wind, the earthquake, and the fire; and heard the "still small voice"—that voice is YET heard among the mountains! St. John preached in the desert;—the wilderness is YET a fitting place to speak of God. . . . [Cole in fact had portrayed Elijah and John the Baptist in two paintings.]

He who looks on nature with a "loving eye," . . . in gazing on the pure creations of the Almighty, . . . feels a calm religious tone steal through his mind, and when he has turned to mingle with his fellow men, the chords of which have been struck in that sweet communion cease not to vibrate.[29]

The superiority of wilderness lay in the fact that its associations were *not* of human deeds. "Those scenes of solitude from which the hand of nature has never been lifted," Cole wrote, "affect the mind with a more deep toned emotion than aught which the hand of man has touched. Amid them the consequent associations are of God the creator—they are his undefiled works, and the mind is cast into the contemplation of eternal things."[30] He concluded "American Scenery" with a ringing plea:

Nature has spread for us a rich and delightful banquet. Shall we turn from it? We are still in Eden; the wall that shuts us out of the garden is our own ignorance and folly. We should not allow the poet's words to be applicable to us—

> *"Deep in rich pasture do thy flocks complain?*
> *Not so; but to their master is denied*
> *To share the sweet serene."*

May we at times turn from the ordinary pursuits of life to the pure enjoyment of rural nature; which is in the soul like a fountain of cool waters to the way-worn traveller; and let us

> *"Learn*
> *The laws by which the Eternal doth sublime*
> *And sanctify his works, that we may see*
> *The hidden glory veiled from vulgar eyes."*[31]

These final two quotations from English poet Edward Young's "The Infidel Reclaimed" and Scottish poet John Wilson's "Nature Outraged" reinforced Cole's message to his fellow painters that they must reveal the Eternal's glory hidden in nature to their materialistic countrymen.

Hence Cole's powerful emphasis on religious feeling in "American Scenery" suggests that *The Oxbow*'s associations tell an essentially religious tale. The painting's wild side displays the power and presence of the Almighty, while the settled side bespeaks the plenty and peace associated with Eden or the Promised Land. The mention in the essay of God's presence on Biblical mountaintops prompts thoughts of Mount Sinai, where, as Exodus 19:16–17 recounts, Moses and the people of Israel encountered

God in "thunders and lightnings, and a thick cloud upon the mount," not unlike storm on the mountains to the left. Reflections on Moses prompts thoughts of his view from Mount Pisgah westward across the Jordan into the Promised Land of Canaan in Ex. 34:1, perhaps meant as a parallel to the view from Mount Holyoke into the prosperous Connecticut Valley. Odd-shaped clear-cuts on the distant hills suggest another association. As Matthew Baigell observed, they resemble the Hebrew characters נח ("Noah").[32] The reviewer in the *New-York Evening Post*—probably editor William Cullen Bryant or critic William Dunlap, friends of Cole's who may have heard this simile from the artist himself—wrote that "the mists are rising like altar smoke from the hills in the distance."[33] Taken with the letters inscribed on the hill, the "altar smoke" would allude to Genesis 8:20–22, when Noah burned an offering on an altar he built after the waters of the Flood subsided: "And the LORD smelled a sweet savour; and the LORD said in his heart, I will not again curse the ground any more for man's sake. . . . While the earth remaineth, seedtime and harvest, and cold and heat, and summer and winter, and day and night shall not cease."[34]

Cole included other details that in conjunction with his essay suggest a further religious reading of *The Oxbow*, one which balance the associations of the left side to the Old Testament God of the Mountains with associations of with the New Testament millennial restoration of Eden on the right. In the lower right, near the river, flocks graze "deep in rich pasture," in Edward Young's phrase, as if to affirm we are still in Eden. To reinforce the New Testament promise of the right side, the poles of the camp chair form a distinct cross. In later work, Cole made the cross an increasingly common motif. The cross leans to the right parallel to the furled umbrella to point toward the Edenic portion of the painting, which is the direction the artist is also facing, as if to direct the viewer's gaze to the peaceful, happy scene below. The religious tale *The Oxbow* therefore tells is of the presence of the God of Sinai on the left side, while the right alludes to God's renewed covenant with mankind after the Flood and his blessing on the land in Genesis 3:17, alongside intimations of a millennial return to Eden.

Northampton's Associations: Calvinism, God, and Natural Beauty

The setting of *The Oxbow* was remarkably beautiful. Englishwoman Harriet Martineau traveled the region in 1835 and spoke for many visitors

when she wrote, "The villages of New-England are all more or less beautiful, and the most beautiful of them all is, I believe, Northampton."[35] The
cross formed by camp chair leans northward as if to point to Northampton,
which lay just outside the frame to the right. Cole specifically named the
town in the painting's full title, *View from Mount Holyoke, Northampton,
Massachusetts, after a Thunderstorm,* and so directed viewers' attention to
a place with deep and plentiful associations with the history of Protestant
radicalism. Northampton lay at the geographical heart of a Puritan realm
of villages and farms stretching down the river past Hartford to New
Haven, upstream into Vermont and New Hampshire, and back into the
green hills and valleys on either hand.

Here the Connecticut flows gently through the former bottom of
an ancient glacial lake 200 miles long. The waters drained, Noah-like,
to leave the well-watered, fertile Promised Land that drew so many
Puritans from New England's otherwise generally thin, rock-strewn
soils. In September 1653 a group of Puritans came up from Connecticut
and purchased the great meadow along the west bank of the oxbow
from local Pocumtuc Indians, who called the place Nonotuck. Sixteen
families from four Connecticut towns arrived the next spring with their
cattle and goods and built houses and a meetinghouse. The settlers
named the place after Northampton, England, a staunchly Puritan town
in the east Midlands where several had lived. Other Northamptonians
who joined this exodus to America included Anne Bradstreet, English
America's first published poet. For their first minister, the townfolk
called Eleazer Mather, one of America's most famous family of ministers. When Mather died in 1669, his widow married his successor, Solomon Stoddard. The Stoddards' grandson, the great Puritan
theologian Jonathan Edwards, assumed Northampton's pulpit upon
Stoddard's death in 1729. Edwards's grandson Timothy Dwight, born in
Northampton in 1752, had a distinguished career as poet, author, minister, theologian, and president of Yale.[36]

With the scope of the concept of associations expanded beyond any
that Cole might have intended or his viewers have known, this history and
these Puritans tell the tale of the unfolding of Calvinist doctrines of God,
nature, and humanity into American ways of seeing nature in spirituality, art, science, and landscape. These expanded associations embellish
and elaborate *The Oxbow*'s tale into a virtual Genesis of American conservation and environmentalism. It begins as Anne Bradstreet leaves old
Northampton for New England in 1630, flashes back to John Calvin in

Geneva, continues via the lives of the Mathers, Edwards, and Dwight, and ends in the world of Thomas Cole.

Eighteen-year-old Bradstreet arrived in Massachusetts aboard the *Arbella,* the flagship of the first convoy of Puritans to Massachusetts Bay Colony, which her father, Thomas Dudley, had helped organize. She was wife and daughter of future governors of the commonwealth. Her clever, lively, and well-crafted verses were published in 1650 in London in *The Tenth Muse Lately Sprung Up in America.* In 1678, six years after her death, a second edition came out in Boston with several new poems that reflected life and religion in Massachusetts. Chastened by the frequent absences of her prominent husband, by illnesses, by deaths of family members, and by a fire that burned down her home and consumed her library, Bradstreet wrote of submission, resignation to God's will, and the vanity of worldly things.

Whenever Bradstreet's faith faltered, she turned to nature. In a private note to her children, she wrote, "That there is a God my Reason would soon tell me by the wondrous workes that I see, the vast frame of ye Heaven + ye Earth, the order of all things night and day, Summer & Winter, Spring and Autumne, the dayly providing for this great household upon ye Earth, ye preserving + directing of All to its proper End."[37] ("Nature's household" was an early term for what is now called "ecology," from οἶκος, Greek for "house.") Bradstreet expanded on this theme in "Contemplations," a meditation on creation and her most enduring poem. "Contemplations" begins with the poet walking along a riverbank in late afternoon surrounded by the glorious color of a New England autumn. The sun, the trees, the seasons, and animal and insect life all turn her mind to their Creator. Blissful creatures offer Him their praise, an allusion to Psalm 148. Bradstreet bemoans humans' comparative ineptitude, due to Adam's Fall, to sing the Creator's praises. Contemplation of Adam and the beauty of Creation lead her thoughts to Eden, where Adam and Eve brought sin and death into the world. With their children came the first envy, hate, and murder. "Contemplations" concludes on a hopeful note that, however beautiful, all that is created will fade away, while man alone may gain immortality.[38]

These themes of beauty of creation, nature's effortless praise of the Creator, blissful Eden, postlapsarian misery and sin, and hopes for salvation occupied Reformed minds for centuries. Moreover, of various paths have long led doubting Christians back to belief, Reformed Protestants like Cole and Bradstreet have favored the road from nature to God that theologian John Calvin had chosen. In 1536, in the slender first Latin edition (of five) of *Institutes of the Christian Religion,* Calvin systematically laid out what has been characterized as "a profoundly original theology" upon whose foundations Huguenots, Dutch and Swiss Reformed, Scottish Presbyterians, English Puritans, and many others erected the churches of Reformed Protestantism.[39] As Calvin passed through Geneva in 1636, town fathers prevailed upon the author of the *Institutes* to stay and assist in the Reformation in the city. This chance event made Geneva his home for most of the rest of his life. Calvinism demanded complete Christianization of every aspect of personal and communal life, religious as well as political, economic, and cultural. There has been no better exemplar of the stereotypical Calvinist than Calvin himself. Of medium build, quiet and almost shy (although with a temper that he fought to control), studious, "remarkably religious" and censorious since childhood, zealous, abstemious, frugal, grave but pleasant, and ceaselessly industrious—late in life he rebuffed advice to take better care of his declining health, saying, "What, would you have the Lord to find me idle?"[40]—Calvin had few close personal relationships but loved the natural world. Perhaps even dour Calvin could not resist Geneva's stunningly beautiful situation on the shores of Lake Geneva with gleaming Mont Blanc, the highest peak in western Europe, rising majestically behind the stone face of Mont Salève.

In his theology, Calvin honored Creation in far greater measure than any Christian theologian of his era. In the opening chapters of the *Institutes* he argued that nature was the most important source of knowledge of God outside the Bible, an ancient doctrine that Calvin gave pride of place as the starting point of all theology. To him, the Lord had made the universe "as a spectacle for God's glory" or as a "dazzling theater" of his glory.[41] Because Adam's Fall had clouded human reason and rendered worthless all proofs of God and all "empty speculation" of natural philosophy,[42] "we know the most perfect way of seeking God . . . is not for us to attempt with bold curiosity to penetrate to the investigation of his essence, . . . but for us to contemplate him in his works whereby he rendered himself near and familiar to us, and in some manner communicates himself."[43] So great was his respect for creation that Calvin confessed "that it can be said reverently, provided it proceeds from a reverent mind, that nature is God."[44] Calvin was no poet, but thoughts of the Divine glory in nature made him as poetic and dewy-eyed as he ever got, as in this 1535 passage from his preface to the French translation of New Testament of his cousin Pierre-Robert Olivétan:

It is evident that all creatures, from those in the firmament to those which are in the center of the earth, are able to act as witnesses and messengers of his glory to all men; to draw them to seek God, and after having found him, to meditate upon him and to render him the homage befitting his dignity as so good, so mighty, so wise a Lord who is eternal; yea, they are even capable of aiding every man wherever he is in this quest. For the little birds that sing, sing of God; the beasts clamor for him; the elements dread him, the mountains echo him, the fountains and flowing waters cast their glances at him, and the grass and flowers laugh before him.[45]

Following Calvin's lead, Puritan divines placed the knowledge of God in creation in the first line of the Westminster Confession of 1647, the creed of Anglophone Reformed churches: "Although the Light of Nature, and the works of Creation and Providence do so far manifest the Goodness, Wisdom, and Power of God, as to leave men inexcusable; yet are they not sufficient to give that knowledg [sic] of God and of his Will, which is necessary unto salvation."[46] Edmund Staunton, one of the leading divines at the Westminster Assembly of 1647, in his travels always "entertained his Company with Heavenly discourse: And as variety of objects did present themselves to him, he always drew excellent matter out of them; glorifying God for the Wisdom, Power and Goodness which appeared in the works of Creation, and Providence."[47] American Puritans learned the principle in works of such theologians as William Ames. His *Medulla Theologiae* (1623) (translated as *The Marrow of Theology*), required reading into the eighteenth century for ministerial students at Harvard and Yale,[48] asserted that "God is known in the creation. . . . From this consideration of creation our faith ascends above the order of nature and *Apprehends the light of the glory of God, to be shown in the face of Jesus Christ, because it is God who commanded the light to shine forth from out of darkness,* 2 Cor. 4:6."[49] In Northampton, Solomon Stoddard preached, "The works of Creation are a standing Monument of the power, and wisdom, and goodness of God."[50] Cotton Mather, son of Eleazar's brother Increase, wrote in 1693, "The Great God requires our *Contemplation* to observe ALL HIS WORKS. . . . We should now *Know the Work of God,* and Study as far as we can, every one of *His Works.*"[51] Mather recorded that his pious late brother, Nathanael, "considered that the whole creation was full of God; and that there was not a leaf of grass in the field, which might not make an observer to be sensible of the Lord."[52] In the afterglow of a religious experience, Stoddard's grandson Jonathan Edwards saw "divine glory" in everything:

> God's excellency, his wisdom, his purity and love, seemed to appear in everything; in the sun, moon and stars; in the clouds, and blue sky; in the grass, flowers, trees; in the water, and all nature; which used greatly to fix my mind. I often used to sit and view the moon, for a long time; and so in the daytime, spent much time in viewing the clouds and sky, to behold the sweet glory of God in these things: in the meantime, singing forth with a low voice, my contemplations of the Creator and Redeemer.[53]

What was taught from the pulpits was thought in the pews. Born in Vermont in 1805, Joseph Smith Jr., an unlettered farmer's son and descendant of New England Puritans, recalled his troubled mind as a teenager. After searching the Bible,

> I looked upon the sun the glorious luminary of the earth and also the moon rolling in their magesty through the heavens and also the stars shining in their courses and the earth also upon which I stood and the beast of the field and the fowls of heaven and the fish of the waters and also man walking forth upon the face of the earth in magesty and in the strength of beauty whose power and intiligence in governing the things which are so exceding great and marvilous even in the likeness of him who created him them and when I considered upon these things my heart exclaimed well hath the wise man said that it is a fool that saith in his heart there is no God.[54]

Cole too sought God in nature. As Noble noted,

> If ever there was a mortal that pressed towards the visible works of God with the fresh enthusiasm of one who goes newly to behold the wonderful, that mortal was Cole. He went, at the hundredth time, as one going for the first time,—not in words, not in outward excitement, but in all gentleness and quietness, and in spirit, for he went to seek spirit: and when he found it under the shuck and crust of things, shuck and crust were all beating and throbbing with life;

they were living creatures, ever beautiful, ever new: and so the last time of looking was as the first, and nature grew to him youthful instead of older, and covered with tokens of heaven and immortality in its mouldering trunks, as ashes cover the living coals.[55]

Reformed Protestants could find evidence of the being and attributes of God everywhere from the wide heavens to the smallest blade of grass thanks to Calvinism's radical and truly novel doctrine of the providence of God. Calvin's doctrine of providence rejected a quiet or inactive God. The God of Calvinism could never be "idle." God did not act remotely through primary and secondary causes, as St. Thomas Aquinas had conceived it. Nor did he order all nature in a hierarchy from eternal heavenly spirits down through the ranks of living beings to dead earthly rock, as medieval Christians believed. Nature was egalitarian. At every moment God sustained, ordered, cared for, and guided the tiniest creature individually as well as the vast universe as a whole.[56] Ames in *Marrow of Theology* reaffirmed that God ordained a purpose for everything "for the perfection of the universe" and added that "the creature depends in every way upon the creator—not only for its creation, but also for its being, existence, continuance, and operation."[57] Like Calvin, who often spoke of God's glory shining from Creation, Ames employed the metaphor of light with regard to creation, from which "the power of God shines forth. . . . The goodness of God shines forth. . . . The wisdom of God shines forth. . . . The constancy of God shines forth."[58]

A group of former Puritans led by Ralph Cudworth and Henry More, the so-called Cambridge Platonists, expanded on Calvin's radical providence and set the stage for philosophically more complex modes of thinking about God's presence in nature. They drew from Platonist philosophers like Plotinus to portray the world as an immediate, ongoing creation of the Holy Spirit, an organic unity in its diversity. Creation was an image or shadow cast by the divine Mind, from which the universe emanated like light from a candle or the sun. The believer who meditated on the beauty of this world would find the spirit of God shining forth. Harvard and Yale embraced Cambridge Platonism as an ally against the twin threats of materialism and philosophical atheism.[59] In 1726, in his *Compleat Body of Divinity,* the only complete work of divinity written in colonial New England, Samuel Willard of Boston integrated the Calvinist doctrine of Providence with Cambridge-Platonist language of continual creation by emanation: "This Conserving *Providence of God, is a Kind of* Creation. . . .

In *Creation* all things are *New Made;* . . . whereas in *Conservation* they [have] . . . a *Present Existence,* which . . . would every moment fall back again into Nothing, if it were not held up by a Divine Hand. . . . It . . . is always emanating from God."[60]

Jonathan Edwards wrote American Puritanism's most sophisticated analysis of God's presence in nature, published posthumously in 1765 as *A Dissertation on the End for Which God Created the World.* His theology of creation looked both back to Calvin's *Institutes* and forward to Ralph Waldo Emerson's Transcendentalist speculations.[61] Edwards read More as a senior at Yale and studied More and Cudworth while writing *A Dissertation on the End for which God Created the World.*[62] From the time of his marriage, Edwards had kept a notebook entitled "Images or Shadows of Divine Things" in which he meditated on God in the natural world, treating the natural phenomena symbolically, not unlike emblems, reminiscent of the Platonic idea that the world was but shadows of the divine mind. In *Dissertation,* Edwards conflated Calvinist "communication" and Neoplatonist "emanation." He reinterpreted the standard Calvinist tenet that God created the world for his own glory with a heavy reliance on the Neoplatonist metaphor of light and doctrine of plenitude (creation from the fullness of God). Edwards wrote that "there is an infinite fullness of all possible good in God" which is communicated or emanates, flowing forth like an "infinite fountain of good [sending] forth abundant streams," an "infinite fountain of light . . . [pouring] forth light all around, . . . as beams from the Sun." This was why, Edwards said, we could find "the knowledge of God's glory in other beings, and an high esteem of it, love to it, and delight and complacence in it: . . . these things are but the emanations of God's own knowledge, holiness and joy."[63] Creation emanated from God and communicated God to us.[64]

Cudworth and More had if anything a greater impact on religious thought in Boston and at Harvard, both more theologically more liberal than Northampton and Yale. Emerson read them while a student at Harvard in the 1820s. Emerson adopted Calvinist notions of God's radical presence in nature as amplified in Cambridge Platonism but rejected Calvinism's Biblical literalism and predestination. Ralph Cudworth's *Intellectual System of the Universe* lay at hand in 1835 and 1836 while he was writing *Nature,* the founding text of American Transcendentalism—just at the very moment that Cole was painting *The Oxbow.* "We learn that the highest [truth] is present to the soul of man, that the dread universal essence, which is not wisdom, or love, or beauty, or power, but all in one, and each entirely is that for which all things exist, and that by which they are," wrote Emerson; "that spirit creates; that behind nature, throughout nature, spirit is present. . . . The world . . . is the present expositor of the divine mind."[65] Not unlike Edwards's images and shadows, Emerson believed that physical facts corresponded to spiritual facts. To Calvin, to Edwards, to Emerson, and to Cole, only humankind's blindness prevented them from seeing God in every aspect of nature.[66]

From the "Geneva of Lancashire" to the Crescent of Calvinism

Cole fretted whether a landscape painting as unusually large as *The Oxbow* would sell, but the National Academy of Design exhibition had hardly opened its doors when Charles Nicoll Talbot, a merchant from New York, bought it at its asking price, $500. Talbot was an evangelical Calvinist from an old Massachusetts Puritan family. He sat on the board of trustees of New York's Bleecker Street Presbyterian Church—New York had no Congregational churches—and took a leading part in a number of religious and philanthropic endeavors. Talbot probably bought *The Oxbow* for its connection to Northampton, where his retired father lived in a house in which the painting would hang, and where he spent summers and attended the Northampton Congregational Church.[67] Talbot later became close friends with its minister, William Solomon Leavitt, a former pastor of the Presbyterian church in Hudson, across the river from Catskill. Leavitt's close family ties with Northampton's church included one ancestor who was Jonathan Edwards's uncle and others whose machinations led to Edwards's dismissal in 1750.[68] *The Oxbow* had found a very appropriate home.

The Congregational Church of Northampton had an interesting association with Cole personally that tells of his Calvinist origins. Eleazer Mather's father, Richard Mather, had been minister to a congregation of farmers from Cole's birthplace. The elder Mather had been a fifteen-year-old student in Lowton in southern Lancashire when in 1611 his headmaster sent him to the village of Toxteth twenty miles to the west, in response to its request for a schoolteacher. Lancashire was the most Catholic county in England except for its radically Puritan south and southeast from Liverpool to Bolton to Manchester. Toxteth, a former game park, had been settled in 1592 by Puritans from Bolton, a town

so Puritan that Royalists called it the "Geneva of Lancashire" during the
Civil War of the 1640s. Soon a fervent Puritan, Richard Mather became
Toxteth's minister in 1618. When King Charles I purged Puritans from
the Church of England, Mather sailed for Massachusetts with his family
in 1635 to become one of the colony's leading clergymen.[69]

Cole was born in 1801 in Bolton, still the vigorous center of a region of
religious Dissent.[70] Almost certainly raised a Dissenter, Cole emigrated
with his family to Ohio in 1818 and soon went to Philadelphia in search
of work and art training.The region swarmed with fellow Reformed artists and art patrons. Philadelphia anchored a "Calvinist crescent" that
stretched through New Jersey and New York and across Connecticut
to Boston: Scottish Presbyterians in Pennsylvania, Congregationalists
and Unitarians in New England, and a mélange of Dutch Reformed,
Huguenots, Presbyterians, and New England Congregational migrants
in New York. Cole made his career in New York at the bend of the crescent's bow. Reformed buyers warmly appreciated the moral seriousness
Cole brought to his art. Cole's patrons were all Reformed Protestants.
Robert Gilmor Jr. of Baltimore was son of a Scottish immigrant, grandson of a minister, and leading member in the Presbyterian church his
father cofounded. Gilmor bought many of Cole's early paintings, guided
his early career, and paid for his first trip to Europe.[71] Daniel Wadsworth of
Hartford descended from Puritan founders of Connecticut and was grandson of a minister of the Hartford First Congregational Church, of which he
was a prominent member. He supported Cole's art throughout his career
and in fact had recommended to him the view from Mount Holyoke.[72]
Also of Connecticut stock, Luman Reed moved to New York City and supported both Grace Episcopal Church and the Unitarian Church. Reed
commissioned *The Course of Empire* and bought many of Cole's works.[73]
Samuel Ward, a New York banker whose ancestors included an officer
in Oliver Cromwell's army and a governor of Rhode Island and whose
daughter, Julia Ward Howe, wrote the "Battle Hymn of the Republic," was
an evangelical Calvinist, a low-church Episcopalian, and first president of
the New York Temperance Society. He commissioned Cole's most popular
series, the religious allegory *The Voyage of Life*.[74]

Cole's friends, supporters, and fellow painters were mostly of
Reformed background as well. His good friend Asher B. Durand of New
Jersey, of Huguenot and Dutch ancestry, became a landscape painter after
a sketching trip with Cole in 1837. Durand published an influential series
on landscape art in which he wrote of nature's "influence on the mind

and heart" through its "lessons of high and holy meaning, only surpassed by the light of Revelation." He measured a painting's greatness "in proportion as it declares the glory of God, by a representation of his works, and not of the works of man."[75] Cole's close friend and champion William Cullen Bryant grew up a devout Congregationalist twenty miles northwest of Northampton. A newspaper editor and the nation's leading poet, Bryant often worked with Cole in promoting American arts and landscape appreciation. His "Sonnet to an American Painter Departing for Europe," written upon Cole's voyage to Europe in 1829, urged him to gaze on "fair scenes" in which "everywhere" was "the trace of men" but urging him to "keep that earlier, wilder image bright." Bryant wrote popular poems that praised the divine in nature and asserted that in nature one came closest to God. Like Cole, he desired to spread appreciation of God's works, and attempted to publish books of American scenery delineated by Hudson River School artists, the most successful of which was *Picturesque America* of 1872. Cole's best student, Frederic Church, from a Congregational family of Hartford, painted large, powerful landscapes that won him international fame. Church faithfully honored Cole's moral and religious views throughout his long career.

Landscapes of the Reformed

Cole emigrated to America just at the moment when American Reformed Protestants were developing a taste for landscape art. The moral and spiritual purposes that Cole and Durand expressed in their essays were on everyone's mind by the time *The Oxbow* was hung for its first viewing. Landscape painting exploded onto the American art scene between 1820 and 1850, the years of the great religious revival called the Second Great Awakening. It remained the dominant form of painting for another generation until the mid-1870s. Despite its Reformed connections, landscape art, with its high moral purpose, did not spring up in Calvin's Geneva. Puritans sought God in nature for over two centuries before it occurred to them to adorn their walls with landscapes. In the seventeenth and eighteenth centuries Huguenots, Dutch, Presbyterians, and finally Puritans developed an aesthetic that transformed landscape art as a moral undertaking.

Huguenots, Puritans, and Presbyterians: it is remarkable that the English and American landscape traditions—or any artistic traditions at all—should have emerged from a religious tradition as hostile to images as Reformed Protestantism. Its implacable hostility to "human inventions" in worship and its zeal to uphold the Bible alone as a source of religious truth fostered a culture that trusted texts and mistrusted images. Intent on glorifying the Creator and not the creature, early Calvinists stripped churches of decoration and banished it from their lives and cultural productions. To discourage human vanity and abuse of God's gifts, they preferred a "plain" style of speech, rhetoric, sermons, liturgy, clothing, and material culture. Calvinists rejected utterly the very visual worship of medieval Catholicism that they claimed distracted congregations from the preaching of God's Word and led to glorifying human works. In reaction to Catholic "idolatry" Reformed architects built plain, functional, and completely unadorned places of worship. A Reformed war against images unleashed furious attacks on church art and architecture. In their zeal to return worship to godly simplicity, Calvinists whitewashed paintings on church walls, shattered stained glass windows and replaced them with plain glass, ripped out and burned elaborate altars and choirs, and smashed sculpted saints and crucifixes. Righteous zeal took a special toll in Scotland, where hardly a medieval religious structure survives intact.[76]

Although Reformed Geneva produced no landscape art tradition, Calvin formulated enduring aesthetic principles. He viewed art as a gift from God with such power that artists must take pains to submit their art to the word and will of God.[77] Art for its own sake was false art. Fine art that served no obvious practical or moral purpose disappeared from Calvinist culture. Calvin urged the artist to find inspiration in nature, the work of the divine Artist himself. Historian Léon Wencelius observes that Calvin's conception of art was "simultaneously realist, since the subject of art is earthly; and idealist, since, in order to realize this subject in his work, the artist must sympathize with the creative idea with which the subject was made."[78] Reformed art therefore tends to serve higher purposes while remaining grounded in the facts of nature and the everyday world. Art must above all be *truthful*. Calvinists obsessively sought to expose hypocrisy and established an enduring quest for authenticity in life and art—hence the Puritan hostility to theater, which proffered only lies and illusion.

But for Reformed artists to express the truth of nature, they first had to create a Reformed art. In the beginning, the spread of Calvinism threw artists and sculptors out of work, for the church had been a munificent patron, and they turned to painting portraits or decorative art. The rise of literacy stimulated a somewhat compensatory demand for illustrations for books and broadsides. Artists found employment illustrating Bibles, religious works, and emblem books, but in England in the Puritanic early decades of the seventeenth century, even this work grew rare. In 1635 Francis Quarles published *Emblems,* a popular book for two centuries, in which he linked symbolic illustrations with verses of a moral explanation. He felt constrained to defend his use of images: "An Embleme is but a silent Parable. . . . Our blessed SAVIOUR . . . in holy Scripture, . . . is sometimes called a Sower; sometimes, a Fisher; sometimes, a Physitian: And why not presented so, as well to the eye, as to the eare? Before the knowledge of letters, GOD was knowne by *Hierogliphicks;* And, indeed, what are the Heavens, the Earth, nay every Creature, but *Hierogliphicks* and *Emblemes* of his Glory?"[79] If Nature told of God's glory, then why not pictures of nature? Emblems were pictures that even Puritans could enjoy with an easy conscience. They hugely influenced Reformed art.[80]

In 1660, the Puritan Commonwealth of Oliver Cromwell fell and their enemy Charles II was restored to the throne. This religious catastrophe stimulated a remarkable outpouring of the Puritan creative imagination in both literary and visual art. Milton published *Paradise Lost* in 1667 and *Paradise Regained* in 1671. Between 1678 and 1684 the comparatively unlettered Puritan preacher John Bunyan published three classic works: an elaborate allegory, *The Pilgrim's Progress from This World to That Which Is to Come,* one of the most popular books ever printed; *The Life and Death of Mr. Badman,* a fantasy biography; and *The Holy War,* another elaborate allegory. The dense imagery of Milton's vivid, dramatic scenes in Eden, Heaven, and Hell, and of Bunyan's colorful allegorical spectacles, cried out for illustration. *Pilgrim's Progress* contained illustrations beginning with its original edition. An illustrated *Paradise Lost,* the first illustrated poem, appeared in 1688 and played a crucial role in making Milton's Christian epic a classic bestseller, with over a hundred editions appearing in the eighteenth century. In 1799 illustrations of the poem made the transition from book art to fine art when Swiss painter Henry Fuseli opened his Milton Gallery in London with 47 huge canvases of scenes from *Paradise Lost.* A former Reformed minister, Fuseli had been convinced to become a painter by Joshua Reynolds, taught Constable, and supported the career of Turner, but had the most obvious influence on his engraver William Blake, who would publish his own remarkable illustrations of Milton.[81] Cole, Church, and many other American painters began their careers painting scenes from *Paradise Lost* or *Pilgrim's Progress.*

The Dutch created the first Reformed fine art. The striking realism and detail of their landscapes and genre scenes reflected the Calvinist desire to truthfully render creation. Reformed painters followed the ideal of "art that conceals art," which meant that, as in the plain style of preaching, extensive learning and skill should not be shown off for its own sake but rather hidden beneath deceptively plain presentation. Hiding meaning also appealed to oppressed minorities like the Huguenots, whose artists, architects, and landscape designers encoded moral and religious messages in their work for their Catholic patrons.[82] Art that concealed art also hid the didactic and moral purposes behind Dutch landscapes and domestic scenes. Distracted by impressively detailed realism, later generations missed their moral seriousness and higher purpose of portraying God's creation and redemption of human life.[83] So strong was the Dutch influence on early English landscape art that the English borrowed the word "landscape" itself from Dutch *landschap*. The word "landscape" first appeared in English in Joshua Sylvester's 1605 translation of Huguenot Du Bartas's religious epic *The Devine Weekes*, which compares God's resting and admiring Creation to an artist who has painted "a Land-scape, various, rich, and rare."[84]

Exiled from France after 1685, Huguenot artists and artisans kick-started the enfeebled English arts and crafts scene. With the Dutch example and the assistance of Huguenots, native English fine art developed in the eighteenth century with the clear marks of the Calvinist aesthetic. William Hogarth was the key figure. Raised Presbyterian in a strongly Dissenter neighborhood of London, Hogarth took inspiration from Dutch genre scenes and Puritan book illustration and pioneered the painting of series that illustrated a story or moral. *Pilgrim's Progress* inspired several Hogarth series, including *A Harlot's Progress* and *A Rake's Progress*, which sold popularly as engravings. In 1735, relying on Huguenot instructors, Hogarth organized St. Martin's Lane Academy, precursor to the Royal Academy, in the heart of the London Huguenot expatriate community. At this creative nexus of French and English Reformed culture Hogarth created a distinctively English style of art for the first time since the Reformation.[85]

Reformed moral landscape art made its first entrance with Hogarth's student Thomas Gainsborough and reached its culmination with John Constable. Under the leadership of Gainsborough, Constable, and Sir Joshua Reynolds, English art of the eighteenth century developed a marked excellence in portraits and landscapes—precisely the two places where God's splendor shone forth, according to Calvin.[86] Portraits honored man, created in God's image, and depicted the transience of life, while landscapes displayed the works of God. Gainsborough was born in 1727 to a devout Dissenter family in Sudbury, Suffolk, a Puritan stronghold that sent more emigrants to New England than any other place in East Anglia.[87] He embarked on a career as a painter of landscapes but had to paint portraits to earn a living, albeit portraits that often had landscape in the background, commonly the subjects' estates, with all their implications of the Eden of *Paradise Lost*.[88]

With Constable the British landscape tradition reached its culmination. Born in Suffolk less than ten miles from Sudbury, he grew up in a religious family that had destined him for the ministry, but he showed no talent for it. After study at the Royal Academy of Arts he painted occasional religious scenes and, to make money, quite good portraits, but landscapes were his passion. Gainsborough and Dutch landscapists influenced him strongly. Like the Dutch, Constable preferred to portray rural scenes of everyday life. He insisted on scientific accuracy in painting. The truth of nature was his first concern.[89]

Sir Joshua Reynolds in particular shaped English art theory. Son, grandson, and nephew of Anglican priests, Reynolds was president of the Royal Academy of Art from its founding in 1768 until his death. He wrote the first important English theoretical work on art, the *Discourses*, which popularized the idea of a hierarchy of genres. André Félibien of France had formulated the hierarchy of genres to separate fine artists from artisans and linked a painting's quality to the creativity behind it. History painting—historical, Biblical, mythological, literary, and allegorical subjects—stood first, followed by genre painting, landscapes, and finally still-lifes. In his Ninth Discourse, Reynolds added a Calvinist twist to Félibien. The highest art, he said, had moral purpose above mere gratification of the senses, and that it should teach moral and intellectual truths. The artist must make himself "virtuously useful" to society.[90]

So Cole strove for "truth in nature" in his art, the "imitation of the true in nature"; to nature "the artist must always turn if he would produce a work of immortality."[91] The "grand quality" of Cole's art, according to Noble, was "TRUTHFULNESS TO NATURE." No aspect of Cole's art, even its piety and poetic expression, moved Noble to comment at such length as much as his "marvelous truth to nature."[92] On the basis of their beauty and truth to nature Cole judged others' paintings, and by those standards others judged his as well.[93]

Cole also subscribed to another Reformed aesthetic principle, the doctrine of the sublime and the beautiful, as exemplified in the work "the wild Salvator Rosa, or the aerial Claude Lorrain."[94] Rosa and Lorrain were first singled out in Britain in 1748 in the moralistic and Bunyanesque allegorical poem *The Castle of Indolence* by James Thomson, son of a Scottish Presbyterian minister: "Whate'er *Lorrain* light-touch'd with softening Hue, / Or savage *Rosa* dash'd, or learned *Poussin* drew."[95] After the barely Protestant Edmund Burke published his landmark essay *A Philosophical Enquiry into the Origin of Our Ideas of the Sublime and Beautiful* in 1757, Rosa came to stand for the painterly "sublime"—landscapes that induced emotions of awe and terror—and Lorrain for the painterly "beautiful"— peaceful and pleasant scenes. Archibald Alison in his 1790 *Essays on the Nature and Principles of Taste* and other Scottish writers revised his theory to bring it into greater conformity to Reformed sensibilities. A Scottish Episcopal priest, Alison united the idea of the "true sublime" with morality and divinity in nature.[96] He wrote that a person "in the lone majesty of Nature" would feel "some unseen spirit" touch "all the springs of his moral sensibility" and rekindle the "original conceptions of the moral or intellectual excellence of his nature. . . . In the Sublimity or Beauty of the works of Art, this purpose of Nature is yet more evident."[97] Alison's *Essays* also taught Cole's generation the principle of "associations." Cole and his fellow Hudson River School artists guided their moral landscape-art by the stars of Reynolds and Alison.[98]

Art historians note the influence on Cole of Bunyan's works and Quarles's *Emblems*. When Cole went to Philadelphia in 1818 to become an artist, his first job had been as an engraver of illustrations for Bunyan's *The Holy War. The Cross and the World* series openly alluded to Bunyan's *The Pilgrim's Progress* in following the progress of a similar pilgrim and his worldly companion. *The Cross and the World*, along with Cole's popular series *The Voyage of Life*, recall vividly the emblematic tradition. These series combined themes from Protestant literature and images reminiscent of Puritan emblem books with moralistic narratives like those of Hogarth. In contrast with crowded indoor and street settings of Hogarth's works, landscapes dominated Cole's paintings and underlined the meaning of each image. The gentle landscape of Childhood, the bright and hopeful landscape of Youth, the treacherous landscape of Manhood (Figure 1.2, see color insert), and the serene and darkening landscape of Old Age allegorically represent the stages of life. The individual in *The Voyage of Life* faced his fate alone, accompanied only by an angel. Here Cole epitomized the religion not only of the solitary Protestant soul on its voyage to eternity but of the lone Protestant pilgrimage to nature as well.

Still in Eden? Paradise Lost

"We are still in Eden," Cole had written in "American Scenery." He then painted an Edenic American scene into the right half of *The Oxbow.* Eden had long fascinated him. In 1827 and 1828, the ambitious young landscape painter unveiled the large paintings *The Garden of Eden* and *Expulsion from the Garden of Eden* (Figures 1.3 and 1.4, see color insert), his earliest attempts to accomplish, following Reynolds, what he called a "higher style of painting" than landscapes. The two paintings tell a moral story of rise and ruin not unlike *The Course of Empire. The Garden of Eden* depicts the bliss of Adam and Eve "still in Eden" before the Fall, while *Expulsion* shows the misery of the pair after the Fall, "[shut] out of the garden" by their "own ignorance and folly." More broadly, Cole's Milton paintings express the same Calvinist fascination with and yearning for an earthly natural Paradise that Bradstreet expressed in "Contemplations." This nostalgia for Eden in no small part kindled the rise of an American landscape ideal that in the decades to follow would inspire artists, landscape architects, and nature preservationists.

Reformed fascination with Eden and the Fall began small in the sixteenth century and grew into something akin to an obsession in the seventeenth. In his *Commentaries on Genesis,* Calvin had betrayed an interest in the earthly Eden by inserting a map of its likely original location in Mesopotamia. English editors included a version of Calvin's map in the Geneva Bible, the translation long favored by Puritans. The spell of Eden strengthened in the next generation of French Protestants, the Huguenots, when Guillaume de Saluste du Bartas reimagined Eden in verse. In answer to Calvin's calls to Christianize all aspects of life, including poetry and the arts, and to glorify God in all undertakings, Du Bartas wrote the first long poems in French on sacred subjects and popularized the adaptation of classical forms of poetry for Christian instead of pagan or secular themes. In 1578 he published *La Sepmaine; ou, Creation du monde,* his poetic retelling of the six days of creation. This colossal international bestseller appeared in at least 42 editions and numerous translations and inspired commentaries and imitators.[99] James I of England, a poet himself and a friend, translator, and fan of Du Bartas, commissioned Joshua Sylvester's translation of *La Sepmaine* and its sequel *La Seconde Sepmaine,* published in 1605 as *The Devine Weekes and Workes. The Devine Weekes* had many fervent devotees among the Puritans, not least Anne Bradstreet, whom a dedicatory poem in *The Tenth Muse* called "a right Du Bartas Girl."[100]

Du Bartas's detailed description of Eden in his Eighth Day inspired a Puritan version that surpassed *Las Sepmaine* in every way. Milton knew *The Devine Weekes* from boyhood and may have had it at hand in the 1650s and 1660s while writing his own great epic of Genesis, *Paradise Lost*.[101] Its publication in 1667 proved to be a momentous event in the development of the ideal of Eden (which he located in accordance with Calvin's map, 4.210–214). For two centuries *Paradise Lost* would rank with Bunyan's *Pilgrim's Progress* as the most popular works of Reformed literature. Still hugely popular and deeply influential in Cole's day, the poem retold dramatically and unforgettably the familiar story of joy and contentment in Eden, of sin and expulsion from the Garden, and of the divine curse on all humanity.

Nature was much more than just the background for Milton's epic, for the poet described nature in Eden in exquisite, loving detail and endearingly portrayed humanity's blissful life in effortless harmony with each other, with the Creator, and with creation. When Britons and Americans read Genesis they imagined Milton's Eden, with its naturalistic groves, meadows, waterfalls, and meandering streams surrounded by craggy wilderness walls, "A happy rural seat of various view" (4.247)—not unlike, one is tempted to say, the view from Mount Holyoke. The splendor of the world, whose beauty the poet repeatedly compares to Heaven itself, stunned Satan when he first looked upon it.[102] In Book 4, Milton described the "lovely . . . Lantskip" of Eden (4.152–153)—an early example of the artistic term, still spelled in imitation of Dutch pronunciation, that both echoed *Devine Weeks* and foreshadowed the nineteenth-century linkage of Eden with landscape art. Milton envisioned Eden as the work of God, not man, which therefore resembled a particularly pleasant and beautiful natural spot rather than the artificial garden of traditional imagination— "not nice Art / In Beds and curious Knots, but Nature boon / Powred forth profuse on Hill and Dale and Plaine" (4.241–243). In Eden, natural phenomena delight. Milton's striking description of evening (4.598–609), the first in English literature, spawned a genre of evening poetry.[103] Nature also played moral or metaphorical roles.[104] Nature led Adam to knowledge of God and then suffered moral transformation under the Curse along with Adam and Eve's Fall.[105] An important aspect was Milton's treatment of light, which always symbolized God's presence, as darkness did his absence.[106] It was during "Twilight upon the Earth, short Arbiter / Twixt Day and Night" (9.48–51) that Satan slipped into Eden. Smoke and darkness represented God's wrath. Hell combined these elements of fire, smoke, and "darkness visible" (1.60–63). A volcano stood in Hell, the fiery smoking counterpart to the mountain of God in Eden.

Milton portrayed Adam and Eve living and working harmoniously with God and nature, and seeing God's attributes in his works. Their Morning Hymn—probably the poem's most beloved passage—began, "These are thy glorious works, Parent of good, / Almightie, thine this universal Frame, / Thus wondrous fair; thy self how wondrous then! / Unspeakable, who sitst above these Heavens / To us invisible or dimly seen / In these thy lowest works, yet these declare / Thy goodness beyond thought, and Power Divine" (5.153–159). The Morning Hymn was a metrical version of Psalm 148. Calvinists sang versified psalms, which God himself had provided for worship, disdaining hymns written by fallen man, and in fact Milton's first poetic work was metrical psalms. Psalm 148 was a perennial Reformed favorite, which Stoddard for example cited to urge young people to learn to praise the Creator.[107] Milton like the psalmist enjoins all creation to sing the Creator's praise: the angels, the sun, moon and stars, the elements, the plants, the waters, the singing bird, and the animals of land and sea. The Morning Hymn epitomized the harmony of humans with God and nature in a world where Adam did not kill animals for food or any other purpose, where human labor kept Eden beautiful and productive, where Adam and Eve took only what they needed and knew no greed or want, and where humanity and all nature together praised and glorified God—as they could never do as well or as effortlessly again, as Bradstreet also lamented. Their spontaneous praise dramatized the Reformed rejection of human invention in worship and the belief that, as the Westminster Shorter Catechism of 1648 famously put it, "the chief end of man" was "to glorify God, and to enjoy him forever." Nineteenth-century Romantics responded enthusiastically to this scene of praise and glorification of God in a beautiful natural setting, the true and original worship service.[108]

Paradise Lost's sympathetic depiction of nature has "green" overtones. Milton lovingly and accurately detailed the various plants and trees of Eden, in contrast to animals, which he treated comparatively cursorily, but much of the poem was simply a love song to the earth. Book 7 contains a remarkable, exuberant visualization of the six days of creation.[109] The poem notes how the Fall of Adam and Eve led to environmental destruction. In Reformed theology, greed exiled us from Paradise, when Adam and Eve "serve[d] ungovern'd appetite" (11.517). After Satan first entered Eden in order to look it over, he sat in the tallest tree disguised as a cormorant, emblem of insatiable greed, not knowing he perched in the Tree of Life itself merely for the view. The demon of greed, Mammon, loved gold and plundered the earth. From his teachings humans "Ransack'd the Center, and with impious hands / Rifl'd the bowels, of thir mother Earth / For Treasures better hid" (1.679–688). The long reign of *Paradise Lost* in popular culture from late seventeenth to the early twentieth century coincided with the era when education rarely included any science. Many readers learned their first scientific concepts in passages that alluded to or discussed astronomy, physics, chemistry, or botany. *Paradise Lost* endorsed Adam's search for understanding nature, but only if understanding Creation led to glorifying God.[110]

Paradise Lost ended on a curiously hopeful note despite the tragedy of sin, the Curse, and expulsion from Eden. With Archangel Michael's promise of "a Paradise within thee, happier farr," the angels escorted Adam and Eve out of the garden. "The World was all before them, where to choose / Thir place of rest, and Providence thir guide. / They hand in hand with wandering steps and slow, / Through *Eden* took thir solitarie way" (12.646–649).

Although Paradise was an enduring theme throughout the history of Christianity, never had it received the concentrated attention that Reformed Protestants gave it. There was something about this religious tradition, perhaps the undercurrent of fear of God's wrath, or the implacable decree of predestination, or the prophetic calls for reform and righteousness, or the censoriousness of its theologians and preachers, that stirred nostalgia for an imagined era of bliss and peace with God. Very likely, too, the Calvinist emphasis on God's presence in nature inspired a longing for that long-lost moment in time when God could be enjoyed in a beautiful landscape without the impairing effects of the Fall.

The Works of God, Not Man

The rugged summit of Mount Holyoke in the foreground of *The Oxbow* did not much resemble the actual place. Writing in *American Scenery* in 1840, Nathaniel Parker Willis described the spot as it truly looked: "The ascent at the side is easy; and it is a fashionable climb for tourists, whose patronage of ginger-beer and sunrises maintains a shantry [*sic*] and a hermit on the top."[111] Cole removed all evidence of human presence from the much-visited spot to show a wild, lonely mountaintop with a Salvatorean twisted, broken tree. No fashionable tourists drink ginger-beer and no hermit in his shanty sells refreshments. Just the lone painter views the scene, taking in the sublimity of God's presence in the wilderness of the left side and the beauty of a godly landscape on the right. By the same token, it was no accident that the picturesque town of Northampton lie just beyond the frame, rather than inside it.

To Reformed Protestants, the works of fallen humanity distracted from the divine beauty of the works of the Creator. Humanity seemed despicable when compared to nature's theater of divine glory. Bradstreet's contemplations of creation gave her pleasure, until the creatures' effortless praise of God made her think of her own "imbecility" and then thoughts of Eden led to contemplation of sin and death. Likewise, Ebenezer Hazard, a Philadelphia businessman, elder in the Presbyterian Church, member of the American Philosophical Society, and Fellow of the Academy of Natural Sciences, aptly expressed the Calvinist mode of thinking when in 1780 he wrote a friend, "I never critically contemplate any of the works of Nature without such views of the wisdom, the power, and the majesty of God, as are rapturous and transporting. These views often carry me quite beyond the creature. I get lost in the Creator; come back to earth, and despise myself. They are worth having, notwithstanding they produce this consequence."[112]

Calvinism encouraged believers like Bradstreet and Hazard to "despise" themselves in creation. The world was made for man, Calvin affirmed: "Heaven and earth being thus most richly adorned and copiously supplied with all things, like a large and splendid mansion gorgeously constructed and exquisitely furnished, at length man was made—man, by the beauty of his person and his many noble endowments, the most glorious specimen of the works of God."[113] However, by and large the goodness and beauty that Calvin found in nature he was quite unable to see in humans, who were by nature "vicious, perverse, corrupt, void, and deprived of all good, rich and abundant in evil."[114] The sins that led to the Fall of Adam and Eve demanded particular condemnation for having brought sin and death into the world: pride and disobedience, first of all, and then ambition, ingratitude, greed, and desire.[115] In contrast to the works of God, the works of man—"human inventions"—bore imperfections and pollutions that mirrored the vanity and corruption of depraved human nature.[116] Calvin therefore forcefully proclaimed the Bible and Creation as sole places to seek the pure and the godly. Anything adverse or unpleasant in nature he ascribed either to the direct effects of human action or to God's curse on nature to punish Adam for his sin.[117] Upon the twin tenets of human depravity and God's total sovereignty in the universe rested the principle that individuals by their own weak efforts could not attain salvation, which God freely gave for his own glory—the fearful and characteristically Calvinist doctrine of predestination.

Reformed theologians followed suit as they scorned the works of men in nature and man's inventions, or unscriptural innovations, especially in worship. One of Ames's major books, for example, *A Fresh Suit Against Human Ceremonies in God's Worship* (1633), carried on its title page an epigraph from Psalm 119: "I hate vayn inventions: but thy Law doe I love." Not only worship was sullied by human works, but all also that came from the hand of man. After the Fall, wrote Milton in *Paradise Lost,* "Sin / With vanity had fill'd the works of men" (3.446–7). In his treatise on Original Sin, Edwards asserted that man's first invention was Adam's eating of the forbidden fruit, whose consequence was the "many Lusts and Corruptions of Mankind" in their own inventions.[118]

Worse, the works of man perverted the works of God. Willard noted, "There is an *Universal Vanity* which like an overflowing Deluge hath covered this lower World; and all these Creatures suffer under it: The Apostle [Paul] tells us it is not the Creature's Fault, that doth not patiently sustain it, but groans under it (*Rom.* 8. 20, 21, 22); that Acts up to its Ability, Serves to its End; but being [made?] to pass thro' the hands of Sinful Man it is there spoiled: *That* stands pointing to God and his Glory, but *Man* takes it, and makes it Serve himself; yea & Arms it in Rebellion against his Maker."[119] Edwards put it more memorably in his famous sermon "Sinners in the Hands of an Angry God": "God's Creatures are Good, and were made for Men to serve God with, and don't willingly subserve to any other Purpose, and groan with they are abused to Purposes so directly contrary to their Nature and End. And the World would spue you out, were it not for the sovereign Hand of him who hath subjected it in Hope."[120]

Therefore, Reformed Protestants sought to distance themselves from artificial environments in order to immerse themselves in the unsullied works of God. Dissenter minister Isaac Watts, in his often-reprinted *Improvement of Mind* of 1741, remarked, "When we are in the *House* or the *City,* wheresoever we turn our Eyes, we see the *Works of Men;* when we are *abroad in the Country,* we behold more of the *Works of God.* . . . Read the Wisdom of God, and his admirable Contrivance in them all: Read his Almighty Power, his rich and various Goodness, in all the Works of his

Hands."[121] In 1853, Theodore Parker, the great Boston Unitarian preacher, though a strong foe of Calvinism as a theology, still held the Calvinist doctrine of nature: "In cities men tread on an artificial ground of brick or stone, breathe an unnatural air, see the heavens only a handful at a time, think the gas-lights better than the stars, and know little how the stars themselves keep the police of the sky. Ladies and gentlemen in towns see Nature only at second-hand. It is hard to deduce God from a brick pavement. . . . In the country men and women are always in the presence of Nature, and feel its impulse to reverence and trust. . . . The material world is the element of communion between man and God. To heedful men God preaches on every mount, utters beatitudes in each little flower of spring."[122]

Worshipping in a Congregation of One

One figure appears in *The Oxbow*—the conspicuously solitary artist glancing back toward the viewer. Reformed Protestants appreciated God in nature much better in solitude, in communion with the Divine in the plantations of God, far from the works of fallen humanity. Bradstreet implied as much in "Contemplations," whose stanzas tell of the poet walking alone through natural scenes and meditating on the creatures. While this was a consequence of the Protestant doctrine that salvation was an issue between the individual and God, it was also reinforced by Puritan devotional practices. Puritans preached the value of what Puritans called "secret prayer," after Matthew 6:6, an old Christian tradition that Puritans observed widely and frequently. The Mathers, for example, encouraged it. Increase Mather published a sermon on secret prayer in 1682.[123] Cotton wrote *The Religion of the Closet* in 1705 and recommended, "The Works of GOD are well worthy of your *Meditations;* and you are to *Meditate* on them, till you *Glorify* Him."[124] Small houses and large families drove fathers, mothers, and even children to fields and woods in search of solitude for secret prayer.[125] Militia captain Roger Clap instructed his offspring to "*Pray in Secret,* though you have not a Closet or Door to shut; you need none: You may Pray alone in the Woods, as Christ did in the Mountain: You may Pray as you walk in the Field, as *Isaac* did."[126] From childhood, the missionary David Brainerd often prayed "secretly," apparently in the woods, and enjoyed numerous profound religious experiences. Sometimes, like Bradstreet, Brainerd "envied the birds and beasts their happiness, because they were not exposed to eternal misery."[127] Born in 1772 to poor Calvinist farmers in Royalston, Massachusetts, and raised in frontier Bridgewater, Vermont, Abner Jones recalled, "I used frequently to resort to secret prayer. The place which I chose for this purpose, was at the foot of a rock, where it seemed there was a place carved out on purpose for me to kneel down in."[128]

Edwards frequently practiced meditation and prayer alone in the woods and fields. Like Brainerd and Jones, as a boy he "used to pray five times a day in secret. . . . I with some of my school-mates joined together, and built a booth in a swamp, in a very retired spot, for a place of prayer. And besides, I had particular secret places of my own in the woods, where I used to retire by myself."[129] After graduating from Yale, Edwards took his first position at a Presbyterian church in New York City, where he walked, meditated, and prayed at "a solitary place, on the banks of Hudson's River."[130] Later, at Northampton, he regularly rode into the woods to reflect, pray, meditate, and now and then see visions, perhaps at times near the oxbow, or perhaps in the distant hills, or even atop Mount Holyoke, where he could look out over the magnificent works of creation that Cole immortalized in *The Oxbow*.[131] "No wonder the beauty and majesty of nature stamped themselves unforgettably on his early thought," wrote Edwards's biographer Ola Elizabeth Winslow.[132]

In the nineteenth and twentieth centuries, when Reformed Protestants went alone to the woods for spiritual purposes, they followed an already long-established tradition of retiring privately to a natural spot to meditate, pray, and find God. When Emerson advised the solitary individual to seek mystical union with the Divine in the woods, he simply restated long-standing Calvinist advice. Puritans had worn a broad path into the wild long before Transcendentalists discovered it and marked the trail for spiritually inclined nature-lovers.

Nature's Tales of Divine Glory

It should not be strange that Cole expected his viewers to read the landscape of *The Oxbow* for the tale it told, because Reformed Protestants were fond of thinking of nature as a holy book to be read. Dating from the works of St. John Chrysostom and St. Augustine in the fourth century, this traditional Christian doctrine taught that the book of revelation (the Bible) and the "book" of nature both told of God's existence and attributes and furthermore must agree because both came direct from the same Author. Although Calvin himself never referred to God's two "books,"[133] an early

Calvinist creed, the Belgic Confession of 1561, picked up the book meta-phor and inserted it after the opening declaration of the existence and attributes of God: "We know [God] by two means: first, by the creation, preservation, and government of the universe; which is before our eyes as a most elegant book, wherein all creatures, great and small, are as so many characters leading us to contemplate the invisible things of God, namely, his eternal power and Godhead, as the Apostle Paul saith (Rom. 1:20). . . . Secondly, . . . by his holy and divine Word."[134] From this point on, the book of nature was Calvinists' second Scripture.[135]

Calvinists eagerly read the "characters," the "pages," the "manu-scripts," or the "book" of nature. Du Bartas's *Devine Weekes* declared, "The World's a Booke in *Folio*, printed all / With God's great Workes in Letters Capitall: / Each Creature, is a Page, and each effect, / A faire Caracter, void of all defect."[136] In Milton's *Paradise Lost*, the angel Rafael tells Adam that "Heav'n / Is as the book of God before thee set, / wherein to read his wondrous works."[137] Increase and Cotton Mather's publica-tions mentioned the book of nature before any others in New England. Cotton Mather used the metaphor often. He wrote in *The Christian Philosopher*, "*Chrysostom*, I remember, mentions a *Twofold Book* of GOD; the Book of the *Creatures*, and the Book of the *Scriptures*: GOD hav-ing taught first of all us διὰ πραγμάτον, by his *Works*, did it afterwards διὰ γραμμάτον, by his *Words*."[138] Mather's colleague Samuel Willard, in *A Compleat Body of Divinity* of 1726, extended the metaphor with the images of "leaves" and "characters": "the *book of nature,* the great and admirable works of God; . . . there is never a leaf in this Book, but hath something of God written legibly upon it, and many Characters of his Divine power, wisdom and goodness there engraven."[139] Edwards liber-ally sprinkled his writings with references to the book of nature. From sermons, books, and hymns, the book of nature gained popular currency as well. Watts's hymns are a notable example. Long beloved and sung in countless churches of many denominations, they often praised the book of nature and the presence in creation of God and his attributes, such as his metrified psalm, Psalm 19: "All nature joins to shew thy praise; / Thus God in every creature shines, / Fair is the book of nature's lines, / But fairer is thy book of grace."[140] The metaphor turned into an inescap-able cliché in the nineteenth century. Scores of nineteenth-century sci-ence textbooks for the young, replete with moral and religious lessons from the Creation, bore variations of the title *The Book of Nature*. No less was the phrase met with in college science courses until the second half of the century. The phrase "book of nature" finally faded from use around 1920.[141]

Cole painted *The Oxbow* in the midst of a popular vogue for natural history, which Reformed Protestants pursued with special enthusiasm and religious devotion. If Cole's paintings were to be true to nature's truths and read the characters on nature's pages aright, he must make them scientifically accurate. He read geology and included geological terminology on his sketches in order to incorporate geologically correct details into his landscapes. In his paintings Cole frequently included such elements as erratic boulders left by retreating glaciers, which at the time were interpreted as relics of Noah's Flood. Cole's 1829 *The Subsiding of the Waters of the Deluge* (Figure 1.5, see color insert) illustrated current geological theory regarding the origins of dramatic geological formations. In *The Course of Empire* series, a high bluff in the background with an erratic boulder on its summit served as a reminder of how God brings low the vain works of man at last. Nevertheless, his geological details were often incorrect, both because Cole, following Reynolds, valued creativity over slavish reproduction of reality and because he painted in his studio from memory and from sketches made at the spot.[142]

Cole's interest in science would connect him with another person with an association with Northampton. Sometime in the 1830s Daniel Wadsworth introduced him to his relation Benjamin Silliman, Yale's first professor of science. Silliman and Wadsworth were married to nieces of John Trumbull, the celebrated Connecticut painter who had discovered Cole and introduced him to Wadsworth in 1825. Cole corresponded with Silliman, sent him geological specimens to identify, and visited him in New Haven. For Silliman, as for Cole, geology and art served higher, spiritual ends. In 1830, Silliman had written in the *American Journal of Science and Arts* that the two pursuits, "the one so interesting to science, and the other to taste and moral feeling, are capable of being blended, in a manner both highly instructive and delightful."[143]

By Silliman's time, Calvinists had long dominated the establishment and progress of American science. With the exception of Quakers for a time, members of other denominations (however well educated) lagged considerably in advancing the field. Many of the most influential acquired their interest and expertise in natural history while studying abroad. Barred from Oxford or Cambridge, which were reserved for Anglicans, Congregationalists and Presbyterians studied at the universities of Leiden and Edinburgh, where the latest advances in natural history were taught in the medical curriculum by eminent professors.[144] Colonists, especially such Scottish immigrants as Cadwallader and Jane Colden of New York, Alexander Garden and John Lining of Charleston, South Carolina, and William Smith, first provost of what is now the University of Pennsylvania, corresponded with and sent specimens to leading European scientists.[145] Three cities, Charleston, Philadelphia, and Boston, formed early centers of scientific activity. Charleston's natural science tradition passed its hey-day by the antebellum era. Most prominent was Charleston Lutheran pastor John Bachman, native of New York. Stephen Elliott, tutored by a Connecticut Congregational clergyman and educated at Yale, published the two volumes of *A Sketch of the Botany of South-Carolina and Georgia* in 1816 and 1824. Charleston doctor John Edwards Holbrook, born in Beaufort to New Englanders, raised in Massachusetts, and trained at Brown University and in Europe, produced the landmark five-volume *North American Herpetology* in 1842.[146] Outside Charleston, Southerners published little natural history, with the exception of Edinburgh-trained John Mitchell of Virginia.[147]

Philadelphia Quakers and Reformed Protestants led the late colonies and early nation in natural history. American Quaker interest in the natu-ral world went back to Pennsylvania founder William Penn, whose interest in botany led in 1681 to his election to the Royal Society. Quaker natural-ists included James Logan and three generations of Bartrams: William Bartram, his son John Bartram, and his grandson Thomas Say. Quaker natural history faded as Reformed science thrived.[148] Benjamin Franklin, a Presbyterian from Boston, cofounded the American Philosophical Society in 1742. The first professional naturalist in the United States, Benjamin Smith Barton studied at the universities of Edinburgh and Göttingen before teaching natural history at the University of Pennsylvania.[149] Dutch immigrant Gerard Troost, a graduate of Leiden, cofounded in 1812 the Philadelphia Academy of Natural Sciences and served as its first president, succeeded in 1817 by Scottish-born geologist William Maclure.[150] Another Scot, Alexander Wilson, published the landmark nine-volume *American Ornithology* between 1808 and 1814, which inspired John James Audubon and John Burroughs.[151]

No city matched Boston in enthusiasm for natural history, which extended deep and wide in the local population. Even New England farmers recorded the day the first spring flowers opened or the first birds returned for the summer, and took walks in the woods.[152] Bostonians founded a short-lived Linnaean Society in 1814, succeeded by the Boston Society of

Natural History in 1830. Instruction in natural history began in America at Harvard, where botany numbered among topics of instruction from its earliest days.[153] In 1846, Swiss zoologist Louis Agassiz's Boston lectures instigated the establishment in 1847 of Harvard's Lawrence Scientific School with a professorship for Agassiz. In 1857, New England poet Henry Wadsworth Longfellow wrote a famous birthday tribute in which Nature invited the infant Agassiz to "read what is still unread / In the manuscripts of God."[154] Agassiz, who was the son and grandson of Reformed ministers and the famed advocate of the revolutionary theory of the Ice Age, gave Harvard the benefit of his prestige and charismatic teaching until his death in 1873.

Cole's friend Silliman played an especially important and leading role in American education in natural history. A train of associations leads from *The Oxbow* to Silliman by way of his mentor, President Timothy Dwight of Yale. Dwight's grandfather Colonel Timothy Dwight had been Edwards's leading ally in the unsuccessful battle against his dismissal in 1750. Dwight's son Timothy Jr. married Edwards's daughter Mary. The Dwights raised their thirteen children in an intellectual and orthodox Calvinist household in which the name of Grandfather Edwards was spoken with reverence. One of their children, also named Timothy Dwight, was destined to be a major player in the history of American Calvinism as well as an important facilitator in the rise of American science. Precocious and full of promise, he graduated from Yale at the head of his class in 1769 at age 17 and earned his master's degree in 1771, and was ordained a Congregational minister. Dwight successively served as chaplain to the Continental Army; founded an academy in Northampton; served as Northampton's state representative; pastored the church at Greenfield Hill near Fairfield, Connecticut, where he founded a second academy; led Connecticut's Federalist Party; and helped found Calvinist Andover Theological Seminary. A poet and hymn writer, Dwight also found time to write America's first published epic, modeled on *Paradise Lost,* entitled *The Conquest of Canaan* (1785), and two other long poems, *The Triumph of Infidelity* (1788) and *Greenfield Hill* (1794). After his death in 1817, two sons published several volumes of Dwight's sermons, his *Theology Explained and Defended,* and Dwight's best-known work, *Travels in New England and New York.* In 1795, he was appointed to a position he long coveted, president of Yale.[155]

In 1802, Dwight hired Silliman to fill a new position in chemistry and natural history. Dwight led the fight against "infidelity," his word for religious skepticism and liberalism, in effectively the first campaign in America's so-called culture wars. Nature and science were weapons in the arsenal of orthodoxy, as he wrote in *The Conquest of Canaan:* "So round th'immense, on fair creation's breast, / In endless pomp the GODHEAD shines impress'd; / His love, his beauty, o'er all nature burns; / Each sun unfolds it, and each world returns."[156] To lessen the lure of "infidelity" for New England's young men, he expanded Yale's offerings in mathematics and science to show their harmony with religion.[157] American colleges had offered mathematics and science courses for decades, but Dwight turned Yale into the leading scientific educational institution in American science.[158] He invited Silliman, of Fairfield, Connecticut, to join the faculty. Silliman was a bright young lawyer, recent Yale graduate, and son of a close friend, but had no knowledge of science whatsoever. No matter. Dwight chose his professors for their politics (Federalist), denomination (Congregational), and theology (Calvinist), and Silliman was safe on all counts.

Silliman surely exceeded all expectations. To gain necessary scientific background, he attended the University of Pennsylvania in Philadelphia and the University of Edinburgh. At Yale, Silliman taught chemistry and the first course on geology in an American college and in 1810 spearheaded creation of the Yale medical school. In 1818 he founded *The American Journal of Science,* the first successful American scientific journal, and for two decades was its editor. He also cofounded the Yale Scientific School in 1846–1847 (renamed the Sheffield Scientific School in 1861), whose example Harvard followed the following year, and which awarded the first doctorates of philosophy in the United States. Additionally, Silliman gave popular lectures across the country, always harmonizing science and faith, which like Dwight he insisted rightly understood were in perfect agreement.[159]

Nature Study as Moral Pursuit

Even the glacial lake that formerly flooded the Connecticut Valley at the Oxbow has associations with Reformed love of natural science. Its name, Lake Hitchcock, honors Congregational minister Edward Hitchcock, the geologist who discovered it in 1818. Born in Deerfield, eighteen miles upriver from Northampton, Hitchcock fell under Silliman's spell at Yale and the two became lifelong friends and colleagues. In 1825, due to ill health, Hitchcock resigned the pulpit of the Congregational Church in

Conway and accepted an invitation to be the first professor of chemistry and natural history at Amherst College, across the Connecticut from Northampton. He would serve as State Geologist of Massachusetts and of Vermont, first president of the Association of American Geologists and Naturalists (later the American Association for the Advancement of Science), and president of Amherst. America's foremost Christian geologist and defender of natural theology, Hitchcock published *The Religion of Geology* in 1851.[160]

The interest of Cole, Dwight, Silliman, and Hitchcock in science—especially geology and biology—as an aid to religion was the fruit of a long development in Reformed countries. Already in the middle of the seventeenth century, Reformed clergy were researching and writing about natural science. English Puritan minister John Ray penned many important scientific books. His *The Wisdom of God Manifested in the Works of Creation* of 1691 presaged a popular new genre, "physico-theology," an updated form of natural theology. In 1713, Anglican vicar William Derham published the widely influential *Physico-Theology* to admiring audiences on both shores of the Atlantic. Derham's purpose foreshadowed Dwight's: "for the Proof of the Christian Religion against Atheists and other Infidels, to improve this occasion in the Demonstration of the *Being* and *Attributes* of an infinitely wise and powerful Creator, from a Cursory Survey of the Works of Creation."[161] Anglican priest William Paley drew from Ray, Derham, and others in his popular *Natural Theology; Or, Evidence of the Existence and Attributes of the Deity, Collected from the Appearances of Nature* of 1802, which went into innumerable editions in England and America and became required college reading for generations of students.

In English America, the first native-born scientists were New England ministers, most notable among them Increase and Cotton Mather. In 1684, Increase Mather cofounded the (short-lived) Boston Philosophical Society on the model of England's Royal Society, the world's first scientific society. He published a book on comets, *Kometographia,* and in 1685 two more books on scientific subjects, *An Essay for the Recording of Illustrious Providences* and *The Doctrine of Divine Providence,* but lamented his inability to contribute more to science. His son Cotton would be the most important American Puritan scientist.[162] Medicine and science fascinated the younger Mather his whole life. Between 1712 and 1724 he sent a string of dispatches he called "Curiosa Americana" to the Royal Society, which elected him Fellow in 1713. He wrote the only comprehensive medical book in colonial America, the extensive but unpublished *Angel of Bethesda.*[163]

Ray, Derham, and Puritan scientist Robert Boyle inspired one of Mather's best-known books, *The Christian Philosopher* of 1721, the first American general book on science. It developed the notion of "the Twofold Book of GOD," nature and revelation, to assert that scientific knowledge of creation led to "a PHILOSOPHICAL RELIGION; And yet how *Evangelical!*" As the priest of the temple of God which is creation, man could well answer the end of his existence, "To glorify GOD." To Mather, every creature was a preacher, and even the smallest blade of grass proof of the existence, power, and glory of God. Science would evangelize for Reformed Protestantism.[164]

Hitchcock forms a leading example for how study of the works of God in nature offered an easily available, innocent, and morally profitable activity to small-town ministers with free time. Parson-naturalists would dominate English natural science in the late eighteenth and nineteenth centuries and still made significant contributions into the twentieth. Curate Gilbert White in 1789 published his beloved *Natural History and Antiquities of Selborne* to move "his readers to pay a more ready attention to the wonders of the Creation, too frequently overlooked as common occurrences."[165] Natural science was equally a safe, moral, and "improving" subject for children and women. In 1761, English children's-book publisher John Newbery, writing under the pseudonym "Tom Telescope," pioneered the genre with his *The Newtonian System of Philosophy, Adapted to the Capacities of Young Gentlemen and Ladies*, in print for eighty years, and replete with religious and moral lessons.[166] In 1777 the Dutch pastor Jan Floris Martinet, realizing that his young catechism students wanted more than just the Heidelberg Catechism, published his hugely popular *Katechismus der Natuur*, in print in many languages into the twentieth century. Martinet took his young readers by the hand and walked them through parks, woods, and fields, attaching inspiring moral lessons as he went.[167] Nature books for children and for home use soon flooded America. In the late 1780s and 1790s the important Worcester, Massachusetts, printer Isaiah Thomas published popular American editions of English and Scottish moralistic natural-history books and was followed by other Massachusetts printers. Gradually the science overshadowed the moral lessons, without displacing them entirely. Publishers relied less on reprints from England and Scotland, and American works appeared abroad. The popular 1832 *Youth's Book on Natural Theology* by Connecticut Congregational minister Thomas H. Gallaudet went into several editions, including London and Bombay editions and a Hawaiian translation.[168] Women and children throughout the Reformed world walked out into woods and fields for the lessons in natural history and religion that they would find there. By 1850 natural history became a popular avocation for adults as well. Women increasingly were drawn to the socially acceptable life sciences and many made significant contributions, particularly in botany and ornithology.[169]

The nature study movement injected nature into the schools and gave new impetus to the connection between childhood and the good moral effects found in nature. The movement began in the summer of 1873 when, to spread the love of nature among young people, Agassiz founded a school for teachers on Penikese Island off Massachusetts on teaching natural history. Beginning in the 1890s, Congregationalist professor Liberty Hyde Bailey of Cornell and his Quaker colleague Anna Botsford Comstock made natural history (with religion mostly removed) a popular school program for another quarter century or more. Comstock's 1911 *Handbook of Nature Study* has never been out of print.[170]

From Providence to Cosmos

In 1851, Silliman made a pilgrimage from Yale to the Berlin home of Agassiz's mentor, the great hero of American natural science Alexander von Humboldt. His trek symbolized the natural sympathy that Calvinistic science held for the holistic science that Humboldt championed. Calvin was certainly no scientist, but his doctrine of an active God in an active creation of mutually interacting parts had profound implications for the work of Reformed scientists. Creation in Calvinism was no static universe but a world of development and change. Calvinist ways of thinking about nature promoted biological holism and acceptance of change and process in natural history. No Reformed scientist before Darwin would have greater influence than the early nineteenth-century explorer-scientist Humboldt, who was absolutely lionized in Reformed nations and especially in America. His multivolume *Personal Narrative,* published beginning in 1814, was avidly read in England and America. In vivid prose it regaled the reader with adventures and discoveries from Humboldt's scientific journeys of exploration between 1799 and 1804 into the interior of South America. In 1849 he brought out a widely read series of lectures published in English as *Aspects of Nature* or *Views of Nature.* The five volumes of his great masterwork, *Cosmos,* were released serially in the 1840s and 1850s to huge anticipation and acclaim in America, just before Humboldt's death in 1859.[171]

Humboldt founded a characteristically Reformed style of science. He grew up in a pious Calvinist household, admired Swiss-Calvinist author Jean-Jacques Rousseau, and modeled his career as scientist-explorer after that of his friend and mentor Georg Forster. Forster and his father, Prussian naturalist and Reformed pastor Johann Reinhold Forster, had accompanied Captain James Cook on his voyage of discovery. Forester argued for a holistic approach to the sciences to attain a unified understanding of the diversity of nature as the immediate revelation of God and thereby to draw nearer to the Creator.[172] Humboldtian science combined detailed measurement of natural phenomena with observation of their interrelations, an insistent focus on the unity in the diversity of the world. Despite their overall secular tone (no gushing over God's presence in nature), Humboldt's works contained noticeable Calvinistic moralism and hints of spiritual wonder at the unity in diversity of the cosmos. He decried the sins of man but expressed love of the natural world. In *Views of Nature* Humboldt noted the vanity of human works, much as Calvin had and Cole would in the paintings of *The Course of Empire* series: "Thus pass away the generations of men!—thus perish the records of the glory of nations! Yet . . . when in the storms of time the monuments of man's creative art are scattered to the dust—an ever new life springs from the bosom of the earth. Unceasingly prolific nature unfolds her germs,—regardless though sinful man, ever at war with himself, tramples beneath his foot the ripening fruit!"[173] To Humboldt, nature has moral influence upon those humans who know to see and to listen. All of nature stands "in an ancient and mysterious communion with the spiritual life of man." The sounds of living things are the "voices of nature revealed to the pious and susceptible spirit of man."[174]

Cosmos similarly celebrated nature instead of humanity. It lacked an anthropological volume but had five volumes about the natural world and its moral, spiritual, and intellectual affect on humanity.[175] As the very title *Cosmos* indicated, the central concept underlying all Humboldt's work was nature's unity in diversity: "Nature considered *rationally*, that is to say, submitted to the process of thought, is a unity in diversity of phenomena; a harmony, blending together all created things, however dissimilar in form and attributes; one great whole (τὸ πᾶν) animated by the breath of life. The most important result of a rational inquiry into nature is, therefore, to establish the unity and harmony of this stupendous mass of force and matter."[176]

The scientific advances of Cole's era dovetailed nicely with the Reformed notion of landscape painting. Landscape painters read geology to correct their portrayal of rocks, biology for depiction of plants, and meteorology for precise rendering of the new nomenclature of cloud types: nimbus, cumulus, and cirrus. Humboldt's science played a role. His descriptions of nature were to science what landscapes were to art. His proto-ecological science emphasized measurement and study of individual species within the broad unity of the environment. He had both an implied and explicit interest in landscape painting. Young Romantic landscape painters in Germany, Britain, and the United States insisted on the truth of the individual components of the landscape, primarily in the correct delineation of identifiable plant species and geological formations, in an overall composition.[177]

Cole's art was Humboldtian art. Noble claimed that "Cole clearly saw, and heartily rejoiced in the great and all pervading principle of the universe, *unity arising out of infinity,*"[178] that fundamental tenet of Humboldt's cosmos. *The Garden of Eden* and *Expulsion from the Garden of Eden* show more evidence that Cole incorporated Humboldt-inspired science to make his version of Eden distinctive. Just prior, English artist John Martin had brought art, landscape, and *Paradise Lost* together in innovative and hugely successful engraved illustrations published between 1825 and 1827. Previous illustrators had focused on the poem's characters; Martin made landscape an essential part of the story. Immediately Cole began to rework Martin's engravings of Adam and Eve's Morning Hymn and of the expulsion in a novel interpretation of Eden as lush and tropical. In *The Personal Narrative,* Humboldt vividly described his ascent of the volcano on Tenerife and his encounters with the tropical landscape of South America. Considering his interest in geology and science,[179] surely Cole was familiar with *Personal Narrative,* which may even have inspired Cole to journey to the Caribbean island St. Eustatia in 1819, where he sketched the luxuriant tropical vegetation. Martin's engravings of a very English-looking Eden must have prompted Cole to recall his trip as he himself imagined what Eden looked like. The volcano in the *Expulsion* had no precedent in illustrations of *Paradise Lost,* which had only a volcano in hell. Did Humboldt's Tenerife volcano inspire Cole to add one?[180] Certainly in *Expulsion* Cole intended the very earth to express God's wrath against mankind, while a wolf-like carnivore's attack on a stag and swooping vulture at lower left illustrated how the Fall caused suffering in nature.

The career of Charles Darwin epitomized the connections between Reformed Protestantism and the development of the modern sciences of biology and ecology. Originally intent on taking holy orders, Darwin decided instead to study medicine. While a student at Edinburgh, he became more interested in the natural science courses than the medical curriculum. He studied William Paley's *Natural Theology*. Chosen to accompany the captain of the H.M.S. *Beagle* on its five-year voyage of exploration, Darwin always carried his copy of Milton's *Paradise Lost* when he expected to have any extended time on shore. Humboldt's *Personal Narrative* was an absolute inspiration to him. When he returned to England, he modeled his own *The Voyage of the Beagle* on it, the book that made him one of the nation's most celebrated scientists twenty years before *Origin of Species* of 1859. *Origin of Species* itself grew naturally out of the ideas of the interconnectedness of nature within a harmonious whole in a cosmos that was never "idle" but constantly creating itself. It was a natural theology without a creator.

The Calvinist Crescent: Cradle of Modern American Environmentalism

Living at the heart of the Calvinist crescent, Cole became the nation's best-known and best-beloved artist by expressing on canvas the Reformed mind in the early nineteenth century. From his brushes flowed visions of God in wild nature, of Eden still all around us, of the scientific study of creation in its details and its unity, and of humankind's moral duty to seek higher things than just worldly success. Cole's landscapes minimized human presence and human works as inferior to the glorious works of the creator. They and his works in general taught moral lessons and evangelized for a higher and holier view of the world.

Cole died in 1848, too early to see the ways that this heartland arc of the Reformed would put these principles into action. The Congregationalists of the Connecticut Valley and the New England diaspora would give the nation conservation in all its aspects: parks, which preserved God's natural world for the benefit of the people; forestry, which conserved natural resources for the common good; and agricultural improvement, which conserved the soil while providing sustenance for the people. They also midwifed the birth of ecology, the science behind the conservation agenda: the foundational work of American ecology was done by Stephen Forbes, Henry Chandler Cowles, and Charles Bessey, all Congregationalists, and their students.[181] Unitarians of Massachusetts fostered Transcendentalism, which popularized the return to wild nature to seek the spirit of God. Presbyterians from Pennsylvania and the spreading

Scottish diaspora across the Midwest and California shaped American environmentalism, from its manifestation in national parks, forests, and conservation agencies to its climax in the 1960s and 1970s. From Calvinism American environmentalism acquired many traits that would distinguish it, from its moralism to its suspicion of humans in the landscape to its urgent evangelism. These elements shaped its program and invested it with tremendous social, cultural, and political power.

2

Origins of Conservation in the Puritan Landscape

The Puritan Landscape of West Rock, New Haven

Nineteen-year-old Frederic Edwin Church craved success and recognition, not unlike his teacher, Thomas Cole, at the same age. Eager to follow the trail Cole blazed to the pinnacle of the American art world, Church decided to paint a "higher type of landscape" than those he had done in nearly two years as Cole's student. Familial expectations spurred his ambition. His father, Joseph Church, a wealthy businessman and devout Congregationalist in Hartford, Connecticut, had wanted his son to enter a more practical occupation than painter. Reluctantly indulging him, Joseph asked friend and neighbor Daniel Wadsworth to recommend the boy to Cole, whose high moral reputation eased his concerns. Cole could hardly refuse the request. Wadsworth was his early patron and staunch champion, while Church and others had commissioned a picture from him for the grand opening in 1844 of the new Wadsworth Atheneum, America's first public art museum. Besides all that, Cole needed money and Church had invited him to name his price.

Grateful to be the first student of the nation's preeminent painter, Frederic assured Cole that "my highest ambition lies in excelling in art. I pursue it not as a source of gain or merely as an amusement. I trust I have higher aims than these."[1] The sentiment surely pleased Cole, although, perhaps egged on by his father, who persisted in calling painting his son's "business," Church before too many years would be very wealthy from skillful painting and clever self-promotion. Cole recognized an unusually gifted artist when his student arrived in Catskill. The National Academy of Design showed two of the teenager's landscapes at its 1845 exhibition in New York City. For the 1846 exhibition, Church's painting in a higher style followed Cole's Alisonian principles that great paintings depicted historical or Biblical subjects or had associations with significant people or events. He chose an American scene, perhaps mindful of Charles Lanman's criticism of Cole in the *United States Democratic Review* in 1843, reprinted in *Letters from a Landscape Painter* in 1845. "Excepting his actual views of American scenery, the paintings of Cole might have been produced had he never set foot upon our soil, . . ." Lanman complained. "Let our young painters use their pencils to illustrate the thousands of scenes, strange, wild and beautiful, of our early history."[2]

Cole had contemplated painting such scenes and several years earlier included several on a list of potential subjects. One still-unpainted item, Thomas Hooker's journey through the wilderness with his Puritan congregation to found Hartford in 1636, perfectly suited Church's need to reassure friends and skeptical family back home. Filial piety ran strong in Connecticut, especially in families like his whose ancestors came with Hooker. "About the beginning of June, Mr. Hooker, Mr. Stone, and about a hundred men, women and children, took their departure from Cambridge, and travelled more than a hundred miles, through a hideous and trackless wilderness, to Hartford, . . ." as Hartford native Benjamin Trumbull recounted the oft-told story in 1820 in *A Complete History of Connecticut*. "They drove with them a hundred and sixty head of cattle. . . . Mrs. Hooker was borne through the wilderness on a litter."[3] Church followed these details closely as he set to work on an ambitiously large five-foot canvas.

Frederic Church's *Hooker and Company Journeying through the Wilderness from Plymouth to Hartford, in 1636* (Figure 2.2, see color insert) portrayed nature's religious and moral connotations within a more specific Reformed tradition than *The Oxbow*'s broadly Calvinist associations.[4] As critic Henry Theodore Tuckerman noted in 1867, "Church exhibits the New England mind pictorially developed."[5] Intended as a critique of Church's lack of poetic imagination and love of hard facts, Tuckerman's barb struck a larger truth. *Hooker and Company* and the series of New England landscapes that it launched celebrated the region's Puritan heritage and its example to the nation. When Church painted orderly, prosperous, moral landscapes of Connecticut Valley towns with explicit Congregational references and implicit associations with Puritan history and values, he sought to extol the American republican culmination of the most perfectly realized Calvinist society ever created. As a Congregationalist Whig and then

Republican, Church hoped to preserve and disseminate Connecticut's founding ideals of an orderly, godly society. Ministers Hooker in Hartford, John Davenport in New Haven, and John Warham and John Maverick in Windsor had guided the founding of a conservative Puritan society, which prospered and spread throughout the Connecticut Valley. From their principles a powerful ideology of conservation developed in the nineteenth century with three interconnected themes: agricultural improvement, conservation of forests and natural resources, and public parks. While the Calvinism that informed *The Oxbow* bequeathed to the environmental movement a tradition of the solitary individual in communion with God in Eden or studying his unsullied works, the Puritanism pictorially developed in Church's art left a legacy in the conservation movement.

Hooker and Company shows colonists in late afternoon crossing a stream on their descent into the beautiful Connecticut Valley. The rays of the setting sun give a glory to the scene suggestive of the Israelites' descent into the Promised Land, or perhaps of a return to Eden itself. Church's entirely imaginary composition brings together scattered natural features from the Connecticut Valley. The Puritan at the center—Hooker himself, perhaps—points to Hartford's Charter Oak. Behind him the Connecticut River makes its oxbow at Northampton. On the horizon lies New Haven's West Rock.[6] Symbolically *Hooker and Company* represents the religious and ideological origins of Connecticut-Valley Puritan civilization. Charter Oak and West Rock carry associations with the orderly, godly, free people about to rise in the region. Church turned to these emblematic natural features for several subsequent paintings. Twice more he portrayed Hartford's Charter Oak, a tree that symbolized resistance to political and religious tyranny. According to legend, Captain Joseph Wadsworth had hidden Connecticut's charter in a hollow of the oak to prevent representatives of tyrannical (and Catholic) King James II from seizing it. Church implicitly honored Daniel Wadsworth's ancestor but, more importantly, probably intended these pictures of Charter Oak to applaud Connecticut's tradition of resistance to arbitrary government. By implication as well, they criticized the ongoing Mexican War, which New England Whigs like the Churches vehemently opposed as unjust.[7]

West Rock appeared in Church's 1848 painting of another subject from Cole's list, the story of the Three Judges. After his Restoration in 1660, Charles II had hunted down the Puritan judges, or regicides, involved in the trial and execution in 1649 of his father, Charles I. Many escaped abroad to sympathetic Reformed countries. Three sailed for New Haven, where Davenport and his congregation concealed them. John Dixwell lived unrecognized under a pseudonym, but William Goffe and Edward Whalley had to hide in a cave on top of West Rock when the king's men came looking for them. When Charles's agents returned a second time, Goffe and Whalley fled upstream and settled in Hadley, directly across the river from Northampton.

Instead of another historical scene like *Hooker and Company*, Church's *West Rock, New Haven* (Figure 2.1, see color insert) relies on associations to suggest the heroic judges who dealt death to unrighteous tyrants and the godly Connecticut farmers who gave them refuge. The white spire of a Congregational Church rises meaningfully before West Rock, while in the foreground, men (church members, presumably) gather hay. West Rock, the solid, enduring natural emblem of Puritan resistance to ungodly monarchs, presides over a scene of religion, industry, prudence, virtue, peace, and plenty. The haying scene hearkens to the paintings of everyday life by the Dutch and Constable, but also to the smiling landscape in the right side of *The Oxbow*. As Cole's student, Church had painted a study of *The Oxbow*.[8] He seems here to allude to the neat hayfields in Nonotuck meadow nestled in the round swerve of the Connecticut River on land that belonged to Hadley, Goffe and Whalley's final sanctuary.

Cole had singled out such scenes for special praise in "Essay on American Scenery":

> The imagination can scarcely conceive Arcadian vales more lovely or more peaceful than the valley of the Connecticut—its villages are rural places where trees overspread every dwelling, and the fields upon its margin have the richest verdure . . . Seated on a pleasant knoll, look down into the bosom of that secluded valley, begirt with wooded hills—through those enamelled meadows and wide waving fields of grain, a silver stream winds lingeringly along—here, seeking the green shade of trees—there, glancing in the sunshine: on its banks are rural dwellings shaded by elms and garlanded by flowers—from yonder dark mass of foliage the village spire beams like a star . . . Those neat dwellings, unpretending to magnificence, are the abodes of plenty, virtue, and refinement.[9]

Both *The Oxbow* and *West Rock* depict just those wooded hills, those enamelled meadows, those waving fields, and that silver stream, and in *West Rock* that beaming village spire rising above yonder dark foliage. Both pictures honor modest plenty, virtue, and refinement of the New England village.[10]

West Rock, New Haven was Church's ticket to artistic recognition. Critics at the 1846 National Academy exhibition gave it positive notice, and the Academy elected him as its youngest full member. The Wadsworth Atheneum bought the painting. Church ended his studies with Cole and set up a studio in Hartford before moving to New York. In 1850 his rapid rise to prominence attracted two students, barely younger than he was: William James Stillman, who soon left bitterly dissatisfied with him; and Jervis McEntee, who became a lifelong friend. Not long afterward, Church roared past Cole's friend and successor Asher B. Durand to soar above other Hudson River School painters as the nation's leading artist.

Church lauded the landscape of New England and its religious associations in several more paintings. *View near Stockbridge* of 1847 featured the bucolic town in western Massachusetts where, after his ouster from Northampton, Jonathan Edwards preached and wrote his great works of theology. *New England Landscape* of 1849 and *New England Scenery* of 1851 were imaginary compositions of typical New England subjects. White church steeples beam above the green woods in *Stockbridge* and *New England Scenery*. Church also hiked and sketched in Vermont and on Mount Desert Island in Maine, which inspired several canvases of wilder landscapes. The best-known of this period of his career was symbolic *Beacon, Off Mount Desert Island,* which he painted at the peak of the political crisis over the Compromise of 1850.

Although after 1852 Church abandoned New England subjects for good as he turned toward new interests, he never forsook the interest he shared with Cole (and probably learned from him) in religious associations of landscape. When Church came to study with him, Cole was exclusively painting religious subjects and had joined Catskill's Episcopal church. Its pastor, Louis Legrand Noble, was a passionate and apparently persuasive advocate of his church who married Cole and Maria Bartowe in 1836. Cole's second journey to Italy in 1841–1842 and extensive exposure to Roman Catholicism seemed to have deepened his interest in liturgical, hierarchical Christianity. Upon his return, Noble baptized him and later Maria, too, presumably because Episcopalians did not recognize Dissenter baptisms. Like Cole, Church took subjects from the Bible and from Puritan literature for historical paintings. Church's grand painting for 1847 impressively imagined a scene from John Bunyan, *Christian on the Borders of the "Valley of the Shadow of Death," Pilgrim's Progress.* He also produced *Moses Viewing the Promised Land* in 1846, another *Pilgrim's Progress* and *The River of the Water of Life* in 1848, *The Plague of Darkness* in 1849, and *The Deluge* in 1850. The title of the 1850 painting *Twilight, "Short Arbiter 'Twixt Day and Night"* alluded to the line from *Paradise Lost* describing Satan's entrance into Eden as darkness fell, which underscored the ominous looming anthropomorphic rocks to the right and lent a sense of impending doom to the apparently peaceful landscape. This imagined scene—inspired by landscape Church had seen in Vermont, with a tranquil sunset and a small cabin in the wilderness, like *Beacon, Off Mount Desert Island* of the same year—may also comment on the great 1850 political crisis over slavery.

As Cole gravitated toward Episcopalianism, crosses increasingly appeared in his art and sneaked into his devoted student's as well. Cole painted *Cross in the Wilderness* in 1844, *The Solitary Cross* in 1845, and *Cross on a Hilltop* in 1846–1847. *Cross at Sunset* and the five-painting series *The Cross and the World* were unfinished in his studio at his death in early 1848. To most Protestants of the day, crosses signified papist superstition and idolatry and were rarely seen in American Protestant churches, although some Episcopalians would have been comfortable with crosses.[11] Church, "a nineteenth-century type of the old Puritan," according to his friend Charles Dudley Warner,[12] cleaved to the Reformed traditions of his upbringing. Modern critics have noticed how often Church included cruciform objects in his paintings and interpret this as injection of religion into landscape. Given Reformed aversion to crosses, he perhaps meant them also or even primarily to honor Cole, whom he always venerated. "Church never rose superior to Cole in his own esteem," Warner noted, "and all through life he was wont to speak of him with the same affectionate veneration that he must have felt for him in the first weeks of his tutelage."[13] After Cole died, Church painted *To the Memory of Cole* with a cross shaped like that in Cole's unfinished *Cross at Sunset* rising prominently on a hill with a view of the Catskills.[14] The small crosses and cruciform objects scattered throughout his paintings of the 1850s may therefore pay similar homage to his master.

Also like Cole, Church was close to clergymen. He and Noble traveled together in search of icebergs in 1859 and to Jamaica in 1865. Noble wrote the program books for Church's *Heart of the Andes* and his iceberg paintings. Nevertheless, Church remained true to Reformed Protestantism and did not follow Cole into the Episcopal Church. His family attended Hartford's Center Congregational Church, which

Hooker had founded, and which conservative, orthodox Joel Hawes pastored. After he moved to New York, Church attended the Dutch Reformed Church of George Washington Bethune, an art connoisseur and close friend. Church contributed an illustration (an engraving of *West Rock*) and Bethune an essay to *The Home Book of the Picturesque: or American Scenery, Art, and Literature* of 1852. Bethune retired to a home on a hill south of the town of Hudson with views of Catskill village, the Hudson River, and the Catskill Mountains. Church bought the neighboring property in 1860 and built a Downing cottage on it the next year. When Bethune died in 1862, he purchased his property and built his fantasy mansion, Olana, on the hilltop. There Church was active in Hudson's Presbyterian church, whose minister, W. S. Leavitt, was later called to Edwards's church in Northampton and befriended Charles Nicoll Talbot, owner of *The Oxbow*.[15]

Mutual Subjection According to Rule: The New England Town

The Calvinist and Puritan associations of Cole's *The Oxbow* and of Church's *West Rock, New Haven* and his New England pictures have their symbol in those Congregationalist spires rising above New England towns, beaming like stars. In the constellation of community churches spread across the green landscape from the Gulf of Maine to the Long Island Sound, townspeople fashioned the moral basis, the practical ethic, and the legal precedents from which conservation would arise in the nineteenth century. The New England town calls to mind a picture-postcard image of a columned church with a white steeple rising above the village green amidst gloriously colorful autumn foliage, its bell summoning townfolk for church or for that enduring symbol of American democracy, the town meeting. Despite Puritans' reputation as spoilers of fun and hangers of witches, Americans look upon no other colonial English settlements with the soft-focus sentiment that they do the Puritan town. Forged from an amalgam of Old English social, political, and economic practices and molded in the discipline of a powerful Reformed social ethic, the New England town reached its classic form just as Cole was painting *The Oxbow*. Until the end of the century, the children of the New England town became its evangelists. Like preachers pressing the Gospel on wayward sinners, they offered it as salvation for a nation staggering from one environmental, social, and economic crisis to another. They failed at making all America

a New England but succeeded in establishing an extraordinary and enduring intellectual and moral framework for the work of conservation.[16]

The New England town arose out of Puritans' determination to take
advantage of a land far from wicked Europe. Here they had a historically
unique opportunity to establish a commonwealth from a coherent social,
economic, and religious ethic grounded in the Word of God.[17] To organize
a godly community in what they saw as an amoral, disorderly wilderness,
Hooker and his hundred colonists followed the general pattern for Puritan
towns (Figure 2.3). These communities arose somewhat haphazardly, but
under leadership of ministers like Hooker. A powerful regional cultural
force, Puritan clergy provided some uniformity of purpose and principle.[18]
The governments of Massachusetts Bay Colony and Connecticut rejected
the individualist ethos of the earlier colony of Virginia and granted townships to groups rather than private individuals. Town leaders distributed
to each family property sized according to social station. Each received
a mix of the types of land needed for agriculture: houselot, cropland,
meadow, and woodlot. Emigrants in the Great Migration, the Puritan
influx between 1630 and 1642, came in numbers so large—between
15 and 20,000—that colony officials could not closely oversee how the
towns organized and divvied up their lands. Towns therefore reflected
the diverse regional agricultural, economic, and political ways of the first
settlers. Some chose open field systems, others closed fields; some conservatism, others entrepreneurship; some a traditional economy, some
capitalist; some town meetings, some selectmen; and so forth. All towns
retained common land, some of it for such communal purposes as the
common upon which the meetinghouse sat, but most reserved for future
generations. One meetinghouse served as both town hall and church and
embodied the community covenant to be God's people.

After the first wave of colonists settled Connecticut, boatloads of
Puritans increasingly radicalized by the policies of Charles I arrived but
stayed in Massachusetts, ensuring that orthodoxy sang not in unison but
in a fugue of different voices. Connecticut churches were more open in
their membership requirements than those of Massachusetts, and the colony never restricted suffrage to church members as the Bay Colony did.[19]
More moderate and homogeneous than Massachusetts Bay colonists,
Connecticut-Valley Puritans created a "land of steady habits" long before
the state received that nickname in 1801.[20]

In 1691 King William imposed a secular charter on Massachusetts that
dealt Puritan ideals a severe blow, with its provisions for royally appointed

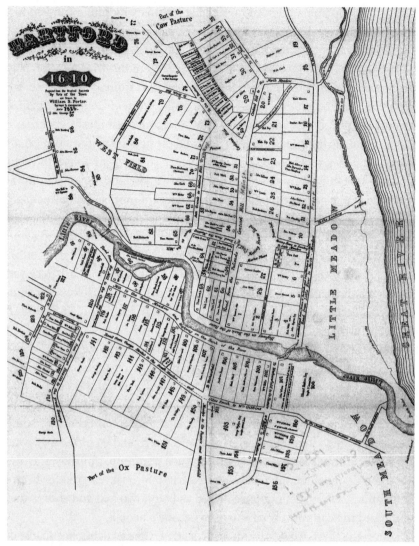

FIGURE 2.3 Hartford in 1640 prepared from the original records by vote of the town and drawn by William S. Porter. Connecticut Puritans sought to establish a godly community, clustered loosely together and each family on its plot as distributed in 1639–1640. Sprinkled across the town are names that afterward became prominent: Hooker owned lot 3; Wadsworth, 66; the Olmsteds, 5, 58–59, and 133; Marsh, 12; Church, 35 and 48; James Cole, stepfather of Jonathan Edwards's great-grandfather, 8 and 155. For scale, note that lots 60–63 today constitute a large city block between Main, Gold, Wells, and Arch Streets.

governor, separation of the state from the church, and toleration of Protestant denominations. Puritan (now Congregationalist) ministers lost their sympathetic governor, religious monopoly, and role as the colony's official conscience. Clergy in eastern Massachusetts fell under the spell of a new mood in the Church of England that stressed morality over creed and reason over fervor. Natural theology—that uncreedal, dispassionate search for the evidences of God in nature—became the fashion of the day, which Boston adopted with greater enthusiasm than Connecticut. The stage was set for the rise of anti-Calvinism in Boston and its successors Unitarianism and Transcendentalism.[21]

Connecticut preserved Congregational sway by keeping a low profile. Leaders avoided direct confrontation with the king and understated the strength of the economy in order to make the colony as invisible to royal authorities as they could. Connecticut retained its original charter, along with the right to choose its governor and freedom to run its own affairs. England's Act of Toleration forced Massachusetts to allow non-Congregationalists in their midst, but Connecticut's hostile and unequal application of the law kept numbers of Anglicans, Baptists, and Quakers very low for a very long time. Even in the early nineteenth century, when Episcopalians (formerly Anglicans), Baptists, Quakers, and now Methodists made up a majority of voters, Congregationalists dominated Connecticut politics, society, economy, and culture. Like Connecticut, the upper Connecticut Valley drew its Congregational ministers from conservative Yale rather than liberal Harvard. Connecticut Congregationalism's quiet cultural hegemony stretched unbroken from eastern Long Island to the Canada frontier.

Puritan colonists all agreed that everyone should live in a community, and that religion required that each must put the common good ahead of himself. Since the Bible did not have a fully worked-out social and economic doctrine, Reformed thinkers drew on humanist, Renaissance, medieval, and classical sources, albeit always backed with Biblical proof-texts. Calvin's theology had an especially strong social-ethical component.[22] Fundamental to Calvin's thinking was that Christians must dedicate body, soul, and worldly goods to the glory of God and the good of society. In Thomas Hooker's words, "Mutuall subjection is as it were the sinewes of society, by which it is sustained and supported. Hence every man is above another, while he walkes according to rule; and when he departs from it, he must be subject to another. Hence every part is subject to the whole, and must be serviceable to the good thereof, and must be ordered by the power thereof. . . . It is the highest law in all Policy Civill or Spirituall to preserve the good of the whole, at this all must aime, and unto this all must be subordinate."[23]

Communal values endured even after London ended the practice of granting land only to groups and curtailed clerical influence. New England colonies now granted land to individuals, who still organized townships along similar lines as before, although privately and for profit. Puritan law restrained individuals and favored communities, because, as Hooker had said, the godly could be trusted to put the common good ahead of their own interests, but the behavior of others must be constrained. The line between self-interest and community interest, however, is rarely starkly drawn. Sometimes the two clearly coincide, while at other times they clearly conflict, but most often they need weighing by a disinterested referee. While neither ministers nor most townspeople truly abandoned the communal ideal, it required constant negotiation to put into practice.[24]

The passage of time produced two recurring problems for the towns. First, large families and relatively low mortality meant that every few decades towns faced the task of dividing common lands to accommodate rising generations. When good land grew scarce, young men went elsewhere. New towns were founded in more and more agriculturally marginal areas until after 1815, when the pacification of Indian tribes and the opening of the Erie Canal drew many young men west to a band of settlement in better land across upstate New York, northern Ohio, and Chicago to Wisconsin and Iowa in search of good land and economic opportunity.

A second challenge for New England towns was that such leading families as the Wadsworths and the Churches accumulated ever greater wealth. The 1640 map of Hartford illustrates how Puritans generally ensured that original settlers had sufficient land but did not receive equal portions. Puritans did not believe in economic leveling. As generation succeeded generation, families that had initially larger allotments acquired more land through purchase or intermarriage with other leading families. By the eighteenth century the Connecticut Valley was dominated by a relatively wealthy elite, who have been referred to as "river gods," descended from the first settlers, or proprietors, of the first towns.[25] Resentment among those who felt left out could fester into alienation from both Congregationalism as well as the Puritan system of rules and mutual subjection, which over the years looked from the bottom or the outside like a conservative system that functioned to protect and preserve the status of the elite.

Wise ministers kept on the good side of these powerful families and the factions that clustered around them. Jonathan Edwards was one who did not. Edwards himself belonged to a prominent family, since his great-grandfather William Edwards was stepson of a proprietor of Hartford and sat in church among Wadsworths, Churches, Olmsteds, and Marshes to hear Hooker preach.[26] Edwards's unbending insistence on the religious foundation of the community was his undoing. Throughout his ministry at Northampton, one of the largest towns in the valley, Edwards decried the growing power and greed of the wealthy. He repeatedly reminded his congregation of their obligation to the community and to the poor. He alienated all the river gods but his formidable Uncle John Stoddard and Colonel Timothy Dwight. Stoddard died suddenly in 1748, and within two years the church had forced Edwards out over matters that would not normally result in the dismissal of a pastor. His more accommodating successors would fare better.[27]

Times changed and the Puritan world evolved, yet in the conservative land of steady habits an essentially Puritan ethos and government thrived, nourished by Yale's staunch Calvinist orthodoxy and by regular religious revivals. In response to Connecticut's perpetually contentious political and religious scene, a conservative party coalesced to preserve and promote the Puritan founders' vision of an orderly and moral society. With great continuity, these principles successively animated the politics of the region's Federalist, Whig, and Republican parties.

The Congregational Church maintained considerable influence even as its numbers steadily declined relative to the Anglican, Baptist, and Methodist churches, until at its disestablishment in 1818 it comprised less than half of Connecticut's population. The openly Federalist politics of Congregational ministers drove Jeffersonians into other churches and some resented the economic power of its wealthier members. Some disgruntled parishioners found in Baptist and Methodist churches greater individualism, fervent preaching, and untutored religion of the heart. Smaller numbers sought the liturgical beauty and claims to ecclesiastical authority that the Episcopal Church offered. The river gods themselves remained stalwart Congregationalists.[28]

New England towns evolved in the early nineteenth century into the classic picture-postcard image so famous today. Small towns still dominated the region, except for a few major ports, and in Connecticut as late as 1820 only New Haven, Hartford, and Middletown exceeded 5,000 in population and no town had as many as 9,000.[29] Religious toleration forced

separation of the religious and civic purposes of meetinghouses into different structures. When the time came to replace old or outgrown buildings,
Congregational churches would be built not on publicly owned commons
but on private land facing greens, as commons came to be called, with the
town hall nearby. A perfect example is the church that Daniel Wadsworth
designed and built for the First (or Center) Congregational Church in
Hartford in 1807 (Figure 2.4), built on the Ancient Burial Ground around
the corner from the meetinghouse's original site on the common. Like
other Congregational churches of the time, it was designed in an elegant
modern style with classical portico and tall steeple often topped by a useful
weather vane (instead of an all-too-Catholic cross) and adorned by a clock,
that epitome of the well-regulated Puritan life. Congregationalists adopted
this style in the belief that good taste would influence public morals and
order for the better, the same conviction that later inspired the layouts of
public parks and the City Beautiful movement. The physical settings of
the towns also changed. In the decades after the Revolution, people moved
from scattered farmhouses into commercial centers to create nucleated
towns. In addition, cheap grain from rich, newly cultivated Western lands
forced farmers to switch from convertible husbandry to more-profitable
dairy farming. Consequently, pastures moved down from the hills onto
former farmland and cattle browsing in the woods kept forests open.
Towns looked as if they were set in parkland (Figure 2.5).

In the 1830s New Englanders beautified their villages and created a
landscape of captivating charm. English actress and author Fanny Kemble
wrote of her 1833 visit, "The exterior of the houses,—their extreme neat-
ness and cleanliness,—the careful cultivation of the land,—the tasteful
and ornamental arrangement of the ground immediately surrounding the
dwellings,—. . . above all, the church spires pointing towards heaven, from
the bosom of every village,—. . . presented images of order, of industry, of
taste, and religious feeling, nowhere so exhibited in any other part of the
Union."[30] Thomas Cole loved villages of the Connecticut Valley. Flowing
from "the wild mountains of New Hampshire," he wrote in "Essay on
American Scenery," the Connecticut River

> soon breaks into a luxuriant valley, and flows for more than a hun-
> dred miles, sometimes beneath the shadow of wooded hills, and
> sometimes glancing through the green expanse of elm-besprinkled
> meadows. Whether we see it from Haverhill, Northampton, or
> Hartford, it still possesses that gentle aspect; and the imagination

FIGURE 2.4 Center Congregational Church and surrounding businesses, Main Street, in Hartford. Around 1888. Altered for clarity. While the original meetinghouse had been on the common next to the Old State House, this building, the congregation's fourth, was built on part of the Ancient Burial Ground, land originally owned by Richard Olmsted. Not visible, the Wadsworth Atheneum is to the photographer's left diagonally across the street from the church.

FIGURE 2.5 John Warner Barber, *N. West View of Farmington from Round Hill,* ca. 1836. The park-like setting of a New England town appears in this view of Farmington, Connecticut, in 1836. The spire of the Congregational Church rises on the right, topped by a weather vane. The shorter towers of the Methodist Church and the academy are to its left.

can scarcely conceive Arcadian vales more lovely or more peaceful than the valley of the Connecticut—its villages are rural places
where trees overspread every dwelling, and the fields upon its mar-
gin have the richest verdure.[31]

Like Kemble and Cole, New Englanders romanticized this ideal village
with its tasteful steepled church on the town green as representative of
traditional communal, devout, prosperous, and harmonious society that
the rest of nineteenth-century America had forgotten and left behind.[32]

Improvement and Stewardship: Calvinist Roots of Conservation

Frederic Church belonged to the generation or two who were raised in
this apparent model of democracy, morality, industry, sobriety, and natural
beauty that was the New England town. In the same era, they also learned
the fundamental doctrines of conservation, preached from the pulpits of
Congregational churches. The Puritan civilization that nestled in the loveliness of the valley and hills along the Connecticut River, with its heart

in Church's hometown of Hartford and its head in Yale in New Haven, fostered a most impressive roster of conservation leaders, usually raised in the Congregational Church, often educated at Yale, and imbued with its values and traditions.

Conservation's moral concern was rooted in the Reformed Protestant duties of improvement and stewardship. Calvinist ministers scarcely favored a word more than "improvement." Improvement meant an overriding and never-ceasing responsibility to improve one's soul, one's intellect, and one's possessions. Calvinists were ever conscious that as in Christ's parable of the steward (Luke 16:1–13), God would call them to give account of their stewardship. "Let him who possesses a field," Calvin wrote in his commentary on Genesis 2:15, "so partake of its yearly fruits, that he may not suffer the ground to be injured by his negligence; but let him endeavor to hand it down to posterity as he received it, or even better cultivated. . . . Let every one regard himself as the steward of God in all things which he possesses."[33] This teaching, which dates to the patristic period but which Calvinists revived, became axiomatic to Reformed thought. In 1676, in a foreshadowing of the significance the term would take in the twentieth century, Puritan Sir Matthew Hale expanded the concept to include stewardship of the earth as well as personal possessions, in his essay "The Great Audit, with the Account of the Good Steward." This popular essay had long influence and went into many editions into the 1830s, including one late edition published in Hartford in 1802.[34]

Another standard Biblical support for the ideal of improvement, Matthew 25:14–30, was Christ's parable of the talents, a favorite passage for Calvinists. Jesus told of a man who gave talents (of money) to three servants to take care of while he was away. Upon his return, he praised the two servants who invested and earned a return ("Well done, thou good and faithful servant") while he cast the "unprofitable servant," who buried his talent for safekeeping, "into outer darkness: there shall be weeping and gnashing of teeth." Reformed believers interpreted this passage to mean that God's gifts, whether spiritual, intellectual, or material, must be improved or increased for His greater glory.

Ministers regularly reminded their congregations of the parables of the talents and good steward and of the virtues of improvement. Chauncey Whittelsey warned Yale graduates in 1744, "But they that had been foolishly negligent; and had unjustly misimprov'd their Time and Talents, were frowned upon, condemned and punished."[35] "We must remember," Jonathan Edwards admonished, "that we must all of us give account of our stewardship, and how we have disposed of those goods that our master has put into our hands."[36] Puritans sternly condemned idleness, which uselessly produced nothing for self, family, or society, and equally abhorred waste, which lost that which might have been useful.[37] "God's Creatures are good, and were made for Men to serve God with" rather than Mammon or sin, preached Edwards.[38] In the only complete system of theology produced in Puritan New England, Samuel Willard summed up the doctrine of stewardship that thundered repeatedly from pulpits across New England, "*Those that do* Excell *in Gifts, ought to improve them readily for the Benefit of others, who need the Help of them.* God hath bestowed them for that end; and made them the Stewards thereof, 1 *Pet.* 4.10. And if they do not thus Improve them, they hide their Talent under a Napkin."[39] Willard added,

> Tho' every Man hath a proper Right to such an Estate as he comes to Possess in a Lawful and Honest way; yet he is not the *absolute Lord* of it, to do with it what he sees meet; but is put into it as a *Steward* under God, and to follow His Directions in the *Improvement* that he makes of it. GOD is the supream Lord of all; we Ourselves are His, and then surely what we have must be so: And it is He who hath deposited this *Portion* into our hands, be it *more* or *less;* so that by whatever *Media* we come by it, He Governed it, and ordered the Success of it; and we must run it up thro' all *Second* causes to Him, else we derogate from His Glory. . . . And it is certain the He will ere long call every one of us to give an Account of our *Stewardship.* . . . And these things belong to the *Talents,* which our Lord hath betrusted us withal; and He will come, and strictly enquire of us, how we have *Occupied* them.[40]

Stewardship and improvement were woven into the fabric of the Reformed tradition. From its earliest days, Calvinism promoted ideals of conservation as a moral duty of individuals and communities. Reform was in the air in the sixteenth century not only in religion, but also in schemes to improve society and the economy. Sixteenth-century Huguenots first brought together the goals of reform into a general program to return the church to its earliest principles, increase knowledge, improve agriculture, and abolish poverty.[41] Calvin had taught that Christians must work to eliminate poverty, which hindered people's ability to live fully for the glory of God.[42] Huguenots felt that France's poverty held back the material and moral progress of its people, and poor treatment of its forests and fields lay at the root of its distress.

Two remarkable books by the famous Huguenot potter Bernard Palissy laid out the agenda better and more completely than any other works. Palissy cited the parable of the talents to justify the audacity of an unlearned potter to question accepted wisdom and put forward his own ideas. His *Recepte véritable, par laquelle tous les hommes de France pourront apprendre à multiplier et augmenter leurs thrésors* ("True Formula through which all Frenchmen may learn to multiply and augment their treasures,"[43] 1563) bore a printer's emblem on its title page depicting a man leaping from barren plowed ground (Figure 2.6). A winged arm stretches upward toward a crowned figure in the clouds who holds three fingers up in blessing or sign of the trinity, while a heavy stone tied to his other arm holds him back. The motto explains, "Povreté empêche les bons espritz de parvenir" ("Poverty prevents the advancement of clever men"). Drawing the lesson that God expected his gifts to be improved and righteously used, Palissy offered *Recepte véritable* as his use of his "gifts,"

FIGURE 2.6 The emblem of Barthélemy Berton, Huguenot printer of Bernard Palissy's *Recepte véritable,* from the title page, symbolized the Huguenot conviction that alleviation of poverty preceded moral advancement.

containing the knowledge he had won through observation and experiment, and sternly condemned those who neglected God's gifts or lived as
useless parasites on society, especially the Catholic clergy.[44] Palissy urged
Frenchmen to also make best use of God's gifts, such as the land and forests that they neglected.

Recepte véritable laid out what grew into the three branches of
Connecticut-Valley conservation: agricultural improvement, parks, and
forestry. Palissy advocated improvement of agriculture through science,
technology, and moralism. He condemned lack of technical improvement
in farm implements and urged the creation of royal offices, medals, and
rewards for inventors of agricultural machines. He praised marl as a soil
improver and explained the best storage and employment of manure to
preserve its value as fertilizer. He offered scientific explanations for the
growth of plants and fruits and their dependence on nutrients ("salts") in
the soil. His discussion of soils would help inspire the rise of English and
American soil science. Tenantry, he complained, sapped farmers' incentive to preserve soil fertility, while the low status of farm labor led prosperous landowners to neglect the land and use profits to buy offices or seek
worldly advancement.

But the question remained how science might come up with solutions that even the great philosophers of ancient Greece and Rome had
not known. Palissy gave his answer in the 1570s in a pathbreaking series
of scientific lectures in Paris, which he published in 1580 in his celebrated *Discours admirables de la nature des eaux et fontaines tant naturelles
qu'artificielles* ("Admirable discourses on the nature of waters and springs
[or fountains] both natural and artificial").[45] Palissy argued passionately
against speculative theories of Aristotle, ancient authors, alchemists, and
medical writers and pressed the virtues of observation and deduction. In
the book foolish, pompous *Theorique* ("Theory") asked the questions and
clever *Practique* ("Practice") gave the answers. When Theory objected,
"What is your basis for undertaking to contradict so many learned philosophers? . . . you who know neither Greek nor Latin, nor scarcely good
French," Practice responded, "I have no other book than the sky and the
earth, which is known to all, and it is given to all to know and to read in
this beautiful book."[46]

Following Palissy, Huguenots wrote the pioneering works of modern
scientific agriculture. Charles Estienne and Jean Liébault published the
long-popular *L'agriculture et Maison Rustique* in 1572, perhaps the first
major text to deviate from popular classical works to include practical

advice on such subjects as soil types.[47] The 1600 English translation, *Maison Rustique or the Countrie Farme,* enjoyed a long popularity, and copies appeared even in the English colonies as early as 1620.[48] In 1600, Olivier de Serres—whose favorite book was *Recepte véritable*—brought out the huge, landmark *Le theatre d'agriculture et mesnage des champs* ("Theater of Agriculture and Management of Fields"), the founding work of modern agronomy and the first agricultural manual informed by scientific experimentation. De Serres famously based agricultural improvement on "SCIENCE, EXPERIENCE, DILIGENCE."[49] Finally, as if in response to Palissy's call, de Serres's Calvinist minister, Jacques Besson, published plans for new agricultural machines in *Théâtre des instrumens mathématiques et mechaniques* in 1578.[50]

Huguenot influence jumped the English Channel in 1594, when Sir Hugh Plat wrote his pioneering and influential *The Jewel House of Art and Nature,* the founding work of English agricultural chemistry and based on Palissy. Plat's work quoted Palissy at length on soil chemistry and improvement. Also interested in agricultural inventions, Plat devised an early seed drill in 1600 that was an ancestor of Jethro Tull's revolutionary mechanism a century later.[51] In 1616 Gervase Markham, another early agricultural writer, contributed to the dispersion of Huguenot agronomic ideas with his popular second edition of Richard Surflet's translation of Estienne and Liébault's *La Maison Rustique* with additional selections by Olivier de Serres and other French writers. The Huguenot linkage of religion with agricultural improvement did not endure in Protestant England, however. Reformers of the English church had no need to link up with reformers of agriculture and society. If many improvers were in fact quite religious, they lacked consistent links to Puritanism. In America, however, a strong motivation for improving (that favorite Puritan word) farming methods took root and grew on the rocky Calvinist soil of New England.

Recepte véritable also contained Palissy's detailed plan for an elaborate allegorical Edenic landscape garden, a remote ancestor to American parks. The longest and most extensive garden plan produced in Valois France or by any sixteenth-century artist, it took inspiration from Psalm 104 and was intended both as a place of worship and as a refuge from religious persecution. Living elms and poplars—God's creatures, not the inventions of man—would be trained and trimmed to make the walls and roofs of pavilions.[52] The elaborate garden plan in *Recepte véritable* anticipated a century of Huguenot landscape gardening and gardening theory. Salomon de Caus, Jacques Boyceau, and Claude Mollet designed all major

French gardens, wrote the all the handbooks, and spread the French formal garden style to England and Germany. While they either did not know
or maintained a prudent silence over the ethical and religious dimension
of working the earth, they did argue for designing with nature and for
designs that revealed aspects of the natural world, as made known by
experimental science rather than vain speculation. The English-garden
style in the eighteenth century reincorporated overt religious and moral
meaning. Swiss Calvinist Jean-Jacques Rousseau popularized the English
garden in France, and its aesthetics influenced the American parks movement in the next century.[53]

The issue of forest conservation arose in answer to the criticism that
such a garden would waste money that might be better spent on buying
offices and worldly advancement. Like Calvin, Palissy extolled contemplation of the works of God in nature as superior to pursuit of self-interest
or earthly pleasures. Self-seeking people had wreaked a whole string of
abuses on France, including the destruction of France's forests. After a
lengthy meditation on Psalm 104, he concluded,

> All these things have made me such a lover of the fields, that it
> seems to me that there are no treasures in the world so precious, or
> which ought to be held in such great esteem, as the little branches
> of trees and plants, although they are the most despised. I hold
> them in more esteem than mines of gold and silver. And when
> I consider the value of the very smallest branch of tree or thorn,
> I am filled with wonder at the great ignorance of men, who seem, in
> our day, to study only how to break through, cut down, and destroy
> the beautiful forests which their predecessors had been guarding
> as so precious. I should not find it wrong in them to cut the forests
> down, if afterwards they planted any portion of the soil; but they
> think not at all of times to come, not considering the great harm
> they are doing to their children in the future.

This consideration of the needs of future generations would constitute
a fundamental rationale for conservation. Palissy then remarked, in
a passage that nineteenth-century foresters would rediscover and cite
repeatedly,

> *Question.*—And why do you find it so wrong that forests should be
> cut down in this manner?. . .

Answer.—I cannot enough detest such a thing, and can call it not a fault, but a curse and a misfortune to all France; because when all the woods shall have been levelled, there must be an end of all the arts, and artisans may go and browse on herb, like Nebuchadnezzar. I have sometimes attempted to put down in order the arts that would cease, if there came to be an end of wood; but when I had written a great number of them, I could see no way to an end of my writing; . . . all navigation and all fisheries must cease, and that even the birds and several kinds of beasts, which nourish themselves upon fruits, must migrate to another kingdom, and that neither oxen, cows, nor any other bovine animals, would be of service in a country where there was no wood. . . . It would even be necessary, if we had no wood, for the office of the teeth to become vacant, and where there is no wood there is no need of wheat nor any other grain for making bread.[54]

Then Palissy enumerated the advantages to landowners of planting trees. He conspicuously omitted the military purposes that a century later would motivate both Colbert's celebrated forestry laws and John Evelyn's famous *Sylva*. Palissy described only the benefits of forests for human society and God's creatures.

Huguenots got their best chance to put their agenda into effect when the Protestant champion Henry IV converted to Catholicism in 1598 to assume the crown of France. He issued the tolerant Edict of Nantes and ended the bloody wars of religion that had bled France for decades. Intelligent and energetic, Henry and his Protestant minister Sully drew up France's first far-reaching and effective forestry law. Giving top priority to increasing agricultural production, Henry encouraged new agricultural inventions, drained marshland for agriculture, promoted silk-growing (for which de Serres wrote a handbook, which King James I had translated into English), and instigated publication of de Serres's *Le theatre d'agriculture*, said to be Henry's favorite book. Henry's assassination in 1610 abruptly ended these initiatives. Growing religious repression culminated in the Revocation of the Edict of Nantes of 1685, which forced hundreds of thousands of Huguenots into exile and the remainder underground. Their conservation initiatives faded into history.[55]

Stymied in France, the Reformed Protestant religious and social agenda scored success in Puritan America, in a rocky wilderness land severely depeopled from European diseases.[56] Puritans fled to New England to build Palissy's own great unrealized fantasy, a Protestant place of refuge, and erected a godly social order beyond the fantasies of the Huguenots. They built communities that regulated forest use, equitably divvied up resources, emphasized agricultural improvement, avoided tenantry, and gathered the people into Calvinist churches. The sale of land to outsiders and nonresidents was generally prohibited or discouraged. Tenantry was rare. Knowing better than to expect virtuous behavior from sinful man, Puritans regulated and controlled their fellow townsmen for the common good and the good of succeeding generations. To preserve forest resources, towns and colonies regulated the timber trade, a vital sector of the New England economy, and acted to preserve for future generations woodlots on both private and common land.[57] As equitably as they knew how, New England townships parceled out to every member of the town the agricultural, meadow, and wood lots that made sustainable agriculture possible. As historian Brian Donahue has shown, in a virtually endless cycle, annual spring floods enriched meadows that produced hay that fed cattle through the winter, when they generated the manure that restored fertility to cropland. Hay was so essential for this cycle that Puritans scouting sites for new towns looked for broad meadows.[58] It was in fact its meadows (rather than theological differences) that ostensibly justified the move to Hartford (see Figure 2.3). Thus the hay meadows in the center of *The Oxbow* and *West Rock* symbolized prudent husbandry and proper care of the land.

Such a scheme was the stuff of Palissy's dreams. The efflorescence of conservation thought and dreams of improved communities that Huguenots produced when they adopted Calvinism would in fact be matched four centuries later by a similar flowering of conservation ideas among New Englanders raised in Reformed communities, even as they abandoned the Calvinist theology that fostered it. Inspired by the godly beauty of New England towns and imbued with Reformed ideals of improvement, care of the land, and social justice, Frederic Church's generation of Connecticut-Valley Congregationalists preached the example of the New England town to a mostly careless and prodigal nation.

3

Building the Moral Society: Farms, Forests, and Parks

Frederic Church's Widening Vision

Fresh intellectual winds carried Frederic Church in new directions in 1852 and 1853. Three of the five volumes of Alexander von Humboldt's *Cosmos* had appeared in English, and John Ruskin was publishing a modern version of the Reformed landscape aesthetic. Humboldt and Ruskin hit the American Reformed art scene like a whirlwind. The reputations and influence of Reynolds and Allison never recovered. Freed from its low rank in the hierarchy of genres, landscape art rose in critical estimation, with particular emphasis in the scientific accuracy of the details of God's works. Such principles played to Church's strengths as an artist. For a time he neglected New England subjects and sought new vistas in South America. When he returned to painting American landscapes, they showed less Yankee chauvinism and greater nationalistic fervor. His artistic development paralleled changes in his fellow New Englanders, who also lifted up their eyes from their focus on New England and took in the prospect of a fast-growing nation with a desperate need of their tradition of improvement, regulation, and preservation of land and resources for community and future generations.

Humboldt spurred Church to travel in search of unpainted views. Church's celebrated accomplishments as a painter-explorer fired the aspirations of painters from Albert Bierstadt to Thomas Moran. Humboldt urged landscape painters to depict geology and botany realistically, and he lamented that no landscape artists had yet painted the astonishing tropical and alpine scenes of South America. Taking up Humboldt's challenge, in 1853 Church and his wealthy friend Cyrus Field of Stockbridge,

Massachusetts, followed Humboldt's path through modern Venezuela to Ecuador. Back in his New York studio, Church turned out a stream of dramatic South American pictures that enthralled the public.

Not all critics had been friendly, however, which prompted Church to pick up Ruskin's *Modern Painters* and read it with great care in order to find a way forward. In his discussion of the art of the painter, Ruskin tinted Humboldtian hues with earnest Scottish-Presbyterian moralism. Church applied Ruskin's critical palette to his ambitious painting *Niagara,* which lifted him to the pinnacle of the Anglo-American art world. His newfound fame also led to prominent involvement with the nation's leading advocates and creators of parks, forest conservation, and agricultural improvement. With the exception of one Prussian forester, every one of them either like Church grew up in New England Congregationalism or was no more than one generation away. The American conservation and environmental movements were born in the elegant steepled churches rising above the greens of Connecticut Valley towns.

American artists had received the first volume of Ruskin's *Modern Painters* with enthusiasm when it appeared in America in 1848, the year of Cole's death. Ruskin propounded an aesthetic theory that reigned in the United States for a generation. Raised Scottish Presbyterian, Ruskin expressed with a clarity of no other author the Reformed aesthetic emphasis on artistic material and moral truth. He urged artists to infuse obsessive faithfulness to fact with moral or religious purpose. Minute detail might be true to nature, but it must always be "detail referred to a great end,—sought for the sake of the inestimable beauty which exists in the slightest and least of God's works, and treated in a manly, broad, and impressive manner." Consciously following Humboldt, Ruskin declared it the landscape painter's "imperative duty" "to descend to the lowest details with undiminished attention. Every herb and flower of the field has its specific, distinct, and perfect beauty; it has its peculiar habitation, expression, and function. The highest art is that which seizes this specific character, which developes [sic] and illustrates it, which assigns to it its proper position in the landscape, and which, by means of it, enhances and enforces the great impression which the picture is intended to convey. Nor is it of herbs and flowers alone that such scientific representation is required. Every class of rock, every kind of earth, every form of cloud, must be studied with equal industry, and rendered with equal precision."[1] American painters took these Humboldtian-Ruskinian principles as gospel.[2]

People receded even more from the landscape. Humans had generally diminished presence in Hudson River School paintings during Cole's
lifetime. American landscape art grew wilder and less peopled as Ruskin
explicitly pushed man and his works from the canvas. Here he was more
like Calvin than Humboldt in his insistence that landscape art was "a
witness to the omnipotence of God," not "an exhibition of the dexterity
of man," that had "lifted our thoughts to the throne of the Deity," and
not "encumbered them with the inventions of his creatures." The viewer
should "depart with the praise of God in his heart." Otherwise, the landscape was the product "of a debased, mistaken, and false school of painting." Ruskin "attach[ed] to the artist the responsibility of a preacher."[3]
Modern Painters had chapters on skies, clouds, the earth, mountains, and
water but none on man in the landscape, who apparently did nothing to
elevate the mind to God. When at the end of the second volume Ruskin at
last discussed human beauty, he defined it in terms of freedom from the
visible effects of sin.

The Andean landscape seems to have inspired Church to seek out God's
best works back in his native land as well, because in 1856 he began to consider how to paint Niagara Falls. Countless painters from rank amateurs
to Cole had painted the falls, yet vast, powerful Niagara had defied every
effort to capture it on canvas. For over six months Church returned often,
sketching the scene from every conceivable angle, in every light, and at
every time of day.[4] Back in New York he experimented in oil sketches until
he got the perspective he wanted. He studied Ruskin's chapter on painting water. He chose an unusually shaped canvas, twice as wide as high.
Church selected a vantage point on the edge of Horseshoe Falls where the
falls themselves were not visible until the eye followed the edge to where it
curved back around to disclose the power and majesty of the falling water.
His stroke of genius was to eliminate the near bank altogether. Viewers
felt as if they were looking directly over and down into the rushing, swirl-
ing waters about to tumble over the edge, as if there were danger of falling
into the current.

Church unveiled *Niagara* (Figure 3.2, see color insert) on May 1, 1857,
and it was an immediate sensation. The painting and its effect were entirely
original. Thousands came to view his Niagara Falls with everything but the
roar, paying twenty-five cents apiece for the privilege. Thousands ordered
copies of the forthcoming chromolithograph. Church sent *Niagara* for exhibition in London and a year later sent it back for a tour of the Lancastrian
metropolises Liverpool and Manchester, Edinburgh, and London again.

It amazed British audiences and critics just as much as it had American. No higher tribute could have come than Ruskin's astonished praise of the "truthfulness" of the painting's unprecedented portrayal of moving water, which has rarely been so convincingly painted. *Niagara* prompted English critics to hail Church as the first great American painter and the heir of J.M.W. Turner himself, who had died in 1851 with no clear English successor. *Niagara* returned to the United States in 1858 universally regarded as the greatest of American paintings and its artist as the greatest American painter.[5]

Church returned from another journey to South American in 1857 to paint even greater Humboldtian-Ruskinian masterpieces of the Andes. His huge *Heart of the Andes* of 1859 was so laden with exquisite, scientifically accurate detail that with the help of a descriptive pamphlet viewers inspected it through opera glasses or tubes so that they could isolate and study small sections at a time. In 1859, in company with Cole's pastor Louis Legrand Noble, Church headed north to paint icebergs. The resulting paintings, most notably *The Icebergs* of 1861, set off a fad of Arctic landscape art. Church continued to produce great paintings for many more years, but this was his heyday.

Church at the Cradle of Conservation

Church's *Niagara*, along with his Hartford river-god connections and close friendship with the Cole family, would gain him entrance to the circles of leading proponents of the nascent conservation movement. In 1879 art connected him with the very birthplace of the conservation movement, the estate of George Perkins Marsh's boyhood. Looking to buy some Cole pictures, wealthy lawyer Frederick Billings contacted Church, who acted as broker for sales of Cole's paintings still in the family's possession. Billings needed appropriate paintings to decorate the Marsh house, which he had bought in 1869 upon his return to his picturesque hometown of Woodstock, Vermont, after a successful law career in Gold-Rush San Francisco. He acquired three Cole landscapes, which hung alongside paintings by Hudson River School artists Albert Bierstadt (whom he and his wife had met in California), Asher B. Durand, Sanford Gifford, John W. Casilear, and John F. Kensett. Later he added works by William Keith and Church himself. An apparent Ruskinian, Billings was "attracted to [Church's] landscapes empty of human beings," as biographer Robin W. Winks put it.[6]

The Reformed aesthetics of the house's art mirrored the Puritan landscape around it. The grandest residence in Woodstock, "the Marsh house was set into a moral landscape that represented the old Vermont values of thrift, good craftsmanship, and success handsomely but not vulgarly expressed," Winks noted.[7] For Billings as for Marsh, the moral landscape evoked agricultural improvement, forest conservation, and appreciation of nature as the handiwork of God and as resource for social improvement. Billings had read Marsh's conservation classic *Man and Nature* when it came out in 1864 and now dedicated himself to making the author's former home and estate a monument to conservation. He established a model farm, still operating today as the Billings Farm and Museum. As a member of the Vermont State Forestry Commission, Billings would write most of its 1884 report. In one of the first and most successful efforts at forest restoration, he reforested denuded Mount Tom overlooking Woodstock. Billings built carriage roads for public recreation and in effect transformed Mount Tom into a public park.

Just a year before he brokered the sale to Billings of three Coles for the Marsh house, Church joined into a different restoration project of much greater scale than Mount Tom: the movement to create an international park around Niagara Falls and restore the natural beauty of its banks. His famous *Niagara* forever linked him in the public mind with one of America's most famous and impressive wonders. Probably inspired by the park in Yosemite established five years earlier, Church first suggested a park at the falls around 1869. Frederick Law Olmsted, friend to both Church and Billings, mounted the campaign to make the park a reality. Church had known Olmsted, a distant cousin, in Hartford, where both had attended the same school and Center Congregational Church.[8] Olmsted had become principal designer and builder of New York's Central Park in 1857. When corrupt politicians ousted him from his job as overseer of park construction in 1862, he found employment in California managing the Mariposa mine near Yosemite Valley, where he worked with Billings, the mine's lawyer. Billings helped make sure that Olmsted sat on the first Yosemite Park Commission in 1864, for which he designed a plan for its development (never carried out). Billings also facilitated commissions for Olmsted for the designs of the campus of the new University of California in Berkeley, a park system for San Francisco, and the plan for the new city of Tacoma, Washington. Olmsted returned to New York in 1865 to resume work on Central Park. By the time of the Niagara campaign, he was the nation's greatest and most influential landscape architect.

These men—Church, Billings, and most especially Marsh and Olmsted[9]—were members of a generation or two of Connecticut-Valley Congregationalists who successfully brought about a nineteenth-century rebirth of the Huguenot conservation program, designed for another country in another time but representing the same religious, moral, and social values. This generation formulated a powerful conservation ideology for agricultural improvement, forest conservation, and parks, and vigorously worked to realize its vision of a righteous republic.

Improving the Land

Church painted the idyllic New England farm scene in *West Rock, New Haven* before expanding his vision to produce the grand vista of national pride in *Niagara*. The conservation careers of Billings, Marsh, and Olmsted developed in close parallel, starting with agricultural improvement and expanding to forests and parks later. Conservation sprang up from a seed of worry about the decline of New England farming and with it the New England town. Although agricultural reformers arose in all sections after 1820, from the beginning Connecticut-Valley Congregationalists, often educated at Yale, led the movement for scientific agricultural improvement. They put their faith into advancement in new agricultural methods pioneered by experimental farms, educational institutions, and experimental stations. They informed farmers of the latest advances and inventions through publications, government agencies, and agricultural colleges.[10] Nowhere can the evolution of the conservation and parks movements appear more clearly than in the career of the man who was essentially a Yankee Palissy, Church's friend and kinsman Olmsted, who had been a gentleman farmer pursuing horticultural experiments on Staten Island before he ever thought about designing a park.

Conservation rested on foundations of the Calvinist and Puritan ideal of improvement of one's land and possessions, which explains why Congregational agricultural improvement was so moralistic and why ministers played such surprisingly prominent parts. American scientific agriculture began with Congregational minister and Yale graduate Jared Eliot, born in Guilford, Connecticut, to a prominent family of ministers. A critic of religious and political divisiveness, Eliot defended the ideal of an orderly and righteous commonwealth and extolled New England towns' beneficial effect on morals, industriousness, and order.[11] Improvement of New England's stingy soils, he was sure, would preserve moral order. Keen to use his talents for the public good, between 1748 and 1757 he published essays about his observations and in 1760 gathered them into the first American book on agriculture, *Essays upon Field-Husbandry in New England.* Eliot discussed agricultural techniques but also agricultural inventions, including his plans for a simplified version of Jethro Tull's new seed-drill.[12]

A half century later, competition from abundant harvests on fertile, newly settled Western lands threatened the political and the moral economy of New England towns. Agricultural improvers mustered with the weapons of science and education to battle twin evils: New England's poor soil and emigration of their young to the disorderly, godless frontier. Local elite and farmers experimented with crops and methods. In 1794, the Society for the Promotion of Agriculture, one of the nation's first state agricultural societies, appeared in New Haven County, with General James Wadsworth and Timothy Dwight among its presidents.[13] Charles Nicoll Talbot, buyer of *The Oxbow,* involved himself in the effort to uphold the peaceful, prosperous landscape that Cole's painting depicted so gloriously. Talbot sat on the board of the Northampton Silk Company, which in 1836 introducing silkworm culture to the region to give New England farmers a valuable product that did not have competition from the bountiful West.[14] Thanks to such efforts, a silk industry thrived for decades in Connecticut. Another attempted improvement, William Jarvis's introduction in 1810 of Spanish Merino sheep to Vermont, succeeded too well. Sheep overran the country and produced the disastrous environmental consequences that would inspire Marsh's *Man and Nature.*

A number of monthly journals informed farmers of agricultural advances. Thomas Green Fessenden, the son of the Congregational minister of the Connecticut River town of Walpole, New Hampshire, founded the *New England Farmer* in 1822, one of the earliest and most influential American agricultural journals. Jesse Buel founded and edited *The Cultivator,* America's leading agricultural periodical, and authored several books on agriculture before his death in 1839. Born in Coventry, Connecticut, in 1778 and raised in Rutland, Vermont, after 1790, Buel like Calvin proclaimed it the farmer's religious duty to improve the soil: "The new system of husbandry . . . regards the soil as a gift of the beneficent Creator, in which we hold but a life estate, and which . . . we are bound to transmit, UNIMPAIRED, to posterity."[15]

Hence it was particularly appropriate that Olmsted, after a single semester at Yale taking courses from Benjamin Silliman, decided in 1846 on a career as a modern scientific farmer, the first step on a winding path to an illustrious career as the nation's first landscape architect. As an ambitious novice, Olmsted sought advice at the Albany office of Buel's successor, Luther Tucker of *The Cultivator*, for which his father had been the Hartford agent.[16] Born in Vermont to Connecticut natives, Tucker had recently founded *The Horticulturist* and would found *The Country Gentleman* in 1853. By good fortune, there Olmsted met Andrew Jackson Downing, whom Tucker had recruited as editor of *The Horticulturist*. From his Staten Island farm, Olmsted corresponded with Downing, sent contributions to *The Horticulturist*, and bought plants from Downing's nursery.[17]

As supplement to agricultural journals, Buel and others supported a national government agency to aid farmers, which Henry Leavitt Ellsworth established in 1839. Distant cousin of W. S. Leavitt, Church's minister in Hudson and Talbot's in Northampton, Ellsworth was a native of Windsor, Connecticut, graduate of Yale, and founder of the Hartford County Agricultural Society in 1817. As first commissioner of the US Patent Office in 1835, Ellsworth established the US Bureau of Agriculture to collect and distribute seeds for farmers, publish agricultural statistics, and engage in chemical, botanical, and entomological research. Its successor, the Department of Agriculture, was created in 1862 and organized along lines proposed by Buel a quarter century before.[18]

Along with journals and a national agricultural bureau, agricultural schools arose in New England to teach useful, improving knowledge to farmers and mechanics. In 1824 two Yale graduates, Josiah Holbrook and future Congregational minister Truman Coe, established the first, the Agricultural Seminary in Derby, Connecticut.[19] In the following decades, a hodgepodge of agricultural and industrial schools sprang up across the country. Congregational minister and Illinois College professor Jonathan Baldwin Turner campaigned for a national system of land-grant colleges. Born in Templeton, Massachusetts, and educated at Yale, Turner believed that agricultural improvement served religious purposes and also hastened the Millennium.[20] Connecticut-born Senator Lyman Trumbull of Illinois persuaded Congressman Justin Smith Morrill of Vermont to sponsor the Morrill Land-Grant Act of 1862, which passed with vital lobbying assistance from Congregational minister Amos Brown.[21] Over the next three decades Morrill introduced many bills in the House and then Senate to expand funding until 48 land-grant agricultural colleges had been founded by century's end. Morrill retired to Vermont in 1898 as a gentleman farmer, living in a Downing cottage and surrounded by Downing-inspired gardens.[22]

By 1866, Olmsted had been approached to design the campuses for two of these new agricultural colleges and would in succeeding years prepare designs for Amherst College near Northampton, Trinity College in Hartford, Mount Holyoke College in South Hadley, Smith College in Northampton, Yale, Stanford University, and several others. That year he published *A Few Things to be Thought of before Proceeding to Plan Buildings for the National Agricultural Colleges* on the layout and landscape design of these new institutions of democratic, useful knowledge. Quoting Turner, Olmsted presented his belief that the landscape, architecture, and instruction of the new institutions should not only raise the educational level of farmers but also further a greater sense of community that he found lacking in the South and Midwest.[23] He rejected the popular plan for a single, large building in the center of college land for a campus of smaller buildings dedicated to specific purposes, modeled on the New England town.[24]

To further experimentation for improvement of farming, George W. Atherton campaigned for agricultural experiment stations in states with land-grant colleges, which the Hatch Act funded in 1887.[25] Born in 1837 in Boxford, Massachusetts, educated at Yale, and married by Dwight's son Timothy Dwight, Atherton was inspired by Yale professor Samuel W. Johnson, a Kingsboro, New York, native of Connecticut ancestry,[26] who established the nation's first agricultural experiment station in 1875 at Wesleyan University in Middletown, Connecticut, before it moved to Yale two years later. As Yale President Arthur Twining Hadley said, "The whole system of agricultural experiment stations may well be regarded as his monument."[27] One of the Connecticut Agricultural Experiment Station's most noteworthy achievements was development of modern high-yield hybrid corn by Donald F. Jones, born in 1890 in Hutchinson, Kansas, to New England natives who descended from Hartford's founders.[28] The Hatch Act spread experimental stations across the nation.

In 1867, Olmsted began a long relationship with Cornell, an early land-grant college whose campus he designed and which employed the most energetic and prolific agricultural reformers of the age, Liberty Hyde Bailey.[29] Bailey's father was a Congregationalist, native of Vermont, and prize-winning Michigan farmer who raised his son on an intellectual fare of the Bible, *Pilgrim's Progress, Paradise Lost,* and Charles Darwin. As horticulture professor at Michigan State Agricultural College, Bailey in 1888 was offered a chair in horticulture at Cornell's new Hatch-Act experimental station, from which he made Cornell's agricultural program the foremost and largest in the nation. He was one of the instigators of the extension system that would bring advanced agricultural practices to local farmers. To keep bright young people from leaving the farm, he endeavored to educate rural children about the natural world around them so that they would love and appreciate it. A major proponent of the nature-study movement, he wrote monthly pamphlets for distribution to elementary teachers. He founded and edited *Country Life in America* and *Cornell Countryman* to make rural life more attractive to live in. President Theodore Roosevelt asked him to chair his Country Life Commission and Bailey wrote most of its 1909 report. He was also convinced that good farmers were religious farmers. In his best-known and most philosophical book, *The Holy Earth* of 1915, he wrote, "If God created the earth, so is the earth hallowed; and if it is hallowed, so must we deal with it devotedly and with care that we do not despoil it, and mindful of our relations to all beings that live on it."[30]

By the twentieth century, these fervent, earnest proselytizers of the gospel of improvement had produced a morally and materially compromised agricultural system. Faith that science would rescue and improve the farmer's physical and moral state had led instead to a modern industrial agribusiness tightly tied to the US Department of Agriculture and the nation's agricultural schools. Not only has the family farmer vanished from the land, vast chemical-dependent monocultures of Jones's hybrid corn and other hybrids and modified plants have produced major environmental and health issues. Yet Yankee agricultural improvement has also bred Yankee agricultural counterimprovement. The old Puritan tenets of sustainability and efficiency led to the first stirrings of organic farming by USDA soil scientist F. H. King. Born in Whitewater, Wisconsin, to a native of North Pomfret, Vermont, King became first Chair of Agricultural Physics at the University of Wisconsin in 1888 and began a series of publications from the Wisconsin Agricultural Experiment Station beginning in 1891. A fanatic for efficiency, he introduced the iconic cylindrical Wisconsin (or King) silo, which lacked corners where silage might spoil and (that old Puritan sin) be wasted and lost to beneficial, useful purposes. After a tour of East Asia in 1909 to study how Asians farmed sustainably by recycling virtually all waste, King published the foundational work of Anglo-American organic agriculture, *Farmers of Forty Centuries; or, Permanent Agriculture in China, Korea and Japan.* Although no record of stewardship of the land could beat forty centuries of farming the same soil, Bailey and King's colleagues dismissed his book because they could not imagine that poor Chinese rice growers formed any sort of example for American farmers. However, republished in London in 1927, *Farmers of Forty Centuries* became a classic in the nascent English organic-farming movement. The Rodale family brought out an American edition after World War II, and it has since enjoyed resurgence as a prophetic work. Recently, several land-grant colleges have established organic research programs.[31] Agricultural improvers continue to find new ways to teach the duty to leave the land unimpaired for future generations.

Forest Conservation

Concern for agriculture extended to woodlands. Every farm needed a woodlot for fences, lumber, and fuel. In this way, American forestry and conservation emerged from concern for preserving the agricultural resource base for communities and future generations of New England towns, which in colonial times for the same purposes had passed ordinances to regulate timber cutting. Billings's reforestation of Mount Tom complemented his model farm, while Olmsted's horticultural experience prepared him to choose and place trees, bushes, and flowers in his park designs and led him to an interest in forestry.

Similarly, Billings's hero Marsh had discovered forestry and conservation during his efforts to bolster declining New England agriculture and New England towns. His *Address delivered before the Agricultural Society of Rutland County, Sept. 30, 1847* laid out the prospect for further improvement of American agriculture, which he linked to civilization and social progress. To this commonplace observation Marsh added the need for "the introduction of a better economy in the management of our forest lands." He lamented how, "in the physical geography of Vermont, within a single generation," terrible changes had occurred: "The signs of artificial improvement are mingled with the tokens of improvident waste, and the bald and barren hills, the dry beds of the smaller streams, the ravines furrowed out by the torrents of spring, and the diminished thread of interval that skirts the widened channel of the rivers, seem sad substitutes for the pleasant groves and brooks and broad meadows."[32]

After two decades of thought and research, Marsh addressed these issues in *Man and Nature; or, Physical Geography As Modified by Human Action,* the single most powerful and influential work in the history of international conservation. Marsh, too, descended from Connecticut river gods whose forebears journeyed in 1636 with Hooker and the Wadsworths, Edwardses, Churches, and Olmsteds to Hartford. The Marshes were a restless clan who from generation to generation moved up and down the Connecticut Valley. Religious quarrels after Hooker's death provoked John Marsh and his son John II to join disgruntled church members to found Hadley, Massachusetts, in 1659, and John II soon resettled across the river in Northampton. John III returned to Hartford. His son Joseph was a founding proprietor of Lebanon, Connecticut, in 1697. Joseph II's widow and children settled in 1773 in Hartford, Vermont, where Joseph III was a proprietor, county judge, and lieutenant governor. In 1790 his son Charles set up a law practice in nearby Woodstock, where George Perkins was born in 1801. George Perkins Marsh, just as restless, spent nearly half his 81 years far from New England, in Washington, DC, as a politician and in the Ottoman Empire and Italy as a diplomat.[33]

Marsh's international, cosmopolitan outlook and reputation should not obscure their origins in quite provincial concerns and values. His wife remembered him as "the last of the Puritans"[34] and as a promoter of New England's "intellectual, moral, and material prosperity. He regarded New England as the mother who was chiefly to form the character of the rising States of the West."[35] However, he observed in dismay as Vermont farmers struggled to survive economic pressures that led them to overcut their forests for timber and then overgraze their hilly meadows during the Merino sheep craze. Treeless mountains baked in the sun and eroded in the rain. Fish died as clear streams turned muddy. Towns declined as their young people sought out richer western lands. Not agricultural improvement, Marsh thought, but Puritan-style regulation of timber, grazing, and fisheries would solve Vermont's problems.[36] While a diplomat in Italy, Marsh wrote down his conclusions in *Man and Nature*. He drew examples from his extensive travels in the devastated landscapes of the Holy Land and the Mediterranean but he took his key insights from observations of his home state. Hoping to preserve New England villages from ecological ruin, and with no slight inspiration from Palissy, whom Marsh repeatedly praised, quoted, or cited, he argued for preservation of forests. Forests, in addition to supplying wood to future generations, would maintain the purity and flow of water and prevent soil erosion.[37]

Marsh's provincial Congregational experience thoroughly informed the book, with its epigraph from a sermon by Congregational minister Horace Bushnell and its outbursts of Puritan moralism. The righteous farmer and citizen must give heed "to the necessity of restoring the disturbed harmonies of nature, whose well-balanced influences are so propitious to all her organic offspring, of repaying to our great mother the debt which the prodigality and the thriftlessness of former generations have imposed upon their successors—thus fulfilling the command of religion and of practical wisdom, to use this world as not abusing it." Marsh warned, "Man has too long forgotten that the earth was given to him for usufruct alone, not for consumption, still less for profligate waste."[38] With Calvinist-Miltonic overtones, he noted that "man, who even now finds scarce breathing room on this vast globe, cannot retire from the Old World to some yet undiscovered continent, and wait for the slow action of such [natural] causes to replace, by a new creation, the Eden he has wasted."[39] Man had been a poor steward, and would be surely called to account for neglecting the welfare of future generations.[40] With forests, of course, considering the very long period needed to regenerate woodland, the need to plan now for future generations is a great deal more obvious and necessary than most other human endeavors.

Billings was far from the only son of the Connecticut Valley to answer Marsh's call to action. Having read *Man and Nature,* Franklin B. Hough, born in Martinsburg, New York, to a native of Connecticut, supervised the 1865 state and 1870 national censuses in New York, whose falling statistics on timber production alarmed him. Hough's pivotal paper "On the Duty of Governments in the Preservation of Forests" for the 1873 meeting of the American Association for the Advancement of Science, citing Palissy and Marsh, noted the need to plan for future generations but the lack of incentive for individuals to do so. He proposed popular education on the economic value of planting trees, forestry schools to train educators and engineers, and government regulation of forests, all of which came to pass. Hough emphasized protection of Adirondack forests, having sat on a legislative commission to study their preservation in 1872. His actions were instrumental in the creation under Governor Grover Cleveland in 1885 of a forestry commission and state Adirondack and Catskill Forest Preserves. The federal government tapped Hough in 1876 to assess the state of the nation's forests, and in 1881 he became the first chief of the new Division of Forestry in the Department of Agriculture to advise farmers on care of their woodlands. The following year he helped organize the American Forestry Congress and edited the *American Journal of Forestry.*[41]

In 1883, American Forestry Congress vice-president Nathaniel H. Egleston succeeded Hough. Another Marsh disciple, Egleston was a native of Hartford, graduate of Yale, and Congregational minister in

Jonathan Edwards's old church in Stockbridge. Egleston had come to forestry through his interest in improving rural life and the New England village as his paradigm. His 1878 *Villages and Village Life: With Hints for their Improvement* recommended planting trees in towns for beauty and in the countryside for utility.[42]

In 1886 Bernhard E. Fernow, born and trained in Prussia, replaced Egleston as head of the Forest Division, the first professional forester to hold the post. Fernow redirected the Division of Forestry away from advising farmers and toward managing forests under federal control. He played a role in the passage in 1891 of the Forest Reserve Act, which provided for reservation of federal forested land from public sale, and in 1897 of the Organic Act, which defined the purpose of the forest reserves and mandated their management and protection and was sponsored by South Dakota Senator Richard F. Pettigrew, native of Vermont.[43]

In the meantime, Olmsted took an interest in forestry that would have major consequences for American conservation. Olmsted had worked with Billings in California when Billings read *Man and Nature* in 1864, and surely knew the book. His 1866 proposal for the grounds for the land-grant Massachusetts Agricultural College, now University of Massachusetts at Amherst, assigned the hill on the site for forestry demonstration.[44] Olmsted repeated Marsh's points when he published a report on the Chicago fire in *The Nation* in 1871.[45] Then in 1888 George W. Vanderbilt, son of neighboring Staten Island "farmer" William H. Vanderbilt and grandson of railroad magnate Cornelius Vanderbilt, consulted with Olmsted regarding land with spectacular views that he had bought in the mountains of North Carolina. Olmsted considered the Biltmore estate's exhausted soil and cutover forests were poor material for the park his client wanted. "My advice," he told Vanderbilt in 1891, "would be to make a small park into which to look from your house; make a small pleasure ground and garden, farm your river bottom chiefly to keep and fatten life stock with a view to manure; and make the rest a forest, improving the existing woods and planting the old fields."[46] Olmsted needed a forester to assist him, and at that moment aspiring forester Gifford Pinchot walked through the door while on a tour of American forests.

Pinchot's Biltmore experience would be his springboard to success and fame as America's greatest forester, and it was hardly coincidental that he appeared at that moment. His family knew Olmsted and had employed his services.[47] Olmsted might even have had young Pinchot in mind when he suggested reforesting Biltmore. Pinchot had graduated from Yale in

1889; ambitious to be America's first native-born professional forester, he attended French forestry school for one year, toured managed forests in France, Germany, and Switzerland, and returned home hoping one day to replace Fernow. Pinchot started at Biltmore in 1892, reported on his work at a forestry exhibit he prepared for the Chicago World's Fair in 1893, and hired a German forestry assistant, Carl Alwin Schenck, who soon took over the work and in 1898 also established at Biltmore the first American forestry school. Schenck would credit Olmsted, not Marsh or Hough or Pinchot, as "the inspirer of American forestry."[48] When Fernow left the Division of Forestry in 1898 to be the first dean of the Cornell College of Forestry, the nation's first state forest school, Pinchot succeeded him as head of the Forest Division. In 1901 the Pinchot family funded the foundation of the Yale Forestry School, the nation's first postgraduate forestry program, to train professional foresters. Pinchot's greatest achievement was the creation of the Forest Service in 1905, when the forest preserves were moved from the Department of the Interior to the new Forest Service. Two years later he renamed the preserves National Forests in order to emphasize their efficient and scientific use for the benefit of the nation.

Pinchot, who declared, "I was born a Connecticut Yankee,"[49] built American forestry on Connecticut Puritan values. He was born in 1865 in grandfather Amos R. Eno's house in Simsbury, Hartford County, Connecticut, to a maternal lineage of Puritans and Huguenots. Gifford was close to his pious mother, who instilled in her son strong moral and evangelistic sentiments. He at first was inclined to a career in church work.[50] His father, James Pinchot, turned him from religion to forestry. Gifford's grandfather, a French immigrant, made a great deal of money deforesting swaths of Pennsylvania and his father became interested in forestry in order to reforest family property. In his autobiography, Pinchot recalled the moment his father suggested a career: "'How would you like to be a forester?' asked my foresighted Father one fortunate morning in the summer of 1885, just before I went to college.... He was fond of quoting the great saying of one of his heroes, Bernard Palissy, the inspired potter, naturalist, and philosopher, who died in the Bastille, that neglect of the forest was 'not merely a blunder, but a calamity and a curse for France.'... He was sure that Forestry must come to America,...and...the time was ripe."[51] For Pinchot's twenty-first birthday in 1886, his uncle gave him the 1882 edition of *Man and Nature*.[52]

The forester never displaced the New England preacher in Pinchot, now a preacher of the forest "gospel of efficiency," in historian Samuel

P. Hays's apt phrase.[53] "The conservation issue is a moral issue," he wrote, "and the heart of it is this: For whose benefit shall our natural resources be conserved—for the benefit of us all, or for the use and profit of the few?" He decried "the prodigal squandering" of natural resources, waste which was "often not merely without benefit but to the serious injury of the community." He insisted, "We, the American people, have come into the possession of nearly four million square miles of the richest portion of the earth. It is ours to use and conserve for ourselves and our descendants, or to destroy."[54]

For protection of private forests, Pinchot held that moral communities like New England towns would take better care of soil and forests. The key to maintaining moral communities was a strong country church. In 1908, at the peak of his forestry career, Pinchot promoted the "country life" move-ment to make rural living more attractive and served on the Country Life Commission with like-minded Liberty Hyde Bailey. In the 1910s Pinchot and his cousin Charles Otis Gill, a Yale classmate and a Congregational minister, coauthored two influential studies of country churches, which Pinchot funded: *The Country Church: The Decline of Its Influence and the Remedy* in 1913, and *Six Thousand Country Churches* in 1919.[55] At a 1916 con-ference on country churches, Pinchot sermonized, "The country church can be made again what it was during the early days in New England, the strongest power not only for righteousness, which it is now, but also for the general success of country life and for the welfare of country commu-nities." Like the missionary he once thought of becoming, he concluded, "The work which lies before the country church may well be second to no other in the power of its thrust toward a social order founded on the eth-ics of Jesus Christ."[56] Pinchot's forestry reinterpreted the Puritan goal of a moral, orderly society in terms of the nation's resources.

When Pinchot left the Forest Service in 1910, his friend Henry S. Graves succeeded him. Son of a professor from West Fairlee, Vermont, Graves graduated from Yale and followed his friend Pinchot into forestry. He served as the first dean of Yale Forestry School and was appointed dean again when he left the Forest Service in 1920.[57] Graves's successor from 1920 to 1928 was William B. Greeley, the last Connecticut-Valley Yankee to head the Forest Service. Greeley was born in Oswego, New York, and raised on a ranch in Santa Clara County, California. His father and grandfather had been Congregational ministers in Chicopee Falls, Massachusetts (fifteen miles downstream from Northampton). Greeley was the first graduate of the Yale Forestry School to head the Forest Service, yet he and Pinchot had a dramatic falling out. Having worked his way up through the ranks of the Forest Service, Greeley's understanding of lumbering was more practical than that of Pinchot, whose experience on the ground was limited to a year on the Biltmore Estate. While on the one hand Greeley sought to expand public ownership of forests to replenish the cutover lands east of the Mississippi, on the other he sought a rapprochement of sorts with the lumber barons. The result was the Clarke-McNary Act of 1924, drafted by Greeley with the support of the lumber lobby, which made it easier for the Forest Service to buy land and encouraged greater cooperation with industry. Pinchot bitterly opposed it as a complete sellout to the lumber industry. Thereafter, Pinchot's moral view of forestry was marginalized, and communally based forestry as an aspect of farming had wholly given way to commercial forestry of large tracts of nonagricultural land. The model of the New England town vanished.[58]

Puritan forestry died but its moral spirit survived in conservation, perhaps the greatest legacy of Pinchot's career. Here was a clear expression for the twentieth century of the Reformed traditions of stewardship of the earth and the interconnectedness of nature, along with the Puritan priority of community over self-interest. Pinchot realized in 1907 that the "possible use or waste of natural resources . . . fitted into and made up the one great central problems of the use of the earth for the good of man," which "must be solved if the generations, as they came and went, were to lived civilized, happy, useful lives in the lands which the Lord their God had given them." He discussed the idea with W. J. McGee, formerly of the Bureau of Ethnology. McGee formulated a succinct definition: "the use of natural resources for the greatest good of the greatest number for the longest time" and convinced Pinchot "that monopoly of natural resources was only less dangerous to the public welfare than their actual destruction."[59] Shorn of its Puritan moralism, conservation today remains the least controversial and least politicized aspect of the American environmental movement.

Public Parks

Olmsted's chance meeting with Downing in the office of *The Cultivator* in 1846 set in motion his dramatic rise from gentleman farmer to the nation's foremost landscape architect, parks advocate, and city planner. Child of Massachusetts natives and owner of a nursery in Newburgh, New York, Downing in fact preceded him in all these fields and had published three books and many articles in American, English, and French journals by the time Tucker recruited him to edit *The Horticulturist.*[60] The books, *A Treatise on the Theory and Practice of Landscape Gardening, Adapted to North America* of 1841, *Cottage Residences* of 1842, and *The Fruits and Fruit Trees of America* of 1845, had quickly become classics on both sides of the Atlantic. Downing added *The Architecture of Country Houses* in 1850, a brisk seller popular with critics and readers alike. He peppered his books and essays with quotations from all the standard authorities, including Milton (Book 4 of *Paradise Lost*),[61] Uvedale Price, Horace Walpole, William Wordsworth, Sir Joshua Reynolds, Darwin, Jean-Jacques Rousseau, Louis Agassiz, Alexander von Humboldt (*Cosmos*), William Hogarth, and Ruskin, not to mention classical authors, the Bible, and the "Book of Nature," seasoned with allusions to the art of Cole, Claude, Poussin, and Turner.[62] Such citations document the debt of American gardening, landscape architecture, and parks to the Reformed aesthetics of Hogarth, Reynolds, and Ruskin and to the Reformed science of Agassiz, Humboldt, and Darwin.

Just as importantly, they acknowledge how much was owed to the Reformed Edenic ideal of landscape. The naturalistic Eden that Milton imagined in *Paradise Lost* inspired English landscape gardeners to abandon French geometrical formal gardens, consciously revive gardens' moral purpose, and create the naturalistic "English garden." Visitors wandering the grounds of English estates admiring the views would "spontaneously" recite Milton's description of Eden in Book 4 or the Morning Hymn in Book 5.[63] The subjects of many of Gainsborough's portraits sat before vistas of their naturalistic gardens and estates in implicit testimony to their moral sense and good taste. Horace Walpole's 1771 treatise on the English garden, "On Modern Gardening," gave Book 4 of *Paradise Lost* whole credit for inventing the English garden.[64] Uvedale Price and others continued to quote Milton as they pushed the English garden in the wilder direction of the picturesque. Swiss Reformed author Rousseau's lovingly detailed description of an English garden in *La nouvelle Heloïse* set off a Continental craze for the style.[65]

Downing sought to disseminate tasteful landscape gardens and architecture throughout America, as the full title of his journal reflected, *The Horticulturist and Journal of Rural Art and Rural Taste.* Like the builders of New England's Congregational churches, he believed that a tasteful physical environment promoted a moral and orderly society and likewise that "a beautiful rural church" would have "as much to do with awakening devotional feelings, and begetting an attachment in the heart, as the unmistakable signs of virtue and benevolence in our fellow-creatures, have in awakening kindred feeling in our own breasts."[66] His well-known essay "Moral Influence of Good Houses" asserted that "a taste for beautiful and appropriate architecture" promotes "public virtue and the general good."[67] Extensive citations of Timothy Dwight's *Travels in New-England and New-York* supported Downing's contention that New England had the most tasteful American towns:[68] "There is one part of the Union where the millennium of country towns, and good government, and rural taste has not only commenced, but is in full domination. We mean, of course, Massachusetts. . . . [Elsewhere,] you feel little or nothing of that sense, of 'how pleasant it must be to live here,' which the traveller through Berkshire, or the Connecticut valley, or the pretty villages about Boston, feels moving his heart within him."[69] Downing urged town planning after the example of the New England town for new towns and suburbs fast springing up across the nation.

New England towns provided the model for the rise of city parks, themselves models for the first state and national parks. His 1850 essay "Our Country Villages" recommended "a large open space, common, or park, situated in the middle of the village . . . well planted with groups of trees, and kept as a lawn. . . . This park would be the nucleus or *heart of the village*, and would give it an essentially rural character, . . . for the common use of the whole village, . . . and broad, well-planted avenues of shade-trees."[70] Downing noted the beautiful avenues of elms that graced New England's towns, most memorably in Northampton, Springfield, New Haven, and Stockbridge (Figure 3.1, see color insert).[71]

Old England, not New, alerted Olmsted to the democratic possibilities of large urban public parks. Olmsted set sail in 1850 for a walking tour of England and Scotland intending to make notes on agricultural practices for articles in *The Horticulturist*. Just after disembarking in Liverpool, Olmsted had a revelation. He and his companions took the ferry across the Mersey to Birkenhead (opposite Toxteth, incidentally), where a resident enthusiastically recommended they see the new public park, built in 1847 and the first anywhere developed with public funds. Birkenhead Park's playgrounds, winding paths, little lake, and presence of all classes and ages fascinated Olmsted. He reported, "Five minutes of admiration, and a few more spent in studying the manner in which art had been employed to obtain from nature so much beauty, and I was ready to admit that in democratic America there was nothing to be thought of as comparable with this People's Garden."[72] Olmsted had surely read editorials

by William Cullen Bryant in his *New York Evening Post*. Born to orthodox Congregational folk in Cummington, Massachusetts, twenty miles
from Northampton, Bryant had argued since 1844 in favor of a public
park in New York City for its effect on "good morals and good order."[73]
Horace Greeley, a New Hampshire–born Universalist of old Puritan stock,
joined the campaign from his *Tribune*.[74] Downing published articles in
1848 and 1849 in *The Horticulturist* that advocated parks for America. At
Birkenhead, Olmsted had found a pattern for New York's park. His "The
People's Park in Birkenhead, Near Liverpool" in *The Horticulturist* in 1851
prompted Downing to write "The New-York Park" urging the mayor to act
on a park for the fast-growing city. The New York legislature authorized
Central Park in 1853, but political wrangling and lack of appropriations
delayed progress until 1857.[75]

Without any training or experience, Olmsted found himself the
landscape architect of New York's new park, which had it not been for
Downing's death in 1852 in a steamboat accident would surely have been
the job of Downing and his partner Calvert Vaux. Increasingly owners of
estates who desired Downing's gardening services also wanted an architect for their homes, so he had gone to England in 1850 for an architectural
assistant and brought back Vaux, of Dissenter background and Huguenot
lineage.[76] In 1857 Vaux partnered with Olmsted in a design proposal for
Central Park, "Greensward," in the English-garden style, which became
the plan for America's first major city park and model for urban parks
from Boston to San Francisco.[77] The approval of Central Park in 1853
prompted Hartford Congregational minister Horace Bushnell, Olmsted's
friend and former next-door neighbor, to lobby city fathers for a park. In
1854 Hartford became the first municipality to purchase land for a public
park with city funds, Bushnell Park.[78]

Olmsted was the first person known as a "landscape architect."[79] After
his partnership with Vaux ended in 1872, Olmsted moved away from
Vaux's Gothic-revival style to work with H. H. Richardson, pioneer of the
naturalistic Shingle Style. In 1883, he established his firm, Fairsted, at
Brookline, Massachusetts—a suburb of Boston so beautiful that Downing
had described it as "a kind of landscape garden."[80] Named for the city
in England from which Olmsted's Puritan ancestors had emigrated,
Fairsted functioned as the country's first landscape-architecture school
until Harvard established the first true school, funded by the Eliot family
in 1900 in memory of Charles Eliot, Olmsted's protégé, and directed by
Frederick Law Olmsted Jr.

Central Park's design and purpose manifested the Puritan social ethic. One goal was religious. Olmsted wrote that "it is one great purpose of the Park to supply to the hundreds of thousands of tired workers, who have no opportunity to spend their summers in the country, a specimen of God's handiwork that shall be to them, inexpensively, what a month or two in the White Mountains or the Adirondacks is, at great cost, to those in easier circumstances."[81] So skillfully did Olmsted hide the artificiality of the park that many religious visitors thought they were looking at the works of God. Eliot described his mentor's "fundamental principles": "Mr. Olmsted . . . preferred . . . undulating meadows fringed with trees, quiet, farstretching pastoral scenery, and groves which preserved the underbrush and the rough surface of the natural forest. . . . Artificial features were not the object of any landscape undertaking, but its necessary impediments."[82] The works of man must be hid or intrude as little as possible.

Central Park represented an Eden in the midst of an urban Hell. Olmsted generally avoided explicit references to Eden, perhaps in deference to the city's contentious political and religious scene or to the many different purposes that the park served in different minds: recreation, nature preservation, democratic ideals, civic pride, and a symbol of the good taste of the upper classes. Explicit Edenic language did emerge, however, in an 1881 plea against overdevelopment of a naturalistic park he designed for Mount Royal in Montreal: "If you can but persuade yourselves to regard them as sacred places and save them from sacrilegious hands and feet, the original Gardener of Eden will delight your eyes with little pictures within greater pictures of indescribable loveliness."[83] While the park was at least a generation too late to inspire people to spontaneously recite passages from *Paradise Lost,* pious visitors nevertheless found their thoughts leading to Eden. In an 1864 sermon inspired by a stroll through the park, "Moral Analogies of Central Park," Presbyterian minister Horace Eaton mused how depraved man still created parks out of a yearning for the beauty of Eden.[84] Five years later, Congregational minister Matthew Hale Smith called Central Park "an area of beauty, charming as the Garden of the Lord,"[85] and Methodist minister John Francis Richmond in 1872 compared the city to the capital of Hell in *Paradise Lost* and the park to Eden: "Who can press . . . through its neglected sinks, without thinking of pandemonium; or its cultivated parks, without thinking of paradise?"[86]

Olmsted saw parks' purpose as primarily moral and social. Opportunities to relax the mind amidst beautiful expansive scenery, to exercise the body, to escape the crowded, noisy, stressful city streets, as well as to leave the works of man for those of God, enabled people to be industrious, useful, moral citizens. People could not exercise their talents or contribute fully to the community if they were ill, weak, or enticed by the multitude of immoral amusements that cities offered.[87] Matthew Hale Smith concurred: "The whole influence of the Park," he wrote, "has been to educate and elevate the public taste, and to inspire a love for the beautiful."[88] Like New England church architecture and Downing's tasteful houses and villages, well-designed parks would expose the public to good taste and healthy influences, and thus promote good morals and good order.

Olmsted and Vaux's park designs consciously translated the Reformed aesthetics of the Hudson River painters into landscape, a reversal of what painters do. After all, Olmsted observed, "A park is a work of art, designed to produce certain effects upon the mind of men. There should be nothing in it[,] absolutely nothing—not a foot of surface nor a spear of grass—which does not represent study, design, a sagacious consideration & application of known laws of cause & effect with reference to that end."[89] In a brilliant move that illustrates the inextricable interrelationship of art and landscape from the very beginning, Olmsted and Vaux had enlisted Jervis McEntee, Church's student and Vaux's brother-in-law, to paint "before" and "after" scenes of the park as part of their winning "Greensward" proposal. Fellow members of the Century Club, Olmsted and Vaux also knew Church. Church commissioned Vaux to make the initial design for his mansion, Olana. Olmsted sometimes sought out artists for their advice. After joining the new Yosemite park commission in 1864, Olmsted had consulted with Thomas Hill and other artists then camping there on how best to preserve the features of the valley. In 1871, at Vaux's suggestion, Olmsted had Church appointed to the commission overseeing construction of Central Park in the belief that "the public utility of devotion to art and the study of Nature in a public service of this kind should be recognized and Church seemed on the whole the most appropriate and respectable man to express this."[90]

Through New Englanders like Olmsted, the Reformed Edenic landscape manifested itself in state and national parks, beginning with the first park, Yosemite in 1864. Yosemite park was the creation of New Englanders. Israel Ward Raymond, representative of the Central American Steamship Transit Company of New York born in New York to former Connecticut Congregationalists, wrote the letter to Senator John Conness in early 1864 that instigated creation of a park at Yosemite.[91] The Yosemite commission headed by Olmsted included Raymond, Josiah Dwight Whitney, William Ashburner, and Galen Clark, as well as two local businessmen and an attorney. Whitney, a native of Northampton, relative of the Dwights, and former student of Silliman at Yale, headed the California Geological Survey.[92] Stockbridge native Ashburner was a mining engineer on the California Geological Survey.[93] Former New-Hampshire Congregationalist Galen Clark owned a tourist station near the Mariposa Big Trees on the southern route into Yosemite and was appointed Guardian of the Yosemite Valley and the Big Tree Grove, his title for most of the rest of his long life.[94]

New England Congregationalists, Universalists, and Unitarians publicized Yosemite. Congregational minister John Calvin Holbrook preached the first sermon in the valley in 1859.[95] Unitarian minister Thomas Starr King brought Yosemite to the attention of New Englanders with a series of letters from the valley to a Boston newspaper in 1860 and 1861.[96] George Fiske, son of a New Hampshire Congregational deacon, was the early Yosemite photographer whom Ansel Adams ranked first among his predecessors and whose photographs illustrated Clark's *The Yosemite Valley* of 1910.[97]

From the day white Americans discovered it in 1851, Yosemite had inspired Reformed Protestants to religious reactions. Yosemite represented the holiest "church" of nature, the very "Rome" of Reformed nature pilgrimage, a notion popularized in Bryant's oft-quoted "Forest Hymn" of 1824, which proclaimed, "The groves were God's first temples," and Ruskin's comparison of the Alps to cathedrals and temples in the fourth volume of *Modern Painters* of 1856.[98] Jonathan Edwards's great-granddaughter Sara Jane Clarke Lippincott, editor of the children's magazine *Little Pilgrims*, wrote an account of the trip she and "fellow-pilgrims to the sacred Sierra" took in 1872 to Yosemite, "the temple of [Nature's] ancient worship, with thunderous cataracts for organs, and silver cascades for choirs, and wreathing clouds of spray for perpetual incense, and rocks three thousand feet high for altars."[99] Josiah Letchworth, a Presbyterian from Buffalo, New York, in a letter described his entry into Yosemite in 1880 as "a pilgrimage to some vast cathedral shrine of Nature" where he was "baptized" in the spray of Bridal Veil Fall; the valley was "Nature's own great cathedral, where her votaries come from all lands to wonder and admire—whose cathedral spires point to Heaven, whose domes have withstood the storms and tempests of all the ages, seem set apart from all the world to show forth the mighty works of Omnipotent Power, and you feel as did the Apostle of old. What you have seen are 'unspeakable things,' which no pen or pencil can describe. . . . A dream, more of Heaven than of earth, has been revealed to you."[100]

When Reformed Protestants wrote letters, articles, books, or poetry about Yosemite, they regularly compared it to Eden, particularly Milton's Paradise. In a typical response, Fitz Hugh Ludlow, son of a Presbyterian minister, noted his initial skepticism—"If report were true, we were going to the original site of the Garden of Eden"—but found himself transported at his first sight of the Valley in 1863: "We did not so much seem to be seeing from that crag of vision a new scene on the old familiar globe, as a new heaven and a new earth into which the creative spirit had just been breathed. . . . Never were words so beggared for an abridged translation of any Scripture of Nature."[101] In Ludlow's party was Bierstadt, in his first visit to the Valley, who wrote, "We are now here in the garden of Eden. . . . The most magnificent place I was ever in."[102] Jean Bruce Washburn's popular 1872 poem "Yo Semite" compared it to "that Paradise so fair of old," "that Eden, so supernal bright!"[103] San Francisco Presbyterian Charles Warren Stoddard, native of Rochester, New York, remembered approaching "with silent, devotional steps" toward Yosemite: "The new world lies below there, illuminated with the soft, delicate tints of Eden."[104] English traveler William Simpson raised the possibility in 1874 that Yosemite might be the original Eden itself.[105]

Many quoted or alluded to *Paradise Lost*. In fact, Yosemite Valley resembled Milton's Eden physically, with its meadows, groves, waterfalls, lake, and meandering river surrounded by a "steep wilderness, whose hairie sides / With thicket overgrown, grottesque [picturesquely irregular] and wilde." In 1859, New Englander Joseph Lamson wrote, "Filled with emotions such as Adam and Eve may be supposed to have felt when, 'They, hand in hand, with wandering steps and slow, / Through Eden took their solitary way,' we cast one sad look at the scene behind us, and bade a sorrowful and final adieu to the wonderful Yosemite Valley."[106] English tourist William Minturn identified with "one of Milton's angels perched on a cloud" as he gazed down into the valley.[107] A rattlesnake inspired this vision from Sara Jane Clarke Lippencott: " 'Ah, fellow-pilgrims, here . . . is Paradise!' As if to make the words true, . . . just at this point the Serpent started up from the grass and the flowers. . . . [A] rattlesnake! Ah! if the 'grand old gardener' of Eden had served the father of serpents and lies as Mr. Hutchings served this rash intruder,—mashed his head and cut off his rattles,—what a different world we should have had of it! Then, every first family could have had a Yo-semite to itself,—a private Paradise, with no angel of expulsion to drive us down the valley and up the trail."[108] Like Lamson and Lippencott, California poets Joaquin Miller in his popular "Yosemite" and George Sterling in "Yosemite: An Ode" also would both liken departure from Yosemite to expulsion from Eden.[109] Very commonly authors and poets claimed to hear nature praising God in Yosemite, like all creation in the Morning Hymn.[110]

Creation of Yosemite Park immediately inspired proposals to do something similar for Niagara. Massachusetts editor Samuel Bowles visited Yosemite with Olmsted in 1865 and reported, "This wise cession and dedication by Congress . . . furnishes an admirable example for other objects of natural curiosity and popular interest all over the Union. New York should preserve for popular use both Niagara Falls and its neighborhood and a generous section of her famous Adirondacks, and Maine one of her lakes and its surrounding woods."[111] Church, the famous painter of *Niagara,* proposed such a park for the falls in 1869. Olmsted and architect H. H. Richardson went to inspect the falls. Like most visitors, they were utterly appalled at the "sordid interests" that had turned the falls into part industrial complex, part carnival, and part tawdry tourist trap. Olmsted began the campaign for the park and prepared a design with Vaux that removed the works of man from the American bank and restored its "wild" condition. Church brought the Canadians in on plans for an international park. Against fierce political and commercial resistance the legislature approved funds, and in 1885 Governor Grover Cleveland signed the bill. In Yosemite the government for the first time set aside public land to preserve its natural beauty; the Niagara Fall State Park represented the first time that government had purchased land for the same purpose, and moreover removed the works of man in order to restore natural beauty.[112]

Connecticut Valley Congregationalists continued into the next century to lead and guide the American parks movement. Ferdinand V. Hayden and Cornelius Hedges of Westfield, Massachusetts, were the principal proponents of Yellowstone, the world's first national park in 1872. William Kent, son of Connecticut natives and a Yale alumnus, cofounded the Save-the-Redwoods League in 1918, donated the land for Muir Woods National Monument, worked to establish California's Mount Tamalpais State Park, and coauthored the 1916 bill to create the National Park Service.[113] Two other cofounders of the Save-the-Redwoods League, Frederick Russell Burnham and Henry Fairfield Osborn, descended from Connecticut Congregational ministers.[114] Yale graduate George Bird Grinnell, grandson of the Congregational minister of Greenfield, Massachusetts, led the creation of Glacier National Park in 1910, and landscape architect Ernest F. Coe, New Haven native and Yale graduate, spearheaded establishment of Everglades National Park in 1934.[115]

Among the most influential was the National Park Service's first director, Stephen Tyng Mather, born in San Francisco to a native of Darien, Connecticut, and descendant of Richard Mather, several Congregational ministers, and a deacon. Mather, a deeply religious man, believed that "from Nature can be learned the scheme of creation and the handiwork of the Great Architect as from no other source."[116] As National Parks director, he sought to develop parks tastefully to give public access to their moral and religious influence. National parks would play an essential role in the moral development of twentieth-century America and their spiritual power be preserved even as the Park Service encouraged millions to visit. In a 1923 visit to New York's Coney Island amusement park, Mather told Gilbert Stanley Underwood, the young architect who soon would design the Ahwahnee Hotel in Yosemite, "Our job in the Park Service is to keep the National Parks as close to what God made them as possible and as far as we can," and he gestured at Coney Island, "from a horror like this."[117]

Mather asked landscape architects to oversee and plan the development of a coherent, integrated system of national parks. He would have agreed wholeheartedly with professor of landscape architecture Frank Albert Waugh, who wrote in 1917 that landscape architects were "the men best trained in the love of the landscape and in the technical methods by which it alone can be conserved, restored, improved, clarified, made available and spiritually effective in the hearts of men and women."[118] A Congregationalist born in 1869 in Sheboygan Falls, Wisconsin, to a family with origins in Litchfield, Connecticut, Waugh studied landscape and horticulture at Cornell. In 1903, he founded the nation's second landscape architecture program at the land-grant college now named the University of Massachusetts at Amherst. Waugh's publications laid a theoretical basis for the design of recreation areas in parks and national forests. He either trained or profoundly influenced the nation's young landscape architects. One of his students, Conrad Wirth, the son of Hartford's parks superintendent and of Swiss ancestry, directed the Park Service between 1951 and 1964 and oversaw the massive Mission 66 development plan for the Parks system.[119]

The Nature Vacation

While Olmsted was tastefully bringing the moral effects of nature to the masses, Congregational ministers were bringing the masses to the woods, streams, and mountains. As Bushnell said in a speech to Phi Beta Kappa in Cambridge in 1848 on "Work and Play," a man cannot work well who is broken down with care and overwork, nor if he chases money all day can he dedicate himself to higher or moral things. He needs periods of play. The most moral, religious, creative, loving, and inspired moments of life do not occur during hard work. Especially after the Civil War, other ministers in the early "muscular Christianity" movement picked up Bushnell's point that play makes better Christians and argued for healthy, muscular manly Christians (womanly Christians apparently not being in short supply).[120] In the midst of America's growing industrial cities, Olmsted's parks provided the perfect place for innocent yet healthy play, away from urban vices like drinking, gambling, cardplaying, dancing, and worse. Then, in 1866, Congregational ministers discovered the health effects of a vacation in the woods when Hartford landscape painter John Fitch, who regularly spent summers painting in Keene Valley in the Adirondacks, took Congregational minister Joseph Hopkins Twichell along. Today best known as Mark Twain's Hartford pastor and closest friend, Twichell returned in 1868 with Bushnell and Yale president Noah Porter. These "climbing clerics" summered annually in the Adirondacks with their families, camping, hiking, fishing, and occasionally preaching in a little church in Keene Valley.[121]

In that same year of 1866, a parishioner took Congregational minister William Henry Harrison Murray of Meriden on a camping trip to the Adirondacks. Congregational ministers had started taking vacations to get away from the relentless year-round duties of pastoring and preaching and to have time to think and meditate. Of course, resorts and urban recreations were no places for men of the Gospel, so where could they go? Murray, native of Guilford and graduate of Yale, published *Adventures in the Wilderness: Or, Camp-Life in the Adirondacks* in 1869 and told them to enjoy innocent and morally improving recreation in the woods and mountains amidst the works of God. "It is in the ministry that you find the very men who would be the most benefited by this trip," said Murry. "For when the good dominie came back swarth and tough as an Indian, elasticity in his step, fire in his eye, depth and clearness in his reinvigorated voice, would n't there be some preaching!"[122]

Adventures in the Wilderness incited a camping craze. A wilderness vacation good for the minister must be good for the congregation, too. Murray provided how-to tips, touted the health benefits of the Adirondacks, and excited the reader with his tales of fish and game. Cabins, camps, hotels, and resorts sprang up all over the Adirondacks. All this attention to the forest of the Adirondacks also raised the question of how to preserve this treasure. By steps beginning in 1883, the legislature created the vast Adirondacks State Park to protect and preserve the forests and waters. The 1894 constitution of New York included a provision protecting the state park from development: the Adirondacks "shall be kept forever as wild forest lands."[123]

Connecticut Congregationalists felt that young people especially should enjoy nature's health and moral benefits. Frederick William Gunn, head of a boys' school in Washington, Connecticut, led the first organized camping trip for boys in 1861, tenting with them for two weeks and leading in the sort of activities that have been common in summer camps ever since. Murray's book inspired Congregational minister George W. Hinckley of West Hartford to found the first permanent church camp for boys in 1880. A second church camp, at Camp Harvard, New Hampshire, soon appeared in 1882, established by Harvard Seminary students. In 1885, Congregationalist Sumner F. Dudley founded the first residential youth camp for the Young Men's Christian Association (YMCA), first at Orange Lake, New York, and later on Lake Champlain.[124] In the 1890s summer camps for boys sprang up all over New England and upstate New York, a region that by 1920 contained about 90 percent of all summer camps, and introduced boys (and after 1900, girls as well) to outdoor life. Hartford's Center Church joined the movement in 1909, when it established Camp Asto Wamah on the banks of Columbia Lake, Connecticut.[125]

Making America Beautiful

Like Downing inspired by New England towns, Olmsted hugely influenced American urban and suburban design. Beginning in 1870 with Riverside, near Chicago, Olmsted designed suburbs with parks, called "Commons," and winding lanes, a pleasing mix, he said, of the "ruralistic beauty of a loosely built New England village with a certain degree of the material and social advantages of a town."[126] Olmsted's fellow leaders of the field of landscape architecture, H.W.S. Cleveland, Robert Morris Copeland, and Olmsted protégé Charles Eliot, who had all had New England childhoods, spread the ideal of the New England town in suburbs from Boston to Omaha.[127] In his aptly named *Rural Improvement: The Principles of Civic Art Applied to Rural Conditions, including Village Improvement and the Betterment of the Open Country,* Frank Albert Waugh held up the New England village as a model for agricultural communities. "Nothing could be finer," he wrote, "from the standpoint of civic design, nor as representing the civic life of a community, than the large, beautiful, dignified (usually Congregational or Unitarian) church, fronting on the town commons in many New England villages. These come the nearest to representing the ideals, both of civic design and church influence, of anything we have ever seen in America."[128]

Large, crowded, industrial cities however required something beyond the New England town. Olmsted began to design coordinated citywide systems of parks, with landscaped, tree-lined roads called "parkways" linking them, for such cities as San Francisco (never built); Buffalo, New York; Milwaukee, Wisconsin; and most famously, Boston, with its Emerald Necklace system of parks. The culmination of his career, in a sense, was the commission to design the grounds of the World's Columbian Exposition in Chicago in 1893 under the supervision of architect Daniel Burnham. Olmsted was the most important figure in the founding and development of the City Beautiful movement, which this Chicago World's Fair publicized to the nation. Its integrated design and unified style showed how cities might beautify water-fronts, waterways, streets, public buildings, and open spaces and install pub-lic art. With Olmsted's retirement in 1895, Burnham assumed leadership of the City Beautiful movement. Descended from New England Puritans, Burnham had dropped ministerial ambitions to become an architect.[129] He worked with Frederick Law Olmsted Jr. and architect Charles McKim on the design for the Mall in Washington, DC, which made it the world's most beautiful capital city. A successful plan for Cleveland followed. A plan for San Francisco was unfortunately abandoned in hasty rebuilding follow-ing the devastating earthquake and fire of 1906. His crowning work, the Chicago Plan of 1909, in Frank Lloyd Wright's estimation made Chicago the world's most beautiful city.[130] By the time he died in 1912, Burnham had left a monumental legacy, in more senses than one.[131]

The Chicago World's Fair inspired a poem that perfectly sums up the Connecticut Valley Congregational vision of a society of plentiful farms, natural splendor, and beautiful cities, all blessed by God. Katharine Lee Bates visited the fair on her way to Colorado Springs, Colorado. Daughter of a Congregational minister and a professor of English literature at Wellesley College in Massachusetts, Bates not long afterward climbed Pike's Peak, near Colorado Springs overlooking the Great Plains.[132] Exhilarated, she wrote a poem published in 1895 in *The Congregationalist* which became the much-loved American patriotic anthem, "America the Beautiful":

> O beautiful for spacious skies,
>   For amber waves of grain,
> For purple mountain majesties
>   Above the fruited plain!
>   America! America!
>   God shed His grace on thee,
> And crown thy good with brotherhood
>   From sea to shining sea!
>
> O beautiful for pilgrim feet,
>   Whose stern, impassioned stress
> A thoroughfare for freedom beat
>   Across the wilderness!
>   America! America!
>   God mend thine every flaw,
> Confirm thy soul in self-control,
>   Thy liberty in law!
>
> O beautiful for heroes proved
>   In liberating strife,
> Who more than self their country loved,
>   And mercy more than life!
>   America! America!
>   May God thy gold refine,
> Till all success be nobleness,
>   And every gain divine.
>
> O beautiful for patriot dream
>   That sees beyond the years
> Thine alabaster cities gleam
>   Undimmed by human tears!
>   America! America!
>   God shed His grace on thee
> And crown thy good with brotherhood
>   From sea to shining sea!

"America the Beautiful" perfectly expressed the New England Congregational agenda that gave the country agricultural improvement, conservation, parks, and urban planning. It was all there: natural beauty, bountiful land, white "alabaster" cities, oversight of God, "stern, impassioned" Puritan ("pilgrim") heritage, restraint of selfish individualism for the common good (through both "self-control" and "liberty in law"), rejection of greed for gold for desire for nobleness (more clearly stated in the third stanza of the 1895 version: "God shed his grace on thee / Till selfish gain no longer stain / The banner of the free"), abolitionist-tinged ideal of sacrifice for others, and millennial hope for brotherhood. "America the Beautiful" was a vision of the beautiful, godly, orderly, and moral New England town spread by God from sea to shining sea.[133]

Local Color: The End of Connecticut Valley Congregationalism

On June 27, 1867, Twichell joined Edward Slosson and Annie Trumbull in marriage in the sanctuary of his new Asylum Hill Congregational Church in Hartford. Annie Trumbull Slosson rose to be one of the leading figures of the New England local colorists, who for a time were counted among the nation's leading authors. Along with Harriet Beecher Stowe, Rose Terry Cooke, Sarah Orne Jewett, Mary Wilkins Freeman, Alice Brown, and Elizabeth Stuart Phelps, Slosson wrote stories that illustrated the decline of the New England village. Indeed, the New England town had been in steep decline since the 1830s, the very time when Cole, Martineau, and Kemble were singing its praises. Olmsted had commented on the problem in a paper he read before the American Social Science Association in 1870, in which he told of a man who returned to a New England town "such as fifty years ago were the glory of New England. . . . But as he found them now, they might almost be sung by Goldsmith [in his "Deserted Village"]. The meeting-house closed, the church dilapidated; the famous old taverns, stores, shops, mills, and offices dropping to pieces and vacant, or perhaps with a mere corner occupied by day laborers; but a third as many children as formerly to be seen in the schoolhouses, and of these less than half of American-born parents."[134] As the town declined, so did the old Puritan world. Congregationalism drifted away from Calvinist theology and the Puritan imperative to morally reform society from top to bottom. Virtually all leading conservationists and parks advocates—from Church and Olmsted to Marsh and Pinchot—had themselves abandoned

the New England town and its Calvinist church on the green as too narrow to live in, even as they labored to save it and held it up as a model for
the nation.

Slosson and the New England local colorists interwove themes
of religion and declining Calvinism with themes of nature. These
Congregational women chronicled in fiction the other side of the story
that men had outlined in the literature of conservation, but from the
point of view of women, the home, and the town rather than from the
standpoint of natural resources. While men like Marsh and Pinchot
were out saving the nation, women writers told the stories of women
hemmed in by declining opportunities and constricted social expectations. Their salvation lay not in machines or sustainable farming
methods but in discovering inner strength through religion or nature,
or finding quiet strength and courage to face and overcome their challenges. Consequently, in contrast to men, these authors do not rue the
decline of the New England town and its agriculture.[135] Local colorists
echoed conservationists' concerns about deforestation, but always with
a central concern with the domestic world of women and framed in a
post-Calvinist moral concern.[136] New England women actively supported
parks and forest conservation, but their voices have been rather absent
from American agrarian thought.

The popularity of local color fiction coincided with the rising popularity of natural history for women and of nature study for children.
Slosson in particular heavily emphasized themes of nature in her stories.
Born in 1838 to a prominent Connecticut family, a graduate of Catherine
Beecher's famous Hartford school for girls, Slosson rejected Calvinism
but remained a devout Congregationalist. Two brothers went into the
ministry and one became a supporter of evangelical fundamentalism.
After 1900 Slosson wrote mainly sentimental didactic religious stories
for children. Her most famous story, "Fishin' Jimmy" of 1888, was a
religious parable.[137] Far more than her fellow local colorists, Slosson
also immersed herself in the natural world. After her husband's early
death in 1871, she grew close to her widowed brother-in-law W. C. Prime,
with whom she frequently vacationed at resorts at Franconia Notch, New
Hampshire, Florida, the Delaware Water Gap, and elsewhere. When
logging and sawmill pollution threatened forests and streams around
Franconia Notch, she and Prime joined the campaign to create Franconia
Notch State Park, for which Slosson contributed a dialect poem, "Riled."
Two typical stanzas:

Say! Where on airth be the rivers,
Them shinin' old mountain rivers,
A-flashin' an' a-dashin', a sparklin' in the sun?
They uster look jes' like silver,
The shiniest kind o' silver,
My! It's more'n a month o' Sundays sense I seen a single one.

. . .

Don't call them streams here rivers,
This porridge o' sawdust rivers;
These sewers o' chips an' shavins choked up with sudsy mush,
Why, nary a fish can now live in 'em;
A sensible trout wouldn't live in 'em;
An' a fisherman. My! Think o' castin' a fly on that gutter o' slush![138]

As Prime fished for trout or the pair went on hikes, Slosson botanized. In 1886 she discovered entomology and became a recognized and
often-published entomologist, with numerous species and even a genus
named after her.[139] The classic New England town declined, but in Slosson
and other women the Reformed complex of religion, nature, and moral
activism lived on.

The End of Congregationalist Conservation

By the 1870s, when Church worked with Olmsted to establish the state
park at Niagara Falls, his art career had passed its peak. Artistic tastes
changed but he was unwilling to change with them. Rheumatic arthritis
also made it more difficult to paint and slowed his output. He retreated to
his family and Olana, the mansion he in effect made his last, great work
of art. Church died in 1900, mostly forgotten and his art scorned. His
son and daughter-in-law maintained Olana unchanged until by 1964 both
had died. A plan to sell the land to developers prompted a public campaign to raise money to buy and preserve it, signaling revival of interest
in the Hudson River School and resurrection of Church's artistic reputation. Today it is the Olana State Historic site and has been painstakingly
restored and maintained.

After Billings's death in 1890, his wife and daughters also preserved
the Marsh estate. In 1934, granddaughter Mary Billings French married
Laurance Spelman Rockefeller in the Woodstock Congregational Church.
Rockefeller's grandfather, John D. Rockefeller, had been a staunch Baptist,

but the Rockefeller men all married strong Congregational women who exercised formative influence over their sons. John D. Rockefeller married Laura Spelman, a devout Congregationalist whose father had been active in church affairs. John D. Rockefeller Jr. married Abby Aldrich, a Congregationalist from Rhode Island. Temperamentally like his mother, John Jr. played a major role in conservation during the twentieth century. He befriended Parks director Horace Albright, donated land and money to Grand Teton, Acadia, Great Smoky Mountains, Yosemite, and Shenandoah National Parks, and contributed to the Save-the-Redwoods League. Named for Laura and close to Abby, Laurance made conservation central to his life's work. As Rockefeller generations go on, many have continued to engage in environmental causes, including John D. III's daughter Alida Rockefeller Messinger; Nelson's son Steven C. Rockefeller, Professor Emeritus of Religion at Middlebury College in Middlebury, Vermont; and David's son David Rockefeller Jr., active especially in Alaska and marine conservation, and daughter Eileen Rockefeller Growald, cofounder with her husband of the Champlain Valley Greenbelt Alliance of Vermont. Mary Billings French Rockefeller inherited the Marsh estate, which she and Laurance donated to the National Park Service in 1992 as the Marsh-Billings-Rockefeller National Historic Park.[140] On its odyssey from private home to national treasure, the Marsh estate has journeyed through the three phases of Congregational conservation: agricultural improvement, forestry, and parks.

Pinchot's idea of "conservation," drawn from the work and example of Marsh as well as many Congregationalist forerunners, fragmented almost as soon as it was pronounced. When Pinchot unhooked conservation from the Puritan-town ideal and hitched it to Progressivism, he broadened its appeal at the expense of its focus on the moral community. Less than a year after William Howard Taft's inauguration, Taft fired him over Pinchot's accusations that Secretary of Interior Richard Ballinger was in league with private interests, and a fissure opened in the Republican Party that never healed. Pinchot had also fought unsuccessfully to have the national parks managed by the Forest Service, itself an agency of the Department of Agriculture, which would have been a neat and logical nesting of the three agencies born of Connecticut-Valley Congregational activism, and a symbolic synergy of the three goals of Reformed conservation since the days of Palissy. Despite the fact that the National Park Service Organic Act of 1916 was written by Frederick Law Olmsted Jr. and sponsored by William Kent, the battle over damming Hetch Hetchy Valley in Yosemite

National Park in 1913, which Pinchot supported, had left national park advocates with bad feelings toward the Forest Service. A kind of sibling rivalry between the two agencies for forestry and parks—children of the same mother but located in separate departments of the cabinet and lacking any sort of unifying ideology—has never entirely abated. Democrat Franklin D. Roosevelt came to office in 1933 as a staunch supporter of conservation and new parks, which politically severed these causes from their roots in Republican New England. Three years later he proposed a single Department of Conservation, not much different from Pinchot's desire to unite parks and forests in one department. By then, however, so many people from so many backgrounds had loaded the concept of conservation with definitions of their own, that the proposal died amid rancor and contention. Even Pinchot opposed it.[141]

Congregational conservationists vanished from leadership of conservation and environmentalism. The classic New England town was nearly gone. Industrialization, urbanization, and immigration made the Puritan heartland nearly unrecognizable. The once-powerful authority of Congregational ministers dwindled dramatically. Rising mass media, commercialism, and consumerism overwhelmed the power of pulpits and parents to perpetuate Puritan virtues of "self-control," selflessness, the common good, living lives useful to society, and leaving the world unimpaired for future generations. The old Puritan type of New Englanders like Marsh and Church became objects of fun and derision. Journalist H. L. Mencken relentlessly lambasted the "Puritans" of the 1920s. Grant Wood skewered the stereotype of the ancestry-proud New England upper crust in his satiric painting "Daughters of the Revolution" of 1932. Movies ridiculed them as humorless, moralistic meddlers, like Almira Gulch in *The Wizard of Oz* of 1939, who for the most of the picture is transformed into the Wicked Witch of the West and was played by Margaret Hamilton, a character actress specializing in the stereotypical New England spinster. By the second half of the twentieth century, restraint on individualism was often seen as a violation of rights and even psychologically harmful.

The Connecticut River Valley produced no Emerson, no Thoreau, no John Muir. Congregationalists could commune with God in the woods with the best of them, but these practical-minded folks rarely lost themselves in airy mysticism and never defended wilderness for its own sake apart from its social benefits. Truth be told, many did leave the Congregational Church and moved spiritually in similar directions as the Transcendentalists. University of California geologist Joseph LeConte, a Huguenot descendant raised Congregationalist on a Georgia plantation, described his religious metamorphoses, typical for his generation: "I was first orthodox of the orthodox; later, as thought germinated and grew apace, I adopted a liberal interpretation of orthodoxy; then, gradually I became unorthodox; then in deep sympathy with the most liberal movement of Christian thought; and finally, to some extent, a leader in that movement."[142] Yet there remained a difference between Bostonian and Connecticut Transcendentalism. Even those members of Emerson's Transcendentalist circle who came from the Connecticut Valley—Bronson Alcott, Orestes Brownson, Sylvester Judd, George Ripley—interested themselves strongly in the *practical* implications of Transcendentalist ideals, from education to the problems of the working class to social reform.[143] Emerson produced philosophy. Congregationalists produced agricultural inventions and methods as well as governmental and educational agricultural institutions; conservation and forestry reservations, educational institutions, and the Forest Service; and city, state, and national parks, and the Park Service. Today it might well be said that American ideals and dreams may be Emersonian but American landscaping, suburban communities, public conservation institutions, public parks and public forests, and even agriculture to a large extent are Congregational.

FIGURE 1.1 Thomas Cole, *View from Mount Holyoke, Northampton, Massachusetts, after a Thunderstorm (The Oxbow)*, 1836.

FIGURE 1.2 (*top*): Thomas Cole, *The Voyage of Life: Manhood*, 1842.
FIGURE 1.3 (*bottom*): Thomas Cole, *The Garden of Eden*, 1828.

FIGURE 1.4 (*top*): Thomas Cole, *Expulsion from the Garden of Eden*, 1828.
FIGURE 1.5 (*bottom*): Thomas Cole, *The Subsiding of the Waters of the Deluge*, 1829.

FIGURE 2.2 (top): Frederic Edwin Church, *Reverend Hooker and Company Journeying through the Wilderness in 1636 from Plymouth to Hartford*, 1846.

FIGURE 3.1 (bottom): Asaph Willard, *Eastern View of the Public Square or Green in New Haven, Connecticut*, c. 1849. From the left, the three churches are Trinity Church (Episcopal), Center Church (Congregational) and North Church (Congregational).

FIGURE 3.2 Frederic Edwin Church, *The Falls at Niagara*, 1857.

FIGURE 4.1 Ansel Adams, *Clearing Winter Storm, Yosemite National Park*, c. 1937 (negative); 1976–77 (print).

FIGURE 4.2 (*top*): John Marin, *Quoddy Head, Maine Coast*, 1933.
FIGURE 4.3 (*bottom*): Georgia O'Keeffe, *Black Mesa Landscape, New Mexico/Out Back of Marie's II*, 19

FIGURE 4.4 (*top*): Arthur Dove, *Nature Symbolized Number 2,* c. 1911.

FIGURE 4.5 (*left*): Georgia O'Keeffe, *Blue No. 3,* 1916.

FIGURE 4.6 (*top*): Marsden Hartley, *New Mexico Landscape*, 1919–20.
FIGURE 5.1 (*bottom*): William Keith, *Mount Lyell, California Sierra*, 1874.

FIGURE 5.2 William Keith, *Yosemite Valley*, 1875.

FIGURE 5.3 (*top*): William Keith, *San Anselmo Valley Near San Rafael*, 1869.
FIGURE 5.4 (*bottom*): William Keith, *Evening Glow*, 1891.

FIGURE 6.1 West Fraser, *Atlantic Moonrise*, 2006.

FIGURE 7.1 Sanford Robinson Gifford, *Hunter Mountain, Twilight*, 1866.

FIGURE 8.2 (*top left*): Leo Twiggs, *Philips Gate,* Hugo Series, 1990.

FIGURE 8.3 (*top right*): Leo Twiggs, *Blues at the Beach,* The Blues series, 1999.

FIGURE 8.4 (*bottom*): Leo Twiggs, *High Cotton Down Home Blues,* The Blues series, 2008.

4

Nature, Parks, and Emersonian Modernism

Storm Over Yosemite

The wet winter of 1935 should surely have been an inauspicious time to take one of the world's most celebrated nature photographs. Banks of clouds swept in from the chilly Pacific Ocean over the still unbridged Golden Gate. Storms poured rain on the green hills of the California coastal range before rolling on east and drenching the vineyards and almond groves of the Central Valley. Heavy, wet, low gray skies surged up the Sierra Nevada, which forced them to drop their ballast of snow over canyons and crags. They then passed on, lean and dry, high over the deserts of the vast Great Basin.

One day in January, the clouds broke between storms and shafts of sunlight found the earth again. Stepping out of his Yosemite studio, photographer Ansel Adams saw his opportunity. He drove down the valley and steered steeply up the southern route of the two that exited the park. At the mouth of the new Wawona Tunnel, he pulled over and stopped. Here, 500 feet above the valley floor, visitors from the world over have paused year after year in a ritual of speechless wonder at their first view of Yosemite. Early tourists dismounted or climbed from stagecoaches at Inspiration Point 2,000 feet above. Modern ones step out of cars and buses at Tunnel View. Then or now, they gather and gaze in reverent silence. Massive El Capitan towers in the middle distance and, across the valley on the right, graceful Bridalveil Fall descends, a bright ribbon on gray granite cliffs. Between them the Merced River winds tranquilly through level meadows and groves as the valley passes through the grand portal formed by El Capitan and Bridalveil. Beyond, one of the world's most beautiful valleys curves gently out of sight beneath the looming flat granite face of Half Dome in the distance.

As soon as Adams stepped out of the car, he saw the possibility of a very good photograph. He attached his boxy eight-by-ten-inch camera to its tripod and carefully positioned it. He precisely measured the light, framed the view through the camera, set the aperture and exposure, attached a filter, inserted the negative, wiped a few water drops from the lens, and covered it with a cap. Then he waited. Presently, the clouds opened and sunlight streamed onto Bridalveil Fall. With a quick practiced motion, he pulled off the lens-cap and snapped the shutter.

Adams had often photographed this view and would many times again, but this time, with this image, he had captured a truly magical moment. Wispy clouds wreathed dark granite masses and obscured Half Dome. Light fell on the silvery filament of Bridalveil Fall and illuminated the cover of bright snow behind shadowy trees. Thousands—perhaps millions—of amateur and professional photographers and painters from around the world have captured the same view, yet this photograph, *Clearing Winter Storm, Yosemite* (Figure 4.1, see color insert), numbers among a half dozen of Adams's most famous photographs and among the best loved of all images ever made of Yosemite Valley. Invited in 1975 to the White House to meet President Gerald Ford, he brought a print of *Clearing Winter Storm* for a gift. A mural of *Clearing Winter Storm* would greet visitors in 1979 to *Ansel Adams and the West,* a major exhibition at the New York Museum of Modern Art, which broke attendance records everywhere as it traveled to art museums across the country. The show's catalog, *Yosemite and the Range of Light,* with *Clearing Winter Storm* on its cover, sold over 250,000 copies. An unending stream of posters, datebooks, calendars, and books has spread reproductions of *Clearing Winter Storm* into offices, homes, apartments, and dormitories around the country. *Clearing Winter Storm* along with his other Yosemite photography has made Adams the best known photographer in the history of the United States and perhaps of the world.[1]

With the tremendous popularity of his photographs, Adams joined Thomas Cole and Frederic Church in the pantheon of American landscape artists. His work's unpeopled natural grandeur and obsessively crisp detail point to their common Reformed Protestant aesthetic. Born in San Francisco, Adams traced paternal ancestry back to Maine and ultimately to Ulster Scottish immigrants. Yet he was no Congregationalist.

Nominally Episcopalian, Adams grew up unchurched among "heathens," as he joked.[2] He owed no conscious artistic debt either to Cole's heroes Sir Joshua Reynolds and Archibald Alison or to Church's master John Ruskin. Adams was an enthusiastic partisan of Modernism. He absorbed Reformed cultural elements, particularly his intense moralism, from his father and learned Reformed values and aesthetics by catching his father's contagious enthusiasm for Ralph Waldo Emerson. Emersonian Transcendentalism reinforced Adams's unchurched spirituality as well as his Modernist photography. He encountered Emerson's ghost repeatedly in his life, for Emersonianism was the guiding spirit for the first genera-tion of American Modernist artists, craftsmen, and architects. Because the National Parks system was born in the same decade as American Modern art, Emersonians often designed and built its infrastructure. The "natu-ral" places that Adams photographed had already been transformed into Transcendentalistic spaces.

Histories of conservation and environmentalism conventionally bestow on Emerson and the Transcendentalists full laurels for spreading nature spir-ituality through the land.[3] Certainly by the middle of the twentieth century Transcendentalism had completely eclipsed outworn Congregationalism as environmentalism's effective spiritual creed. Transcendentalists however did not first lobby for and design parks, push for forest conservation, advo-cate agricultural improvement, or popularize wilderness vacations. New England Congregationalists, many of them ordained ministers, did those things, in hopes of resuscitating decaying New England towns.

Yet the Puritan community continued to decay, as did Puritan theol-ogy. Advances in Biblical criticism, archeology, and geology, not to men-tion publication of Charles Darwin's *Origin of Species* in 1859, undermined trustworthiness of the Bible and theological certainty, two axioms of Calvinist thought.[4] The cataclysm of the Civil War further shook faith in America's providential destiny.[5] Many New Englanders left their churches. To these Reformed seekers of a new dispensation, and especially to their children, Emerson offered moral and spiritual guidance based on the Book of Nature, so to speak, rather than the now rather problematic Book of Revelation. Last of a line of Puritan ministers and product of the more liberal coastal branch of Puritan civilization, Emerson released the genius of Reformed Protestantism from its theological cage and clothed it in glit-tering, seductive colors. His focus on fulfillment of individual potential without reference to demands of community appealed to denizens of the new industrial cities and suburbs rising in gritty smoky majesty across the country. By the end of the century, a generation was enamored of Emerson like no generation has venerated any other American intellectual.

Born at nearly the same moment—Modernism at the Armory Show in 1913 and the National Parks system in 1916—Modernism and the parks reached maturity in the following two decades. The Modernist search for the spiritual in the landscape took part in the last and fullest blooming of Emerson's Transcendentalism. Under Emerson's tutelage, the Modernist generation learned to trust the self and to revere nature as the highest source of all things spiritual, moral, and creative. The Emersonian spirit moved quietly but powerfully most particularly among the children of New England. It was the spirit of the solitary seeker alone in nature in the twentieth century. It is also the spirit of the Reformed relationship of individual, spirit, and nature, which this generation adapted to parks for the uplift of a democratic people.

Adams the Emersonian

Like an evangelist seeking converts, Adams passionately pressed upon people his Emersonian love of nature. "There has always been a touch of the New England preacher about Ansel," friend and collaborator Nancy Newhall said.[6] Adams's images of Yosemite had deep spiritual meaning. He called it "a national shrine," but the valley was a shrine to no particular religion. As a child Adams rejected religious institutions and creeds for a personal, "amorphous sense of deity." He believed that in natural landscapes without human presence "the clear realities of Nature seen with the inner eye of the spirit reveal the ultimate echo of God." Moreover, he wrote in "The Meaning of the National Parks" that humanity's future depended on such places:

> In contemplation of the eternal incarnations of the spirit which vibrate in every mountain, leaf, and particle of earth, in every cloud, stone, and flash of sunlight, we make new discoveries on the planes of ethical and humane discernment, approaching THE NEW SOCIETY AT LAST, PROPORTIONATE TO NATURE.

Compared to the "enormous spiritual and inspirational value" of nature, "no works of man of any kind [have] consequential value." To the artist was given a special role. Because art "is both the taking and giving of beauty, the turning out to the light the inner folds of the awareness of the spirit," writers, artists, and photographers had the power to educate the people to protect the beauty of nature against the power of profit-seeking and material exploitation. His friend the author Wallace Stegner observed that Adams "is, before all else, a poetic and mystical interpreter of Nature. . . . Nature, one says. Not scenery. Scenery for Adams is a dirty word, an invention of the tourist business, an oversized curio. Nature is something else. Scenery is for profit, Nature is for reverence, and the fewer tracks of man there are in it, the better."[7]

Adams often evangelized where converts counted—in Washington, DC. In 1936, on behalf of the Sierra Club he lobbied senators and representatives for proposed Kings Canyon National Park. He bedazzled them with his images of the wild, rugged, beautiful high country, but Los Angeles wanted to dam the canyon for water and blocked the bill. In 1938, he published a book of his photographs of the region in *Sierra Nevada: The John Muir Trail*, and sent a copy to Secretary of the Interior Harold Ickes, who passed it on to President Franklin Roosevelt. With their support, the park was finally created in 1940. Adams was just one of many park supporters, but his work and efforts displayed the power of the artist to halt exploitation of sacred places for profit.[8]

Nature as the work of God and the best place to worship, the inferiority of the works of fallen man, suspicion of avarice, and the duty of the artist to serve religious and moral purposes—all were items from the rich legacy of Reformed Protestantism. Yet in Adam's own mind he was simply and solely spreading the gospel of Emersonianism. When Emerson stood in the woods, on the bare ground, exhilarated by the currents of Universal Being circulating through him, as he put it in his classic 1836 essay *Nature*, his sense of deity was as amorphous as any. "The world . . . [is] the present expositor of the divine mind," he wrote. ". . . We are as much strangers in nature, as we are aliens from God. . . . Is not the landscape, every glimpse of which hath a grandeur, a face of him?" Emerson believed that for the poet (or artist) to find the divine in the landscape, man and his works must be invisible, due to our alienation from God and disharmony with nature: "Yet this may show us what discord is between man and nature, for you cannot freely admire a noble landscape, if laborers are digging in the field hard by. The poet finds something ridiculous in his delight, until he is out of the sight of men." Emerson felt that the more people perceived the Spirit and its moral laws in the beauty of nature, the closer humanity and the world would come to redemption: "then will God go forth anew into creation."[9]

In *Nature* and in such celebrated essays as "Self-Reliance" and "The American Scholar," Emerson advocated throwing off the dead forms of the past that kept the individual from realizing "an original relation to the universe."[10] Instead of relying on the Bible as Calvinists did to escape centuries of human perversion of true Christianity, Emersonians turned to nature to release them from the bonds of the dead past.

> Embosomed for a season in nature, whose floods of life stream around and through us, and invite us by the powers they supply, to action proportioned to nature, why should we grope among the dry bones of the past, or put the living generation into masquerade out of its faded wardrobe? The sun shines to-day also. There is more wool and flax in the fields. There are new lands, new men, new thoughts. Let us demand our own works and laws and worship.[11]

"The faith that stands on authority is not faith," he wrote in "The Over-soul."[12] Emerson asserted that the role of artists and poets was to educate humankind in the things of the spirit, and artists and poets could only fulfill this role if they learned from nature: "Nature paints the best part of a picture, carves the best part of the statue, builds the best part of the house, and speaks the best part of the oration."[13] Art must educate the public to perceive beauty and thus bring humanity into harmony with nature. The artist must therefore follow his vision, scorn unperceptive mass opinion, and reject conventional thinking. "Whoso would be a man must be a non-conformist," he declared. "To be great is to be misunderstood."[14]

Emerson had reformulated Reformed Protestant principles for a posttheological America. He represented a different stream of Puritan thought than the more traditional Calvinist Congregationalism of Yale and the fertile green hinterlands of the Connecticut River Valley. In Boston and coastal New England, European intellectual, cultural, and theological currents washed ashore and eroded Calvinist foundations. When in Northampton Jonathan Edwards was pronouncing judgment on sinners in the hands of an angry God, Boston's ministers were abandoning the steely unbending tenets of Calvinism for the softer, more forgiving doctrines of Arminianism. By the time Emerson was born in 1803, Boston congregations were discarding such mystical doctrines as the Trinity. Before his graduation from Harvard, the old Puritan tradition had split into Congregational and Unitarian churches. Last of a line of Puritan ministers, Emerson was an ordained Unitarian minister at the Second Church of Boston, where Increase and Cotton Mather had once held forth. But German biblical criticism pushed Emerson to the conclusion that Jesus had never intended to begin a new religion, and he resigned his pulpit. He powerfully defended his rejection of Christian doctrines and defended the freedom of the spiritual seeker in *Nature* in 1836 and the graduation address to the Harvard Divinity School in 1838. The normally placid precincts of Unitarianism erupted in vituperative acrimony that took decades to cool. Lapsed Reformed Protestants however understood the language he spoke. In time, Emerson the dangerous radical became Emerson the revered sage.

In exalting the individual, Emerson lost sight of community. Like good Puritans, the Transcendental seeker communed alone in the woods with God. Unlike them, he must free himself from society's conventions in order to realize his true genius. Emerson had in fact not lost sympathy for the needs of the community, but he and his disciples spoke little of that. To a degree this was a reflection of the different experience of eastern New England. The Puritan language of community had long been attenuated in Boston. When Puritans lost control of Massachusetts colonial government barely fifty years after its establishment, intense early communalism weakened but did not die. If Boston and Harvard never led the movements for parks, conservation, and agricultural improvement, Boston in many respects was at the forefront. Grazing was banned on Boston Common in 1830, in effect transforming it into the first American urban park for public recreation. Mt. Auburn Cemetery, across the Charles River in Cambridge, was the first to be opened to the public and helped start a fashion for relaxing and picnicking in rural cemeteries before urban parks became common. Boston's pure public water system and the arrangement and design of its suburbs became national models for America's other fast-growing cities. It built the first metropolitan sewage system and established the first suburban forest preserves.[15] Still, national leadership for parks and conservation came from Hartford, Yale, and the Connecticut Valley rather than Boston, Harvard, and the New England seaboard. Conservation was Congregational, not Unitarian. It was certainly not Transcendentalist.

Emerson's seductive eloquence exalted nonconformity, art and poetry's higher spiritual purpose, and harmony with nature—common enough ideas in the Romantic Era—but Emerson's growing stature and unique oracular style endowed them with tremendous authority. Emerson's reputation continued to grow after his death in 1882 at age 78. The "Emersonian generation" born in the waning decades of the nineteenth century and the first decade of the twentieth grew up with Emerson on parents' book-shelves, in libraries, and in classrooms. Its members absorbed his mes-sage more deeply and profoundly than their elders. While Emerson's own generation ranked him among the nation's top American intellec-tuals and authors, the next generation or two venerated him as spiritual sage, seer, and oracle.[16] Reformed Protestants especially followed him like the Pied Piper out the church door and down paths of spiritual experi-mentation. He gave them a language and a vision. Seekers pursuing and revealing the spiritual meaning of natural landscape, Emersonians wove Transcendentalism into their art, their literature, their architecture, and their preservation and creation of landscape. Through some of America's greatest and most distinctive creative work run the themes of nature, spiri-tuality, and independence.[17]

The Education of Ansel Adams

Adams came by his Emersonian convictions first by education and then through the artists, writers, and photographers in whose company he ven-tured down paths of nature and spirit. Adams was born in 1902 into the Emersonian generation's later years, but his father, Charles, was born in 1868 and rode the generation's rise. A fervent Emerson devotee and owner of a well-used collection of his works, Charles Adams was very close to his son. Both acquired from Transcendentalism an abiding affinity for mystically tinged approaches to nature. Emerson also transmitted to them his ideas about the harmony of science and spirit. Charles was an avid amateur astronomer and introduced Ansel to British astronomer Arthur S. Eddington's *The Nature of the Physical World* (1928) and *Science and the Unseen World* (1929), which ranked material understanding of science with spiritual knowledge of God's all-pervasive creative presence.

American Modernism and Adams also grew up together. Adams began his love affair with Yosemite in 1916, when he also took his first photo-graphs of it. That spring, as the fourteen-year-old boy sat in bed at his home in San Francisco recuperating from illness, he picked up a book about the Yosemite Valley, James M. Hutchings's *In the Heart of the Sierra*, which his aunt had lent him to help pass the time. The excited boy insisted the family take its annual vacation in Yosemite that summer and his par-ents give him his first camera to record the visit.[18] Aspiring to a career first as a pianist and later as a photographer, he mixed with West Coast artists, poets, and writers. Adams and friends joined the Modernist revolt against the flowery genteel tradition of poetry and art, the "scented merde" that E. E. Cummings famously derided in 1923 in "Poem, or Beauty Hurts Mr. Vinal." John Muir's flowery Victorian nature writing never appealed to Adams, despite its Transcendentalist overtones.

Adams followed the typical pattern of the Emersonian generation, many of whom would discover Emerson in a memorable encounter during youth. In the 1910s and 1920s Emersonians often flirted with or passionately embraced a number of spiritual or intellectual vogues whose principles complemented those ideals. In their Modernist zeal after World War I to discover the new and reject the old, they tended not to explicitly discuss Emerson's works. As time moved on ardor for fashionable seers and mystics tended to fade, while quiet devotion to earlier values learned at the knee of the Concord sage persisted through long lives and careers.[19] Adams and his friends in the West Coast avant-garde searched out more modern versions of Emerson's teachings of a spiritual reality beyond the material world. In the 1920s they were swept up in the vogue of interest in Walt Whitman's poems, in English socialist Edward Carpenter's Whitman-inspired *Toward Democracy,* in the mystic philosophy of Russian philosopher G. I. Gurdjieff and his disciple P. D. Ouspensky, and in theosophy. Deeply immersed in this world of ideas in the 1920s, Adams composed and published a number of spiritual nature poems with titles like "And Now the Vision."[20]

Adams's full conversion to Modernist photography began with a 1927 car trip through the Southwest that broadened his intellectual and artistic circle beyond the somewhat isolated and parochial West Coast. Since Adams never formally studied in Europe, as so many artists did at the time, "Taos and Santa Fe were his Rome and his Paris," Newhall wrote.[21] Adams returned in 1929 and 1930 to work on illustrations for *Taos Pueblo,* with text by Mary Austin. A friend introduced him to Mable Dodge Luhan, the heiress, art patron, and dynamic personality who had drawn a cosmopolitan crowd of writers and artists to Taos. At Luhan's sprawling house Adams met a group of artists from the circle of Alfred Stieglitz, the New York photographer and gallery owner: Paul Strand, John Marin, and Stieglitz's wife, Georgia O'Keeffe. They would change his life and art.

Strand's work was an absolute epiphany to young Adams. Strand rejected the popular gauzy pictorialist style of photography that imitated painting, the style that Adams worked in, and advocated "straight" photography. His work took full advantage of the unique capabilities of the new technology of photography: sharp focus, full use of the tonal scale from darkest black through gray to brightest white, and glossy prints. Impressed, Stieglitz in 1915 had given him a one-man show at his gallery, 291, the nation's showcase for American Modernist art, and he soon joined the Stieglitz circle. Straight photography completely won Adams over. He and Strand differed however on their preferred subject matter. Born in 1890 to German Jewish parents, Strand had little interest in Reformed unpeopled spiritual landscapes and on a trip West in 1915 had written, "Things become interesting as soon as the human element enters in."[22] Adams abandoned pictorialism the better to capture the "truth" of the landscape and became unparalleled master of straight photographic techniques, which he popularized in how-to articles and books. In 1932, he joined with Imogen Cunningham, Edward Weston, and other California photographers to found f/16, a group dedicated to the truth of crisp, precise images. Stieglitz, who had not given a photographer a one-man show since Strand's in 1915, honored Adams in 1936 with his own one-man show at his gallery, An American Place, which brought him from the regional to the national stage.[23]

The Reformed Protestant call for truthfulness in art had in the nineteenth century culminated in the minutely scientifically correct detail of Frederic Church's paintings. In the twentieth, it gave rise to both realist and abstract styles. Adams's sharp detail was meant as a statement of a photograph's difference from painting, but it also represented the strand of Reformed aesthetics that emphasized fidelity to the works of the divine. "The photographers who have followed the more-or-less clear path of straight photography," Adams wrote, "clearly show that the medium has its own particular capacities for the revelation of both informational and spiritual truth!"[24] Although out of critical favor by mid-century, realist painters continued to work. Fairfield Porter, descendant of old New England families and brother of nature photographer Eliot Porter, affirmed this aesthetic in 1973: "Facts, the subject matter of experience, and their connections, transcend the ideal. So what makes an artist great, and significant, is not that one approves of his communication, but that his communication is transcendent. It will be so to the extent that it connects to fact."[25] The twentieth century produced a number of major Protestant realist painters, among them Edward Hopper, an Emerson enthusiast raised Baptist of mostly New York Dutch ancestry; Grant Wood, son of strict Iowa Quakers whose preference for truthfulness precluded fiction in the house; John Steuart Curry, child of stern Covenanter Presbyterians in Kansas; Norman Rockwell, heir to a ancient line of Connecticut Yankees who were by turns Puritan, Congregational, Presbyterian, and Episcopalian; and Andrew Wyeth, a descendant of Massachusetts Puritans, brought up on Emerson and Thoreau.

A second thread however led away from representation of exact fact. Here artists cleared away detail in order to expose the inner truth of the subject. In *Modern Painters,* Ruskin himself had justified this approach in his energetic defense of the controversial "indistinct" style of J.M.W. Turner. Turner's later canvases sometimes resembled later Impressionism, but fundamentally the two differed. Turner wanted to convey the truth of nature; Impressionists sought to express their experience. In the twentieth century, Swiss-born abstract artist Paul Klee put into words the central notion behind the abstraction of Reformed-style Modernism. "Formerly we used to represent things visible on earth, things we either liked to look at or would have liked to see," Klee said. "Today we reveal the reality that is behind visible things, thus expressing the belief that the visible world is merely an isolated case in relation to the universe and that there are many more other, latent realities. . . . Art is a simile or the Creation. Each work of art is an example, just as the terrestrial is an example of the cosmic."[26] After World War II, two Reformed Protestant artists, Dutch American Willem de Kooning and American Presbyterian Jackson Pollock, were the foremost leaders of the abstract expressionist movement. Following Pollock's death in 1956, de Kooning returned to that venerable Reformed artform, the landscape.[27]

Emersonian Modernism

Adams grew much closer to Marin and O'Keeffe than Strand. Neither Strand nor another artist in the Stieglitz circle, Charles Demuth, of German stock from Lancaster, Pennsylvania, were Emersonians or landscape artists. Strand flirted with landscapes around the time Adams met him but soon was involved with political photography and film. Adams, Marin, and O'Keeffe went deeper into the art of the unpeopled landscape. Marin fascinated Adams. Around the time Stieglitz decided to champion American Modernist painting, he gave Marin his first show at 291 in 1909. Marin was always disinclined to discuss his art or his influences, but his New England background, preference for unpeopled natural landscapes, and Transcendentalistic comments mark him as a fellow Emersonian. Born in 1870, he was raised by his mother's grandparents and her family—"great Bible readers of Yankee descent," according to his biographer.[28] He was known for his "New England" or "Yankee" personality and art,[29] especially of New England landscapes (Figure 4.2, see color insert). His landscapes lacked people because, he said, "Mountain streams trees and rocks are so sympathetic—damned if I find most humans so."[30] He felt it useless to portray an object exactly, since artists did not have the thing itself, but rejected pure abstraction from the imagination alone. The best art came from "the wedding of man and nature."[31] When pressed in 1922 to articulate his artistic ideals, Marin echoed Emerson's belief in the artist's role as the interpreter of the Spirit in nature. The artistic productions of certain artists, he said, "have an exalted value in that they put in motion the Spirit, through the eye and approach the great Seeing, not as reminders of other seeings but in themselves."[32]

Adams stood forever in awe of O'Keeffe. The year 1916 had major significance for her as well. On May 23, on Fifth Avenue in New York City, Stieglitz opened the doors of 291 for the very first show of O'Keeffe's art. The exhibit marked the beginning of her career, her membership in the Stieglitz circle, and her relationship with her mentor, champion, and future husband Stieglitz.[33] The year 1929 in Taos was another fateful time for both Adams and O'Keeffe, when Adams made the decision to devote himself to photography full-time and O'Keeffe fell in love with northern New Mexico. "Nobody told me how wonderful it is," she told Luhan.[34] O'Keeffe spent almost every summer among its hills and canyons until 1946. Then Stieglitz died and she moved permanently from New York to her house on Ghost Ranch near Abiquiu in the mountains north of Santa Fe.

Maybe it was simply a coincidence that O'Keeffe turned so passionately to landscapes after meeting Adams the landscape photographer. In personality they were opposites: she was as taciturn and solitary as he was talkative and gregarious, the laconic, solemn, black-clad New England Yankee to his New England preacher. Her colorful abstract New Mexican landscapes (Figure 4.3, see color insert) complemented Adams's exquisitely precise black-and-white images. Raised like Adams by transplanted New Englanders, she too had a taste for Transcendentalism, for esoteric mysticism like Ouspensky and theosophy, and for unpeopled landscapes. As she ironically put it, "My pleasant disposition likes the world with nobody in it."[35] "I wish people were all trees and I think I could enjoy them then," she told Marsden Hartley.[36]

O'Keeffe inherited a strong Calvinist streak but unlike Adams, who was born to Emersonianism, she absorbed its doctrines by stages that together demonstrate something of the pervasiveness of Emerson's influence on the Arts and Crafts movement and the birth of American Modernism. Born in Wisconsin in 1887, O'Keeffe had a strong Dutch–New England Calvinist heritage that overwhelmed her warm, big-hearted Irish-Catholic and Hungarian paternal stock. Her strict and dour mother and maiden aunt sent the children to the Congregational Church and closely supervised their upbringing and education. O'Keeffe's spiritual journey in art began in 1912 under the tutelage of art teacher Alon Bement, of Ashfield, Massachusetts. Bement gave her the 1914 translation of Russian artist Wassily Kandinsky's *On the Spiritual in Art*, which she read and reread. More theosophical than Transcendental in origin, *On the Spiritual in Art* articulated notions that Emersonians appreciated and did so in the language of early twentieth-century avant-garde art. Like Emerson, Kandinsky argued for the superiority of the spiritual to the material, the artist as the "solitary visionary" and "priest of beauty" leading society to a higher plane, and the self-reliance of the artist true to "internal truth," beauty's source in the soul. Kandinsky advocated abstraction in art without breaking "the bonds which bind us to nature."[37]

Kandinsky excited in O'Keeffe a desire to create abstract art herself, so Bement gave her a copy of Jerome Eddy's seminal *Cubists and Post-Impressionism*. It contained reproductions of the first abstract paintings she saw, including abstractions of leaves by one American, Arthur Dove.[38] Born in 1880 to Presbyterians in Geneva, New York, Dove acquired a love of nature and art from a Transcendentally inclined neighbor, farmer-naturalist-painter Newton Weatherly, whose influence he treasured throughout his life.[39] By 1911 he was painting a series of canvases he called "Nature Symbolized," which attempted to portray abstract notions like wind on a hillside (Figure 4.4, see color insert). Stieglitz exhibited Dove's work at 291 in 1912 and gave him Kandinsky's book, which drew Dove deeply into Ouspensky and theosophy.[40] O'Keeffe deeply admired Dove, "the only American painter who is of the earth."[41] Her New York apartment would have no art on the walls with the exception of a Dove abstract above the mantel.[42] On New Year's Day, 1916, a friend brought O'Keeffe's experiments with Dove-inspired abstract art (Figure 4.5, see color insert) to Stieglitz, who excitedly gave her the show at 291.[43] In 1923, critic Paul Rosenfeld perceptively paired Dove's work with O'Keeffe's as representing complementary male and female aspects of Modern abstract art.[44]

In 1914 Bement sent O'Keeffe to study with Arthur Wesley Dow of Columbia University, a leading art teacher and ardent Emersonian. Born in Ipswich, Massachusetts, Dow described art in thoroughly Emersonian language as "the highest form of human energy, the creative power which is nearest to the divine." Since nature itself was near the divine, Dow even called landscape art "religious art." Through his classes and his landmark 1899 art manual *Composition*, Dow popularized the style and aesthetics of Japanese prints to a generation of artists and art teachers and was an important inspiration for the Arts and Crafts movement. O'Keeffe acknowledged an artistic debt to him throughout her life.[45]

The most famous as well as the most explicitly Emersonian of the Stieglitz circle was Marsden Hartley, whose influence on O'Keeffe can hardly be underestimated. Born in 1877 in Lewiston, Maine, to immigrants from Lancashire cotton mills, Hartley regarded himself as a true son of New England. At the Cleveland School of Art, his most supportive teacher presented him with a copy of Emerson's *Essays* that he carried in his pocket for years. He remembered, "I felt as if I had read a page of the Bible." "It seemed so made for me—circles, friendship, the oversoul, and all that. . . . I was to read Emerson then assiduously to the neglect of all else." Emerson awakened a fascination with nature and mysticism, which directed his reading, writing, and painting throughout his life. His series of Maine landscapes that Stieglitz exhibited in 291 in 1909, he called "rendering the God-spirit in the mountains." He read Kandinsky's *On the Spiritual in Art* in the original German and brought it to Stieglitz's attention in 1912. Kandinsky brought out his Emersonian predilections and initiated the period of his greatest paintings. Late in his career Hartley returned to Maine and to his Transcendentalist sources. He followed Thoreau's footsteps in 1939 to Maine's highest mountain, Mount Katahdin, and made it the subject of a series of paintings.[46]

O'Keeffe came to New Mexico because of Hartley and his landscapes. Invited to Taos in the winter of 1918–1919 by Mabel Dodge Luhan, Marsden discovered the New Mexico landscape, whose beauty and spirituality overwhelmed him (Figure 4.6, see color insert). Marsden could not get the landscape out of his mind and painted it from memory for the next five years, even while in Europe. He urged Strand and then O'Keeffe and Marin to come out. "On first seeing New Mexico it's like being in an exhibition of Hartleys," Rebecca Strand wrote to O'Keeffe and Stieglitz from Santa Fe in 1926. ". . . Georgia should [come;] . . . she would do some great things."[47] Hartley's New Mexico canvases (some of which, like *Landscape and Mountains* of 1922–1923, had skulls and bones in the foreground) suggested to O'Keeffe the artistic possibilities of the landscape. After she came to New Mexico in 1929, her landscape forms and colors would resemble Hartley's more than Dove's.[48] Her landscapes of sensuous, barren hillsides and floating cow skulls overshadowed her earlier acclaimed Precisionist paintings of New York architecture and rivaled her popular paintings of oversized flowers.

O'Keeffe, Dove, Marin, and Marsden Hartley made up the core group of the 291 painters, all spiritually inclined with a preference for nature themes and unpeopled landscapes.[49] They were searching to express a mystical truth—the ultimate spiritual truth—that cameras could not capture and embraced abstraction against the superficial exactitude of film. Under their influence O'Keeffe's connection to nature grew very Emersonian. "When I stand alone with the earth and sky," she wrote a friend, "feeling of something in me going off in every direction into the unknown of infinity means more to me than any thing any organized religion gives me." She remarked, "I feel that a real living form is the natural result of the individual[']s effort to create the living thing out of the adventure of his spirit into the unknown—where it has experienced something—felt something—it has not understood—and from that experience comes the desire to make the unknown—known." O'Keeffe's "world with nobody in it" was a deeply spiritual place.[50] By the 1970s, she in painting and Adams in photography were the nation's most celebrated landscape artists. She became a national icon and emblem of Southwest art, with a major museum in Santa Fe dedicated to her work.

The Wright Stuff for Parks Architecture

The spiritual bent of the landscape painters of the Stieglitz circle except Adams did not connect them to Yosemite Valley or the national parks. When O'Keeffe visited Adams in Yosemite in 1938 for a week of camping, to his great disappointment she did not even bring her paints. O'Keeffe however was also friends with another member of the Emersonian generation, architect Frank Lloyd Wright, who did link with the young National Park Service, although in different ways. In the spring of 1933 Wright invited O'Keeffe to join and direct his new Taliesin Fellowship, a live-in, hands-on training school for architects and artists in Spring Green, Wisconsin, 45 miles from her hometown, Sun Prairie. Remaining just a "Friend of the Fellowship," she declined because "Wisconsin just wasn't my kind of country," and Wright's wife, Olgivanna, a Gurdjieff disciple, became director.[51] Wright instead followed O'Keeffe to the Southwest. He set up winter quarters in Arizona and in 1937 began building Taliesin West near Scottsdale.[52] Wright visited O'Keeffe in 1942 and she in turn visited her friend at Taliesin the same year, and at Taliesin West in 1947.[53]

Wright was a thoroughgoing Emersonian, born in 1867 in Richland Center, Wisconsin, and raised in New England and Wisconsin in an Emersonian family. His father was a Baptist and later Unitarian minister from Hartford, Connecticut, and his mother was sister, daughter, and descendent of Welsh American Unitarian ministers. He received an education rich in Unitarian and Transcendentalist authors: "[William Ellery] Channing, Emerson, Theodore Parker, and, yes, Thoreau,"[54] as well as such Transcendentalist "fellow travelers" as John Ruskin and Johann Wolfgang von Goethe, and New England poets John Greenleaf Whittier, Henry Wadsworth Longfellow, and William Cullen Bryant. Wright, like Adams and also O'Keeffe, never had any formal training in Europe.[55] In his autobiography, speaking in third person, he claimed that Nature had been his only teacher and inspiration: "In these adventures alone—abroad in the wooded hills to fetch the cows, the barefoot, bareheaded urchin, was insatiable, curious and venturesome. So he learned to know the woods. . . . A listening ear, seeing eye and sensitive touch had been naturally given to him, his spirit was now becoming familiar with this marvelous book-of-books, Nature-Experience, the only true reading. The book of Creation."[56] When asked in the 1950s by broadcaster Mike Wallace if he went to church, Wright answered, "Yes. I go occasionally to this one and sometimes to that one, but my church—I put a capital N on nature and go there. . . . You spell God with a G, don't you?" Wallace replied, "I spell God with a G, you will spell it. . . ." Said Wright, "I spell nature with an N, a capital."[57] Wright worshipped in the church of Nature.

Patterning himself after an Emersonian ideal of the architect as hero, Wright made architecture a thrall of nature and spirit. "True Wisdom is no earthly thing," he wrote. "Wisdom is a spiritual state attained by refraining from selfish competition, imitation or moralizing. And, most of all, by living in love and harmony with Nature."[58] He added, "NATURE gradually apprehended as the principle of Life—the life-giving principle in making things with the mind, reacting in turn upon the makers. Earth-dwellers that we are, we are become now sentient to the truth that living on Earth *is* a materialization of the Spirit instead of trying to make our dwelling here a spiritualization of matter."[59] In 1894, at the start of his career, he wrote, "Go to Nature, thou builder of houses, consider her ways and do not be petty and foolish. Let your home appear to grow easily from its site and shape it to sympathize with the surroundings if Nature is manifest there, and if not, try and be as quiet, substantial, and organic as she would have been if she had the chance."[60] His ideas of an organic architecture that conformed to nature led him to a radically new style in harmony with landscape, the Prairie Style. Prairie Style's founder and leading practitioner, he scattered prominent examples around the Chicago area, including Frederick Law Olmsted's suburb Riverside.[61]

On the twenty-fifth of August, once again in that year of 1916, Congress passed the National Park Service Act. The act authorized a National Park Service to supervise and coordinate the national parks then proliferating haphazardly across the country, to preserve their scenery, antiquities, and wildlife, to make them accessible to the public, and to leave them "unimpaired for the enjoyment of future generations." The first Parks director, Stephen Tyng Mather, appointed like-minded men to develop the parks. They gave the national parks a distinctive look that in their minds harmonized with the natural landscape that they were to promote and protect, in such a way as to minimize the visibility and impact of the people they were encouraging to come. In Mather's vision, national parks would be peopled landscapes designed as much as possible to look like no one was there.

Wright's ideal of building in organic harmony with the landscape and the Prairie-Style principle of landscaping with local native plants impressed Mather's architects in the infant National Park Service. Wright would have designed for the parks himself, but his tendency to speak his mind kept the government from approaching him directly to design park buildings. In 1953 he submitted an unsolicited design for a restaurant in Yosemite, but it was rejected for political reasons related to his criticisms of anti-Communist hysteria.[62] Parks architects however borrowed heavily from Wright's designs. To take a prominent example, Robert C. Reamer drew heavily from the Prairie Style for his magnificent Canyon Hotel in Yellowstone National Park, which opened in 1911. Child of a deeply religious Congregational family in Oberlin, Ohio, Reamer began his architectural career in Chicago in the 1890s, where he possibly knew Wright and certainly knew his architecture. His comment about the design of the Canyon Hotel echoed Wright's principles: "I built it in keeping with the place where it stands. Nobody could improve upon that. To be at discord with the landscape, would be almost a crime. To try to improve upon it, would be an impertinence."[63]

Park Service administrators agreed with Reamer. The quest for the spiritual in nature that the Emersonian generation expressed in landscape art shaped the infrastructure and the very landscape of the national parks. Their managers, developers, and designers, nearly every one of whom had Puritan New England ancestors, strove to create and preserve the illusion of an uninhabited world of otherworldly beauty for the spiritual uplift of the nation. Mather appointed as the parks' first "Landscape Engineer" Charles P. Punchard Jr., a graduate of Harvard's landscape architecture program and descendant of founders of Salem, Massachusetts. Punchard and his successors set out to create a style for the buildings, hotels, and roads of the parks that would hide their mundane or commercial purposes and blend in harmoniously with the landscape. In search of architectural styles appropriate to natural landscape, in addition to Prairie Style they drew from the rustic Adirondacks camp style, the Shingle Style, and architecture of the Arts and Crafts movement, in particular the West Coast architecture of Greene and Greene and Bernard Maybeck.[64]

The rustic camp style had developed in the Adirondack Mountains in upstate New York, a favored vacation destination for New England bourgeoisie. It drew from local building techniques, with historical antecedents in New England vernacular architecture.[65] The Shingle Style, a mixture of English models with native New England wood construction, arose in New England after the Civil War. In the 1880s H. H. Richardson designed many influential buildings in the Shingle Style. He used undressed native boulders and natural forms, which attracted the attraction of architects who followed Emerson's dictum that nature builds the best part of the house. Weathered shingles looked natural to the landscape, unlike conventional painted boards. In the late 1870s and 1880s Richardson collaborated on several parks and estate projects with Frederick Law Olmsted, his neighbor in Brookline, Massachusetts. After his untimely death in 1886, Olmsted frequently incorporated Richardsonian stonework in future parks projects, whence National Parks architects borrowed the style in the 1920s.[66]

From the West Coast came the model of Arts and Crafts architecture. The greatest examples in Southern California came from the drawing boards of Charles Sumner Greene and Henry Mather Greene, two names redolent of old New England and distant kinship with Stephen Mather. Born in St. Louis in 1868 and 1870, respectively, deeply impressed by a New England Emersonian educator with the marvelous name Calvin Milton Woodward, and trained at the Massachusetts Institute of Technology, the brothers began architectural practice in the Boston firm that inherited Richardson's work upon his death. Charles Greene's youthful fascination with "Ideal and Art" and his deep interest by the 1920s in theosophy and Buddhism were typical of Emersonian spiritual eclecticism. Greene and Greene incorporated Spanish and local vernacular elements in place of New England elements in the Shingle Style. Uncut, weathered local stonework complemented design elements like rough timber, redwood paneling, or adobe and made some of their buildings appear to rise naturally from the landscape.[67]

Reamer used them all—Prairie, Rustic, Shingle, and Arts and Crafts—in one or another of the forty buildings he designed for Yellowstone National Park. His Old Faithful Inn of 1904, his great masterpiece and the pride of the park, was a fanciful, exuberant mixture of Rustic and Shingle Styles.[68]

Mather felt that Yosemite deserved an outstanding hotel and called upon another Los Angeles architect, Gilbert Stanley Underwood, to design the Ahwahnee Hotel, his great masterwork. Born in Oneida, New York, raised in Southern California, and trained at Yale and Harvard, Underwood would design many major buildings for the Park Service, including Bryce Canyon Lodge in 1925, the Grand Canyon Lodge (North Rim) in 1928, and Jackson Lake Lodge of Grand Tetons National Park in 1955. For the Ahwahnee, Underwood borrowed not from Greene and Greene but Bernard Maybeck, the leading San Francisco Arts and Crafts architect, and a devout Emersonian. Born in New York City in 1862 to agnostic German immigrants, Maybeck absorbed German transcendental thought from his family and the German American community. A high school teacher, a "frail but stern Yankee named Pettigrew," introduced him to Emerson. German and American Transcendentalism became Maybeck's religion. "There is something bigger and more worthwhile than the things we see about us, the things we live by and strive for," he remarked in 1923. "There is an undiscovered beauty, a divine excellence, just beyond us. Let us stand on tiptoe, forgetting the nearer things and grasp what we may."[69]

In 1890, Maybeck was an architect in San Francisco when he had an encounter that would reveal new architectural (and spiritual) possibilities in harmony with nature. Author Charles Keeler recalled that Maybeck bought "a cottage in the hills back of Oakland, and next door to him the Reverend Joseph Worcester had a little summer retreat. Looking into Mr. Worcester's windows, he saw the interior of the cottage was all of unpainted redwood boards. It was a revelation."[70] An amateur architect and disciple of John Ruskin's Arts and Crafts philosophy, Worcester designed his house himself in 1876, the first Arts and Crafts structure on the West Coast. Son of the founder of New England Swedenborgianism and former teacher of architect and urban designer Daniel Burnham, Worcester moved to California in 1863. He avidly read Emerson and Thoreau, both admirers of Emanuel Swedenborg's ideas of the correspondence between the material and the spiritual.[71] An advocate of designing in harmony with nature and spirit, Worcester influenced an entire generation of San Francisco architects and designers. In 1894 Maybeck codesigned Worcester's Swedenborgian Church of the New Jerusalem in San Francisco, which included such details as local madrone timbers with the bark on, chair seats of local tule cane, and landscape paintings by Worcester's close friend William Keith. Furniture designer Gustav Stickley claimed that the church's tule-grass chairs inspired Mission Style furniture, a style that he largely created.[72]

Maybeck grew convinced that a building "should fit into the landscape as if it were a part of it."[73] Maybeck's great masterwork would be the First Church of Christ, Scientist, in Berkeley, a superb balance of natural forms, exposed and carved wood beams, and Gothic touches. Sunlight filters through wisteria blossoms into the windows in place of stained glass and a redwood tree rises where the steeple should go (Figure 4.7).[74] A frequent visitor to the Sierra, Maybeck designed buildings for Yosemite National

FIGURE 4.7 Bernard Maybeck, First Church of Christ, Scientist, Berkeley, California. Maybeck made nature an organic part of his architectural masterpiece. The steeple is a redwood tree and when the wisteria blooms, the light filters through the blossoms instead of stained glass. This place of worship made from living creation was in effect an Arts and Crafts version of Bernard Palissy's design for a garden with pavilions of living trees, the works of God and not man.

Park and other Sierra parks and resorts. The Sierra Club's 1903 LeConte Memorial Lodge in Yosemite National Park was designed with many elements in Maybeck's style either by Maybeck's brother-in-law John White or possibly by Maybeck himself, for whom White often worked. Maybeck also collaborated in a second Yosemite Park structure, Parsons Memorial Lodge in Tuolumne Meadows.

For the Ahwahnee Hotel, Underwood drew from Maybeck's innovations and took inspiration for the hotel's stone buttresses from Maybeck's 1921 Glen Alpine Springs resort buildings at Lake Tahoe (Figures 4.8 and 4.9). It would not be the last time Underwood borrowed from Maybeck's work for his National Park structures and lodges, but here it produced a glorious effect of a hotel in harmony with its dramatic landscape.[75]

Yosemite's Emersonian architecture played its part in Adams's life. He got a job as caretaker of the LeConte Lodge for several years beginning around 1920, the start also of his lifelong association with the Sierra Club. Adams knew Maybeck personally. Adams loved the house Maybeck designed for a close friend, so after his marriage to Virginia Best he commissioned a house from him in 1928, but the newlyweds could not afford to build it.[76] Ahwahnee Hotel managers helped support Adams through the Depression by buying his photographs for menus, hotel items, and publications. In 1929, Adams acted in the hotel's Bracebridge Christmas dinner pageant, which he helped write, and reprised his role annually until 1975. Adams reserved the Ahwahnee's best rooms for O'Keeffe and friends before they set out on a backcountry camping trip in 1938. In 1962, Eldridge Spencer, Maybeck's former draftsman who had corrected some of Ahwahnee's design and structural flaws in 1931, designed a house in Carmel for Adams and his wife.[77]

In many ways the spirit of the Emersonian generation was with Adams when he created *Clearing Winter Storm*. It was present in his own spiritual ideals and the aesthetic principles, and it was present no less in the management and architecture of the park that he photographed. Devotion to Emersonian principles produced some of the era's greatest, most influential, and best-known photography, art, architecture—and parks. Mather's Park Service recognized the necessity and even the desirability of commercial services and recreational pursuits in the parks but viewed them as compromises of the ultimate spiritual purpose of contact with God's own temples. Certainly other elements contributed to and shaped the National Park system. Even the spiritual purpose required little more than the Reformed sense of God's presence in nature's beauty. No

FIGURE 4.8 Bernard Maybeck, Glen Alpine Springs Dining Room. Maybeck's design looks as though it had grown out of native rock. The pillars echo the mountains and stones of the Sierra setting. Underwood borrowed the idea for the Ahwahnee Hotel in Yosemite National Park.

FIGURE 4.9 Ansel Adams, *Ahwahnee Hotel, Yosemite National Park,* 1943. The angle of Adams's photograph of the Ahwahnee Hotel beautifully emphasizes how the building was intended to fit naturally with the dramatic landscape around it. The pillars that Underwood borrowed from Maybeck are visible.

evidence survives that Mather was an Emersonian, and possibly neither was Frederick Law Olmsted Jr., who oversaw the design and building in 1933 of Wawona Tunnel and the dramatic overlook upon which Adams perched his camera and tripod in 1935.[78] Yet establishment of the Park Service during the apogee of the Emersonian era ensured that to a large degree park officials, architects, artists, and visitors viewed them as places of Transcendentalistic worship. Man and his works, particularly for commercial purposes, must be minimized. Pure, untrammeled Nature must be "made available and spiritually effective in the hearts of men and women," as many of them as Mather could entice into God's mountains, to inspire them to live better lives and "create a new society at last."

So the Emersonian river runs: before, beneath, and beyond the short but intense vogues of Kandinsky, Gurdjieff, Ouspensky, and theosophy; past unpopulated landscapes of Adams, O'Keeffe, Marin, Dove, and Marsden; around the organic architecture of Wright, the Greenes, and Maybeck; to come to the parks at last, the greatest manifestation of natural spiritual landscape in America. One of the Emersonian generation's greatest creative achievements was not landscape art. In the nascent National

Park system, the Transcendental search for the spiritual in nature left an imprint on the very landscape itself. From the vision of an unpeopled landscape of the spirit evolved the ideals and goals of the new National Park Service. The Park Service's managers, developers, and designers strove to create and preserve the illusion of an uninhabited world of otherworldly beauty.[79]

5

Progressive Presbyterian Conservation

Two Scots and a Mountain

In October 1872, three artists followed the young daughter of hotelkeeper James Hutchings through the trees along the Merced River. Waterfalls that thundered in spring were mostly silent now, trickling down Yosemite's towering gray granite walls or altogether dry. Shimmering aspen leaves reflected golden in the placid waters. Not long before, snow had dusted the high country. Floy Hutchings brought William Keith, Benoni Irwin, and Thomas Ross to a cabin among the dogwood where the river curved below the Royal Arches.[1] Sent by Ralph Waldo Emerson himself, Keith had come all the way from Boston to this place in quest of dramatic Sierra views that had never yet been captured on canvas. No one knew the glorious beauty of the Sierra Nevada like the cabin's owner, John Muir. Six years had passed since Keith's first visit to Yosemite as an ambitious novice trailing after Albert Bierstadt, Thomas Hill, and Virgil Williams, painters whose Yosemite landscapes had become an artistic sensation. Soon afterward, like Bierstadt and other American painters before him, he went to study art in Düsseldorf, Prussia. He came back after a year to exhibit his paintings in New York City and open a studio in Boston, where Hill and Williams had located. Bierstadt's triumphant return to the Sierra in 1871 turned his thoughts back to the West. He and his wife went up to Concord in 1872 to see Emerson, her fourth cousin, who told Keith he should look up Muir, a remarkable young man whom Emerson had encountered in Yosemite the previous year. Likely, Emerson gave him the name of Jeanne Carr, wife of a professor in Berkeley and Muir's dear friend, who had sent him to Muir.

Muir opened his cabin door to greet the visitors. They presented Carr's letters of introduction. Of all the distinguished worthies she had sent his way this year, Muir read, the men standing before him were "the best wine of kindred and related spirits. . . . Melt and fuse your spirits in the great Nature baptism in which all Art and Science inspirations are born and replenished."[2] Muir must have been pleased to discover that Keith and his two companions were, like him, of Scottish origin. "Do you know any piece of Alps that would make a picture?"[3] Keith asked. Why, only days before Muir had gazed on a sublime scene that made him wish for paints and brushes. He would gladly take them there. Muir fired off a letter to Carr—"I'm going to take your painter boys into one of my best sanctums on your recommendation for holiness"[4]—and two days later, hurrying to beat coming snows, they set out on horseback for the high country. Muir led them up the route of today's John Muir Trail, climbing past Vernal and Nevada Falls to Tuolumne Meadow, then heading south up the Lyell Fork of the Tuolumne. As they rounded a steep headland late in the second day, Mount Lyell, highest peak in present-day Yosemite National Park, suddenly "stood revealed in the flush of the alpenglow." The awed company stopped still, Muir would recall, and then Keith "dashed forward, shouting and gesticulating and tossing his arms in the air like a madman."[5] "When we got to Mount Lyell it was the grandest thing I ever saw," Keith remembered. "The frost had changed the grasses and a kind of willow to the most brilliant yellows and reds; these contrasting with the two-leafed pine and Williamson spruce (the only trees growing at that elevation), the cold gray rocks, the colder snow, made a glorious sight."[6] Muir left at dawn the next day, leaving the artists to sketch scenes to paint in their studios later (Figure 5.1, see color insert). He hiked past Mount Lyell to Mount Ritter and made the dangerous ascent—the first recorded climb—returning three days later, to the relief of the worried painters.

The kindred souls of artist and mountaineer did melt and fuse. On that October day began a devoted lifelong friendship. Keith and Muir had much in common. Both were born in lowland Scotland in 1838 into the same uncompromising branch of Presbyterianism. Both had immigrated with their families to America at about age eleven, had passed from youthful evangelical fervor to a still-strong spiritual yearning, and were both just launching celebrated careers founded on a spiritual relation to nature. During the next decade they were regular companions. The following spring Keith joined Muir on a camping trip into unexplored Tuolumne Canyon, and a year later they climbed into the high Sierra and down the eastern slope to Owens Lake. During Muir's regular sojourns to the San Francisco Bay Area to write, he stayed near the Keiths' house, often stopping by Keith's studio. The friends supported each other's careers. Muir published a worshipful appreciation of a Keith painting, calling it "a kind of inspired *bible* of the mountains,"[7] and lauded the "devout truthfulness to nature" of another.[8] With Muir cheering him on, Keith became California's most celebrated artist. Keith in turn boosted Muir's emergence as California's best-known nature writer and national advocate of conservation and parks. He brought Muir to San Francisco to be introduced to leading poets and other notables, including Carleton Watkins, pioneering Presbyterian photographer from Oneonta, New York. Watkins's stunning pictures of Yosemite had played a significant role in the creation of Yosemite park in 1864.[9] During Muir's first conservation campaign in 1875, Keith lent a Yosemite landscape to inspire the bashful speaker before an audience at the Sacramento Congregational church. In 1888 they traveled to the Northwest, where Keith sketched illustrations for Muir's *Picturesque California*. The aging companions camped together for the last time in 1907 in Hetch Hetchy valley with hopes that Keith's paintings of the valley would help generate publicity to preserve it from San Francisco's plans for a dam and reservoir.

Keith and Muir belonged to the generation in which Presbyterians replaced Congregationalists as the leading conservationists and transformed conservation, parks, forestry, and agricultural improvement into a national crusade. Their lives and careers reflected changes in Reformed spirituality and ideas about nature. Keith's art evolved from one Reformed extreme to the other, from Frederic Church precision to Turneresque suggestive evocations of nature, while Muir made spiritual transitions from religion to natural history, to reverent love for natural beauty, and to political activism for nature and conservation. A half century after Keith arrived at Muir's Yosemite cabin, Presbyterians had virtually replaced Congregationalists in the leadership of conservation. Whether in the cause of conservation or parks, wilderness or pollution, livable cities or safe workplaces, Presbyterians would dominate environmental discourse and lead the major environmental battles into the 1960s. New England Congregationalists forged the core values of conservation in their advocacy of a moral and orderly society in which community took precedence over the individual. Presbyterians transmuted conservation into mid-twentieth-century environmentalism in the white-hot fires of moral urgency. They were men and women of the word—preachers of righteousness, rather than preservers of godly community. Certain of their cause, like their Covenanter forebears they followed the banner of uncompromising righteousness into the fire and smoke of battle.

For God and Natural History

As Calvinist regions on the edges of the English world, Presbyterian Scotland and Puritan America had a close theological and historical kinship—Glasgow conferred an honorary doctorate on Cotton Mather and Jonathan Edwards found an appreciative audience in Scotland, while Scottish writers and thinkers wielded immense influence on America in the eighteenth and nineteenth centuries. Nevertheless, American Presbyterianism differed from Congregationalism in ways that prepared its children to think differently about nature, environment, and society. Presbyterianism's history shaped it in such a way as to make it a virtual training ground for environmental activism.

Presbyterianism acquired a distinctive Scottish accent from special circumstances of its birth and relations with the state. The Reformation shook Scotland upon the return of John Knox in 1558 from Calvin's Geneva. Scots responded to his holy zeal for Reformed theology and for a church organization called presbyterianism with an enthusiasm they had never shown for Catholicism. Presbyterianism took its name from the elders (Greek *presbyteroi*) who presided over New Testament churches. It was organized into a hierarchical system of sessions, presbyteries, synods, and the general assembly. Teaching elders (trained ministers) and ruling elders (lay leaders) of local congregations made up kirk sessions, which ran the congregation and sent representatives to regional presbyteries. Representatives of the presbyteries met in area synods and in a nationwide general assembly. Each body was responsible for the good order and orthodoxy of bodies beneath it. Presbyterianism was an effective system of church government but provided an easy mechanism for schism. Disgruntled presbyteries hived off into independent denominations. Presbyterian history is a complex story of schisms and reunions.

Charismatic and enormously influential, Knox left a deep and enduring imprint on Scottish Protestantism. His precept and example established traditions of powerful preaching, pervasive biblicism, stark churches, and psalm-singing. Presbyterians loved a fiery preacher declaiming with "thus-saith-the-Lord" certainty. Knox preached without notes and with such power that on at least two occasions he provoked riots. Knox's genius did not extend to writing learned theological treatises, and indeed Presbyterianism has fostered no great Reformed theologian of the caliber of Jonathan Edwards or Karl Barth. Knox said it well in the preface to his only printed sermon: "For considering my selfe rather cald of my God to instruct the ignorant, comfort the sorowfull, confirme the weake, and rebuke the proud, by tong and livelye voyce in these most corrupt dayes, than to compose bokes for the age to come. . . . God . . . made my tong a trumpet, to forwarne realmes and nations, yea, certaine great personages, of translations and chaunges." Scottish preachers modeled their ministries on the prophets of the Old Testament, who as God's messengers called the people to repentance and righteousness and rebuked even nobles and monarchs. Knox declared that "in the publike place I consulte not with flesh and bloud what I shall propone to the people, but as the Spirit of my God who hath sent me, and unto whome I must answere, moveth me, so I speake."[10] He often infuriated the court and once reduced Mary, Queen of Scots, to tears. "The Preacheouris war wonderous vehement in reprehensioun of all maner of vice," wrote Knox; "especiallie avarice, oppressioun of the poor, excesse, ryotouse chear, banketting, immoderat dansing, and hurdome."[11] Four centuries later the "wonderous vehement" Presbyterian clergy would still be decrying these sins with the same enthusiasm. The order of the sins is significant. Avarice stood at the top of Knox's list. Presbyterian environmentalists, too, would often rank it high in their list of environmental sins, as the natural world fell victim over and over to dollar-blinded greed.

The landscape of Presbyterian Scotland never looked like that of Puritan New England, with all that implies for the history of American conservation and environmentalism. Historian Philip Benedict noted, "What the Reformation created was not an ordered, puritanical society, but a political culture in which the language of the godly magistrate, the obligation of the ruler to combat idolatry, and the pretensions of the clergy to moral guardianship over the society all gained substantial resonance, and in which . . . an independent system of church discipline worked with the backing of the state."[12] The political culture of American Presbyterianism fostered far more national politicians than did the common-weal culture of Congregationalism. Moreover, the wider vision of Presbyterianism's national organization contrasted with Congregationalism's more myopic system of independent local congregations. Scotland's traditional, clan-based society promoted little that might be called civic culture. Scottish Protestantism tilted more toward an individualist than a communal ethic.

Sins even against the common good were private and personal, to be disciplined by the sessions. American Puritanism's moral center was the godly society; Scottish religious, moral, philosophical, and scientific thought developed from a more libertarian morality and a practical, commonsense view of social interaction and the natural world.[13]

In further contrast with the New England Congregationalism, Scottish Presbyterianism had to contend with a meddling state. Congregationalists partnered with magistrates to regulate morality, but Presbyterians regularly suspected government of drifting into unrighteousness. Scottish lairds' traditional rights far exceeded the power of Connecticut's river gods. Although Scotland's Reformation Parliament declared in 1560 that Jesus Christ "is the onlie Head of the ... Kirk,"[14] the crown and lairds held fast to their ancient rights to appoint clergy and skim money from ecclesiastical benefices. A growing gap between liberalizing aristocracy and Calvinist commoners worsened the tension. Crises between church and state regularly spawned uncompromising schismatic churches that tenaciously upheld the spirit of Knox and traditions of passionate preaching, austere morality, strict Calvinism, the psalter, and never-ending argument with other Presbyterians. The Covenanter Church formed in reaction to the 1660 Restoration of Charles II. The Secession (or Seceder) Church broke away in 1733, followed by the Relief Church in 1761. Seceders were particularly numerous in Ulster in northern Ireland, where Scots had settled in large numbers. In 1747 the Secession Church divided into Burgher and Antiburgher factions, which each split again into anticreed New Lichts and Calvinist Auld Lichts. The Burgher and Antiburgher New-Licht Secession Churches merged in 1820 into the United Secession Church, which joined with the Relief Church in 1847 to create the United Presbyterian Church. The most traumatic schism was the Great Disruption of 1843, in which a third of the ministers and half the laity left the Church of Scotland to found the Free Presbyterian Church.[15]

During these two centuries of religious controversy the vast majority of Scottish emigrants to America set sail. Presbyterianism came to America by various routes. The first American Presbyterians had been English Puritans, such as Benjamin Franklin's father, who emigrated to Boston in 1683 from Ecton near Northampton (and Franklin himself attended Presbyterian services in Philadelphia). Congregationalists and other Reformed Protestants added to the Presbyterians' numbers by joining the church of their theological cousins when they left their native regions. However, they were swamped by fervent, even militantly religious Scots. A quarter million Ulster Scots arrived between 1717 and 1800 and nearly a million more in the nineteenth century. Between 1755 and 1930 a similar number of Scottish Presbyterians made their way across the Atlantic, some by way of Canada. Schismatic Presbyterian denominations successfully transplanted themselves to the United States despite the absence there of the issues that propelled them to schism. Offspring of English Presbyterian churches would establish on a national level the public parks and forests that Congregationalists had advocated. Children of immigrant Presbyterians censured fallen humankind's sins against nature and society and easily integrated environmental "sins" into their "sermons." Some headed west, where titanic nature and wild open spaces brought out an especially aggressive moralism in defense of wild nature.

Presbyterian immigrants to America mainly arrived first in Philadelphia, by far the largest colonial port of entry, and settled along an axis from New York City to Baltimore. The moral and intellectual center of the axis was the college and later university of Princeton. Presbyterians then spread up the Susquehanna and Delaware valleys and pushed into the backwoods. They swarmed into western Pennsylvania, which still today is the most Presbyterian region of the nation and "the most successful plantation of Scottish religious culture in the western hemisphere," in religious scholar David W. Miller's words.[16] Others moved on to upstate New York or pushed down into the Shenandoah Valley of Virginia and onto the piedmont of the Carolinas and Georgia.[17]

American Presbyterianism consequently had a strong Scottish character, nowhere more strongly than among Seceders and Covenanters, who merged in 1858 into the United Presbyterian Church.[18] Intensely ethnic, United Presbyterians adhered fiercely to Calvinist theology, the Westminster Confession, and the Scottish psalter (until younger generations ceased to understand its Scots dialect) and attracted immigrants who wanted a church like the ones back home. Theological conservatism was complemented by social liberalism and supplemented by natural theology. Many ministers studied at the University of Glasgow, the closest Scottish university to northern Ireland and to the many Seceder churches in western Scotland, where they studied moral philosophy under Francis Hutcheson and later Adam Smith and Thomas Reid. With one of the strongest scientific faculties in Europe, Glasgow also instilled a deep-seated appreciation for natural theology as a bulwark for orthodox Calvinism.[19] Never very large, counting only 100,000 members in 1900, American

Seceder and United Presbyterian churches fostered such environmental figures as Muir and Rachel Carson.[20]

Raised on Fire and Brimstone

Keith and Muir were born in 1838 and raised amidst the gathering storms of passionate religious controversy that led to the cataclysmic Great Disruption of 1843. Keith and his mother left Oldmeldrum, Aberdeenshire, after his father's death, and he grew up in the hamlet of Craigdam with his dour Seceder grandparents, pillars of the local church.[21] In 1850 his mother took him to New York City, where as a teenager Keith had a conversion experience (the experience of grace that Calvinists must undergo for salvation), perhaps during the great urban revivals of 1857. Muir spent his childhood in Dunbar, where his father, Daniel, joined the Seceder Church. In 1847, Daniel heard Alexander Campbell speak in Edinburgh and excitedly adopted his understanding of the Bible alone as a religious authority and the basis for a restoration of pure New Testament Christianity that would precede the Millennium. Campbell's father, Thomas, had been an Ulster Scot, student at Glasgow, and minister in the uncompromising Auld-Licht Antiburgher Secession Church. In 1807 he moved to a Presbyterian church in western Pennsylvania and in 1809 led the schism that created what became the Disciples of Christ. Thomas defended his actions in his *Declaration and Address,* which rejected "any thing of human authority, of private opinion, or inventions of men, as having any place in the constitution, faith, or worship, of the christian church—or, any thing . . . for which there cannot be expressly produced a thus saith the Lord."[22] No "thus saith the Lord" supported creeds like the Westminster Confession or ecclesiastic authorities like presbyteries, so out they went. Seeking religious opportunity and fleeing economic depression, Daniel uprooted his family and settled on the frontier of Wisconsin. The local Scottish community gathered to worship first in the Muirs' and others' houses, after 1858 in the schoolhouse, and after 1865 in "a wee white kirk" affiliated with the United Presbyterian Church.[23]

The Presbyterian family also shaped the style of Presbyterian environmentalism. Both Keith and Muir described their personalities as typically Scottish. Although genial, often kindly, and sometimes playful, Presbyterians had a reputation for being grave, reserved, and dour. They could be argumentative and bitingly critical. Muir disguised or blunted direct criticism with humor. Sharp, dry Presbyterian wit has made many great American humorists—one thinks of Benjamin Franklin, Frances Miriam Whitcher, Mark Twain, Will Cuppy, and Dave Barry (whose father was a minister), not to mention comedians like Jay Leno (whose Scottish mother's maiden name was Muir), David Letterman, and Craig Ferguson. Presbyterian childhood of pervasive criticism and holy correction could leave deep psychological scars. Muir recalled that "father taught us to consider ourselves very poor worms of the dust, conceived in sin, etc., and devoutly believed that quenching every spark of pride and self-confidence was a sacred duty, without realizing that in so doing he might at the same time be quenching everything else. Praise he considered most venomous."[24] Could Muir's long lonely jaunts in nature have brought refuge from a society that he feared judged his every fault? Nature, he often proclaimed, was a safe home, a therapeutic sanctuary, a cathedral for spiritual exaltation. "Thousands of tired, nerve-shaken, over-civilized people are beginning to find out that going to the mountains is going home; that wildness is a necessity; and that mountain parks and reservations are useful not only as fountains of timber and irrigating rivers, but as fountains of life," he wrote. As he told Emerson, hoping to cajole him into camping in the woods, "The mountains are calling. . . . We'll go up a cañon singing your own song, 'Good-by, proud world! I'm going home,' in divine earnest. Up there lies a new heaven and a new earth; let us go to the show."[25] The mountains, as Calvin would have added, were indeed also a show—a theater of God's glory—but to the child of Calvinism they could be a safe, healing, nurturing home.

Scottish Foundations of American Natural History

Muir followed a well-worn Scottish Presbyterian path from religion to natural history. His self-education began with books borrowed from Wisconsin neighbors or cajoled from his father: *Pilgrim's Progress, Plutarch's Lives,* Josephus, Scottish geologist and popularizer Hugh Miller, the travels of Scottish explorer Mungo Park and Alexander von Humboldt, and Scottish Romantic novelist Walter Scott.[26] A lover of poetry, Muir bought Shakespeare and *Paradise Lost.* He read Scottish poet Robert Burns, English poet William Cowper, English religious poet Henry Kirke White, English Dissenter poet Mark Akenside, and Scottish poet Thomas Campbell.[27] The Bible, Burns, and especially Milton would be favorites throughout his life, frequently quoted from memory.[28] Park, Humboldt, and Miller presaged Muir's future course. Park's exploration of Africa inspired him as a youth,

and as an adult he set out follow Humboldt. In the 1870s his articles on
Sierra geology earned him the sobriquet "the Hugh Miller of the West."[29]

A few years of study after 1860 at the University of Wisconsin in
Madison with the liberal Protestant New England faculty undermined
Muir's Biblical orthodoxy but fortified his natural theology. Scots had
long sought God in his works hoping to find evidence to solve their religious quarrels and were the most prolific writers of natural theology
in Europe.[30] Continual religious and intellectual ferment pushed Scots
toward science when natural theology fell short of providing answers.
Dozens of remarkable thinkers produced an explosion of ideas that rever-
berated across Europe and America far out of proportion to Scotland's
small population, including major works and advances in science, technology, engineering, medicine, chemistry, agriculture, mathematics,
geology (including Charles Lyell, namesake of the Yosemite peak), politics, economics, moral philosophy, and aesthetics. The teenaged Muir
read *The Christian Philosopher,* an American bestselling natural theology
by Scottish Seceder minister Thomas Dick.[31] Muir's professors taught science as the study of God's creation. A dozen years later Muir thanked a
professor "who first laid before me the book of Nature" and referred to his
geological research as reading God's "glacial manuscripts."[32] Professor of
chemistry and natural history Ezra S. Carr and his wife, Jeanne, took special interest in him and her potent nature-centered Christianity guided
Muir's spiritual growth.[33]

A fellow student introduced Muir to botany: "This fine lesson charmed
me and sent me flying to the woods and meadows in wild enthusiasm.
Like everybody else I was always fond of flowers, attracted by their exter-
nal beauty and purity. Now my eyes were opened to their inner beauty, all
alike revealing glorious traces of the thoughts of God, and leading on and
on into the infinite cosmos."[34] The word "cosmos" shows his science to
be Humboldtian,[35] but Muir was caught up in an Anglo-American vogue
for natural history that also owed much to the Scots. Since the middle of
the eighteenth century, one of the foremost European centers of medicine and natural history was the University of Edinburgh, which Scots
had founded on the model of the Dutch university at Leiden. Scottish
and Edinburgh-educated amateur scientists working in Charleston,
Philadelphia, and New York first laid the foundations of American natural
history, which new science programs at Yale, Harvard, and Princeton had
begun to build upon. By Muir's day, natural history had become a popular
craze. The study of plants and birds was easily accessible to average people

and had the further recommendation of moral purpose. Scots again played a major role by publishing a torrent of nature books for students, children, and the general public.

Study of the works of God through botany and geology became Muir's passion, but mechanics and inventing were his vocation. He worked and botanized first in Canada and after 1866 in Indianapolis. He was on the track for a successful career as an engineer or mechanic, but his morally admirable useful, industrious, and productive life could not compensate for his yearning to be another Humboldt exploring and studying God's works. In 1867, an industrial accident blinded him. Like St. Paul, he gradually regained his eyesight and emerged from darkness into God's light.[36] "I bade adieu to all my [human] mechanical inventions," he wrote, in good Reformed fashion, "determined to devote the rest of my life to the study of the inventions of God."[37] With a New Testament, Burns's poems, and *Paradise Lost* in his pack, he set off in 1867 on a walk across the Appalachian Mountains to the Gulf of Mexico, botanizing as he went. Miltonic allusions filled his journals. He went as a new Adam, in harmony with nature. He remembered his "envy" at this time of Adam, "the father of our race, dwelling as he did in contact with the new-made fields and plants of Eden."[38] Muir hoped to catch a ship to South America to follow Humboldt, but malarial fever in Florida stopped him.

Having known of Yosemite Valley for about a year, he sailed to California in 1868. Muir took a job in Yosemite Valley that gave him plenty of time for botany, geology, exploration, and mountain climbing. In 1869 Ezra Carr took a position of professor of agriculture, chemistry, and horticulture at the University of California. Jeanne Carr exploited her husband's connections with the scientific world to send a series of famous men Muir's way, among them the nation's leading botanists, Presbyterians Asa Gray of Harvard and his mentor John Torrey of Columbia, in 1872. In 1877 Gray returned with British botanist Sir Joseph Hooker, son of a Glasgow botany professor and kin to Connecticut Puritan minister Thomas Hooker, to climb 14,000-foot Mount Shasta with Muir.[39] Muir published his scientific discoveries findings on the glacial origins of Yosemite in a series of articles in *Overland Monthly* in 1874. For the rest of his life he would take special interest in glaciers and glaciation, discovering the glaciers of Glacier Bay, Alaska, and studying glaciers and their effects in Switzerland and Norway.[40] The Presbyterian path that started in religion led Muir to significant scientific achievement and minor renown.

Spiritual, Not Religious

Like almost every leading twentieth-century Presbyterian environmental-ist, Muir embarked on a religious journey away from orthodoxy toward a spiritual (and not merely scientific) relationship to nature. Presbyterians slowly lost passionate commitment to the vital Reformed doctrines that caused so much ecclesiastical conflict in Scotland and America. Few lapsed-Presbyterian environmentalists became atheists. To them, the spirit creates, shapes, and animates the world, as Calvin and Emerson taught. Muir had learned from Campbell that the Reformed rejection of human invention in worship meant rejection of the Westminster Confession. "I never tried to abandon creeds or code of civilization," Muir wrote to a friend in 1865; "they went away of their own accord, melting and evaporat-ing noiselessly without any effort and without leaving any consciousness of loss."[41]

Muir's contact in Madison with liberal New Englanders smoothed the progress of his pilgrimage to God's own cathedrals. The first visitor that Jeanne Carr sent to Muir in Yosemite was Emerson, whom she had met in 1867 in Madison, and whose visit changed Muir's life. Emerson took a liking to him, corresponded with him, and sent him his books. Muir immersed himself in Emerson's and Thoreau's works. By the time Muir conducted Keith to Mt. Lyell in 1872, he was preaching solely from the text of God's Book of Nature. Every landscape, every mountain, every glacier was a "manuscript" of God to him. He would exult that "the alpenglow is the most impressive of all the terrestrial manifestations of God."[42] Of a quiet place of beauty on a Sierra stream, he wrote, "The place seemed holy, where one might hope to see God."[43] Hearing the Sierra's psalms and ser-mons, he spoke of the time when "the day was divine and there was plenty of natural religion in the newborn landscapes that were being baptized in sunshine, and sermons in the glacial boulders on the beach."[44] Muir's divine spark burned with brilliant intensity in the 1870s. "We almost thought he was Jesus Christ," Keith said. "We fairly worshipped him!"[45] Muir's sister wrote him of his family's awe of him in these years: "For so long a time we considered you the grand exception to the curse, standing as you do on a higher plane, cooling your brow in the pure mountain air and feasting your soul on the absorbing study of sweet soothing nature, untrammeled by either the love, or the fear of society and its folly."[46]

Keith followed a parallel spiritual journey that is visible in his art's changing styles and subjects. Early paintings like *San Anselmo Valley*

Near San Rafael (Figure 5.3, see color insert) had the detail and busy fore-grounds typical of many Hudson River School painters. Out in California, Keith had only vaguely been aware of Ruskin's influence on the New York art scene. In 1871 Muir read Ruskin's works, reading some volumes three times.[47] In the company of Muir, who saw the work of God in every stone and waterfall and his glory all around, Keith injected Ruskinian spiritual-ity and scientific truthfulness to nature into his art. He painted *Yosemite Valley* (Figure 5.2, see color insert) in 1875 at the height of Muir's reli-gious and artistic influence, when Muir admiringly called his friend a "poet-painter."[48] After 1880, when their marriages separated the two friends and Muir took over a fruit ranch in Martinez, Keith grew close to Swedenborgian minister Joseph Worcester, friend to Bernard Maybeck and Daniel Burnham as well as Muir. Under the spell of Swedenborgian landscape painter George Inness, he abandoned Ruskinian realism after 1891 and no longer painted from nature. Rather than depicting God's pres-ence in the landscape, his paintings now expressed the artist's spiritual vision, as in *Evening Glow* (Figure 5.4, see color insert)—to the displeasure of Muir, a Ruskinian to the last.

Presbyterianism gave the world great preachers, not great theologians, and after creeds and codes melted and evaporated former Presbyterians made powerful environmental sermonizers. Muir was the exemplar par excellence. His father was a fervent lay preacher and his mother and Jeanne Carr encouraged him to be a minister. Most of Muir's publica-tions were works of evangelism, sermons to bring people away from the inventions of man into the sacred precincts of God and to "baptize" them through "immersion" in the mountains, forests, and rivers. During the long, bitter, exhausting battle against San Francisco's dam and reservoir in beautiful Hetch Hetchy within Yosemite National Park, Muir evoked his inner John Knox and called down fire and brimstone on the heads of the unrighteous. If human creeds should not come between the believer and the Word, still less should the works of man obscure the divine Book of Nature—no "mantracks" on their pages, as United Presbyterian author and environmentalist Wallace Stegner termed them.[49] When the works of man threatened to intrude on the precincts of God, Muir proclaimed dam-nation of greedy desecrators. The National Parks, said Muir, in a Miltonic passage,

have always been subject to attack by despoiling gainseekers and mischief-makers of every degree from Satan to Senators, eagerly

trying to make everything immediately and selfishly commercial. . . . Thus long ago a few enterprising merchants utilized
the Jerusalem temple as a place of business instead of a place of
prayer; . . . earlier still, the first forest reservation, including only
one tree, was likewise despoiled. . . . This will go on as part of the
universal battle between right and wrong. . . .

The arguments of dam proponents, Muir thundered,

are curiously like those of the devil, devised for the destruction
of the first garden—so much of the very best Eden fruit going to
waste. . . .

These temple destroyers, devotees of ravaging commercialism,
seem to have a perfect contempt for Nature, and, instead of lifting
their eyes to the God of the mountains, lift them to the Almighty
Dollar.

Dam Hetch Hetchy! As well dam for water-tanks the people's
cathedrals and churches, for no holier temple as ever been consecrated by the heart of man.[50]

Muir succeeded in rousing the righteous, but at Hetch Hetchy, both Satan
and Senators had their way. The dam was built and Hetch Hetchy was lost.
Later preachers of environmentalism picked up his fallen standard and
carried on in the universal battle between right and wrong.

Presbyterians, Parks, and Forests

Beginning with Muir's generation, Presbyterians made their mark on
national politics. Far more effectively than New England Congregationalists,
Presbyterians instituted national laws and agencies for conservation, parks,
and forestry. New England Congregationalists thought in terms of individual farmers or communities. They built parks for recreation and implemented agencies focused on education for good agricultural practices or
forest stewardship on farmers' own land. Presbyterians, after the manner of John Knox, called the nation to moral account. The remarkable era
known to history as the Progressive Era was Presbyterians' day in the sun.
Among the first 21 presidents, only three—Andrew Jackson, James K. Polk,
and James Buchanan—were raised Presbyterian. Between 1885 and 1921,
Presbyterians held the White House for nearly 28 out of 36 years, over

three-quarters of the time. No president since 1921 was raised Presbyterian. The administrations of four Presbyterian presidents—Benjamin Harrison, Grover Cleveland, Theodore Roosevelt, and Woodrow Wilson, with the support of three Presbyterian Secretaries of the Interior John W. Noble, Hoke Smith, and Franklin Lane—dramatically advanced the causes of conservation and parks. Between 1889 and 1946, Presbyterians headed Interior for about 43 out of 57 years, again over three-quarters of the time (and only once more since 1946[51]). That they headed Interior far more than any other cabinet department except Agriculture demonstrates with dramatic clarity Presbyterians' elective affinity for moral regulation of public land and landscape for the common good. In an instructive contrast, Presbyterians headed the Departments of "Mammon," Treasury and Commerce, only two years each between 1885 and 1945. Under the administrations of Methodist William McKinley, Unitarian William Howard Taft, Baptist Warren G. Harding, Congregationalist Calvin Coolidge, and Quaker Herbert Hoover, the causes of parks and conservation stalled. (See Appendix).

The presidents and cabinet secretaries of the Progressive Era translated the language of Congregationalist conservation into Presbyterian idiom, whose vocabulary was poor in community and rich in censorious moralism and preaching. Presbyterian determination to conquer avarice and save society, rather than Congregational reverence for the New England town, gave the nation its national conservation and preservation laws. In this era as in no other, natural theology and natural history mixed with national politics.

Muir rode the Presbyterian wave. Under the tutelage of New Englanders, Muir's conservation education began in the years 1874 to 1878, when he annually came down from the mountains to Oakland to write his popular tales of his adventures in the wild. He wrote while staying at the house of John Swett, a Congregationalist from Pittsfield, New Hampshire, and former California superintendent of education. Swett persuaded Muir to write for *Harpers Magazine,* which led to articles for *Scribners* and *Century.*[52] Muir now turned his attention from scientific research to the alarming devastation of California's forests. As a botanist, lover of trees, and worshipper of God in his works, he was horrified by wanton destruction of forests and senseless felling of millennia-old sequoias. Ezra Carr educated him about forests and their preservation. In 1874 he published "Forestry: Its Relation to Civilization," which cited Franklin Hough and George Perkins Marsh.[53] Muir traveled the Sierra in 1875 gathering information about the range of giant sequoias. The next year he launched his first conservation campaign with his talk at the Sacramento Congregational church using a painting Keith lent him as a prop. His first piece of advocacy-journalism soon followed, "God's First Temples: How Shall We Preserve Our Forests?," with its allusion to William Cullen Bryant, in the Sacramento *Daily Record-Union*. Muir used Marsh's arguments to defend forests' utility for protecting water supplies, made a special plea for preservation of the ancient sequoias, and indicted the wasteful destructiveness of logging and the ravages of wanton fires set by sheepherders.[54]

Marriage, family, and making a living then took Muir out of mountains and politics for a decade. He returned to the campaign in 1889 and found the national political battlefield had changed. Presbyterians were now in charge. Benjamin Harrison had just won the presidency. A stereotypical upright, cold, austere Presbyterian known for his moral courage, the devout Harrison sought to put the nation on a more righteous path and combat Mammon's influence in public life. Corporations and their extraordinarily wealthy owners were for the first time making their mark on American life and politics, to the growing dismay of Americans who distrusted their corrupting influence on the republic. To a large degree his one term laid the foundations upon which the Progressives would build after 1900. He launched the political career of young Presbyterian Theodore Roosevelt by appointing him to the Civil Service Commission in hopes of reforming the "spoils system." A momentous achievement was the passage of the Sherman Anti-Trust Act of 1890, which Roosevelt would use effectively against monopolies.[55]

Under Harrison's administration the first expansion of the national parks took place and the historic first forest preserves were established. The new parks resulted from Presbyterian lobbying. In a string of editorials and in letters to Secretary of the Interior John W. Noble, Presbyterian newspaper editor George W. Stewart of Visalia, California, demanded protection of the groves of giant sequoias in the nearby Sierra. His arguments paralleled Muir's that the trees should be saved for their beauty and for their utility in protecting the watershed, upon which local agriculture depended. Stewart corresponded with Muir and later became an active member of the Sierra Club. Noble himself had been born in Lancaster, Ohio, to the founder of the local Old School (Calvinist) Presbyterian church, graduated from Yale, and wed in Northampton.[56] He strongly supported Stewart's proposal. On July 28, 1890, Congressman William

Vandever of Ventura, California, a devout Presbyterian and former trustee of a Presbyterian seminary, submitted a bill to protect the sequoias. Noble took the initiative of officially naming it a national park, Sequoia National Park, the nation's second, after Yellowstone in 1872. He always took great pride in this action.[57]

Vandever also submitted a bill to create Yosemite National Park, the culmination of a campaign by Muir and Presbyterian Robert Underwood Johnson. Johnson, editor of *Century* magazine, had traveled to California in 1889 to organize a series of articles on California, hoping especially to coax Muir out of retirement. He and Muir went on a Yosemite camping trip that Johnson would call a turning point in his life and which transformed Muir's as well. His affection for Muir was likely not unrelated to cherished boyhood memories of his Calvinist Presbyterian grandfather botanizing.[58] Dismayed by the damage sheep caused to Tuolumne Meadow, Johnson suggested a much larger park modeled on Yellowstone which would encompass the watersheds of Yosemite and Hetch Hetchy valleys. Muir would write articles proposing the park and draw its boundaries, which Johnson would publish to raise public support. Johnson would then use his political connections to get the park through Congress. In 1890, Muir wrote the articles for *Century*, Vandever submitted the bill, Johnson lobbied and testified, and America's third national park, Yosemite National Park, became a reality.[59]

In 1889 Johnson also urged Muir to organize an association of leading Californians to support and defend the new Sierra parks. A group of mountain-climbing University of California professors, together with two Congregationalist conservationists, William Colby and Joseph LeConte,[60] founded the Sierra Club two years later. Muir was the club's first president, a post he held until his death in 1914, and Johnson its honorary vice-president.

Attention turned to America's sadly abused forest lands. Concern had been growing in the 1870s and 1880s about timber fraud and depredation on public lands, which were under the jurisdiction of the Secretary of Interior. Dozens of bills were introduced in Congress during the 1870s, 1880s, and 1890s by several individuals, none more persistent than Presbyterian Arkansas Democrat Thomas Chipman McRae, chairman of the House Committee on Public Lands, who was incensed about abuse of public lands.[61] Lobbying by Bernard Fernow, Nathaniel Egleston, Edward A. Bowers of the General Land Office,[62] the American Forestry Association, and the American Association for the Advancement of Science encouraged

Harrison and Noble to support the insertion of a forest preserve provision in a March 1891 bill for public lands reform. A historic section of the law gave the president power to create forest preserves.

Harrison immediately used his new authority to proclaim the first forest reserves.[63] Muir had turned Johnson into a forestry enthusiast. He joined the American Forestry Association and read Marsh's *Man and Nature*. Johnson met with Noble in June and told him of Muir's proposal to make the entire roof of the Sierra Nevada into a large forest reserve. Consequently, in February 1893 Harrison created the huge Sierra Forest Reserve, six million acres stretching across eight California counties from Tuolumne in the north to Kern in the south. Johnson also urged Muir to write his first book, *The Mountains of California,* which *Century* published in 1894. Johnson and Noble corresponded extensively between October 1890 and March 1893. He presented suggestions that Noble carried out, most importantly the creation of a forest reserve around the Grand Canyon that later would be the basis for the national park. In all, Harrison established fifteen reserves with a total of thirteen million acres, for purposes ranging from nature preservation to watershed protection to wildlife sanctuaries. Johnson claimed that, despite the contributions of later conservationists like Theodore Roosevelt and Gifford Pinchot, "Muir and Noble were the two salient leaders and pioneers of forest conservation, and Noble's torch, like those of most of us, was kindled at the flame of Muir's enthusiasm."[64] Later, Noble wrote appreciatively to Muir that "my work . . . was greatly supported, if not inspired by yourself."[65]

When Harrison lost his bid for reelection to Grover Cleveland, Muir capped the decided success of the previous four years with a vacation. He and Keith planned a tour of Europe. After a stop to see the Chicago World's Fair, Muir arrived in New York, where Johnson buttonholed Muir at every opportunity to introduce him to influential people, including popular nature writer John Burroughs and the Pinchot family, joined by young Gifford on a visit from Biltmore in North Carolina. In Boston, at Johnson's suggestion, Harvard awarded Muir an honorary master of arts degree. The introductions continued: Charles Sprague Sargent of the Harvard Arboretum, local-color author Sarah Orne Jewett, and more. The impatient Keith had already left for Europe so Muir traveled alone to Scotland, England, Norway, Switzerland, and France.

On his return, Muir was detoured by Johnson to Washington, DC, to discuss forestry with the new Secretary of the Interior, Hoke Smith, appointed by Cleveland in 1893. Cleveland and Smith, two Presbyterians, would have to fight Congress to dramatically expand the forest reserves. Cleveland's father had been born in Norwich, Connecticut, graduated from Yale, studied theology at Princeton, and served as a Congregational minister in Connecticut and a Presbyterian minister successively in New Jersey, where Grover was born, and Fayetteville, New York. Cleveland could be a natural, lighthearted, even bawdy jokester and switch in a blink of the eye to a stern, uncompromising preacher of righteousness. As governor of New York, Cleveland had supported the pathbreaking Adirondacks and Niagara Falls state parks. As president, Cleveland keenly advocated forest protection. He appointed the obscure Hoke Smith to the Interior Department in part because Smith, son of a New England educator, as editor of the *Atlanta Journal* had editorialized against abuse of public lands, forests, and Indians.[66]

Cleveland created seven million acres of forest reserves, but declined to establish more until Congress provided for their administration. Smith asked Congress for forestry legislation and funds for an advisory forestry commission. McRae submitted the bills, but Western congressmen blocked all forestry bills. In 1895, at the suggestion of Sargent, Pinchot, Fernow, and Wolcott Gibbs of the National Academy of Sciences, Smith successfully requested funding for a forestry commission under the aegis of the National Academy of Sciences which would inspect the forest reserves and write a report. Muir as an ex-officio member helped inspect the Western forest reserves. The commission sent its report to Cleveland's new Secretary of the Interior, David R. Francis, another devout Presbyterian.[67] With Francis's encouragement, the committee recommended the creation of thirteen more forest reserves of twenty-one million acres, substantially larger than Harrison's forest reserves. Cleveland proudly proclaimed their creation on Washington's Birthday 1897. Outraged members of Congress attached to a government funding bill an amendment rescinding the reserves. On March 3, his last day in office, Cleveland vetoed the bill, protecting the reserves but leaving the incoming administration of William McKinley without funding. In a special session, Congress passed an appropriations bill with an amendment based on McRae's early failed bill defining forest reserves purposes narrowly and authorizing the sale of timber. A lull followed Cleveland's hard-fought victories. The administration of McKinley, a Methodist, and his Secretary of the Interior Cornelius N. Bliss, a Massachusetts Congregationalist, would leave little mark on the history of parks and conservation.[68]

Presbyterian Progressive Conservation Crusade

As significant and triumphant as the conservation victories of the Harrison and Cleveland administrations most certainly were, historians always treat them as prologue to the Progressive crusade of the first two decades of the new century. Conservation's more aggressive phase began with a tragedy. On September 6, 1901, six months into McKinley's second term, an anarchist shot the president. Assured that McKinley would recover, Vice President Theodore Roosevelt went on vacation in the Adirondacks. Two days later he climbed Mount Marcy. As evening fell Roosevelt had begun his descent when he saw his guide approaching. The man handed him a telegram. McKinley's condition had worsened. Roosevelt rushed down the mountain, found a wagon and driver, and rode all night over dark mountain roads to the nearest railway station. A special train was waiting with the news that Roosevelt was the nation's twenty-sixth president.[69]

This incident tells much about this man, the most vigorous lover of the outdoors ever to live in the White House. In his almost two full terms, Roosevelt left an astonishing and unequalled conservation legacy. In Roosevelt's first message to Congress he spoke for half an hour on conservation. He established the first bird refuge, at Pelican Island, Florida, and would add fifty more National Bird Reservations from Puerto Rico to Alaska. He authorized four game refuges to preserve such endangered species as the bison. Roosevelt created the National Forest Service in 1905 and quadrupled the acreage of the national forests (the former forest reserves). Five national parks were added during his administration. Under the authority of the Antiquities Act of 1906, he established eighteen national monuments, from Devils Tower in Wyoming to the Grand Canyon. Then there were the first federal irrigation projects, several dams, and the Conference of Governors on conservation of 1908.[70]

Born in 1858 into a wealthy family in New York City, Scottish Presbyterian on his mother's side and Dutch Reformed on his father's, Roosevelt grew up in the Madison Square Presbyterian Church, whose minister after 1880 was the leading social reformer Charles Henry Pankhurst.[71] As a boy he was an avid amateur naturalist, the perfect interest for a son of pious Presbyterians. Roosevelt attended Yale intending to become a naturalist but, unhappy that laboratory work had replaced fieldwork, he went into politics. Natural history remained his hobby. He was an unusually knowledgeable amateur ornithologist and published numerous books on natural history, hunting, and his adventures in the wild.

A lifelong churchgoer, if probably not an entirely orthodox believer, Roosevelt would be not a John Knox preaching truth to power but rather a Knox in the very seat of power preaching truth to the nation. Pinchot commented, "Roosevelt was the greatest preacher of righteousness in modern times. Deeply religious beneath the surface, he made right living seem the natural thing, and there was no man beyond the reach of his preaching and example." William Loeb too called him "essentially a preacher of righteousness." Jane Addams added he was a "veritable preacher of social righteousness with the irresistible eloquence of faith sanctified by work." Senator Henry Cabot Lodge put it most eloquently: "The blood of some ancestral Scotch Covenanter or of some Dutch Reformed preacher facing the tyranny of Philip of Spain was in his veins, and with his large opportunities and his vast audiences he was always ready to appeal for justice and righteousness."[72] "I suppose my critics will call that preaching," Roosevelt famously said, "but I have got such a bully pulpit!"[73]

Roosevelt's political life revolved around moral opposition to corruption in politics and to unrighteous concentrations of wealth. This moral focus applied both to society and to the nation's resources. "I believe that the natural resources must be used for the benefit of all our people, and not monopolized for the benefit of the few," he declared in his important "New Nationalism" speech at Osawatomie, Kansas, in 1910. Although it was Pinchot who popularized the word "conservation," Roosevelt's definition followed Calvin's doctrine of stewardship closely. Hardly any national question "compares in importance with the great central task of leaving this land even a better land for our descendants than it is for us. . . . Conservation is a great moral issue." He recognized "the right and duty of this generation to develop and use the natural resources of our land[,] but . . . not to waste them, or to rob, by wasteful use, the generations that come after us. I ask nothing of the nation except that it so behave as each farmer here behaves with reference to his own children. That farmer is a poor creature who skins the land and leaves it worthless to his children. The farmer is a good farmer who, having enabled the land to support himself and to provide for the education of his children, leaves it to them a little better than he found it himself."[74]

Pinchot, Roosevelt's closest friend in his administration, had also grown up in Madison Square Presbyterian Church. When Roosevelt assumed office in 1901, Pinchot had headed the Forestry Division for three years. Pinchot achieved his greatest success in 1905, when a bill passed Congress rechristening the forest reserves as national forests and transferring them from the Department of Interior to the newborn Forest Service in the Department of Agriculture. Secretary of the Interior Ethan A. Hitchcock, a Presbyterian moralistically preoccupied with rooting out corruption in his department, was too weak an administrator to fend off Pinchot's grand plans. Consequently national forests moved to the Department of Agriculture, but national parks remained under Interior, a situation that has created endless administrative nightmares.

Roosevelt was impressed by Pinchot's top legal advisor, George W. Woodruff, a Pennsylvania Presbyterian and Pinchot's classmate at Yale. Woodruff brilliantly created a strong legal framework for national forest lands when Congress failed to provide one. Roosevelt credited Woodruff with formulating and applying the idea of the federal government as steward of the public lands and resources, the first time that the term "stewardship" was applied to national environmental policy. Congregational minister Charles M. Sheldon, author of the popular 1896 bestseller *In His Steps,* had popularized the concept of stewardship in *His Brother's Keeper: Or, Christian Stewardship* of the same year. A cornerstone of the Social Gospel, stewardship made sense to Woodruff and Roosevelt as a description of the government's role over resources. Roosevelt successively appointed Woodruff assistant attorney-general for the Interior Department, Acting Secretary of the Interior, and member of the National Conservation Commission of 1908.[75]

This was a president whom Johnson realized he could enlist for the fulfillment of his and Muir's plan for Yosemite National Park. The 1864 bill that created the park had given Yosemite Valley alone to the state of California, which Yosemite National Park surrounded after 1890. California refused to relinquish its prestigious park for incorporation into the national park. In 1903, Johnson heard that Roosevelt planned a tour of the Western states and wrote him to suggest Muir as his guide in Yosemite. A fan of Muir, Roosevelt was delighted by the plan. Muir took him into the wilds of Yosemite for three days and the pair had a "bully" time. To Roosevelt it was one of the highpoints of his life, while Muir wrote C. Hart Merriam that he "fairly fell in love with him." Falling under Muir's preacherly spell, Roosevelt wrote of the camping trip, "It was like lying in a great solemn cathedral, far vaster and more beautiful than any built by hand of man."[76] Roosevelt happily supported the successful bill for recession of the valley from California to the federal government. Muir exulted to Johnson, "Sound the loud timbrel and let every Yosemite tree and stream rejoice! . . . You don't know how accomplished a lobbyist I've become under your guidance. The fight you planned by that Tuolumne campfire seventeen years ago is at last fairly, gloriously won, every enemy down derry down."[77]

Not quite down, as it soon turned out. To Muir's alarm, Pinchot wanted to put national parks under the Forest Service and to open their timber and other resources to careful exploitation. Muir's friendship with Pinchot, which dated back to the commission that toured the forest reserves in 1896, was fast fraying. Muir, immigrant Seceder Presbyterian from the frontier, was predestined to preach uncompromising sermons in wilderness cathedrals. Pinchot, wealthy New School Presbyterian (a more liberal strain) from New York City, preached a Connecticut Yankee gospel of the New England town. Their alienation was complete by 1908, when Pinchot did not invite him or Johnson to the Conference of Governors on conservation, which especially embittered Johnson, whose idea the conference was.[78] The rift widened to unbridgeable chasm during the battle over the damming of beautiful Hetch Hetchy Valley in Yosemite National Park. San Francisco coveted the valley for its pure water and hydropower potential. With Johnson's help, Muir opposed it with every weapon known to him, but Pinchot testified that the dam and reservoir would do little harm and serve the greater public good. After years of rancorous debate, Congress approved the dam in December 1913 and dealt Muir his cruelest defeat.[79]

Ironically, Hetch Hetchy was dammed and damned by Presbyterians who soon afterward transformed and expanded the National Park system. Democratic President Woodrow Wilson, elected in 1912, and his Secretary of the Interior Franklin K. Lane were just as preacherly and moralistic as Muir but they fought for righteousness against the powers of Mammon without particular regard for God's works left untouched. Wilson's father was a Southern Presbyterian minister and Princeton professor of Ulster-Scot origin and his mother was Scottish. He was a graduate and former president of Princeton. Deeply concerned about the power of big business to limit individual freedom, he sponsored major legislation to regulate corporations and limit their power. However, he like most Southerners was relatively indifferent to parks and forests.

At first glance, Lane would appear to agree with him. Son of a Presbyterian minister and his Scottish-Canadian wife, Lane had once intended to enter the ministry himself. "Earnest and straightforward," he vigorously combatted corruption as San Francisco city attorney, and Roosevelt appointed him to the Interstate Commerce Commission. Lane loved the company of people too much to appreciate unpeopled wilderness. "Frank can't even enjoy a view from a mountain-peak without wanting to call some one up to share it with him," according to one of his brothers. Lane also had little use for preservation of wild nature and instead pushed his idea of "conservation-by-use." "A wilderness," Lane wrote, "no matter how impressive or beautiful does not satisfy this soul of mine. . . . It is a challenge to man. It says, 'Master me! Put me to use! Make me more than I am!' "[80] Hating San Francisco's private water monopoly, he supported the city's application for a dam and reservoir in Hetch Hetchy for a public water supply and as Secretary of the Interior pushed the project to approval in Congress in 1913.

Perhaps surprisingly, then, Lane created and shaped the National Parks system. The thousands of letters that poured into his office against the Hetch Hetchy dam transformed his thinking and awakened a new awareness of the parks. Lane oversaw significant expansion of the national parks, including Rocky Mountain National Park in 1915, Hawaii and Lassen Volcanic National Parks in 1916, Mount McKinley National Park in 1917, and Acadia National Park in 1919, the first park east of the Mississippi River. He supported the Raker Act of 1916 that created the National Parks Service, a single agency to oversee all the parks. One of Lane's most important acts was to appoint the indefatigable Roosevelt Progressive Stephen Mather as first National Parks director. For assistant director, Mather appointed Horace M. Albright, a Presbyterian from Bishop, California, who succeeded him as director in 1929.[81] As a final token of Lane's love for a park that he had once done so much to spoil, upon his death in 1921, his ashes were scattered according to his wishes from the top of El Capitan in Yosemite National Park.[82]

The Gospel of the Great Outdoors

Presbyterian Progressives also replaced Congregationalists in the movement to bring urban children and adults back to nature. Roosevelt and Muir shared a love of natural history and "roughing it" in the outdoors, but Roosevelt, like many of his generation, furthermore worried that urban life in the nation's rapidly growing cities separated young people from nature. At the 1893 Chicago World's Fair, historian Frederick Jackson Turner, a Presbyterian from Portage, Wisconsin, near the Muir farm, delivered an essay that increased national anxiety, "The Significance of the Frontier in American History." Turner noted that the report of the 1890 census announced that the nation no longer had an identifiable frontier of settlement. Having like Muir grown up on the Wisconsin frontier, Turner believed from experience "that to the frontier the American intellect owes its striking characteristics. That coarseness and strength combined with acuteness and inquisitiveness; that practical, inventive turn of mind, quick to find expedients; that masterful grasp of material things, lacking in the artistic but powerful to effect great ends; that restless, nervous energy; that dominant individualism, working for good and for evil, and withal that buoyancy and exuberance which comes with freedom—these are traits of the frontier, or traits called out elsewhere because of the existence of the frontier."[83] Sharing the widespread concern whether American traits—and American manhood—could survive without the frontier, Roosevelt wrote Turner to praise the essay.[84]

On October 2, 1899, Muir answered the door at his Martinez home and greeted Ernest Thompson Seton, the man who perhaps more than any other would get boys (and girls) back in the woods. Seton made an unimpressive figure, tall, thin, quiet, modest, precise, bespectacled, hatless with a bushy mop of hair, and a grand handlebar mustache. Muir probably had not seen Seton's controversial painting *Triumph of the Wolves* in the Canadian pavilion of the Chicago World's Fair, nor read either "The King Of Currumpaw: A Wolf Story," Seton's story of his life-changing encounter with the wolf Lobo, or his bestselling *Wild Animals I Have Known*.[85] Cool to his visitor at first, Muir warmed when Seton expertly identified tracks in his garden as a coyote's. The two men exchanged wildlife stories. The "Sage of the Sierra," as Seton called Muir, told tales of bighorn sheep from his travels in California, Canada, and Alaska.[86] The pair ought to have recognized one another as "kindred and related spirits." Seton's parents were devout Scottish Presbyterians who emigrated to a backwoods farm in Canada. In the 1880s Seton lived in the wilds of western Canada among Indians and wildlife. A self-trained naturalist, he became an accomplished wildlife artist, nature writer, and storyteller. *Wild Animals I Have Known* made him famous. His claim that the semifictional book was entirely true embroiled him in controversy. In 1903, John Burroughs published "Real and Sham Natural History" in *Atlantic Monthly*, which indicted a group of authors including Seton for passing off fictional animal stories as truth. Roosevelt lept into the fray with both rhetorical fists flying, and the "nature faker" controversy became national news.[87] Seton redeemed himself (and earned Roosevelt's friendship) with the two-volume *Life-Histories of Northern Animals* of 1909. He followed with the landmark four-volume *Lives of Game Animals* of 1925, which included Muir's sheep stories from their meeting in 1899 along with examples of squirrel and grizzly bear behavior drawn from Muir's books, and which contained innovative wildlife range maps and made major steps toward a science of animal ecology.

Like Muir, Seton found God in nature. He was keen to expose urban boys to the natural world and its moral lessons, which he described in *The Natural History of the Ten Commandments* of 1907. A great admirer of American Indians, he identified nature's God with the Great Spirit, as in *The Gospel of the Red Man: An Indian Bible* of 1936.[88] Recognizing that boys of his day shared his fascination with Indians, Seton organized the Woodcraft Indians program in 1902 and wrote a manual, *Birch Bark Roll*, with instructions to boys for organizing "tribes," making Indian clothing and teepees, and playing games. Later editions grew to over 500 pages and increasingly emphasized Indian spirituality. Robert Baden-Powell borrowed heavily from the Woodcraft movement when he organized the Boy Scouts in England in 1907. Seton helped bring the Boy Scout movement to America in 1910, wrote the first Boy Scout Handbook, and sat on its board of directors. However, as World War I approached, the Boy Scouts developed into a patriotic organization to prepare boys for the military. Amidst a barrage of accusations of pacificism, socialism, anarchism, cowardice, and lack of patriotism, Seton resigned in 1915 and returned to the Woodcraft movement.[89]

For a parallel movement for girls, Luther and Charlotte Gulick Jr., in consultation with Seton, founded the Camp Fire Girls in Vermont in 1910. Seton's wife, Grace Gallatin Seton, sat on the organizing board and later served as treasurer, with Seton on the men's advisory committee. Grace Seton drew from *Birth Bark Roll* for girls' activities. When the Woodcraft movement faded away, Camp Fire Girls preserved much of its original scheme.[90]

Gulick himself was a leading proponent of "muscular Christianity," a popular movement that combined evangelism with masculine vigor. Sports and outdoor recreation were healthy and moral activities for manly Christians. Gulick was born in 1865 the grandson of the Old-School Presbyterian missionary Peter Gulick, "austere in his religion, a man of action, decisive, and of strong convictions," and the son of Congregational missionary-physician Luther Gulick.[91] Gulick helped broaden the Young Men's Christian Association (YMCA) from its original evangelical purpose by adding gymnasiums and swimming pools. Already in 1885, the YMCA had sponsored residential boys' camps. As director of the YMCA International Training School in Springfield, Massachusetts, Gulick created physical programs for boys such as the game of basketball, invented with youth director and Presbyterian minister James Naismith.[92]

Like their Congregational predecessors, muscular-Christian Presbyterians ministers headed off into the woods to camp, hunt, and fish. Muir heard Presbyterian missionary Sheldon Jackson lecture at a Sunday School Convention in Yosemite Valley and joined Jackson and other Presbyterian missionaries on Muir's first trip to Alaska in 1879, where he discovered Glacier Bay and Muir Glacier. He befriended missionary S. Hall Young of western Pennsylvania, a son and grandson of Presbyterian ministers. Hall and Muir hiked and climbed together during stops along the way. Muir's vision of the divine in the mountain landscape mesmerized the youthful minister. Young recalled in 1915, "I sat at his feet; and at the feet of his spirit I still sit, a student, absorbed, surrendered, as this 'priest of Nature's inmost shrine' unfolds to me the secrets of his 'mountains of God.'"[93]

Presbyterian clergy became prominent fishermen, most famously author Norman Maclean's fly-fishing father, immortalized in his story (later a movie) "A River Runs Through It."[94] Young once made plans for an Alaskan hunt with Theodore Roosevelt and Henry van Dyke, one of the nation's prominent Presbyterian divines and a passionate fly-fisherman and sportsman. A popular author, van Dyke mixed religion with nature and fishing in many poems, stories, and books. He worked to preserve game and conserve natural resources, pleading in 1883 to preserve the Adirondacks, fighting to preserve wildlife at Yellowstone National Park in the early 1920s, and cofounding the fisherman's conservation organization the Izaak Walton League. He wrote the popular hymn "Joyful, Joyful We Adore Thee," set to Ludwig van Beethoven's "Ode to Joy," replete with stanzas of natural theology: "All Thy works with joy surround Thee, / Earth and heaven reflect Thy rays, / Stars and angels sing around Thee, / Center of unbroken praise! / Field and forest, vale and mountain, / Flowering meadow, flashing sea, / Chanting bird and flowing fountain, / Call us to rejoice in Thee."[95]

The archetypal muscular-Christian fishing minister was Maltbie Davenport Babcock. "A manlier man than Maltbie Davenport Babcock never stood in a Christian pulpit," declared an admirer.[96] Grandson and great-grandson of Presbyterian ministers, Babcock's adroit mixture of nature and religion made him one of the most popular ministers of his day. He was called to the pulpit of New York's prominent Brick Presbyterian Church when van Dyke resigned to teach at Princeton University. Babcock's annual Florida fishing trips helped popularize tarpon fishing (a mounted tarpon hung on his office wall). His penchant for weaving fishing tales into religious lessons made him particularly popular with boys and college students. After Babcock's early death at age 43, his widow published his literary remains in *Thoughts for Every-Day Living* in 1901, filled with poems of joy at the presence of God in nature. One of them, "This Is My Father's World," became another well-loved hymn. It begins, "This is my Father's world. / E'en yet to my listening ears / All nature sings, and around me rings / The music of the spheres." The final stanza proclaims, "This is my Father's world. / He shines in all that's fair. / In the rustling grass I hear Him pass, / He speaks to me everywhere."[97] Ken Burns featured this hymn in the soundtrack of his 2009 documentary film series *The National Parks: America's Best Idea*. "This Is My Father's World" is often included in worship services designed for camping or the outdoors, for instance in the Boy Scout prayer book *Eagles Soaring High: Trail Worship for Christians, Muslims and Jews*.[98]

The Last of Nature's Presbyterian Righteous Warriors

The decline of the Progressive Era began at the moment of its apparent triumph. Roosevelt's hand-picked successor, Unitarian William Howard Taft, handily won the election of 1908. However, almost immediately Pinchot feuded with Taft's Secretary of Interior, Congregationalist Richard A. Ballinger, and was fired in 1910. Bitter and vindictive, Pinchot fanned flames of a scandal that forced Ballinger out of office and contributed to Roosevelt's estrangement from Taft. Hoping to heal his fracturing party, Taft replaced Ballinger with Walter L. Fisher, a son of a Presbyterian minister, leading conservationist, and Pinchot ally.[99] Unmollified, Roosevelt came roaring out of retirement to run for president in 1912. At the Republican National Convention, party bosses gave the nomination to Taft despite Roosevelt's greater popular support. In the age-old Presbyterian way, Roosevelt led the pure and righteous into schism and founded the Progressive Party. Its convention resembled a religious revival. Progressives sang the martial hymn "Onward, Christian Soldiers" and Roosevelt delivered his "confession of faith." He cried out to the cheering delegates, "Our cause is based on the eternal principles of righteousness. . . . We stand at Armageddon, and we battle for the Lord."[100] The Lord, as it happened, had other plans. On March 4, 1913, Democrat Woodrow Wilson took the oath of office. Righteousness would have to wait.

One who waited was Harold L. Ickes, 32-year-old Chicago politician, passionate Roosevelt supporter, loyal worker for the Progressive Party, and later the last and most famous Progressive Presbyterian Secretary of Interior. Ickes went to France to work with the YMCA during World War I. Returning home in January 1919, Ickes stepped off the train in Chicago to hear the stunning news of Roosevelt's death. "Something went out of my life that has never been replaced," he would recall.[101] Ickes voted Democratic in 1920 partly because another Roosevelt, Theodore's distant cousin Franklin, was running for vice president, and in part because the conservative Republican presidents of the 1920s dispirited him. Baptist Warren G. Harding, Northampton Congregationalist Calvin Coolidge, and Quaker Herbert Hoover showed little enthusiasm for conservation or parks. The most active of their four Secretaries of the Interior, Hubert Work, was also the only Presbyterian. A native of western Pennsylvania, Work held office from 1923 until 1928. He expanded the National Parks system into the east by starting the process for Shenandoah and Great Smoky Mountains National Parks, which officially became parks in the mid-1930s, and at Mather's instigation added Bryce Canyon National Park. Work's main legacy was simply to restore Interior's tarnished reputation after predecessor Albert B. Fall's corruption scandal.[102] Momentum for new parks ended when Hoover appointed Ray L. Wilbur, whose conservation legacy was Hoover Dam.[103] When Ickes headed "Progressive Republicans for Roosevelt" in the 1932 election, Franklin Roosevelt gratefully appointed him Secretary of the Interior.

Social justice, not conservation, drew Ickes to the Progressive movement. Born in 1874 in Altoona, Pennsylvania, he grew up in the United Presbyterian Church and intended to become a minister until his Calvinist convictions melted away at the University of Chicago.[104] A lawyer and member of the inner circle at Jane Addams's famous settlement house, Hull House, Ickes defended its residents in court when protest activities landed them unjustly in jail. He married the daughter of one of Hull House's largest benefactors. Historian and *Wilderness* editor T. H. Watkins entitled his biography of Ickes *Righteous Pilgrim* to describe a man scrupulously honest, impatient with social injustice, and implacably hostile to political corruption.[105] Walter Lippman wrote after Ickes's death in 1952, "It was true that he was the greatest living master of the art of quarreling. But it was not true, as he liked to pretend, that he was quarrelsome because he was bad-tempered. He was a kind and generous and warm-hearted man. The Old Curmudgeon business was a false front to protect him against it being generally realized how violently virtuous, how furiously righteous, how angrily unbigoted he was almost all the time."[106] Ickes declared his principles in a speech to a public meeting sponsored by the Presbyterian Church in the U.S.A. in 1934. "Christ wanted men and women to live upright lives, but he also wanted them to have for each other understanding and good will and mutual helpfulness," he said. "He wished them to be good neighbors. He hated injustice with a righteous hatred. His whole life was a fight against oppression. This was the man who drove out the money changers from the temple." He believed that the New Deal embodied these principles in its goals of labor rights, social insurance, aid to the poor, and "an end to wasteful and disregardful exploitation of our natural resources." In an echo of Knox's strong censure of "avarice" and "oppressioun of the poor," Ickes declared that the Roosevelt administration "would make it impossible for a mere handful of ruthless, acquisitive men to accumulate unearned fortunes from the oppression of less fortunate people in no position to protect themselves."[107]

Ickes would be the most active secretary in conservation and parks since John W. Noble. He dramatically expanded and transformed the National Parks system and declared 1934 National Parks Year. Originally a Pinchot-style conservationist, he was converted by Parks director Horace Albright to appreciation of the beauty of undeveloped nature and staunchly opposed more development and road-building within parks. His valued employee Robert Marshall also argued for the preservation of unroaded and undeveloped wilderness.[108] Ickes proclaimed, "If I had my way about national parks, I would create one without a road in it. I would have it impenetrable forever to automobiles, a place where man would not try to improve upon God."[109] He created the first wilderness national parks—Kings Canyon, Olympic, Everglades, and Isle Royale—and had to battle timber, irrigation, and water interests and the Forest Service to do so. When Big Bend became a national park, Ickes proposed naming it and a matching park across the border the Jane Addams International Park, but Texas blocked the idea. Ickes also pushed the creation of the first national seashore, at Cape Hatteras, North Carolina. A less aggressive secretary could never have achieved as much.[110]

Ickes's grandest ambition was creation of a Department of Conservation to replace the Department of the Interior. He wanted to swap agencies with the Department of Agriculture to put the national forests in Interior. Pinchot, who had opposed the National Parks Act of 1916 and advocated inclusion of the parks in the National Forest Service, rallied the Forest Service and timber companies against him. Ickes lost that battle.[111] Unfortunately he also butted heads with the Secretary of Agriculture, another stubborn, argumentative, self-righteous, and preacherly Presbyterian, Henry A. Wallace.

Wallace, like Ickes, was the last Progressive Presbyterian in his office.[112] Presbyterians had dominated Agriculture ever since it was granted cabinet status on February 15, 1889, in the Harrison administration. Three weeks later, Cleveland appointed the first Presbyterian secretary, Jeremiah M. Rusk. Presbyterians would head Agriculture for about 38 of the next 51 years, once again about three-quarters of the time.[113] Most important was devout James Wilson. Wilson immigrated from Scotland as a boy and was brought up on an Iowa farm in Scottish-Presbyterian fashion on "Psalms and oatmeal," as he put it. Wilson experimented with crops and farming methods, went into politics, and retired to teach at the nation's first designated land-grant college, now Iowa State University. Appointed Secretary of Agriculture in 1897, Wilson held the office under three presidents for sixteen years, longer than any other cabinet secretary. He hired Pinchot, oversaw formation of the Forest Service, and was Pinchot's boss for his entire federal career. Wilson's legacy was to firmly orient the department to long-term scientific research in all areas of agriculture, with the goal of making the nation the breadbasket of the world.[114]

Wallace had Presbyterianism and agricultural improvement in his blood. His grandfather, "Uncle Henry" Wallace, born in western Pennsylvania the son of Ulster-Irish Covenanter immigrants, was successively a United Presbyterian minister, farmer, and founder in 1895 and editor of the influential *Wallace's Farmer*. Upon his death in 1916, son Henry C. ("Harry") Wallace published and edited *Wallace's Farmer* while teaching agriculture at what is now Iowa State University. He served as Secretary of Agriculture under Harding and Coolidge. His son Henry A. Wallace learned the Westminster catechism at his beloved grandfather's knee. He took over *Wallace's Farmer* when his father died in 1924. He created a successful hybrid variety of corn, founded Hi-Bred Corn Company to market it, and grew wealthy.[115]

Harding, Coolidge, and Hoover's failure to address farmers' problems disillusioned Wallace and he accepted Franklin D. Roosevelt's offer of Secretary of Agriculture. He modeled himself on his grandfather as a warrior for righteousness, fighting the self-seeking interests that perpetuated poverty and robbed the earth of its fertility and wealth. He filled his speeches with quotations from the prophets and spoke in Social-Gospel tones of bringing millennial peace and plenty. High moral purpose guided a philosophy informed by a firm understanding of science and economics: humankind must learn to live in harmony with each other and with the earth.[116] In 1943, he spoke of his vision of a Christian-led post-war world: "By collaborating with the rest of the world to put productive resources fully to work, we shall raise our own standard of living and help to raise the standard of living of others. It is not that we shall be taking the bread out of the mouths of our own children to feed the children of others, but that we shall co-operate with everyone to call forth the energies of everyone, to put God's earth more completely at the service of all mankind."[117] Roosevelt's cabinet, however, did not have room for two preachers of righteousness. Wallace and Ickes battled the same self-interested corrupt enemies and respected each other's liberalism, yet their eight-year feud ultimately thwarted Ickes's plan for a Department of Conservation. When the press anointed Wallace the "philosopher" of the New Deal, Roosevelt made him his vice presidential running mate in 1940—too late for Ickes, whose Department of Conservation was already dead.

One remarkable man made the transition from Progressive to New Dealer and then to environmentalism—the only New Deal environmental figure to remain in office well into the postwar period. William O. Douglas brought to the nation's highest court the righteous devotion to conservation and wilderness that Ickes had brought to Interior. A rebel against his strict Presbyterian upbringing, Douglas was no churchgoer, although he identified as a Presbyterian, even directing that his funeral service be held in a Presbyterian church and old hymns that his parents knew be sung. Born in 1898 to a Presbyterian minister from Nova Scotia who soon died, Douglas grew up in poverty in Yakima, Washington. He worked his way through Whitman College and Columbia Law School, began a law career, and then joined the faculty of Yale Law School. In 1934 Roosevelt nominated him to the Securities and Exchange Commission, where he made a name in cleaning up Wall Street. Two years later Roosevelt nominated him to the Supreme Court. Douglas remained an associate justice on the Supreme Court until 1975, a 37-year term, longer than any other justice in history. He left a huge legacy in the defense of both civil liberties and the natural world.[118]

Douglas left a dual legacy in environmental law and activism that echoed Presbyterian love of God's works and suspicion of man's and that were imbued with a profoundly Muirian flavor. His friend Charles A. Reich observed,

> Justice Douglas's philosophy of liberty was closely akin to his philosophy about the natural environment. The environment nurtures and preserves all natural life. . . . [The] artificially constructed social environment . . . may nurture and preserve us, or . . . it may produce warped and stunted people who lack the kind of character that a democratic society needs. Douglas . . . often [contrasted] the healthy effects of wilderness on people with the harmful impact of the civilized environment.[119]

Douglas authored a series of wilderness books that chronicled his transformation from Rooseveltian mountain man and Pinchotian conservationist to Muirian environmentalist. He frequently proclaimed the spiritual value of mountains and quoted the Bible. He betrayed the influence of his Calvinist father, to whom he dedicated his first book, *Of Men and Mountains:* "When man ventures into the wilderness, climbs the ridges, and sleeps in the forest," wrote Douglas, "he comes in close communion with his Creator. When man pits himself against the mountain, . . . he becomes meek and humble before the Lord that made heaven and earth. For he realizes how small a part of the universe he actually is, how great are the forces that oppose him." Like Muir, Douglas wrote to encourage people to go to the mountains: "They may discover the glory of a blade of grass and find their own relationship to the universe in the song of the willow thrush at dusk. They may learn to worship God where pointed spires of balsam fir turn a mountain meadow into a cathedral."[120] Two books about his hikes and experiences in America's wilderness regions, *My Wilderness: The Pacific West* of 1960 and *My Wilderness: East to Katahdin* of 1961, cited Muir often. In 1961 he published the juvenile biography *Muir of the Mountains.*[121] Douglas also sat on the board of the Sierra Club from 1960 to 1962.

Douglas stepped from literary advocate and elegist to environmental advocate in 1954, when he led a 184-mile hike along the Chesapeake and Ohio Canal in protest of plans to build a parkway on the recreation area along the former canal. Four years later he led a similar walk to protest a beach road through a wilderness area of Olympic National Park and helped preserve the area in an undeveloped condition. Three books of environmental advocacy followed: *A Wilderness Bill of Rights; Farewell to*

Texas: A Vanishing Wilderness; and *The Three Hundred Year War: A Chronicle of Ecological Disaster.* "For things to change there must be a spiritual awakening," Douglas wrote. "Our people—young and old—must become truly activist—and aggressively so—if we and the biosphere on which we depend are to survive."[122]

Douglas is most remembered for his environmental legal opinions, which inspired biographer Adam M. Sowards to call him "The Environmental Justice" and law professor James O'Fallon to name him "Nature's Justice." Few court cases that came before him before 1960 had any environmental aspect whatsoever, but that changed with his rare dissent in the court's refusal to hear a suit against the spraying of DDT over Long Island in 1957. One interested observer of the case was Rachel Carson, who quoted Douglas's dissent in her explosive *Silent Spring* of 1962 and cited his book *My Wilderness: East to Katahdin* as well.[123] In the 1967 case *Udall* v. *Federal Power Commission,* which involved the question whether a dam should produce public or private power, Douglas in a radical move recommended that the Federal Power Commission revisit the idea whether a dam should be built at all, considering its substantial ecological impact, the first court decision to use the word "ecology." Douglas realized the far-reaching potential of the National Environmental Policy Act of 1970, which required environmental impact statements. He filed several dissents protesting the weak or ineffective application of the act in ways that undermined its power and usefulness. Douglas will be forever remembered for his opinion in *Sierra Club* v. *Morton* of 1972. To the question whether the Sierra Club had standing to sue to stop development of Mineral King in the Sierra, Douglas proposed that natural objects like trees, mountains, and rivers ought, like such legal personalities as corporations, have standing to sue.[124] However, Douglas had little long-term influence on the court. Notoriously uncollegial, he disdained tight legal reasoning in his dissents that might influence future decisions.[125] Like Knox, Douglas had too much preacher in him to compose learned opinions "for the age to come." Like Ickes and Wallace, Douglas was the last Progressive Presbyterian in his office.

The Presbyterian Era in national government came to an end. New School Presbyterianism had pushed denominational focus away from creedal purity and toward ecumenism and liberalism. Righteous certainty faded, as did the denomination's political culture. Before their white-hot fervor and steely righteousness weakened and vanished, they had transformed the locally minded Congregational forms of parks, conservation, and agricultural improvement into lasting law and agencies. Douglas's life and career bridged Progressive conservation and liberal environmentalism. Enough traditional Presbyterian culture survived into the middle of the twentieth century to inspire a somewhat different environmentalism. Presbyterians shaped and inspired the postwar environmental movement, although they remained Knoxes in the pulpit like Muir rather than Knoxes in the seat of power like Theodore Roosevelt. Acting in the Calvinist role of the prophet calling the people back to righteousness, they stirred a nation to restrain the forces of greed and avarice to protect the unsullied works of Nature.

6

Presbyterians and the Environmental Movement

Developers and Druids

West Fraser likes to drive down the coast from his home in Charleston, South Carolina, to where he can cross by boat over to Daws Island Heritage Preserve, a low, four-mile-long island not far from Hilton Head Island. His paints and easel set him apart from the average hiker as he walks along beaches or slogs through marshes, on the lookout for scenery that would make for a good painting. One of his Daws Island landscapes, *Atlantic Moonrise* of 2006 (Figure 6.1, see color insert), he regards as the best representation of his artistic philosophy and his connection to the place. The viewer faces east as shadows lengthen and the golden light of the setting sun illumines the scene. The round rising moon has turned the ebb tide, drawing the waters of the Atlantic back over the salt marshes that are cradle or home to so much life. "The painting," Fraser says, "tells the story of the ebb and flow of the tides and the universal connections that pulse through the veins of all flora and fauna of this place."[1] The ecological sensitivity that pervades Fraser's landscapes mixes with appreciation of long human presence. Indians dwelt on Daws Island from 12,000 to 800 years ago and left mysterious shell rings. Fraser feels "philosophically attuned to the ideals of native American thought, that man is a member of the greater whole of an ecosystem."[2] The island also played a part in the drama of early European exploration. In 1564, a French expedition witnessed Indians venerate an engraved stone pillar that French explorers erected two years earlier to mark their nation's claim, a scene Theodor de Bry depicted in a famous engraving.

Fraser's connection is also more personal. The Fraser family once owned Daws Island. In 1997, his father Joe and uncle Charles Fraser with their partner deeded the island to the state as a preserve after development plans fell through. In the 1960s, the two Fraser brothers had become nationally known for their real-estate development on Hilton Head. They had rejected the common building method of spreading suburbs over bulldozed, clear-cut land and spearheaded the movement to develop in harmony with nature. Joe Fraser had started out working in the lumber business of his father, General Joseph B. Fraser Sr. On the lookout for fresh timber to harvest, Joseph Sr. bought land on Hilton Head Island to cut the tall pines and preserved the oak forest for future development. Charles returned home from Yale Law School in 1956 with a head full of new ideas. He and Joe bought their father's interest in Hilton Head Island and formed Sea Pines Plantation Company. Inspired by the architecture of California and Frank Lloyd Wright, they built houses designed to blend with the landscape. They went to great trouble and expense to save notable trees and natural features. To safeguard their vision of an island developed sympathetically with nature, the Frasers attached lengthy covenants to deeds and exercised absolute control over what homeowners could do. The brothers began similar developments on other coastal islands and Puerto Rico and in nearby states, but the recession of the 1970s forced them to develop more tracts on Hilton Head to keep money coming in. In 1983 they sold control of Sea Pines Plantation. New owners abandoned the strict limits on what owners could do with their Hilton Head properties. The Frasers bought Daws Island for a private use. Inflated rumors of development plans caused them to sell and give it to the state as the preserve that West would continue to visit, explore, and paint.[3]

The Fraser family had been devout Presbyterians. West Fraser however no longer attends church. "My spiritual time is painting outdoors and being outdoors," he says.[4] He is typical of mid-century Presbyterian environmentalists, like David Brower, executive director of the Sierra Club. In 1995, in Lone Pine in the Owens Valley east of the Sierra, as Brower sat gazing up at Mount Whitney and waiting to lead a Sierra Club gathering, he suffered a stroke. The hospital admitting nurse asked Brower's wife, Anne, for his religion for the admitting form. "None," Anne said, but corrected herself: "Put 'Lapsed Presbyterian.'"[5] After the New Deal, Presbyterians concerned with the environment were almost always "spiritual" and not "religious." Prior to the generation of Harold Ickes, Henry A. Wallace, and William O. Douglas, most Presbyterian advocates of parks, conservation, and agricultural improvement attended church, but now most were lapsed. Before Franklin Roosevelt's New Deal, the church-goers had preached Presbyterian conservation from the highest offices in government. Afterwards, lapsed Presbyterians preached environmental-ism revival-style among the people. Though now out of office, they still constituted a potent cultural and political force. For three decades after World War II theirs were the most prominent and effective voices for envi-ronmental causes.

Presbyterianism had changed. It could it no longer hold onto its chil-dren. The nineteenth-century church had a strong sense of its identity and an uncompromising earnestness of purpose in the world. Presbyterian missionaries headed out into the West, onto Indian reservations, up into Alaska, and overseas to Latin America and Asia, and founded strong Presbyterian communities everywhere. Presbyterian politicians strode into national office confident of their duty to secure righteousness in the nation. At the same time, however, declining immigration from Scotland and northern Ireland cut off a crucial source of vitality and renewal. Worship practices grew less distinctive. Obsession with doctrinal purity faded. Hymns, those once-dreaded "human inventions in worship," crowded psalms into a neglected spot in Presbyterian hymnals. The churches threw their righteous energy into the crusade for Prohibition, whose repeal in 1933 demoralized them and led to a retreat from poli-tics. Presbyterians embraced the ecumenical movement, with its goal of Christian unity. Belief in Calvinist doctrine set out in the Westminster Confession of Faith and the Shorter Catechism decayed among believers and in seminaries and pulpits. In the revised Confession of 1967, predes-tination, like Lewis Carroll's Baker, softly and suddenly vanished away. A trendy but anodyne theology of reconciliation took its place. Instead of the Westminster Confession's solemn opening words of the evidence of God in creation, the new Confession substituted contemporary social con-cerns, although near the end it did add a recognizably Calvinist summa-tion: "God's redeeming work in Jesus Christ embraces the whole of man's life: social and cultural, economic and political, scientific and technologi-cal, individual and corporate. It includes man's natural environment as exploited and despoiled by sin."[6]

By the middle of the twentieth century an identifiably Presbyterian cul-ture remained but its political culture, self-assurance, and moral urgency had so waned that it rarely sent Presbyterians into the nation's high-est offices. Instead, lapsed Presbyterians began to abound who became prophets of the new and rising environmental movement, thundering like ecological Knoxes at the sins of government and society. John Muir would be the patron saint of the Era of Ecology, not Theodore Roosevelt.

The Frasers took part in this second wave of Presbyterian crusade for a proper moral relationship of humans to the natural environment. Their innovative development of Hilton Head in harmony with nature was in the vanguard of a revolutionary movement whose leading proponents were two Presbyterian landscape architects, Ian McHarg and John O. Simonds. Born in Scotland in 1920, McHarg pioneered the ideas of ecological regional and urban planning and preached their virtues in classrooms, auditoriums, and on the pages of his seminal 1969 book *Design with Nature*. McHarg's father, thwarted in his ambition to be a Presbyterian minister, bequeathed to his son a "lifetime preoccupation with religious attitudes to nature within a widely religious inquiry" as well as a fiery preacherly temperament. Invited in 1972 to lecture before representatives of the Fortune 500 companies, McHarg spoke on "Man, the Planetary Disease," hoping "to strike terror in the hearts of the villains of the environment." His talk recalled "the Presbyterian sermons of my youth. Sin, guilt, punishment, hell, and damnation. But finally, there is forgiveness. There is absolution if you repent. Wherein lies salvation?" In designing with nature.[7] As he said in an interview in 1997, "I am a censorious Presbyterian. I like this imperative thing: You bastards! Design with nature, or else I'll grind you up for dog food!"[8] At the University of Pennsylvania, in 1957 he developed a new course "Man and Environment." McHarg devised an innovative and influential system of overlays to visualize the various ecological dimensions of a site. His work, most famously his design for The Woodlands near Houston, Texas, with its greenways and open space, hugely influenced the design of suburbs, which became more environmentally conscious.[9]

Although he was the best-known advocate of designing with nature, McHarg followed the same path as John Ormsbee Simonds. Simonds was born in 1913 to a Presbyterian minister, from whom he acquired both an appreciation of nature and a knack for sermonizing. Like McHarg a graduate of Harvard's landscape-architect program, he traveled in Asia and acquired a deep appreciation of Buddhism and Taoism that informed his growing ideas about landscape architecture. His firm, founded in Pittsburgh in 1940, specialized in planned communities and new towns and completed over 80 designs, notably Miami Lakes and Pelican Bay in Florida, as well as projects like Mellon Square in Pittsburgh and the

Chicago Botanic Garden. An avid environmentalist, Simonds wrote the popular 1961 textbook *Landscape Architecture: The Shaping of Man's Natural Environment*. He followed in 1978 with *Earthscape: A Manual of Environmental Planning*. Drawing on their Presbyterian appreciation of nature and knack for preaching, McHarg and Simonds became influential proponents of the postwar ecological transformation of landscape architecture.[10]

In 1970, West Fraser's Uncle Charles famously "encountered" Brower, who came to South Carolina with author John McPhee to meet him—a gathering of three Presbyterians who respectively represent distinctive Southern, Western, and Eastern versions of the postwar Presbyterian environmentalist. McPhee published his account in articles in *The New Yorker* and in the book *Encounters with the Archdruid*. Fraser expected a battle with this "modern druid," his contemptuous term for environmentalists, who he said "worship trees and sacrifice human beings to those trees." However Brower, whom McPhee drily called the "Archdruid," was impressed with the sensitivity to nature with which Hilton Head had been developed. Brower believed development of the coastal islands was inevitable and to Fraser's surprise was supportive. The trio flew to Cumberland Island, a portion of which the Frasers had bought to develop, to the horror of wealthy residents who owned the rest of it. Brower imagined Cumberland Island as a park like Yosemite, with a developed core that concentrated most visitors, surrounded by mostly undeveloped, pristine wilderness, which in fact was what the Frasers planned. In the end, however, an alliance of other environmentalist "druids" and Cumberland Island landowners thwarted the Frasers' plans. Today, as Cumberland Island National Seashore, it is much less developed than Brower or Fraser anticipated and far less visited than Yosemite.[11]

The (Mostly) Missing Southern Presbyterian Environmentalists

West Fraser's family has roots that reach deep into the soil of the South. He was born in 1955 in Savannah, Georgia, and grew up on a farm in nearby Hinesville, where he played in the woods, hunted, fished, and rode horses. The Frasers attended the Presbyterian Church in the United States, in which his grandfather was active. More Calvinist than the larger Presbyterian Church in the USA of the North (with which it would merge in 1983), the PCUS had begun as the Presbyterian Church in the Confederate States in 1861. In 1964 his family moved to Hilton Head Island, South Carolina, five miles from the Georgia line, where he could still ride, fish, sail, and boat in a long youthful idyll. One day bulldozers began clearing the woods. Fraser remembers, "I asked my father ... why he was tearing down the forest and he explained in his logical way. I have always been understanding of business's needs for money since that conversation. Once you start developing it is hard to stop. My father and his brother had a respect for the land, but also believed the Christian ethic of man's dominion over the earth. I have also kept a practical approach to my environmental thoughts. I think the esthetic principals that they adopted have influenced me as well."

West Fraser's Presbyterian upbringing accords with his holistic, ecological view of the landscape, which like Ernest Thompson Seton and so many others he identifies with Native Americans, but he does not disavow the landscape's human history and meaning. "My experience on Hilton Head Island affected me and I do what I do today, in a way, as a response to that," he says. "From my youth I wanted to travel and capture with paint the land of my forebears, the southern coast of Georgia and South Carolina. I believe that with a naturalist's eye I am able to make paintings that give the viewer a true sense of place." His childhood left Fraser with awareness of the vulnerability of the landscape to change. He is active in several conservation groups to promote a greater understanding and appreciation for the natural world: "The work I have done for more than 30 years now will forever capture some of the wild places that have either changed forever, are threatened to be changed, or will be altered due to global climate change. My message has always been subtle. I am developing a respect and new appreciation for the environment I paint, with every new viewer of my work." Fraser's paintings have a moral and a purpose. "My role in the environmental/conservation cause is one of a guide to help individuals gain new respect for the landscape we live in," he says, "and for the ecosystem of man and earth."[12] For all that, however, he firmly believes that conservation need not and should not come at the expense of economic prosperity.

Such attitudes—a certain fatalism about change, approval of humans and their works in the landscape, and concern for the priority of prosperity—are typical of the South and help explain why the region has contributed relatively little to national thought about and activism for nature and the environment. The human associations of even Fraser's "wild" landscapes like *Atlantic Moonrise,* not to mention his many paintings or human and urban subjects, speak to a characteristic preference for people in the landscape. As Charleston's best-known and most widely collected artist, Fraser also paints views of the city, portraits, old plantations, boating scenes, hunters, and other portrayals of humans and their works.[13] Historically, native-born Southern painters of wild landscapes have been rare. During the Hudson River School's heyday, some Northern and foreign artists explored the South looking for new picturesque scenery but found no market for unpeopled landscapes. Southerners preferred portraits or urban or plantation scenes on their walls.[14] Hence Daws Island is a "heritage" preserve and not a "nature" preserve. The state of South Carolina has heritage preserves, bird sanctuaries, boat ramps, fish hatcheries, fishing lakes, scenic rivers, and wildlife management areas, but no nature preserves. Directly or indirectly, in South Carolina nature serves some human purpose. Southern environmentalism works within the limits of the conviction that private individuals exercising their power wisely over their own property is the most appropriate way to manage the land.

Until Charles Fraser went to Yale, the Fraser family's attitudes toward the landscape closely followed common Southern modes of thought. The Frasers' ancestors had profited from nature's bounty in the South long before Fraser Lumber Company and Sea Pines Plantation. They arrived in the seventeenth century and owned slave plantations.[15] Daws Island's human history also includes nearby former rice plantations along the Broad River, whose slaves and freedmen once knew its shores. The Southern attitude that subordinated nature to human concerns formed in the crucible of a slave society. The region's dominant social and political values spread outside the Old South in Southerners' religious and cultural luggage. Westward across the Old Southwest to Texas and Oklahoma, onward to Arizona and southern California, and in a postwar diaspora everywhere across the nation, they brought a distinctive conservative, individualistic taste in religion, culture, and politics and a relative indifference to exploitation of land and labor.

Slavery was the central, sanctified institution of antebellum Southern society, a moral and social monster loosed upon the land, beyond censure or control. Southerners trimmed and warped society to accommodate it. In this profoundly rural society each owner exploited his own land, labor, and resources for personal enrichment. Ideals of civic duty or communal obligation shrank before a cult of individualism. Fatalism, conservatism, and toleration of a brutal social order and of the suffering of others made chimerical any proposal of building a better society. Weak governments had little power to interfere with slavery, and slaveowners easily manipulated them for their interests. Planters wanted few government functions beyond a strong police power to uphold slavery. They escaped much taxation because weak government was cheap government. Tax burdens fell disproportionately on nonslaveowners. In the antebellum era, the moral, religious, philosophical, scientific, sociological, economic, and political leaders of the South closed ranks in slavery's defense. After the Civil War, they remained united in support of Southern racial attitudes and segregation.[16] Silence and averted eyes still met evils of segregation, oppression of the poor and laborers, and social injustice. With its weak governments, unequal taxation, and elite dominance of society and government, the South as a region has always had the nation's greatest gap between the rich and poor, its worst human rights abuses, its most exploited workers, its greatest illiteracy, and its fewest public works and worst infrastructure, as well as its most exploited land and the fewest and worst funded public parks, libraries, or other social goods.[17]

Far from New England Congregationalists and the New England diaspora, Southern Presbyterians adapted Reformed theology to life in a society based on the exploitation of humans, mostly Africans, and of nature. In the former slave states, neither Presbyterianism nor any other denomination could survive if it openly challenged dominant political, social, and economic values. Denominations that accommodated or supported them thrived. Local gentry had controlled the colonial Anglican Church, the predominant church in the South before the Revolution, obliging ministers to support the existing system and avoid moral challenges. In the middle of the eighteenth century, upstart denominations challenged planter dominance of the church. Presbyterian immigrants spread southward from Pennsylvania into the backwoods of Virginia and the Carolinas but often lacked ministers due to poverty and remoteness. Unchurched Presbyterians, along with "plain folk" whose needs the Anglican Church left unfulfilled, were ripe for the evangelical invasion after the 1750s, when Calvinist Baptist missionaries arrived from New England. After the Revolution devastated the Anglican (soon Episcopal) Church, Methodists joined Baptists in reaping the great evangelical harvest. By 1830 Baptists and Methodists dominated the slave states. Preachers who spoke against slavery were beaten, tarred and feathered, whipped, physically attacked, publicly humiliated, jailed, and sometimes lynched. Southerners learned either to accept or to ignore the social and economic values of the plantation system. After the Civil War, these habits of mind evolved into uncritical assent to laissez-faire economics and white supremacy. The churches found or invented Biblical justification for the Southern system. The sins that white Southern Protestants condemned were personal, not social. Beyond church walls, there was no orderly and godly community and no righteous nation to preserve.[18]

Within the limitations of this culture, Southern Presbyterianism has raised up some important if lesser-known environmentalists. Biologist Archie Carr might be the closest counterpart to Muir that the South produced. Carr's reputation spread nationwide because of his skill as a writer. He alternated scholarly works for fellow scientists with eloquent books for the general public. His prize-winning magnum opus, *Handbook of Turtles: The Turtles of the United States, Canada, and Baja California*, published in 1952, established his credentials as an important biologist. A popular account of his Central American adventures followed, the Burroughs Prize–winning *The Windward Road* of 1956, which in part told of sea turtles and their decline from abundance to near extinction. Several readers consequently founded the Caribbean Conservation Corporation (now Sea Turtle Conservancy) with Carr as scientific director. Carr's sea-turtle evangelism grew more pronounced with every subsequent book. He eventually adopted a broader environmental agenda advocating conservation of the Everglades and Africa. *So Excellent A Fishe: A Natural History of Sea Turtles* of 1967 was the culmination of his turtle conservation writings.[19] Carr's intervention in the postwar period when sea turtle populations were plummeting saved some species from extinction.[20]

Carr's research and activism focused offshore, away from the land and society of the South, where it had few social or political implications that might disturb the white Southern conscience. Marriage to a New Englander awakened Carr's inner environmental "Knox" and transformed this son of a Southern Presbyterian minister from pioneering researcher on sea turtles to environmental activist. Carr's grandfather was a Scottish immigrant who settled in Mississippi. His father, a minister in the (Southern) Presbyterian Church in the US, was an avid hunter and fisherman. Carr enrolled at the University of Florida, from which he earned his doctorate and where he spent his entire academic career. In 1937 he married Marjorie Harris, child of Boston Unitarians. Unlapsed, they attended the Gainesville Presbyterian Church.[21] A zoologist herself, Marjorie Carr prodded her husband's activism by her own opinions and example. She acknowledged the Puritan origins of her values: "My feeling is that a lot of the environmentalists here in Florida got their sense of environmental stewardship from . . . Puritanism and early settlers in New England," she observed. "An awful lot of [Floridians] who are interested in the environmental movement originally came from New England."[22] In Florida she was a much better known activist than her husband. She led successful campaigns to save the Ocklawaha River and stop the Cross-Florida Barge Canal. The land set aside for the canal became a greenway 110 miles long and a mile wide, which upon her death in 1998 was renamed the Marjorie Harris Carr Cross Florida Greenway.

The greatest, most original Southern Presbyterian contribution to American environmentalism lay not in the field of activism but in environmental thought. In 2003, philosopher Holmes Rolston III won the Templeton Prize for his work "on the religious imperative to respect nature," which, according to the prize committee,

> has been a major factor in establishing the field of environmental ethics. He has become one of the world's leading advocates for protecting the earth's biodiversity and ecology in recognition of the intrinsic value of creation, including the ongoing evolutionary genesis in the natural world. In philosophical circles he is widely known as the "father of environmental ethics," and in theological circles he is known for his concept of a sacred, prolific, and "cruciform" creation. He gave the Gifford lectures in 1997 at the University of Edinburgh; the lectures were subsequently published as *Genes, Genesis and God* (1999).[23]

An ordained Presbyterian minister and the son and grandson of Presbyterian ministers, Rolston was born in 1932 in Virginia's Shenandoah Valley. He turned toward natural theology out of interest in both theology and science. In 1975 he published the essay "Is There an Ecological Ethics?" in the journal *Ethics* and set off a philosophical debate. Four years later he cofounded the journal *Environmental Ethics*. Rolston continued to break philosophical ground and set the terms of the debate in many other books and essays, among them *Philosophy Gone Wild* of 1986 and the textbook *Environmental Ethics: Values in and Duties to the Natural World* of 1988. He set out a new philosophical approach toward what he termed the "intrinsic value" of nature as a basis for an environmental ethic, controversially claiming that "non-human nature has value independent of humans, and this value is objectively ascertainable."[24] Also controversial was the way that his framing of the issue was fundamentally religious. In a manner consistent with the mind of both Presbyterianism and the South, he grounded his ethics on the value of the natural world and not on social concerns. Although Rolston took pains to address issues of policy and urban society, his environmental ethics formed a clearer and more effective guide to the individual than to policymakers or citydwellers. Social and political concerns remained peripheral, even neglected, adjuncts to his environmental ethics.[25]

Rolston had much in common with the founder of the Templeton Prize, John Marks Templeton. Both were Southern Presbyterians intent on devising a natural theology for the contemporary world. Rolston negotiated the controversial space between Christian theology, science, and ethics. Templeton used his vast wealth to encourage progress in natural theology. Born in 1912 in Winchester, Tennessee, and raised a Cumberland Presbyterian, Templeton graduated from Yale, won a Rhodes Scholarship, and made a fortune as an investor. A Presbyterian elder, he served as a trustee of Princeton Theological Seminary from 1951 to 1988, including twelve years as its president. He believed that theology like science evolved with advances in spiritual or material knowledge, respectively, and that theology and science should work together to further knowledge of the world. Princeton rebuffed these notions, so he established the Templeton Prize for Progress in Religion in 1972 and founded the Templeton Foundation in 1987 to promote the interchange of ideas between science and religion. Despite Templeton's avowed ecumenical purpose, both the Prize and the Foundation have been controversial, particularly among scientists who mistrust its motive and purpose.[26] It represents, however, the modern expression of the old Reformed impulse to find evidence of the spirit in the natural.

Westward the Cause of Environment Makes Its Way

Woodrow Wilson was a deeply Presbyterian Progressive, but a very Southern one. Son of a Presbyterian minister, he was former president of Princeton University. The Virginia native's father had also been a chaplain in the Confederate army, a founder of the Presbyterian Church in the United States, and moderator of its General Assembly. Conservation was not Wilson's priority. Had it not been for Westerner Franklin Lane of the

Department of the Interior, Wilson's administration would have a marginal place in environmental history. The West of sagebrush and sequoias was far more fertile ground for Presbyterian environmentalism than the South of oaks and magnolias. Brower and several eloquent, inspirational postwar environmentalists came out of the land between the Rocky Mountains and the Pacific Coast. Something about the twentieth-century West transformed some Presbyterian men into passionate advocates for nature. Since the days of the Oregon Trail and the Gold Rush, the West outside of Utah has been the least churched section of the country—the perfect haven for lapsed Presbyterians or lapsed anything. Perhaps the open spaces and grand landscape evoked an overpowering sense of the Creator's presence. Perhaps the unprecedented scale of exploitation of natural resources in the West, with its vast deposits of gold, silver, and copper and immense forests of the largest trees on earth, quickened Presbyterian conscience and moral outrage.

Muir of course blazed the trail they followed. Brower in fact cited Muir as the inspiration for his work and was often conscious of his predecessor in the Sierra Club. "From time to time," Brower said, "I remind others of John Muir, perhaps because I keep writing or talking about wild places, as he did."[27] Muir's writings helped inspire him to become a well-known mountaineer, with over seventy first ascents.

Brower, the Sierra Club's first and greatest executive director, was likewise a "dropout Presbyterian," as he called himself, with an implicit nod to Timothy Leary. As a boy, Brower had led his, blind and devout Presbyterian mother on walks in the Berkeley hills overlooking the San Francisco Bay. He first camped with the Pioneers, the YMCA's more religious version of the Boy Scouts. He first found his prophetic voice in the 1930s while speaking during Sierra Club outings. Out of these campfire talks emerged "the Sermon," as he called his standard lecture. Brower gave the Sermon for the first time around 1969 to Presbyterian ministers assembled at the Ghost Ranch retreat (almost in Georgia O'Keeffe's backyard).[28] John McPhee first named it the Sermon and likened it to Billy Graham's evangelism.[29] Noting that "no group was too small for him to evangelize," son Kenneth thought "Sermon" was an apt word, "because for my father environmentalism was religion. . . . The Sermon was a celebration and defense of Creation. Anyone who doubts that environmentalism can make a complete and perfectly satisfactory religion should have grown up in our house."[30] Although Brower had long since left the church, "I think that I will still call myself a believer," he told interviewer Susan Schrepfer in 1980. ". . . I have great respect for the force that created and kept it all going."[31] His friend Harold Gilliam recalled, " 'The Religion,' he called it. Conservation was a religion for him. I'm sure that his experiences of the Sierra contributed to his total philosophy. Love of Nature. Allowing Nature to take its course. Trying to preserve the natural world. It was, again, a statement of *religious* belief that came through so well."[32]

Brower first revealed his enthusiasm, devotion, and skill in environmental activism in Ansel Adams's 1938 campaign for Kings Canyon National Park. The Sierra Club hired Brower as its first executive director in 1952. His charismatic, driving leadership and crusading righteousness transformed it from a small California outdoors club of 7,000 members to a powerful national political force of 77,000. Brower's uncompromising activism and his conversion of the Sierra Club from club to political organization sparked opposition and rebellion, and he was forced to resign in 1969.[33] He founded Friends of the Earth, a loose international affiliation of environmental organizations, and in 1982 created Earth Island Institute to promote new projects for international environmental causes. Only his death in 2000 stopped his earnest activism. Kenneth Brower summarized a lifetime of relentless energy and achievement:

> He was instrumental in the establishment of Kings Canyon, Redwood, North Cascades, and Great Basin National Parks, and Point Reyes, Cape Cod, and Fire Island National Seashores. He led the successful campaigns against dams in Dinosaur National Monument and Grand Canyon National Park. His Exhibit Format Series of large-format photographic books won the Carey-Thomas Award for Creative Publishing. He won the Blue Planet Prize, the Windstar Award, and a garage full of others. He was nominated three times for the Nobel Peace Prize.[34]

Brower rivaled Muir as preacher but not as a writer. When Muir died on Christmas Eve 1914, the mountains and forests of California lost their bard. In 1925, his successor was anointed when James Rorty published a review of Robinson Jeffers's *Tamar and Other Poems,* "a magnificent tour de force." Rorty proclaimed, "Out of [this] volume, the great hills of the coast range rise and take their places, the brown earth cracks beneath the glare of the California sun, the 'earth-ending' waters of the Pacific heap themselves upon the lava beds. California has another great writer to place beside John Muir. America has a new poet of genius."[35] Babette Deutsch of the *New*

Republic concurred: "In Robinson Jeffers we find a poet concerned, like Muir, with the cosmos in which man is but a momentary flicker."[36]

In many respects, though, Jeffers was no Muir, although both were shy, slender men who believed creation was to be glorified and defended against the sins of fallen humanity. Muir was a famous talker. Jeffers was known for his silence. Muir rambled and trekked throughout his long life. Jeffers was rooted in a stone house he built with his own hands on a granite point overlooking the Pacific. Muir preached and lobbied. Jeffers rarely spoke in public and disdained politics. If Muir was beloved, Jeffers could put people off. In its issue for February 2, 1962, *Life* magazine published a full-page portrait of the poet and his grandson, backlit in the entrance to his home, Tor House. The accompanying text offered a forbidding portrayal: "Some time before his death last week at the age of 75, Robinson Jeffers permitted himself a rare public display of warmth by sitting for a photograph with his grandson. . . . His poetry bore the stamp of his dark and troubled credo: that man is only a passing evil defiling the eternal beauty of nature—a 'heartbreaking beauty [that] will remain when there is no heart to break for it.' "[37] With increasing bitterness as Jeffers aged and watched world wars and atomic bombs, his poetry proclaimed a modernized Westminster Confession of Faith: nature is the work and word of God but the works of man bring death and ugliness. In his poems Jeffers wove sermons of nature-Calvinism, as undaunted as Knox decrying the nation's sins "by tong and livelye voyce in these most corrupt dayes."

Jeffers was born in Pittsburgh in 1887, son of a fearfully dour United Presbyterian theology professor and grandson of Covenanter Presbyterians.[38] "Under the stern eye" of his father the boy learned to read from the *Reformed Primer* at age three, studied Latin and Greek, and on Sundays memorized the Westminster Shorter Catechism.[39] Reserved and solemn, Jeffers did not mingle easily with others. When Ansel Adams met him in 1926, Jeffers barely spoke, but as the afternoon wore on the "glacier" "thawed" a bit.[40] After his father moved the family to southern California for his health, the sixteen-year-old enrolled as a junior at Occidental College, a Presbyterian school, graduated with a bachelor of science, and then pursued graduate studies successively in literature, medicine, and forestry without taking a degree. He married in 1913 and settled in Carmel in 1914.

Jeffers thought a landscape as dramatic as the central California coast deserved its own poetry. Each afternoon he quarried stone from the seaside, brought it up from the beach, raised each heavy stone in place as

Tor House and Hawk Tower rose, and composed poetry in his head. The following morning he would write. Composed while the poet was literally in contact with the earth, in the elements of sun, fog, wind, and rain, and amidst a landscape of great beauty, his poems took the critical world by storm. "Jeffers' peculiarly distinctive style . . . has the roll of surf and the jaggedness of rocks about it," Brower wrote. "Something utterly wild had crept into his mind and marked his features. I cannot imagine him as having arisen unchanged in another countryside. The sea-beaten coast, the fierce freedom of his hunting hawks, possessed and spoke through him. It was one of the most uncanny and complete relationships between [a] man and his natural background that I know in literature. It tells us something of the power of the western landscape here at world's end where the last of the American dream turned inward upon itself."[41]

Jeffers's poetry spoke in Reformed idiom of rejection of human creeds and teachings of all kinds. "New Year's Dawn, 1947" concluded,

> There is no valid authority
> In church nor state, custom, scripture nor creed,
> But only in one's own conscience and the beauty of things.
> Doggedly I think again: One's conscience is a trick oracle,
> Worked by parents and nurse-maids, the pressure of the people,
> And the delusions of dead prophets: trust it not.
> Wash it clean to receive the transhuman beauty: then trust it.[42]

Like so many Reformed Protestants, Jeffers found in nature evidence of God's existence and of fallen humanity. He wrote in "The Inhumanist" section of the poem "The Double Axe,"

> . . . there is not an atom in all the universes
> But feels every other atom; gravitation, electromagnetism,
>   light, heat, and the other
> Flamings, the nerves in the night's black flesh, flow them
>   together; the stars, the winds and the people: one energy,
> One existence, one music, one organism, one life, one God:
>   star-fire and rock-strength, the sea's cold flow
> And man's dark soul.[43]

William Everson called them "long, somber and God-tormented poems." A ray of sunny Transcendentalist optimism occasionally broke through the darkness. Jeffers was one of the Emersonian generation, "a transcendentalist gone West and turned inside out," Everson said. Late in his career Jeffers in answer to a query wrote, "Emerson was a youthful enthusiasm, if you like, but not outgrown by any means, only read so thoroughly that I have not returned to him in a long time."[44] In a rare address, at the Library of Congress in 1941, he summed up his beliefs: "Another theme that has much engaged my verses is the expression of religious feeling . . . that the universe is one being, a single organism, one great life that includes all life and all things; and is so beautiful that it must be loved and reverenced; and in moments of mystical vision we identify ourselves with it."[45] Jeffers marveled at God's excessive production of beauty, beyond any bare need: rainbows around the rain, the secret iridescence of seashells, blossoms even on weeds, the music of birds.[46]

The craggy difficulty of Jeffers's poetry did not win him the broad following of fellow lapsed Presbyterian Robert Frost, with his gentle rural verse, or the accolades of poet-laureate W. S. Merwin, the son of a Presbyterian minister whose poems also reflect consciousness of human separation from nature. Jeffers coined "inhumanism" for his religious love of natural beauty and hostility to human self-regard, nakedly expressed in the notorious line from "Hurt Hawks," "I'd sooner, except the penalties, kill a man than a hawk."[47] Inhumanism has attracted some environmentalists but repulsed other readers, like the author of the story in *Life*. Charles Fraser would certainly have thought him one of the "modern druids" who "worship trees and sacrifice human beings to those trees."[48]

On January 20, 1962, a rare snow covered the roof of Tor House when the poet took his last breath. Carmel had grown out to the once lonely spit of land where the house stood and crowded up close to its stone walls. Developers eyed the spectacular coast that stretched south to Big Sur. Jeffers had never acted to slow conversion of wildlands to housing tracts, but the director of the Sierra Club enlisted his poetry in the cause. Brower paired Jeffers's poems with Philip Hyde's photographs in "The Big Sur Country" in the October 1961 *Sierra Club Bulletin*. In 1965 he got together with Ansel Adams, whose *Sierra Nevada* had influenced the campaign for Kings Canyon National Park back in 1938 and whom Brower called "a walking concordance to Jeffers." With Adams's assistance, Brower edited *Not Man Apart: Lines From Robinson Jeffers*, a coffee-table book of Jeffers's poetry illustrated with photographs by Adams and others. It took its title from "The Answer." "Love that," Jeffers had written of the natural world, "not man / Apart from that." Planned as part of a Sierra Club campaign to preserve the wild beauty of the central California coast, the book helped revive Jeffers's reputation. The successful campaign led to restrictions of coastal development. In 1970 Brower again borrowed Jeffers's line to name *Not Man Apart,* the magazine of Friends of the Earth.

At the moment Brower resigned his directorship of the Sierra Club, another Western lapsed Presbyterian was moving onstage. Edward Abbey's uncompromising righteousness inspired the most radical wing of environmentalism yet. Abbey was born fifty miles east of Pittsburgh in Indiana, Pennsylvania, in 1927. His mother was the mainstay of her local Presbyterian church, playing organ, directing the choir, and doing everything but preach, a role her sex denied her. She married a lovable ne'er-do-well of Swiss ancestry, an agnostic anarchist perversely and contentiously anti-everything. Abbey would be a bit of both of them, moralistic preacher and contrarian anarchist. During a hitchhiking adventure he fell in love with the Southwest's sparsely populated natural beauty, still relatively wild and undeveloped in 1944. Abbey returned after two years in the army, enrolled in the University of New Mexico, produced a master's thesis in philosophy on anarchism and violence, and lived the rest of his life in the Southwest.

Abbey's rural Pennsylvania upbringing lasted long enough to watch logging and strip-mining destroy the beauty of the Allegheny hills, kindling a lifelong hatred of the destruction that greedy developers wreak on the beauty of the earth. Perhaps here is the reason why so many Pennsylvanian icons of environmental history went elsewhere—Ickes, Jeffers, Abbey, Rachel Carson, Jane Jacobs, Annie Dillard—and none remained. Massachusetts had its Henry David Thoreau, Connecticut its Frederic Church, New York its John Burroughs, and New York and New England its Thomas Cole and Hudson River School; but the green, well-watered mountains of Pennsylvania have had no great author or painter to praise their natural beauty. From the Poconos in the east, geological fraternal twin of the Catskills, to the deep valleys and verdant mountains of the corrugated Allegheny Plateau, Pennsylvania was less a land for poetry than a realm where industry reigned—Calvinist industry. Pennsylvania Presbyterians resembled Muir the factory manager and inventor of Indianapolis instead of Muir the nature writer and environmental activist of Yosemite. Forests on the eastern mountains, near to cities and river transportation, fell to the ax (and made Pinchot's grandfather's fortune). Under the eastern and southwestern mountains lay deep layers of coal, easy to mine, close to water navigation and rail lines to urban factories and furnaces. Under the western plateau lay great reservoirs of oil. Ulster-Irishman Samuel M. Kier built the nation's first oil refinery in Pittsburgh in 1853 and six years later New Englander Edwin Drake drilled the world's first oil well at Oil Creek. Pittsburgh grew into America's steel center, intensely polluted, "hell with the lid taken off."[49] Muir's contemporary Andrew Carnegie, born in 1835 in Scotland, immigrated there in 1848 and rose from poverty to fantastic wealth as the world's leading steel magnate. In 1967, a son of a Presbyterian minister, historian Lynn White Jr., proposed in his famous essay "The Historical Roots of Our Ecologic Crisis" that Christianity in general and Protestantism in particular fostered an imperial, exploitive attitude toward the natural world. As evidence, he could have done worse than to point to the sober industrious Calvinists of Pennsylvania.[50]

Abbey served stints as park ranger or fire lookout at parks and forests around the West. The loss of the beautiful Glen Canyon upstream from the Grand Canyon on the Colorado River, dammed and inundated under huge Lake Powell, fired up his righteous anger on behalf of wilderness. His first nonfiction book, *Desert Solitaire,* won prizes at its publication in 1968 and became a bestseller in its 1971 paperback reprint. This antidevelopment screed often echoed Muir. "We have agreed not to drive our automobiles into cathedrals, concert halls, art museums,. . ." Abbey wrote. "We should treat our national parks with the same deference, for they, too, are holy places." He added, "Wilderness is not a luxury but a necessity of the human spirit, and as vital to our lives as water and good bread."[51] Abbey's 1975 novel *The Monkey Wrench Gang* followed four people who defended wilderness by "monkeywrenching" development projects to sabotage and stop them. With the rise of Earth First! and environmental radicalism in the 1980s, Abbey found himself hero to a new brand of environmental activist. But beset by health problems, he died in 1989.[52]

Abbey shared much with Jeffers, whose Inhumanism impressed him, and from whom he borrowed for his 1980 postapocalyptic novel *Good News.* Destruction of wild beauty and senseless damming of graceful and spectacular canyons incensed him and, like Muir and Brower, he called damnation down upon the heads of all mammon-worshipping despoilers of nature. "Original sin, the true original sin," Abbey wrote in *Desert Solitaire,* "is the blind destruction for the sake of greed of this natural paradise which lies all around us."[53] Like Knox, Abbey asserted that "the moral duty of the free writer is . . . to be a critic of his own community, his own country, his own government, his own culture." Knox's and Abbey's model was the Old Testament prophet. "The writer, like the ancient

Hebraic prophets, must dare to speak truth to Power and the powerful."[54] He titled one of his books *Vox Clamantis in Deserto,* borrowing from the prophet Isaiah, the "voice of one crying in the desert," decrying the sins of society and calling the people back to righteousness.

Abbey made his tongue a trumpet for these most corrupt days and proclaimed the path to salvation. In "One Writer's Credo," he declared, "I write to entertain my friends and exasperate our enemies. I write to record the truth of our time as best I can see it. To investigate the comedy and tragedy of human relationships. To oppose, resist, and sabotage the contemporary drift toward a global technocratic police state, whatever its ideological coloration. I write to oppose injustice, to defy power, and to speak for the voiceless. I write to make a difference. . . . To honor life and to praise the divine beauty of the natural world."[55] One reviewer said after his death: "Abbey was a true independent, a self-declared extremist and 'desert mystic,' and a hell of a good writer. Irreverent about man and reverent toward nature, Abbey wielded his pen as a weapon in the battle for freedom and wilderness and against arrogance and greed."[56]

David Foreman practiced what Abbey preached, who for all his preaching had been hardly more politically engaged than Jeffers. Disillusioned by the increasingly professionalized and bureaucratized leadership of the Wilderness Society and the Sierra Club, while sitting around a campfire in 1980 Foreman and some friends founded Earth First!, a direct-action environmental movement of self-described "ecowarriors." Foreman probably supplied the name, as he did its rallying cry, "No compromise in defense of Mother Earth!" Foreman was born in 1946 in New Mexico and grew up in the Churches of Christ, a conservative offshoot of Alexander Campbell's Disciples of Christ movement, which had broken away from Presbyterianism. Rejecting creeds and presbyteries as unbiblical human inventions, Campbell taught a libertarian approach to the Bible in which each person should read it as if people had never laid eyes on it before and come to his or her own conclusions. This libertarian mentality pervaded Campbell's movement and in time inclined it toward political conservatism. Foreman had once wanted to become a Churches of Christ preacher. Journalist Susan Zakin described his speeches as "rabble rousing, foot-stomping fundamentalist-preacher speechifying."[57]

To Foreman, humans were the sinners in the Garden. His creed mixed restoration of wilderness with civil disobedience and libertarian or anarchist politics. "The preservation of wilderness," he wrote, "is an ethical and moral matter. A religious mandate. Human beings have stepped beyond the bounds; we are destroying the very process of life."[58] Muir, Brower, Abbey, and Aldo Leopold were his chief heroes. Foreman's solutions to environmental problems had no real social or political implication, disdaining so-called anthropocentric environmentalism and embracing instead the biocentrism of Deep Ecology. He has advocated a restoration of a paleolithic relationship to nature, including spiritualization of nature, and to prevent destruction of what untouched, undeveloped wilderness remains. Earth First! became known for nonviolent obstruction of development threats to wilderness areas. However, by 1990 it was veering toward the political left, and Foreman left it. He now advocates the Wildlands Project, a series of expanded bioregional wilderness areas "off-limits to industrial human civilization, as preserves for the free-flow of natural processes" where nature and evolution can proceed relatively unimpeded by humans.[59]

No Presbyterian preacher of the Age of Ecology of the 1960s and 1970s reached more people than environmentalist pop singer John Denver. For young people of the era, music was the medium of protest and preaching, which radio and cheap vinyl records brought into homes across the nation. In the 1970s Denver recorded a string of hit songs, full of biblical resonances and a strongly moral and religious view of nature and the human relationship to it.[60] Like Muir, who often said that going to the mountains was going home, Denver wrote many songs about leaving and returning home, including "Leaving on a Jet Plane," "Take Me Home, Country Roads," and "Goodbye Again," and he titled his autobiography *Take Me Home*. Denver built a house in Aspen, Colorado, which like Jeffers's Tor House stood on an isolated promontory of land, overlooking an undeveloped mountain valley instead of an ocean. Muir's writings identified him with the Sierra of California while Denver's songs identified him with the Rocky Mountains of Colorado. California featured Muir on its 2005 state quarter. Colorado made Denver's biggest hit, "Rocky Mountain High," an official state song in 2007.

Born in 1943 in Roswell, New Mexico, from an early age Denver knew that he had special talents as singer and songwriter. He knew, too, that as in the parable of the talents he must do something useful with them. Although his parents were not religious—while living in Tucson they dropped him and his brother off at the Presbyterian Church every Sunday and went home to make love—he grew up serious and moralistic. Denver's Presbyterianism lapsed. Aspen attracted all kinds of religious and self-help movements, some of which he experimented with. Denver retained a belief in God and saw nature in a deeply religious light. His first hit album of 1971 was entitled *Poems, Prayers and Promises*. Ostensibly his 1974 hit "Annie's Song" was for his wife, but, as he remarked, it might also be a prayer: "You fill up my senses / Like a night in a forest, / Like the mountains in springtime, / Like a walk in the rain."[61] "Rocky Mountain High" of 1973 was essentially a sermon in song, full of religious phrases and sentiments. It described in third person his experience camping with friends near a mountain lake to watch the Perseid meteor shower, an experience so religiously intense that he was in a sense "born again." Denver sang, "He climbed cathedral mountains. . . . / Now he walks in quiet solitude, the forests and the streams, / Seeking grace in every step he takes. . . . / You can talk to God and listen to the casual reply / Rocky Mountain high." The lyrics preached against avarice and its threat to the works of God, wondering "Why they try to tear the mountains down to bring in a couple more / More people, more scars upon the land." An environmental activist, Denver established the Windstar Foundation in 1976 to inspire a holistic response to the earth's environmental and social problems, including a spiritual response.

Presbyterian Women of the East

Author John McPhee spent a year with Brower and his family while he wrote *Encounters with the Archdruid*. A lapsed Presbyterian who has lived most of his life in Princeton and whose father was a Presbyterian elder and avid fisherman, McPhee weaves into most of his articles and dozens of books an interest in nature and the human relationship with the environment. Yet he never preaches. His work merely implies his environmentalist concerns and his admiration for Brower. McPhee is no preacher of righteousness. He is a quiet, reserved presence in his own books, which say little about their author and let the facts speak for themselves. It would overstate things to make him stand for the postwar male Eastern lapsed Presbyterian environmentalist, but the truth is that few of them made a mark. Yet while McPhee was writing his subtle books, Eastern Presbyterian women took the conservation movement and remade it into modern environmentalism.[62]

In October 1963 Brower played host to Rachel Carson, who was in San Francisco to give a major speech. She wanted to see redwoods. On a beautiful Saturday, Brower drove her across the Golden Gate Bridge, up through the eucalyptus groves of Mill Valley, over golden hills overlooking the

Pacific, and down into the deep shade of Muir Woods National Monument. Brower, Carson, Muir: a marvelous conjunction of three of the brightest stars of Presbyterian environmentalism. Ill with the cancer that would take her life six months later, Carson toured the majestic, towering trees from a wheelchair. On the way back to San Francisco, Brower detoured to Rodeo Lagoon at Fort Cronkite. "In the lagoon just inland," recalled Brower, "were perhaps fifty brown pelicans having a hell of a good time, perhaps celebrating the beginning of their recovery [due to restrictions on DDT] with a pelican ballet, on that sunny day. I have to believe in magic, for what else could have led those pelicans to know that Rachel Carson would have preferred them to redwoods?"[63]

Perhaps the most important environmental figure of postwar America, Carson was no Westerner. This magical trip was her only visit to California. She and other Eastern Presbyterian women remade conservation into environmentalism. The sages of the Sierra, foresters, park rangers, scouts, mushing parsons, manly tarpon-catching ministers, archdruids, and ecowarriors have given the impression that environmentalism is all about nature and wilderness—and that environmentalists are male hikers, sportsmen, and chest-thumping wilderness lovers. Taught to pursue activities useful to society, Presbyterian women far more than Presbyterian men transformed conservation into environmentalism. They insisted that environmental concern include humans and human society and not just mountains and rivers, hawks and bears. "Ecology" to them was meaningless unless its circles and cycles were wide enough to encompass people in their homes, at their jobs, and in their communities. The story of modern environmentalism is incomplete without four Eastern lapsed Presbyterian women (three from Pennsylvania)—Alice Hamilton, Rachel Carson, Jane Jacobs, and Annie Dillard.

Alice Hamilton pioneered the science and medicine of protecting human and environmental health from toxic industrial chemicals. By her death in 1970 at age 101, she had lived long enough to observe the rise of conservation and contribute to the rise of environmentalism. She represented a very different Presbyterian approach to environmental issues, one that had nothing to do with Progressive concerns for parks, natural resources, the frontier, or muscular Christianity. Instead her life and work anticipated the environmental movement's concern for toxic environmental pollutants at work, in the home, and in the air and water.

"We have hard work to do, and loads to lift. / Shun not the struggle; face it," as one of Maltbie Davenport Babcock's popular poems put it, was a Reformed call to action that went out to women, too. By the Progressive Era, opportunity's door had opened just wide enough to let them answer it by entering previously prohibited careers, particularly those related to women, children, or the home. When Hamilton looked into careers in which, in good Reformed fashion, she could be useful, she chose medicine "because as a doctor I could go anywhere I pleased—to far-off lands or to city slums—and be quite sure that I could be of use anywhere."[64] Born in 1869 in Fort Wayne, Indiana, to a devout, prominent Presbyterian family, she learned the Westminster Shorter Catechism at her father's knee. Hamilton entered the University of Michigan Medical School with hopes of becoming a missionary-physician.[65] After study and internships in Minneapolis, Boston, Germany, and Johns Hopkins University, the Women's Medical School of Northwestern University in Chicago hired her in 1897 to teach pathology.

Like many idealistic, religiously raised young women of the day, Hamilton sought to help the poor through work at a settlement house. When a room opened at Jane Addams's famous Hull House, she moved in and remained a resident for twenty-two years. There, Hamilton found opportunities to be useful but she also got an education of an entirely different kind. She saw illness among the poor and working classes caused in workplaces. She read muckraking articles and Thomas Oliver's *Dangerous Trades,* which inspired the title of Hamilton's autobiography, *Exploring the Dangerous Trades.* She became a pioneering researcher and activist in industrial medicine. The governor of Illinois appointed Hamilton in 1910 to a new Occupational Diseases Commission, the first of its kind, from which she resigned to begin investigations of her own. Her journal articles influenced conditions for the better. When Harvard Medical School created a Department of Industrial Medicine and could find no better-qualified man—and it searched for one—it hired Hamilton as the first woman on its faculty. She expanded her crusade against toxic chemicals to the wider environment. In 1925 she led opposition against leaded gasoline (in vain), which cheaply increased the power of engines but filled urban air with a dangerous neurotoxin. Even after her retirement in 1935 Hamilton remained active in health, medical, and political causes until her death in 1970 just before President Richard Nixon signed the Occupational Safety and Health Act, her most important institutional legacy. Hamilton had been the single most important figure in the development of occupational medicine.[66]

Like Hamilton, Jane Butzner Jacobs was vitally interested in improving urban life. She crusaded with righteous indignation against top-down plans for slum clearance, urban renewal, urban planning, and the like, which reached their peak in the middle of the twentieth century. In numerous articles and books she explored what it was that made cities alive and vital. She traced urban vitality to people and supported creating situations and landscapes in cities that allowed people to interact. Interaction then produced innovation, creativity, and prosperity. To her, contemporary urban planners created sterile environments that strangled neighborhoods and urban life. The skepticism toward automobiles and preference for human-scaled cities that she expressed in opposition to dominant postwar thinking helped expand the urban aspect of the rising environmental movement.

Useful service to society was part of Jacobs's moral education, too. She was born in 1916 in the coal-mining industrial town of Scranton, Pennsylvania, to a family of active Presbyterians. Her maternal grandfather taught Sunday School and served as president of the county Sabbath School Association. Her brother would be a federal judge and Presbyterian elder. Jacobs spent six months working at her aunt's community center in western North Carolina for the Presbyterian home mission, a formative experience for her. Working in New York as journalist and editor, she loved Greenwich Village and bought a house there after her marriage to architect Robert Jacobs Jr.[67]

In 1952 Jacobs joined the staff of *Architectural Forum*. Her articles about urban planning and so-called urban blight expressed her growing doubt about the overwhelming consensus in government and planning in favor of urban renewal. She criticized Robert Moses, who had risen to tremendous and almost unopposed power over planning in New York City. She organized opposition to his plans to run an expressway through Washington Park in the middle of Greenwich Village. This campaign stopped Moses for the first time and raised questions about his power and ideas that eventually led to his fall. Her articles in *Architectural Forum* and *Fortune* prompted the Rockefeller Foundation to fund the research and writing of her landmark *Death and Life of Great American Cities* of 1961. It offered both a sermon against the arrogance of planners and a plan of salvation. Recommendations included mixed use, which kept streets alive throughout the day; short blocks to encourage pedestrians; buildings of different ages; and high density. She favored the walker over the driver and regarded suburbs as parasitical communities sucking life out of central cities and automobiles as fatal to city life. City planners reacted with outrage but activists took heart. Within a decade, public protest had stopped dozens of major planned city-killing freeways, from the Embarcadero Freeway across San Francisco's waterfront, to Interstate 40 through Overton Park in Memphis, to Interstate 291 through downtown Hartford.

When Jacobs's book came out, Rachel Carson was working to finish the book often cited as the most important environmental work ever published. Where Hamilton had fought chemical pollutants that industry and vehicles discharged into air and water as by-products, Carson raised alarm about toxic chemicals that humans deliberately spread in the environment with little regard to the consequences for ecological or human health. She followed the familiar Presbyterian track from religion to natural history and then went down Muir's path to sermonizing and lobbying. Her writing career began with books about the wonders of nature and ended with the environmental bombshell and terrifying jeremiad *Silent Spring*.

Born in 1907 in Springdale, fifteen miles up the Allegheny River from Pittsburgh, Carson grew up in the United Presbyterian Church, in which her mother's father and brother-in-law were ministers. Dour, stern, devout, and always dressed in black, her mother did nature-study with Rachel in the backyard. Carson later commended the study of nature for children in her *Teach Your Child to Wonder*. Quiet, solitary, serious, and intensely private, Rachel wrote her high-school senior thesis, "Intellectual Dissipation," on the responsibility of the intelligent to benefit society with their gifts. A theme in all her books would be scientists' moral responsibility toward society and nature. She attended the Presbyterian Pennsylvania College for Women (now Chatham University) because of its Christian ideals, majoring first in English and then biology. After postgraduate study at the Marine Biological Laboratory at Woods Hole, Massachusetts, Carson earned a master's in biology at Johns Hopkins University in 1932, when the Depression ended her studies short of a doctorate. Carson got a job writing and editing for the US Fish and Wildlife Service and soon was publishing her own work. Three bestsellers, *Under the Sea-Wind* of 1941, *The Sea Around Us* of 1951, and *The Edge of the Sea* of 1955, enabled her to quit her job and write full time. Critics showered praise for their elegant style and scientific accuracy. *The Sea Around Us* spent 86 weeks on the *New York Times* bestseller list, an unsurpassed record, and won the National Book Award and Burroughs medal.

Carson ceased attending church but retained a sense of the mystery of creation, of the interconnectedness of life, of the miracle of evolution. "Each time that I enter [the world of the shore]," she wrote in *The Edge of the Sea*, "I gain some new awareness of its beauty and its deeper mean- ing, sensing that intricate fabric of life by which one creature is linked to another, and each with its surroundings. . . . Underlying the beauty of the spectacle [of life] there is meaning and significance. It is the elusiveness of that meaning that haunts us, that sends us again and again into the natu- ral world where the key to the riddle is hidden." She concluded her last sea book with the words that echoed Calvin's view of nature as the place where God communicates himself to us: "Contemplating the teeming life of the shore, we have an uneasy sense of the communication of some universal truth that lies just beyond our grasp. . . . The meaning haunts and ever eludes us, and in its very pursuit we approach the ultimate mystery of Life itself."[68]

The sea was Carson's remnant of Eden before the Fall and brought out her Presbyterian moralism. The sea to her was the last place where nature pursued its timeless processes without human intervention. Greedy "man" could plunder the edges and skim the surface but the sea-life that lived in the great vastness escaped the disruption and extinction that humans caused everywhere on land. Nonscientists rarely appeared in her books except as shadowy unnamed presences, arrogant where they ought to be humble and reverent. Scientists were the exception because they had no economic interest in the sea and sought selflessly to increase knowledge and understanding of the universe. She warned against the inventions of avaricious man and praised the spiritual value of nature. She said in 1954, "I believe natural beauty has a necessary place in the spiritual develop- ment of any individual or any society. I believe that whenever we substi- tute something man-made and artificial for a natural feature of the earth, we have retarded some part of man's spiritual growth. . . . Is it the right of this, our generation, in its selfish materialism, to destroy these things because we are blinded by the dollar sign?"[69]

Everywhere humans were doing just that. Unrestricted atmospheric testing of nuclear weapons caused a perpetual rain of radioactive fallout from pole to pole. Farmers, governments, and homeowners sprayed the new miracle insecticide DDT and other chemicals with abandon. Scientists raised warnings, but when in 1958 Carson began researching the issue even she was shocked. She embarked on a crusade, despite a diagnosis of breast cancer. Operations and radiation treatment slowed but could not stop its spread, and she worked through growing pain and exhaustion. Her first crusade would be her last. Famous and beloved, Carson called upon friends and connections in government and around the world for evidence that no other researcher could have compiled from such scattered and even hidden places.

Silent Spring came out in 1962. Despite the overwhelming scientific evidence that backed the book's argument, it was as a moral indictment that the book succeeded so powerfully and outraged the chemical and agricultural industry so thoroughly. Again, Carson specifically named only scientists and biologists, as they respected and studied nature, and left unnamed the corporations and their researchers. She assailed industry men just as Jacobs attacked arrogant brute-force experts. Greedy corporations oversold dangerous products. Entomologists from the "Neanderthal age of science" threw large amounts of deadly chemicals at a single or minor pest, regardless of wider ecological effects. Researchers blinded by arrogance and desire to conquer nature concocted chemicals not found in nature, poisons undreamed of by the infamous Borgias, "elixirs of death" "brewed in laboratories" to which pests acquired immunity and returned in greater numbers than before. These chemicals entered human bodies to cause illness, cancer, and death. Like a good revival sermon, *Silent Spring* ended with an altar call, to accept salvation now or risk eternal damnation. We have a choice, said Carson, to choose to work in harmony with nature, using biological solutions based on understanding of living organisms and their ecological relationships, or to continue down the path of arrogance that leads to destruction of both nature and ourselves.

Silent Spring awakened a generation to the environmental crisis, from Secretary of the Interior Stewart Udall to teenaged Al Gore and millions more across the nation. It also raised a firestorm. The chemical industry launched a counterattack belittling Carson's qualifications and her understanding of complicated questions that only male scientists really understood correctly. President John F. Kennedy's council of scientific advisors studied its claims and vindicated it. Congress held hearings and Carson testified. With diminishing strength, she determinedly defended her book until shortly before her death in 1964. Still powerful over half a century later, *Silent Spring* remains in print and retains a firm reputation as one of the century's most important books.

A dozen years after Carson's death, a young lapsed Presbyterian woman from western Pennsylvania stepped onto the literary scene with a book that revived the wonder in Carson's earlier work at the miracle of creation. In the late 1960s and early 1970s, Meta Ann Doak Dillard lived with her then-husband in a house at the foot of Tinker Mountain, Virginia, where a small creek ran at the edge of the lot. She read a book of nature writing and decided she could do a better job. She did. Annie Dillard's *Pilgrim at Tinker Creek* won the 1975 Pulitzer Prize for Nonfiction. Her many subsequent books revived and modernized that Presbyterian avocation, exploring the evidence of the attributes of God in nature, and have won many awards and much critical praise.

Born in 1945 in Pittsburgh, Dillard attended Presbyterian Church and spent four summers at Presbyterian summer camp. Her interests tended toward science, mixed with a love of literature and art. Dillard approached nature with wonder, but soberly, with profound questions about pain in the natural world that little troubled Muir or Jeffers. Where Jeffers marveled at God's excessive production of beauty, Dillard wondered at the immense fecundity of life, amazed that God wasted so many spores, seeds, larvae, and offspring to produce so few adults.[70] Muir's biblical starting point was Saint Paul's understanding of "the invisible things" of God in "the things that are made." Dillard was more intrigued by the problem of Job, who questioned God about pain in the world and whom God answered from the whirlwind with four chapters of mysteries of the natural world.[71] Her three best works grapple with this issue: *Pilgrim at Tinker Creek, Holy the Firm* (1977) and *For the Time Being* (1999). In each, she seems to find the search for God in nature as a quest freighted with irony. Her path leads her through nature but bypasses questions of the human relationship to nature and the environment. In this, perhaps she most resembles Thoreau, to whom she has been often compared and whose work she analyzed in her master's thesis.[72] In her works as in Calvin's, humans continue to go to nature, where God communicates himself, but unlike Calvin, she wonders what exactly God is communicating.

Presbyterians and Environmentalism

Modern American environmentalism has been remarkable among world environmental and Green movements for its vitality, power, and intense moral critique, which to a large degree were gifts of the Presbyterian tradition. Emerging from an immigrant church concerned with doctrine and the creation in all its aspects, Presbyterians took the conservation movement from Connecticut-Valley Congregationalists and nationalized it. Presbyterian women later threw the gates of environmentalism wide open

and created a broader and more comprehensive view of ecological problems that included humans and human communities. This wider, more
humane conception of environmentalism has appealed to people from
many religious traditions.

After 1946 Presbyterians rarely sat in national office, but others gladly
did the work. None of them was ever as identified with environmentalism in the popular mind as was John Muir, Theodore Roosevelt, Gifford
Pinchot, David Brower, Rachel Carson, Edward Abbey, or even John Denver.
They lacked the Knox fire and brimstone, that "furious righteousness"
that made these figures popular heroes. During the environmental era
between 1961 and 1981, the most activist Secretary of the Interior, Stewart
Udall, was Mormon. Of the three presidents whose administrations put
in place the framework of modern environmental laws, agencies, and policies, Lyndon B. Johnson was raised Disciples of Christ, Richard M. Nixon
Quaker (although his environmentalism was politically motivated[73]), and
Jimmy Carter Southern Baptist. The environmental leader of the Senate,
Edmund Muskie, was Catholic. Senator Gaylord Nelson, who instigated
the first Earth Day in 1970, was Methodist. And so it goes, down the list of
national officials, with not one Presbyterian. Instead, Presbyterians in the
mode of the prophets called the people to righteousness, preaching the
word and raising a righteous anger. They did not perhaps cause riots or
bring monarchs to weep as Knox did, but they did inspire a major political
and historical movement.

Presbyterian culture also gave American environmentalism some of
its historical limitations. John Muir was a forerunner here as well. As biographer Donald Worster has pointed out, although Muir became a commercial farmer in the 1880s, he looked with a jaundiced eye on the work
of his in-laws, the Strenzels, and his friends the Carrs to foster agricultural
communities.[74] Because Presbyterianism lacked a vision of a righteous
community, it never presented a coherent plan for a just and ecological
society such as the one Congregationalists once envisioned. Presbyterians
were quick to condemn sin, especially avarice and oppression of the poor,
but could suggest no solution besides prohibition of the sin or reform of
the sinner. Even the perennial Socialist candidate for president during the
1930s and 1940s, the ordained Presbyterian minister Norman Thomas,
advocated policies that tended more toward righteousness than ideological consistency. Jacobs so harshly criticized planners and showed so little
appreciation for the need for infrastructure and some degree of order
that *Life and Death of American Cities* shows up on libertarian booklists.[75]

Carson focused so intently on the ecological webs in nature that *Silent Spring* offered no critique of capitalism or society that might remedy the chemical problem at its root.[76] Where there is no vision, the people perish.

During a century and a half, passionate, committed Presbyterian advocates for nature accomplished an enormous number of achievements and victories. Today, however, the forces of avarice and greed are more powerful and organized than ever before. Who will oppose them? Presbyterians are vanishing. Divisive controversies over ordination of women and homosexuals and other issues of the culture wars—a term coined by fundamentalist Pennsylvania Presbyterian Francis Schaeffer—cause fractures, schisms, and defections. The church cannot staunch the loss of its young people. Presbyterianism has fallen from above 6 percent of the American population a century ago to below 3 percent today. It will never again be the cultural force it once was. Environmentalists of the coming century must look elsewhere for passionate leadership.

Nature and New England's Outsiders

Hunter Mountain, Twilight

On a sunny summer morning in 1844, twenty-year-old Sanford Gifford stepped out of his home in Hudson, New York, with a troubled mind. He headed south out of town and climbed to the summit of Mount Merino. A scenic panorama spread before him. Wooded Red Hill stretched from the southwest flank of the mountain toward a magnificent view of the widening Hudson River sliding gently by the Catskill and Shawagunk Mountains. To the west Gifford looked down on sailboats gliding silently up and down the sparkling river. On the far bank lay the picturesque village of Catskill. Beyond it the ancient Catskill Mountains rose wave upon wave to the blue bulk of 4,000-foot Hunter Mountain on the horizon. Gifford rested in the shade of a tree and pondered. He had finished his third semester at Brown University. His father, the prosperous owner of a foundry, was pressing him for decisions about a career. Gifford felt that "any of the pursuits which had been suggested were good enough for him, but that he was good for nothing for any of them." As he gazed across the river at Catskill village, one house stood out as if surrounded by a halo—the home and studio of Thomas Cole. At that moment, Gifford decided to be a painter.[1]

Gifford so admired Cole's landscapes that not long into the course of his art study he painted landscapes only, which critics soon took notice of. In 1855 he sailed to Europe, as Cole had, to study and paint. He puzzled over J. M. W. Turner's luminous later paintings, so different from the style of the Hudson River School. Gifford's conversations with John

Ruskin, Turner's champion, transformed his art. His landscapes now displayed Turneresque concern for the effects of atmosphere and light. Gifford's nature scenes, however, did not imitate Turner subjects, nor did they resemble the grand unpeopled wilderness scenes of his friend Albert Bierstadt. Gifford portrayed rural scenes in a day when the United States was rapidly industrializing and its cities growing. That smoky, crowded, bustling world appeared in Gifford's art not at all. The nature he painted was conservative and nostalgic. Although of New England ancestry, he did not paint individuals who clearly belonged to a community the way that Frederic Church did in *West Rock, New Haven*. He painted atmospheric effects more to represent nature truly and not, like William Keith, to invest his images with spiritual or mystical meaning.

Gifford's attitudes typified the deep-rooted dissenter values of his Baptist upbringing. The work of Baptist-bred landscape artists, nature writers, agrarians, and natural scientists often contain elements of conservatism, nostalgia, individualism, and aversion to mysticism. Joined before 1820 by Quakers, Episcopalians, and Methodists, Baptists were New England's most vocal dissenters from Puritan communalism. Baptist evangelists discovered that these values struck a chord in the South, where Baptists quickly multiplied. Their outsider-born religious attitudes survived and thrived and emerged to create a sort of outsider environmentalism in the twentieth century.[2]

Hunter Mountain, Twilight, perhaps Gifford's best work (Figure 7.1, see color insert), in many ways gives expression to Baptist attitudes concerning the human relationship to nature. In the fall of 1865, having served in the Union Army in the Civil War, Gifford and Worthington Whittredge went on a sketching trip to the Catskills. From those sketches Gifford painted *Hunter Mountain, Twilight* over the winter in his studio in New York's Tenth Street Studio Building, where friends Whittredge, Bierstadt, Frederic Church, and Jervis McEntee also had studios. In the painting, in the shadow of one of the tallest mountains in the Catskills, a farmer at the close of an autumn day herds cattle home through a stark landscape of rocks, stumps, and scattered logs. They cross a small meadow that trees no longer shade. A beckoning fire gleams from a window of a log house nestled within the twilit gloom of remnant virgin forest. Most of the trees are gone, cut to supply hemlock bark to tanneries for their tannin. The cleared forest of the middle distance and smoke rising in the valley from aptly named Tannersville make plain the environmental toll of one of New York's largest tanneries. The family will eke out a living with a few dairy cows on rocky, hilly land by selling milk to the population of the growing industrial cities of the Hudson Valley—like foundry workers working for Gifford and Sons—until the thin mountain soil is too worn out to even support cattle profitably.[3] Pervading the painting is the Baptist worldview of individual choices and interiorized spirituality. Despite the Turneresque light, Gifford was not painting a lesson in natural theology. To him the moral and spiritual value of a landscape lay in its beauty. *Hunter Mountain, Twilight* suggests no solution and envisions no sustainable society or harmonious relation to nature. The family has settled in cutover land, not virgin soil in the wilderness. No New England village offers comfort, cheer, church, or society. No community regulates the use of the land and forest for the common good and future generations. Only the snug, warm home intimated a hope that a proper relation to nature might emerge from the hearts and minds of the farmer and his family.[4]

Gifford's patron James W. Pinchot swiftly bought *Hunter Mountain, Twilight*. If the picture warned that, as Cole feared, through barbaric ravages of the ax we would one day no longer be in Eden, the message was familiar to both Gifford and Pinchot. Quite possibly the painting symbolized regret for artist and patron both. Gifford's grandfather had been a tanner, as had his father before joining the Hudson foundry in 1823. Both tanneries and foundries consumed prodigious quantities of timber. James Pinchot's wealth originally derived from razing many square miles of Pennsylvania hemlocks.[5] Pinchot's remorse and determination to atone and, what is more, to also get his countrymen to atone for the ongoing, heedless, and profit-mad rush to cut down American forests led to a passion for advancing modern forest management methods in the country.[6]

Pinchot was a close friend. On August 11, 1865, on the eve of the Catskill sketching trip, Pinchot named his first son Gifford and asked Sanford Gifford to be the godfather. The career of the painting was bound up with the life of Gifford's namesake. The imposing 54-inch-wide *Hunter Mountain, Twilight* was permanently embedded in the wall above the mantle of the Pinchot home in Washington, DC. Gifford Pinchot of course would grow up to become the nation's most famous forester. Not until after his and his wife's deaths would the painting come down from the wall where it had hung for most of the Chief Forester's life.[7]

Despite the affection of both forester and his father for *Hunter Mountain, Twilight*, Gifford was no conservationist. This landscape and some of his others implied regret for abuses but conveyed no unambiguous moral critique. The new home of a pioneer family in the wilderness was a favorite theme with Gifford, just as it had been with Cole, Church, and other Hudson River School painters. He painted many landscapes with cabins and stumps that implied no judgment of the pioneer. They presented a neutral or positive view of those who, like one of his brothers in Wisconsin, carved homes and bountiful farms out of unproductive wilderness. At the unveiling of *Hunter Mountain, Twilight* at the National Academy exhibition of 1866, critics took no notice of the painting's cutover foreground.[8] Perhaps they were too accustomed to cabins and stumps to read any message in them.

Baptist Nature

Gifford's New England ancestors were Baptists and Quakers, not Puritans. Both groups rejected the ideal of a community church in a communal order governed by conservation measures for the common good. Their theologies revolved around individuals' spiritual states. The Puritan ideal of a Christian commonwealth contrasted with the Baptist vision of a commonwealth of converted Christians. John Burroughs's father underwent a classical conversion experience: "Father 'experienced religion' in his early manhood and became a member of the Old School [Calvinist] Baptist Church. To become members of that church it was not enough that you wanted to lead a better life and serve God faithfully; you must have had a certain religious experience, have gone through a crisis as Paul did, been convicted of sin in some striking manner, and have descended into the depths of humiliation and despair, and then, when all seemed lost, have heard the voice of forgiveness and acceptance and felt indeed that you were now a child of God."[9] Baptists linked the centrality of conversion to Christ's command to evangelize, because only universal conversion of every individual could create Christian communities.

Originally Baptists branched off from Puritanism. They retained Puritans' radical Biblicism and congregationalism but rejected state intrusion in the church and church meddling in government or society. Baptists found no Scriptural warrant for tax-supported churches or for church-led advancement of society. Gospel purity required that churches be free of obligation to the state. Baptists refused to recognize Congregational society in covenant with God and saw only individuals in need of regeneration and baptism. If Congregational churches gathered the community, Baptist churches gathered the converted. Congregationalist imposition of a godly order according to God's will and Biblical plan provoked Baptist resentment of government's suppression of individual conscience as a violation of Scripture. The New England Puritan establishment regarded Baptists as dangerous radicals and forced them to the edges of New England or harassed them. They long had no presence in Connecticut at all.[10] The first Baptist church was founded in 1639 in non-Congregationalist Rhode Island, where Baptists and others established Brown University in 1765. Drawn together by persecution, independent of any other congregation or religious authority, Baptists stubbornly championed principles of complete separation of church and state and of freedom of individual conscience.[11]

The Congregational vision for the nation in "America the Beautiful" makes an instructive foil to the patriotic song "My Country 'Tis of Thee," a Baptist tribute from the individual to God and country. The former expresses the divine beauty of the fruitful landscape and a vision for a moral, orderly society in "alabaster cities." Baptist minister Samuel Francis Smith wrote "My Country 'Tis of Thee" in 1831 while a student at Calvinist Andover Theological Seminary. Mixing religion and patriotism, every verse celebrates freedom and liberty. One verse honors filial piety— "Land where my fathers died / Land of the Pilgrim's pride"—and another the love of the land—"I love thy rocks and rills / Thy woods and templed hills." Aside from this oblique allusion to New England's steepled landscape, the lyrics say nothing of community or of "self-control" and "law." The Congregational God of "America the Beautiful" crowns the nation's good with brotherhood. The Baptist God of "My Country 'Tis of Thee" is "author of liberty." The two most important words in Smith's religious and patriotic vocabulary were "liberty" and "freedom"—that is, freedom from government restraint.[12]

Hence Baptists and other religious outsiders developed ideas about nature and the environment at odds with those of Congregationalists. Although they acknowledged the presence of God in his works, they spoke mostly of his power in the salvation of sinners. Baptist religious life had no room for mystical experience of God in nature. As they saw matters, the facts of inerrant Scripture needed no corroboration from the Book of Nature. Baptists constructed what they thought of as a scientific method of Scripture interpretation that logically ordered Biblical texts to produce truth. This cold rationalism tempered the hot emotionalism of Baptist sermons and conversions. Unsurprisingly, then, former Baptists have turned more easily to a scientific than Transcendental worldview. Emerson's doctrine of self-reliance and his exaltation of individual genius resonated with many Baptists. His principle of mystical union with the Over-Soul in Nature did not.[13] Exalting the individual in the face of hostile society, Emerson had much in common with spiritual outsiders like Baptists and Quakers.[14] Agricultural improvement and proper care of woodlots fell to individual responsibility. Good converted Christians would exercise godly stewardship of their possessions. Baptists refused to look to the magistrate in these matters. Consequently, the Baptist church has fostered very few major advocates of conservation through government regulation.

As Calvinism's appeal to young Congregationalists and Baptists waned, many in Gifford's generation sought a spiritual life to replace predestinarian Christianity. Emerson pointed the way. At Brown, Gifford read Emerson, Carlyle, and Coleridge. He surely responded to Emerson's ringing calls for self-reliance and for an American art and literature and his insistence on the role of the artist and poet to translate nature's truths to society. He did not adopt Emersonian spirituality. The successive shocks of Charles Darwin's *Origin of Species* in 1859, the Civil War, and the Depression of the 1870s made many regard Transcendentalism and all spiritual optimism as a hollow sham.[15] Gifford joined the New York church of Octavius B. Frothingham, president of the Free Religious Association. Founded in 1867 by those for whom even Unitarianism was too conservative, the association regarded all religions as equal and accepted the conclusions of science.[16] Emerson helped make Gifford a seeker but not a painter of sacred landscapes of the spirit.

For their part, Quakers shook off the gloomy implications of the doctrine of Original Sin and looked for the divine inner light in each person. Somber optimists and gregarious individualists, these exiles from the house of Calvin were more interested in people than in unpeopled wild nature. Aside from important eighteenth-century naturalists like John and William Bartram and minor figures like Anna Botsford Comstock of the nature-study movement, the history of conservation and environmentalism counts no prominent Quaker authors or activists.

Burroughs, Baptist Birder

Around the time of Gifford's transformative conversations with Ruskin, Emerson's essays were converting a young Baptist who would absorb Emerson to the bone, far more deeply than Gifford, and who would become the best-loved popular nature writer of his time, ahead of Henry David Thoreau and John Muir. John Burroughs's Connecticut ancestors had migrated to the Catskills after the Revolution. In 1795 his grandfather Eden settled in Roxbury, thirty miles west of Tannersville, where his father was born. Burroughs was also born in Roxbury, in 1837, a year before Muir and Keith. The Burroughs family was Old School Baptist.[17] Yearning for faith and the touch of God's spirit, in the spring of 1856 Burroughs went to a camp-meeting on the banks of the Delaware River. The preacher's words carried him away. He stepped forward to be baptized and came up from immersion shouting hallelujah and praising Jesus. But he climbed dripping out of the Delaware and made his way home disappointed. He had asked God to "take possession" of him but felt "nothing."[18]

Instead, Emerson would take possession of Burroughs. Later that year, he saw Emerson's books in a bookstore. "I looked into them and said to myself: 'Why, this is good! This is what I want.' And I bought the whole set," he recalled. "For a long time afterward I lived, moved, and had my being in those books. . . . I kept my Emerson close at hand and read him everywhere. I would go up under the trees of the sap-bush there at home and read and be moved to tears by the extreme beauty and eloquence of his words. For years all that I wrote was Emersonian. It was as if I was dipped in Emerson." In 1860 he submitted his first major essay to *Atlantic Monthly*, which editor James Russell Lowell initially suspected was a plagiarized Emerson essay. Burroughs recalled, "I quickly saw that this kind of thing would not do for me. I must get on ground of my own. I must get this Emersonian musk out of my garments at all hazards. I concluded to bury my garments in the earth, as it were, and see what my native soil would do toward drawing it out. So I took to writing on all manner of rural themes—sugar-making, cows, haying, stone walls."[19] Burroughs became a writer of birds and natural history by chance. In 1863, he came across the celebrated double-elephant folio of John James Audubon's *The Birds of America*. Audubon ignited an inextinguishable passion for birds.[20] His embrace of Darwin diluted his Transcendentalism even more. He published his first nature essay, "The Return of the Birds," in 1863 and proudly placed it first in *Wake-Robin*, his first book.

Burroughs's essays make it plain that for all his love of Emerson, the Baptist-bred farmer kept his feet planted on solid ground. Emerson's essays send the soul soaring into the empyrean blue; Burroughs's muddy the boots. Burroughs felt that Emerson seemed never to go out among the people or take notice of everyday things and doings. As for Thoreau, he was too moralistic and antisocial. Burroughs liked best Thoreau's wilder, less philosophical *Maine Woods*.[21] Burroughs loved nature for its personal pleasures. He had a genius for entering into the lives of the birds without sentimentality or moralizing. Burroughs treated nature sympathetically but pragmatically. He killed snakes that threatened birds. He hunted, especially the woodchucks that lent their name to his cabin Woodchuck Lodge. Like other scientists of the day, he killed the birds he admired, mainly to examine them scientifically or to preserve for study, although later he preferred field glasses to the gun. Burroughs's nature essays were celebrations of the local. His favorite nature writer was Gilbert White, the pastor of Selborne in England, who in his classic 1789 *The Natural History of Selborne* investigated the animals and plants of his local parish. Even though he did not discover White until he was forty, Burroughs in many ways was White's American counterpart, the ecologist of the local. Surely part of Burroughs's great popularity and appeal was his "invitation" (the name of the last chapter of his first book) to his readers to open their eyes to the wonders of nature around their own homes and neighborhoods.

Burroughs's huge popularity also owed much to the overt nostalgia of his writings.[22] Homesick and far from his native New York mountains, he began writing while a clerk in Washington, DC, to recreate the familiar wildlife of home. After a short career as a bank examiner, he retreated to rural life. In 1873, as soon as he had the money, Burroughs bought a farm, which he named Riverby, on the banks of the Hudson south of Kingston and raised grapes. In 1895 he added a rustic writing cabin, Slabsides, and in 1910 when visitors grew too many, made a farmhouse near family land in Roxbury into a writing retreat. Even at the beginning of Burroughs's writing career, the world that he grew up in was declining and vanished entirely by the time he died in 1921. The opening of cheap and fertile lands to the west along with railroads and steamships to bring crops to market undercut Catskill farmers just as they did New England townsmen. Cheap California grapes put even Burroughs out of business. Nostalgia attracted some of his most famous fans, to whom Burroughs's essays called to mind the rural America of their youth. Financier Jay Gould, a friend of Burroughs's childhood, owned a well-thumbed set of Burroughs's works.[23] His essays delighted industrialist Henry Ford, who befriended him in 1912 and did him many favors.[24]

This was same rural world that New England Congregationalists were trying to save, yet Burroughs did not ascend the pulpit and preach salvation. Marsh's *Man and Nature* did not stir him to action. He responded weakly to calls for moral, social, or political reform.[25] In Baptist fashion, Burroughs sought no government help for farms, forests, or mountains.

In June 1866, while *Hunter Mountain, Twilight* with its hemlock stumps was hanging in the galleries of the National Academy of Design's annual exhibition, Burroughs's "In the Hemlocks" appeared in *Atlantic Monthly*. It portrayed in words the same abused landscape and also did not comment or moralize. Burroughs described the rich natural world awaiting the intrepid explorer of remnant hemlock forests, then added, "Their history is of an heroic cast. Ravished and torn by the tanner in his thirst for bark, preyed upon by the lumberman, assaulted and beaten back by the settler, still their spirit has never been broken, their energies never paralyzed."[26] Three years later in "Birch Browsings," Burroughs noted without judgment how Catskills tanneries had eliminated all but a remnant of the hemlock forests.[27] Burroughs surely knew that childhood friend Jay Gould had cut down a Pennsylvania hemlock forest for his first business venture, a tannery. Yet never did he ever raise any greater reproach than Gifford implied in *Hunter Mountain*.

Burroughs was an early member of the Audubon Society of New York, but he was no conservation activist. He knew both of birds' value to farmers and of their indiscriminate and unconscionable slaughter, but he only occasionally decried overhunting of passenger pigeons or songbirds.[28] Burroughs also noted the slaughter of wildlife. "Deer are still met with, though they are becoming scarcer every year," he commented. "Last winter near seventy head were killed on the Beaver Kill alone. I heard of one wretch, who, finding the deer snowbound, walked up to them on his snowshoes, and one morning before breakfast slaughtered six, leaving their carcasses where they fell. There are traditions of persons having been smitten blind or senseless when about to commit some heinous offense, but the fact that this villain escaped without some such visitation throws discredit on all such stories."[29] A Congregationalist or Presbyterian would have used such a tale as an opportunity to call for rules, regulations, and prohibitions to control the immoral, wasteful destruction of wildlife and timber. Burroughs merely bemoaned the absence of divine retribution.

Immersed in the beauty of the long-inhabited Catskills, Burroughs did not believe the works of fallen man sullied the landscape. Human presence could be beneficial. He observed that farms and settlements created habitat for birds and animals: "Yet, notwithstanding the birds have come to look upon man as their natural enemy, there can be little doubt that civilization is on the whole favorable to their increase and perpetuity, especially to the smaller species. With man, come flies and moths, and insects of all kinds in greater abundance; new plants and weeds are introduced, and, with the clearing up of the country, are sowed broadcast over the land."[30] Late in life his friendship with John Muir did increase his appreciation for the wilder places. The old Baptist however was skeptical of Muir's religious language. "Mr. Muir is a nature-lover of a fine type, one of the best the country has produced," Burroughs wrote in 1912. "But it may be the reader gets a little tired at times of the frequent recurrence in his pages of a certain note—a note which doubtless dates from his inherited Scottish Presbyterianism. . . . Wild nature . . . very often seems on her way to or from the kirk. All his streams and waterfalls and avalanches and storm-buffeted trees sing songs, or hymns, or psalms, or rejoice in some other proper Presbyterian manner."[31] Muir had tried to "baptize" Burroughs in wilderness, but the experience left Burroughs almost as unaffected as his Baptist baptism had.

Man and nature harmonized, and if some effects of human activity in the landscape were lamentable, they did not call for vigorous campaigns of condemnation or new laws and regulations. Muir's great crusade against the dam in Hetch Hetchy Valley in Yosemite National Park left Burroughs indifferent, and he rebuffed Muir's attempt to enlist him in its defense.[32] In the most political act of Burroughs's life, he traveled with Ernest Thompson Seton to Washington in 1913, at Ford's request and at his expense, to successfully lobby two senators who were blocking passage of the Weeks-McLean Act. This landmark bill, sponsored by two New England congressmen, regulated the hunting of migratory birds and banned importation of wild-bird feathers to decorate fashionable ladies' hats.[33] Burroughs played his part and the bill passed, but politics was a game he played rarely.

The Baptist mind imposes on its children significant limitations on action on behalf of the environment that Burroughs was not immune to, particularly an apolitical and almost fatalistic attitude toward human damage to the environment. It is a measure of the importance to Burroughs of people over landscape that, quite unusually for a famous nature writer, only about a third of his books and essays deal with the natural world. Burroughs wrote literary criticism, philosophical pieces especially about science and religion, and travel essays. He published important essays in national magazines about the great intellectual and literary men of his day, notably Emerson, Walt Whitman, and Scottish author Thomas Carlyle. Perhaps because of his engagement with contemporary human affairs, his nostalgic farm pieces, and his backyard natural history, this once popular writer is nearly forgotten today.

Novelist Willa Cather wrote from a similar point of view. She fatal-istically if sadly accepted the passing of traditional farmers who care-fully manured the soil and preserved wildlife habitat. No doubt Cather's childhood amid Virginia's green mountains and valleys and youth on the flat grasslands of Nebraska prompted her nevertheless to support tree-planting and urge farmers to preserve such native trees as cotton-woods that they cut to make way for more wheat fields.[34] She lectured and wrote in defense of native flora and fauna. No writer of nature essays or conservation activist, Cather once sardonically defined "a naturalist of the old school" as "some old gentlemen from the more inaccessible parts of New England, who could still recall Thoreau and Audubon, and who took nature as seriously as Burroughs."[35] Cather, like Burroughs, was skeptical that nature preached sermons and like Gifford thought the beauty of the landscape was God's beauty. "In nature God does not teach morals," she wrote in 1894. "He never limits or interferes with beauty. His laws are the laws of beauty, and all the natural forces work together to produce it. The nightingale's song is not moral; it is perfectly pagan in its unrestrained passion. The Mediterranean at noonday is not moral, the forests of the Ganges have no sermons in them. God's nature is just a great artistic creation, and the zones and climes are only moods of a Divine Artist."[36]

Born in 1873 to Baptists in the Shenandoah Valley, Cather lived in Red Cloud, Nebraska, after 1883.[37] After a stint as a magazine writer and editor, she found a mentor in local-color author Sarah Orne Jewett. Cather published her first novel in 1912, the first in a series of best-selling elegiac novels of life in harmony with nature on farms of the Great Plains, which won her a Pulitzer Prize in 1923. Her masterful prairie trilogy about nineteenth-century Nebraska, *O Pioneers!* of 1913, *The Song of the Lark* of 1915, and *My Ántonia* of 1918, portrayed charac-ters whose fundamental decency was reflected in their care for the land. Deeply pessimistic after World War I, Cather believed modern capital-ist values had prevailed over love of the land. Like Burroughs, Cather never in her work suggested social, political, or environmental reform. Instead, she evoked nostalgia for the disappearing farms of her youth. Conservative socially and politically, "she hated Franklin D. Roosevelt and the New Deal and big government," noted Joan Acocella.[38] Neither she nor Burroughs was going to reform the world. It was up to decent, moral individuals to do what they could to brighten their little corners of the universe.[39]

New England's Environmental Outsider Hero

Part of Burroughs's literary legacy was to keep the name of Thoreau before the reading public's eye in a time when Thoreau's reputation was at its low point. He published three essays on Thoreau in the 1880s.[40] Still, Burroughs had a mixed opinion of Thoreau. Thoreau's prickly attitude put him off and his weaknesses as a naturalist bothered him. It also annoyed him that people regularly compared him to Thoreau. In 1876, Henry James reviewed Burroughs's *Winter Sunshine* for *Nation* and called him "a sort of reduced but also more humorous, more available, and more sociable Thoreau."[41] William Sloane Kennedy preferred Burroughs, commenting in 1897 that Burroughs "has abundance of humor; Thoreau had very little. Thoreau is ever pounding the pulpit; Burroughs never preaches,—except by indirection, which is the best way after all. He has little of the *sæva indignatio* of the brave Concord thinker and reformer; but you feel that in the make-up of this gay angler and forest roamer, bird-lover and horticulturist, there is an ample supply of that moral fire hidden somewhere out of sight. . . . He makes you in love with life: Thoreau makes you dissatisfied with it."[42] After Dallas Lore Sharp published an essay in *Atlantic Monthly* in 1910 comparing Thoreau unfavorably with Burroughs, Burroughs protested, "Thoreau is nearer the stars than I am. I may be more human, but he is as certainly more divine. His moral and ethical value I think is much greater, and he has a heroic quality that I cannot approach."[43] Today often contrasted with Muir, in his lifetime Burroughs's inescapable rival was Thoreau.

Thoreau was no Baptist, which explains much about the contrasts with Burroughs that James and Kennedy pointed out. Yet like a Baptist or a Quaker he was one of New England's outsiders, and today in environmental literature his name is better known than any other outsider environmentalist. Thoreau was an ethnic outsider: his grandfather John Thoreau, a Huguenot immigrant, married a Scottish Quaker. He was a political outsider: many of his mother's Loyalist family fled after the Revolution. He was a religious outsider: the Thoreaus had seceded from the Concord church when it hired a Unitarian minister and joined a Calvinist Congregational Church. He was a social outsider: his father was a humble artisan. Finally, he was an economic outsider: his family had been in poverty before his father began a successful business making pencils. Marginality was the theme of Thoreau's life. Sent to Harvard at great financial sacrifice to his family, the shy student's rustic manners and his greenish homemade suit stood out among higher-class undergraduates, clad in black.

Thoreau shared with Baptists the values of fierce individualism, alienation from politics, and resistance to laws that punished conscience. Fitting for a descendant of Loyalists, Quakers, and Huguenots, who faced persecution for conscience' sake, in "Civil Disobedience" of 1849 he urged people to resist unjust laws and overthrow them by filling up jails through civil disobedience. He spent a night in jail in 1846 for not paying taxes to a government that supported slavery and in 1838 would have been jailed if someone had not paid his church tax for him. Baptists had preceded him. In 1773, in the nation's first campaign of civil disobedience, they planned to refuse to pay church taxes and fill up the jails. The coming Revolution distracted authorities, who jailed no one, and the campaign fizzled.[44] Thoreau also rejected the Puritan ideal of the orderly, moral community as an imposition from above and an obstacle to self-improvement. Transformation of individual lives would solve the problem of lives lived "in quiet desperation" better than any law, regulation, or state or private agency. Ironically for such an environmental icon, Thoreau ignored Congregational programs of conservation. "The Bean-Field" chapter in Walden portrayed agriculture as a vehicle for self-culture and a moral problem without scientific, technological, or government solutions. Farmers drawn into commercial agriculture became slaves to their farms. In Thoreau's version of Emersonian self-reliance, New Englanders would grow their own grain for the flour in their bread. Of forest conservation or public parks or nature preservation, Walden said not a word.[45]

Outsiderness permeates Thoreau's classic Walden. The acerbic first chapter, "Economy," reads like a screed against all those, even Emerson (or perhaps especially Emerson), against whom he bore an outsider's resentment. A skillful builder, he avowed that students would gain a fuller education if they built their own quarters at college, an implicit dig at his less-handy classmates. An inheritance, possessions, and even civilization, he claimed, were encumbrances to the soul. Men were slaves to their work ethic and to their tools. Age had no wisdom from experience worth imparting. Walking was superior to riding the train. Trade was a curse. On the other hand, lest the reader think him only a skilled handyman, in the chapter "Reading" Thoreau posed as an educated man of culture and snobbishly insisted that everyone should read Greek and Roman classics in the original languages.

Young Thoreau had talent at engineering but yearned for a poet's life. His neighbor Emerson took him as his protégé, but Thoreau began to imitate his mentor just as Burroughs would. Emerson noted in his journal, "I am very familiar with all his thoughts,—they are my own quite originally drest."[46] Thoreau retreated to Walden Pond to write *A Week on the Concord and Merrimack Rivers* as a tribute to his beloved brother, dead of lockjaw in 1842. Emerson praised *A Week* until its total failure in 1849 began an estrangement between the two. Thoreau's accomplishments never measured up to the potential that Emerson saw in him. Thoreau often thought himself a failure.

In writing *Walden*, Thoreau too got the Emersonian musk out of his garments by burying them in the earth. Its chapters trace his Burroughs-like transition from Transcendentalist to naturalist. About 1849 Thoreau began a scientific self-education, reading books about science and scientific discovery. The works of Alexander von Humboldt and Charles Darwin's *Voyage of the Beagle* profoundly affected him. He less and less looked for the moral meaning of nature and more and more measured and catalogued facts, like Humboldt, looking for patterns. The final chapter, "Spring," was a thoroughly Humboldtian meditation on the parallels between patterns in thawing sandbanks and the structure of leaves. After *Walden*'s publication in 1854, he continued to measure, catalogue, and observe, filling his notebooks with the obsessive minutiae of natural history that have perplexed scholars. In 1859, he read the life of Bernard Palissy while working on manuscripts on the dispersal of seeds and the succession of forest trees and preparing sections in *The Maine Woods* about the value of forests and the dangers of deforestation. Unfortunately, his death from tuberculosis in 1862 at age 44 cut short his scientific studies.[47]

Thoreau's solitary sojourn on the banks of Walden Pond will forever symbolize the individual's search for meaning and fulfillment in accordance with conscience. That outsider naturalist perspective that put people off in the nineteenth century would attract them in the twentieth. In parallel with the Presbyterian shift from government leaders to independent prophet-preachers, an "outsider" environmentalist mode replaced the old "insider" conservation ethic. Thoreau's reputation rose spectacularly. During the countercultural 1960s and 1970s Thoreau was canonized as the greatest saint in the environmentalist pantheon.[48]

Waldens for All

In 1954, one hundred years exactly after *Walden* came out, Scott and Helen Knothe Nearing published *Living the Good Life: How to Live Sanely and Simply in a Troubled World*. Often called the *Walden* of the twentieth century, *Living the Good Life* did owe much to Thoreau. It quoted him eight times and drew much of its spirit from him.[49] No one could miss how the book's purpose closely echoed Thoreauvian simple living:

> We left the city with three objectives in mind. *The first was economic.* We sought to make a depression-free living, as independent as possible of the commodity and labor markets, which could not be interfered with by employers, whether businessmen, politicians or educational administrators. *Our second aim was hygienic.* We wanted to maintain and improve our health. We knew that the pressures of city life were exacting, and we sought a simple basis of well-being where contact with the earth, and home-grown organic food, would play a large part. *Our third objective was social and ethical.* We desired to liberate and dissociate ourselves, as much as possible, from the cruder forms of exploitation: the plunder of the planet; the slavery of man and beast; the slaughter of men in war, and of animals for food.[50]

Living the Good Life must rank among the most erudite homesteading manuals ever written. Copious quotations from Burroughs and Frank Lloyd Wright illustrated the section on building a home appropriate to the site. It cited agricultural literature dating as far back as Jared Eliot and John Evelyn in the discussion of how to live and to raise food, with lines from Emerson and Lin Yutang thrown in for good measure.

Living the Good Life was fundamentally Baptist. Born in 1883 to a prosperous family in a Pennsylvania mining town, Scott Nearing studied to be a Baptist minister and joined a prominent Philadelphia Baptist church. Then its minister, bowing to political pressure, abandoned a campaign against corruption. Shocked and disillusioned, Nearing concluded the church was "an instrument of reaction and corruption" and embraced political radicalism.[51] He took a position as professor of economics at the University of Pennsylvania Wharton School of Business. In a celebrated academic-freedom case, educational administrators (perhaps the ones he was seeking independence from in *The Good Life*) fired him in 1915. In the 1920s and 1930s Nearing rose to become a leftist leader, but with his independence of mind he bounced from one socialist and communist organization to another. His socialism had more than a hint of Baptist to it. Biographer John A. Saltmarsh noted that it "provided a conceptual framework for criticizing industrial capitalism and envisioning the construction of a society that would pierce societal restraints and release individual potential. Society would have to be changed, but more important, the individual would have to be transformed." A socialist variant of the Baptist conversion experience would create a society of individuals with heightened moral conscience.[52]

Having seceded from Christianity and politics, Nearing seceded from society.[53] In 1932 he left New York City with his mistress, Helen Knothe, a theosophist and Krishnamurti's former lover whom Nearing married in 1947 after his wife died. They started a self-sufficient farm in Vermont. When neighbors moved too close, they moved in 1951 to Maine and started over. The Nearings built all structures by hand with stone. "Stone buildings seem a natural outcropping of the earth," they argued in *Living the Good Life*, citing Wright. "They blend into the landscape and are a part of it."[54] With Scott Nearing as theorist and Helen as publicizer, they published a string of autobiographical accounts of their work: *The Maple Sugar Book* in 1950, *Living the Good Life* and *Man's Search for the Good Life* in 1954, and *Continuing the Good Life: Half a Century of Homesteading* in 1979. The Nearings' self-reliant ethic, rejection of artificial pesticides and fertilizers, organic architecture, pacifism, and vegetarianism looked quaint and eccentric to most Americans until the 1960s. Suddenly young people dropped out from racist, warmongering, materialistic, commercial society and founded back-to-the-land communes from Vermont to Oregon. Sales of *Living the Good Life* shot up.[55] The countercultural bible *The Whole Earth Catalog* placed articles about the Nearings and Thoreau alongside each other.[56] Scott Nearing, the modern Thoreau, fallen Baptist, and exiled radical, his radical dreams of a communist society forgotten, turned toward individualistic self-reliant agriculture of the past—a conservative, nostalgic solution for the crises of the modern age—and found himself a prophet leading the way to the Promised Land of self-fulfillment and organic local foods.[57]

In 1932, the year Nearing and Knothe moved from New York City to Vermont, their hero Frank Lloyd Wright invited a circle of friends, including Georgia O'Keeffe, to join him at Taliesin, his home and studio near Spring Green, Wisconsin, to lead and advise "a new Fellowship of Apprentices." Wright envisioned a community based on the integration of art, industry, and everyday life. "Fellowship work in its manifold branches," Wright wrote, "will come directly under the influence of an organic philosophy: organic architecture for organic life."[58] Idealistic young people answered his call for apprentices. In 1937, Wright began building Taliesin

West on a desert mountain near Scottsdale, Arizona, where the Fellowship wintered until Wright's death in 1959. To make buildings that seemed to rise naturally out of the Arizona mountainside, Wright made wooden forms, placed local stones within them, and filled spaces with concrete, a technique the Nearings copied.

Wright was also a Baptist Transcendentalist. His father was a Baptist preacher from Massachusetts and his maternal grandfather a stern Unitarian minister. He grew up reading Emerson, Thoreau, and Unitarian radicals William Ellery Channing and Theodore Parker. He distilled the Gospel message in the alembic of Transcendental-Baptist individualism: "Jesus taught the dignity and worth of the individual developed from within as an individual, although Christianity perverted the teaching," he wrote in 1932.[59] Wright adhered throughout his life to the Emersonian idea of Nature as church and teacher. Nature taught the lessons of "organic" architecture that grew from the earth. In his role as the Fellowship's architect-guru, Wright read Emerson and Whitman aloud to his apprentices.[60]

A Baptist-style mistrust of centralization and government manifested itself in Taliesin and in Wright's decentered concept of community. "The Big City is no longer a place for more than the exterior applications of some cliché or sterile formula, where life is concerned, he wrote. "Therefore the TALIESIN FELLOWSHIP chooses to live and work in the country."[61] Taliesin West, especially, was as self-sufficient and independent of the government as possible. Like the Nearings on their self-sufficient farm disconnected from the capitalist market, apprentices grew the food that the Fellowship ate. For decades Taliesin West had no municipal water, telephone, or electricity.[62]

Wright's individualist wariness of community presented itself with special clarity in his plans for an ideal city. In 1932, Wright published *The Disappearing City,* an appropriately named plan for a model town named Broadacre City (or "the Usonian City"[63]), in which, as at Taliesin West, decentralization and self-sufficiency complemented reverence for the land (Figure 7.2).[64] Wright was Jane Jacobs inverted. Cities made people "unnaturally gregarious."[65] His town protected and fostered individualism. Families lived in a vast grid of streets on one-to-five-acre allotments which allowed them to grow their own food, each independent in its own Walden, like Thoreau raising his own beans, or the Fellowship or the Nearings their own produce. Man's "social right" was a "right to his place on the ground as he has had his right in the sun and air: land to be

FIGURE 7.2 Frank Lloyd Wright, *Living City, Aerial View*. Wright came up with an answer to "unnaturally gregarious" American cities, called in various incarnations Broadacre City, the disappearing city, or the living city. His utopian plan placed individuals on their own few acres, with nature beautified by human use.

held only by use and improvements."[66] Broadacre City had no place for pedestrians or public transit but relied completely on automobiles. Office buildings and apartment buildings were scattered to keep population density low. Markets, churches, and civic and cultural buildings sat on green spaces at major intersections. However organic the design for houses might be, nature was thoroughly subordinated to human needs.

> Most landscape architects would say, "But I love the natural scenery." Well, so do we. We augment natural "scenery." We develop for it by way of human nature, a collateral complementary scenery in the block of tree plantings in the ordered fields, even more beautiful than "nature." . . . Tillage and consideration for the ground make a fresh and vitally humanized landscape.[67]

Broadacre City was the Baptist alternative to the Puritan village: nature and individual did not serve the common good, but rather community and nature yielded to the individual.

Mad Farmers

Variations of this libertarian, individualistic ideal of society can be found throughout the country but it is nowhere so dominant as in the South, where surely by no coincidence Baptists have their greatest numbers and cultural, social, and political sway. Virginian Thomas Jefferson, a nominal Anglican and Baptists' political ally, penned the classic statements of a republic of yeoman farmers. Southern states had no mechanism and no will to maintain the egalitarian world implicit in a land of Jeffersonian yeoman farmers (or in Broadacre City, for that matter), each prospering on his own plot of land. Nothing prevented accumulation of wealth and power in a few hands. The slave plantation became as emblematic of the South as the steepled town of New England. The implications are enormous: the New England town could become an enduring symbol of American grassroots democracy, piety, moral order, and harmony with nature; but the Southern plantation could only symbolize a moral order based on hierarchy and obedience to authority in which great wealth, gracious living, and perfect freedom flourished together with poverty, debasement, and servitude.[68]

In contrast with the moral and communal purposes of antebellum New England agricultural writing, Southern agricultural thought bolstered the values and enhancement of slave society. The agricultural reformer Edmund Ruffin, Virginia planter and nominal Episcopalian, viewed agricultural improvement as means of shoring up the plantation system. Through speeches, publications, and his agricultural journal, the *Farmers' Register*, he spread his message of soil improvement, particularly the use of marl to adjust the acidity of Southern soils. Southern planters' resort to marl and then guano fertilizer presaged modern agribusiness's reliance on chemical inputs to compensate for worn-out soils from commodity agriculture. Southern agriculture was terribly hard on soil and the environment. Farmers cleared and planted until the land produced no more and then left it, gullied and barren, for virgin soil further west.[69]

By the twentieth century, Southern farmers surveyed a landscape showing centuries of neglect. Still under the spell of antigovernment individualism, Southerners regarded agricultural improvement, conservation, and environmentalism as personal moral issues. A planter's son and slaveowners' grandson, Hugh Hammond Bennett from Anson County, North Carolina, enlisted the government's aid but only to bring scientific information to farmers to combat the terrible Southern erosion problem. He insisted that farmers, not government, organize soil conservation districts and control whether and how to implement advice from government experts. Although an Episcopalian, Bennett's family tree was leafy with Methodists, Baptists, and even a Primitive (or Old School) Baptist preacher, who perhaps inspired Bennett to become the "evangelist" of soil conservation. Appointed director of the Soil Conservation Service in the Department of Agriculture at its creation in 1933, Bennett preached the gospel of soil conservation with moral fervor: "good" farmers adopted it; "bad" farmers did not. In publications like *Our American Land: The Story of Its Abuse and Its Conservation,* Bennett appealed to farmers' self-interest and emphasized conservation's cash value.[70]

A generation later, a Baptist author, like a preacher decrying his generation's moral decline, preached a return to the good old days. Author, environmental activist, and self-described "mad farmer" Wendell Berry fights the evils of agribusiness with protest and civil disobedience while proselytizing the gospel of traditional agriculture. He envisions communities of voluntarily engaged people reforming and healing society's relationship with the earth. Under a kind of alter ego called the "Mad Farmer," Berry wrote a series of visionary poems in the early 1970s about the return of the

Jeffersonian yeoman farmer. Unlike Burroughs, the poems announced Berry's greater activism, which, in the Baptist way, has tended toward petitions, manifestoes, and civil disobedience rather than organizations to pressure government for agencies or programs. His is an environmentalism of nostalgia.

To be a writer, Berry realized, just as Burroughs had, that he needed to write what he knew,[71] the passing rural world of his boyhood. He populated his fiction with course, violent people who inadvertently abuse the land. Berry was born in 1934 in Henry County, Kentucky, to Southern-Baptist farmers. After a master's in English from the University of California and a fellowship in Wallace Stegner's writing seminar at Stanford University, he took a job at the University of Kentucky. Again like Burroughs, he bought a farm near where he grew up and writes in an isolated cabin inspired in large part by Thoreau's cabin on Walden Pond. Berry's enthusiasm for Thoreau coincided with alienation from institutional Christianity. In the 1970s he tired of Thoreau, Ted Olson notes, due to "concern for agriculture, a deepening commitment to marriage, family, and community, and growing faith in Christianity."[72] Berry turned conservatively toward the past. A fan of Gilbert White, Berry felt deeply that this lost way of life was a superior way to live. He bemoaned how mechanized agricultural efficiency consolidated old farms into large agricultural operations, depopulated rural areas, and destroyed farm communities. The rise of environmentalism gave him an additional reason to preserve this way of life, which seemed to him less alienated from the land and better suited to preserve it—despite the evidence of his fiction and his own experience that traditional family farmers often did not treat the land well. In dozens of essays Berry evangelized on behalf of traditional farming. His best-known book, *The Unsettling of America: Culture and Agriculture*, published by the Sierra Club in 1977, presented a comprehensive argument against corporate mechanized faming. Return to the horse-powered farm became an environmental duty.[73]

Like Cather, Berry distrusts government, and he criticized Lyndon Johnson's Great Society programs. Instead of asking the government to preserve a moral order, Berry calls for traditional farming in traditional, voluntary communities that could resist the power of greed and capitalism that threatened them from the outside.[74] "By community, I mean the commonwealth and common interests, commonly understood, of people living together in a place and wishing to continue to do so," Berry wrote. ". . . It has the power . . . to influence behavior. And it exercises this power not by coercion or violence"—by government, that is—"but by teaching the young and by preserving stories and songs that tell (among other things) what works and what does not work in a given place."[75] He argued, "This has become, to some extent at least, an argument against institutional solutions. . . . One must begin in one's own life the private solutions that can only *in turn* become public solutions."[76]

Berry's work says little about forest conservation or parks, the two companions to agricultural improvement in New England conservation. The destructive strip-mining of the Kentucky followed by a dam proposal in Kentucky's Red River Gorge in the 1970s—what Berry saw as the destruction of the earth forever for short-term profit of outsiders—stirred him to environmental activism. Berry still today fights such corporate menaces to the community as mountaintop removal in the Appalachians. Yet despite his essays and letters of protest and his actions of civil disobedience, although he "recognize[s] the need for conservation organizations," he has like Burroughs and Nearing in the main kept his distance from them. They "are not enough. If they are to succeed in any way that is meaningful, or perhaps if they are to succeed at all, their work must be augmented by an effort to rebuild the life of our society in terms of a decent spiritual and economic connection to the land. That can't be done by organizations, but only by individuals and by families and by small informal groups."[77] Berry is an evangelist for personal environmental transformation.

The Sociobiological Baptist

In cultures without a strong moral environmental impulse, human-caused ecological ravages can impel alarmed biologists to environmental activism. Today the South's best-known environmental figure is Edward Osborne Wilson. Raised Southern Baptist, he shares several characteristics with Burroughs and Berry: his environmentalism came later in life, does not emphasize government solutions, and favors individual action, which he bases on a kind of internal sociobiological morality called "biophilia." Unlike them, his urban childhood gave him no farm to be nostalgic for. Wilson was born in 1929 in Mobile, Alabama, was baptized by immersion at fourteen, and read the entire Bible twice. He grew deeply interested in natural history. The adventures of tropical explorers Ivan Sanderson, Frank Buck, and William Beebe (rather than Muir, Thoreau, or Burroughs) excited his youthful imagination.[78] Wilson discovered evolution in his classes at the University of Alabama and was converted to secular materialism. At Harvard, he has become one of the world's foremost experts on ants.

For Southerners humans are the measure of nature. Wilson's biological research emphasized social aspects of ants and ant "societies." In 1975 he turned the glass around and trained it on human societies. His *Sociobiology: The New Synthesis* took the notion that ants evolved as colonies rather than as individuals and applied it to other social animals, most controversially humans. Implications were intriguing but also disturbing. Wilson argued that because human societies evolved, universal human activities must have had competitive evolutionary advantages, including religion, art, culture, and intellect. Controversy arose because of the theory's fatalistic and conservative implications that what is, is right, because it helps humanity survive, which suggestively parallels Southern and Baptist accommodation to society as it is.

Wilson paid little attention to the environmental controversies of the 1960s and 1970s. In 1979, when he was past his fiftieth birthday, the first estimates of the destruction of rainforests, where he did research, alarmed him. A decade early Wilson had written a path-breaking study with Robert MacArthur, *The Theory of Island Biogeography,* which proposed that the number of species an island or isolated ecosystem could support was proportional to its size and degree of isolation. As urbanization, agriculture, or deforestation cut up large ecosystems into fragments, these smaller ecosystem "islands" could only support reduced biological diversity. A collection of essays that Wilson edited in 1988, *BioDiversity,* gave a popular name to the issue, and Wilson followed up with *The Diversity of Life* in 1992 and *The Future of Life* in 2002. His 2010 environmental parable *Anthill* told the parallel stories set in human and ant societies and illustrated the notion that both societies were "superorganisms" that evolution can cause to spin self-destructively out of control.[79]

Wilson in effect made science a new religion. As a student at the University of Alabama, his biology class introduced him to evolution, which nothing in the Bible or Southern Baptist teachings could explain—his "epiphany," he called it. "Science became the new light and the way."[80] He became a materialist with the same enthusiasm and devotion that he had previously been a Baptist. "The shedding of blind faith gave him the intellectual fearlessness to explore human evolution wherever logic and evidence took him"—Wilson wrote those words about Charles Darwin, but they also apply to him.[81] Wilson became an evangelist for his new religion, and his many books were his sermons. He has come to realize this himself.[82] "And you will find in the structure of *Diversity of Life* a Baptist sermon I didn't recognize until I'd written it," he commented to me: "it starts with a story from Sacred Scripture, followed by apocalypse and hellfire, redemption, and the altar call."[83] In the 1990s, Wilson proposed biology as the foundation for "consilience," a unified system of all knowledge, arts, and religion—effectively a new comprehensive religion. "Biophilia," an innate sympathy with life, would stop environmental destruction.[84] Evolution "retold as poetry" provided the grand mythology.[85] Biology would provide meaning, structure ethics, and unify mankind with its universal validity.

Wilson's science effectively undermined religion. His opening salvo in *Sociobiology*, "The Morality of the Gene," proposed the idea that a human was simply a gene's strategy for perpetuating itself, which implicitly confronted traditional morality.[86] Most controversially, the final chapter treated most common aspects of human society purely in terms of evolutionary adaptation and survival. "The theory of group selection," he wrote, "has taken most of the good will out of altruism. When altruism is conceived as the mechanism by which DNA multiplies itself through a network of relatives, spirituality becomes just one more Darwinian enabling device,"[87] just like self-righteousness, gratitude, sympathy, and sincerity. Evangelism was "moralistic aggression."[88] The chapter "Man: From Sociobiology to Sociology" assailed religion, philosophy, social science, and the humanities for harboring ideas that biology proved to be false or unfounded. Wilson's conception of religion paralleled the Southern Baptist ethos: a powerful force for tribal unity in competition with other tribes (for Baptists, other denominations) that created an all-embracing universe of meaning.

In 2006 Wilson offered a religious olive branch, *The Creation: An Appeal to Save Life on Earth,* to open dialogue with the Southern Baptist Church, although without surrendering his materialism or "provisional deism."[89] By using the Christian word "creation" and focusing on the importance of preserving biodiversity for moral as well as practical reasons, Wilson hoped to find common ground and to enlist religion's help in combatting the world's mounting environmental problems.[90]

Aloof from politics or environmental activism, Wilson also has been short on specific recommendations. Sociobiology lacks political prescriptions. Concerned over loss of biodiversity, he supports pragmatic groups like the World Wildlife Fund and the Nature Conservancy but not activist groups like the Sierra Club. Instead of a Congregational-style vision of a just and sustainable society, sociobiological theory proffers biophilia, an instinctual love of life that comes from inside the individual, not from society or its institutions. Sociobiology implies that the current society has evolved for the best. Only if individuals recognize and act according to the innate love of nature that has evolved within us, the sustainable society will emerge. It is the Southern Baptist way.

Former Vice President Al Gore was also inspired by science to make environmentalism his cause, culminating in his Nobel Prize–winning campaign against global warming and 2006 movie *An Inconvenient Truth.* Gore was born in 1948 in Tennessee and raised Southern Baptist. (Biographers note the influence on him of his mother, formerly Churches of Christ.) Gore ascribes the origins of his environmental interests to his mother's discussions of Rachel Carson's *Silent Spring* at the dinner table. Oceanographer Roger Revelle's lectures on global warming at Harvard made him an activist. A tour of duty in Vietnam, studies at divinity school and law school, and a journalism career preceded elections first as representative, then senator, and finally vice president. Two unsuccessful campaigns for the Democratic presidential nomination in 1988 and 1992 with a strong environmental platform prompted Gore to write *Earth in the Balance: Ecology and the Human Spirit.* The subtitle emphasized Gore's conviction that the "global environmental crisis" is a "spiritual" crisis, for "what other word describes the collection of values and assumptions that determine our basic understanding of how we fit into the universe?" Like a Baptist preacher, he asserted that "each of us must take a greater personal responsibility for this deteriorating global environment; each of us must take a hard look at the habits of mind and action that reflect—and have led to—this grave crisis." He frequently used the word "faith," especially in the conclusion. Like Wilson's book, *Earth in the Balance* had an altar call "to convince you to be a part of the enormous change our civilization must now undergo. . . . I hope you, too, will make a commitment to help bring the earth back into balance. . . ." Gore concluded, "The choice is ours; the earth is in the balance."[91]

Skeptics and Deniers

Southern culture and individualistic churches like the Baptists have more typically fostered skepticism or even hostility to environmentalism than enthusiasm, such as in the careers of Gregg Easterbrook and Dixy Lee Ray. Born in 1953 and raised in a suburb of Buffalo, New York, where his father was deacon in the American Baptist church, Easterbrook is no great friend of environmental organizations and prefers individualistic environmental solutions.[92] In 1995, in *A Moment on the Earth: The Coming Age of Environmental Optimism*, Easterbrook presented a putative moderate, skeptical environmentalism that he called "ecorealism."[93] Easterbrook affirmed the necessity and effectiveness of most environmental laws, regulations, and programs already in place. However, ecorealists like himself—"cooler," more "rational," and less "sentimental" than other environmentalists—should resist demands for new or expanded governmental laws and regulations. A whole range of problems from offshore drilling to global warming gave him no cause for alarm. Easterbrook changed his mind about global warming a dozen years later, when, presumably, it was safe for cooler, more rational, less sentimental minds to do so.

With Dixy Lee Ray, skepticism shaded into outright hostility toward environmentalism. Born in 1914 in Tacoma, Washington, to a family of staunch Southern Baptists from Tennessee (her sister became a Baptist missionary), Ray was a respected marine biologist in the Puget Sound region. Although she considered herself an environmentalist, she avoided all environmental organizations or causes and disdained "pseudo-environmentalists" with their "emotional fancy to a part of the landscape or a notion with little basis in research or reality."[94] A supporter of nuclear power, she was appointed by the Nixon administration to chair the Atomic Energy Commission in 1973, less for her credentials as a marine biologist than for her gender and lukewarm environmentalism. President Gerald Ford appointed her the first Assistant Secretary of State for Oceans and International Environmental and Scientific Affairs in 1975. In 1976 Ray won election as governor of Washington as a Democrat. She tangled constantly with her party over her conservative positions on environmental and energy issues and lost her bid for reelection in the primary in 1980. Like Easterbrook, she called herself a scientific, commonsense environmentalist but more often attacked other environmentalists than promoted solutions to problems. Complaining about "the lyrical hysteria of Rachel Carson's book, *Silent Spring*," Ray perhaps originated the allegation that DDT "could have saved millions of lives from malaria and other insect-borne diseases had not political pressure brought by environmentalists like Rachel Carson banned its use in the U.S. and reduced it use worldwide," a claim that has been repeatedly disproved while corporate-funded libertarian sources keep it alive.[95] She attacked "out-of-control" environmentalism in 1990 in *Trashing the Planet: How Science Can Help Us Deal with Acid Rain, Depletion of the Ozone, and Nuclear Waste (Among Other Things)* and in 1993 in *Environmental Overkill: Whatever Happened to Common Sense?* She assailed "exaggerated" claims for global warming, thinning of the ozone layer, acid rain, and other environmental problems. In the Southern and Baptist way, she rejected most solutions that called for government regulation and infringement of the rights of private property. Ray died in 1994 before she could follow Easterbrook and repent her environmental sins.

Some of the nation's fiercest antienvironmentalism is in the South and Southern churches. In 2006, the Southern Baptist Convention, which separated from Northern Baptists in 1845 over the issue of slavery, passed a "Resolution on Environmentalism and Evangelicals" that claimed that "some in our culture have completely rejected God the Father in favor of deifying 'Mother Earth,' made environmentalism into a neo-pagan religion, and elevated animal and plant life to the place of equal—or greater—value with human life"; that "some environmental activists are seeking to advance a political agenda based on disputed claims [that is, global warming], which not only impacts public policy and in turn our economic well-being, but also seeks to indoctrinate the public, particularly students in public institutions"; and that "environmentalism is threatening to become a wedge issue to divide the evangelical community and further distract its members from the priority of the Great Commission [Christ's charge to evangelize the world, a central Baptist tenet]."[96] Such prominent Southern Baptists as R. Albert Mohler Jr., president of the Southern Baptist Theological Seminary in Louisville, Kentucky, regarded "radical environmentalism" as a religion of nature, and environmental issues as distractions from evangelism and the battles with atheism, secular humanism, and other perceived dangers to Christian America.[97]

Young Southern Baptists, however, have begun to warm to environmental issues. Prominent among them is Jonathan Merritt, son of a former president of the Southern Baptist Convention. Merritt graduated from Liberty University, founded by fundamentalist Baptist Reverend Jerry Falwell; conservative Southeastern Baptist Theological Seminary in Wake Forest, North Carolina; and Candler School of Theology at Emory University in Atlanta, Georgia. A self-described "recovering anti-environmentalist," he experienced his epiphany in seminary. In a discussion of the principle that God revealed himself in both the Bible and creation, the professor added that destruction of creation resembled "tearing a page out of the Bible."[98] In light of the near bibliolatry of conservative Protestants, this remark pierced Merritt's conscience to the core. In 2008 he founded the Southern Baptist Environment and Climate Initiative. Relying on traditional Christian theological arguments about God, creation, and human stewardship, which have not received much attention in conservative evangelical discourse, Merritt published *Green Like God: Unlocking the Divine Plan for Our Planet* in 2010 to make a case that conservative Christians could and should be environmentalists. Still, environmentalism remains very much a minority movement and bucks huge skepticism within the church.

The Southern Baptist Church vied with the Methodist Church for dominance in Southern states. At one time the largest Protestant denomination, Methodism has fostered few major environmental figures, especially in the South. Methodism arose outside the Reformed tradition and lacks its strong engagement with culture and society. Like the Baptists, Methodists concerned themselves more with personal rather than social sin. Methodist Ron Arnold, born in 1937 in Houston, Texas, became one of environmentalism's most persistent critics. A college dropout, with the generous support of industry sources he has authored a string of articles and books framing environmentalism as a danger to and practically a conspiracy against freedom and the economy.[99] The holiness and charismatic traditions, which grew out of Methodist theology and ecstatic worship, have no significant moral environmental component at all. Although they originated outside the former slave states, these movements prospered through the South and the Southern diaspora. They teach that salvation is assured through experience of the Holy Spirit, which in Pentecostalism manifests itself in speaking in tongues, faith healing, sometimes serpent handling and drinking of poison, and other miracles. Worship services use emotional preaching, music, and dancing to incite ecstatic expression of religious feeling. The personal experience of the divine at the heart of these churches has virtually no social or political implications, aside from fatalistic conservatism. The one Pentecostal in environmental history books was prodevelopment Western lawyer James G. Watt, Secretary of the Interior from 1981 to 1983. Watt raised such a storm of criticism that President Ronald Reagan asked him to resign. For environmentalism, the holiness and charismatic traditions are dead ends.[100]

The Outsider New England Town

Even the American land system favored individualism over community. The New England town did not prove easy to export to the rest of the United States. Congress designed the system to sell public land as efficiently as possible, which discouraged group settlement. A handful of attempts to plant towns on the New England pattern did succeed. Greeley, Colorado, for example, was planned and led by Nathan C. Meeker, agricultural editor of Horace Greeley's *New York Tribune*, who modeled it on Northampton.[101] Blessed with reliable water and good land, Greeley prospered as few colonies in Colorado did.

Meeker had been inspired by Mormons, who had successfully transplanted a version of the New England town to Utah after 1847. Whereas other New England religious outsiders rebelled against the Puritan communal ideal, Mormons embraced it. Early Mormons were mostly from the lower classes of New England society and planned their communities without leadership from river gods.[102] Joseph Smith, Mormonism's founder and prophet, was born in 1805 of old Puritan stock in Sharon, Vermont, a dozen miles north of Woodstock, and raised in Palmyra, New York.[103] His successor, Brigham Young, also of Puritan ancestry, was born in 1801 in Whitingham, Vermont, and also raised in New York.[104] The Mormon town revised the Puritan model according to Mormon eschatology and interpretation of Biblical accounts of Jerusalem. Parallels with the Puritan town are nonetheless striking: towns were settled by groups under the oversight of colony government; colonists settled together in planned towns near essential resources; communal settlements made watchful control of townspeople by church and neighbors possible; and close settlements kept people close to churches and safer from enemies. Both Puritan and Mormon towns regulated natural resource use. Necessity reinforced community. Mormons worked cooperatively in order to build and maintain irrigation works, without which settlements would have been impossible. Still, Mormon towns looked little like Puritan communities. Like typical American towns elsewhere, they were planned on a grid oriented to the points of the compass and spaciously laid out with broad streets.

Although Mormon and Puritan theology differed profoundly, their ethic was similar. The faith preserved such Puritan ideals as theocratic church government, affirmation of a close and personal God, a providential view of history, and a gospel of works. Smith articulated a doctrine of stewardship that asserted explicitly that earth was made for man, who was

God's steward. Eden played a prominent role. Mormons made their first attempt to build a town in Missouri, which Smith identified as the original site of Eden. In Utah, Mormons saw themselves as restoring the Edenic condition of the earth in preparation for the Millennium. Mormon leaders also urged believers to put community interests ahead of private interests and to bury greed and selfishness. Mormonism's work ethic is reflected in Utah's nickname, the Beehive State, and motto, "Industry." The town ideal and the Puritan communal ethic were transformed by Mormonism's unique religious system but basic principles survived quite recognizably.[105]

After about two decades, the American land tenure system and ecological problems put an end to the Mormon town. The Homestead Act of 1862 drew Mormons out along section lines in so-called string settlements and encouraged speculation, commercial agriculture, and ranching. The arid land was not as forgiving as New England's and not suitable for convertible husbandry. Since irrigated fields dominated the lowlands, cattle roamed upland grasslands, overgrazed, and caused floods that silted up canals. Arid lands easily scarred and eroded. The railroad brought in outsider economic interests and ended church domination of the economy and colonization.[106] Mormons moved steadily away from their radical origins and closer to the Christian mainstream and evolved from anti-American pacifists to conservative Republican patriots. They tend to emphasize that part of their heritage centered on settlement and development of the West, rather than communal conservation of natural resources or preservation of parks.[107]

Hence, unlike Congregationalists, few Mormons have been known for their environmental thought or leadership, with some exceptions. Hugh Nibley (1910–2005) was a Mormon theologian, Democrat, and strong conservationist, which he justified with quotations by Brigham Young.[108] The prominent Udall family also embraced the Democratic Party and environmental causes. Secretary of the Interior under John F. Kennedy and Lyndon B. Johnson, Stewart Udall was shocked and inspired by Rachel Carson's *Silent Spring*. In 1963, he published *The Quiet Crisis*, an environmentalist book by a major politician and a precursor to *Earth in the Balance*. It used the common language of Congregationalism and Mormonism: "It is not too late to repair some of the mistakes of the past, and to make America a green and pleasant—and productive—land. We can do it if we understand the history of our husbandry, and develop fresh insight concerning the men and the forces that have shaped our land attitudes and determined the pattern of land use in the United States. This book . . .

is dedicated to the proposition that men must grasp completely the relationship between human stewardship and the fullness of the American earth."[109] Like Udall a lapsed Mormon,[110] award-winning author and environmentalist Terry Tempest Williams published *Refuge: An Unnatural History of Family and Place* of 1991 to trace the growth of her environmental activism. She was inspired by love of the land and by outrage at government open-air testing of nuclear weapons in the 1950s and 1960s that silently exposed Mormons downwind to radiation. Born in 1955, Williams blamed testing for the high rate of cancer among her relatives, including her mother.[111] Her concern for the impact on community and family of environmental problems appear to reflect Mormon values. Yet although Nibley's, Udall's, and Williams's examples attest to the possibilities of Mormon environmentalism, Mormons as a group tend toward the same patriotic, free-market attitudes as conservative Baptists and Southerners, and its members have contributed relatively little to the environmentalist tradition.

New England Outsider Environmentalism

New England's outsiders rebelled against the moral, orderly Congregational community. The Puritan founding principles of the town run by its godly residents and the church run by its godly members could not withstand centrifugal forces of dissent and individualism. The logic of Puritans' own theology fed the impulse to separate from less godly. Most separatist groups instead advocated voluntaristic communities of believers along with evangelism to convert the world. Ideals of religious freedom slowly dissolved the bonds of church and community. Outsider denominations sprang up, grew, proliferated, and swamped the established order. Alienation from mainstream culture, individualism, and resistance to governmental solutions remain hallmarks of these groups. For the most part, these ideals run counter to the stream of environmentalism and sometimes overwhelm it altogether. Some environmentalist voices have arisen from these groups and supported solutions based on assumptions that in other contexts bolster the antienvironmentalist impulse. Outsider Protestant environmentalists have enriched environmental thought and have conceivably provided a bridge across which former or would-be opponents can cross, but they have not established a basis for a powerful environmental politics.

8

A New Era

Southern African-American Environmental Justice

Developers tempt fate when, like the Fraser brothers, they build on the hurricane-prone coastal islands of Georgia and the Carolinas. In 1989, panicked residents fled Hilton Head when forecasts put the island directly in the path of powerful Hurricane Hugo. At the last minute the huge storm, the strongest in South Carolina's history, turned and went ashore near Charleston, sixty miles to the north. Hugo roared straight through St. Stephens, Leo Twiggs's home town, forty-five miles inland. As soon as the wind and rain had passed, Twiggs rushed to the town to check on his mother. St. Stephens was largely destroyed, but to his immense relief he found her alive. Twiggs is an African-American artist. For two decades his unique, powerful batik paintings depicted the fortitude and endurance of African Americans facing the hardships of slavery, segregation, and racism. The series *Commemoration* meditated on the emotion-laden Confederate battle flag, and *Targeted Man* portrayed blacks with targets on their backs. Other batiks drew from family history or the Holiness church of his childhood. Hugo moved him to think for the first time about the role of nature in the Southern black experience.

At first Twiggs depicted nature as another trial for blacks to endure. The *East Wind Suite: The Hugo Series* (Figure 8.2, see color insert) "began as paintings about a storm," he said, but "became an exploration of the strength and resiliency of the human spirit in the face of adversity."[1] Twiggs explored the more benign black relationship with nature in *We Have Known Rivers* (Figure 8.1, see color insert), a series inspired by Langston Hughes's 1921 poem "The Negro Speaks of Rivers," with its themes of black pride and the connection of black history in Africa and America with great rivers. The poem had "always fascinated" Twiggs. "Perhaps it was the childhood stories my mother told us of my great-grandfather being sold to a plantation owner 'over the river,'" he wrote. ". . . Perhaps it was because my father . . . told us of his life as a cook on a riverboat floating down the Mississippi River."[2] Twiggs's rivers reflect black faces along with trees, stars, and a crescent moon, with ancestors and old African gods symbolizing the great antiquity of the relationship with great rivers that Hughes had written about. Other batiks implied the injustice inherent in the way racism and segregation separated blacks from enjoyment of nature or its benefits. The series *Blues at the Beach* (Figure 8.3, see color insert) centered on Atlantic Beach near Myrtle Beach, the only public beach in this part of the Carolinas open to blacks under segregation. Across the South and sometimes in cities like Chicago, blacks had access to public recreational spots only in segregated or separate state parks and beaches, always less attractive than facilities for whites, and in the South were allowed to use urban parks and pools only on certain days of the week.[3] Never a desirable beach, Atlantic Beach today is the only undeveloped beach in Myrtle Beach. A nearby jazz club added to the scene and lends the series its name. The series *High Cotton Down Home Blues* (Figure 8.4, see color insert) juxtaposed the implied prosperity of "high cotton" with a looming white figure with a tattered Confederate flag behind him. A black family works in the cotton field around him. Their small poor home stands in the background beneath a crescent moon. In the foreground a guitarist sings the blues in a world where, amidst the beauty of nature, black hands harvest her bounty, but white landowners grow rich.

In all these series, Twiggs, like other Southerners, prefers people in the landscape to give it meaning. As an African American, Twiggs discovers in nature aspects of history and injustice for his people. This African-American social understanding of nature and environment parallels that of Catholics, Jews, Methodists, and Episcopalians. Since the 1960s and 1970s, when Presbyterians strutted their last hour upon the environmentalist stage, people from these religious traditions have taken leading roles in the environmental movement and remade it. Environmental concerns broadened beyond traditional emphases on nature, wildlife, and resources. Blacks and Catholics spearheaded the environmental justice movement, while Jews also saw environmental issues in terms of their social consequences. Reacting to the thoroughgoing patriarchy of their religions, Catholic and Jewish women stood in the vanguard of ecofeminist thought. The hierarchical liturgical Catholic and Episcopalian churches fostered grand cosmological theorists. Moreover, Jews played a prominent role in popularizing organic agriculture.

This social understanding of environmental issues clearly marks the career of Carl Anthony, prominent black environmental activist and friend of David Brower. Born in 1939 in Philadelphia, he acquired from his deeply religious, Bible-reading mother a "very strong" "sense of moral principles." Anthony's mother came from the mixed-race elite of South Carolina and was Episcopalian.[4] Mixed-race blacks living in cities like Charleston or New Orleans occupied a relatively privileged position above their darker brethren and often joined denominations like the Episcopal Church that they associated with elite respectability. After studying architecture and city planning at Columbia University, Anthony realized that urban planners and authorities ignored the needs of poor and minority communities. When he joined the faculty of the University of California at Berkeley in 1971, he criticized the gap between professors and practitioners of architecture and urban design. Anthony founded the Urban Habitat Program and cofounded the journal *Race, Poverty, and the Environment.* He was skeptical of mainstream environmentalism. "The desire of a tiny fraction of middle- and upper-class Europeans," he said, "to hear the voice of the Earth could be in part a strategy by people in these social classes to amplify their *own* inner voice at a time when they feel threatened, not only by the destruction of the planet, but also by the legitimate claims of multicultural human communities clamoring to be heard. . . . Why is it so easy for these people to think like mountains and not be able to think like people of color?" In 1991 he accepted Brower's invitation to be president of Earth Island Institute. He resigned in 1998 when white colleagues resisted integrating social justice with environmental issues in the national forests of northern New Mexico. His association with Brower did give Anthony an appreciation of the John Muir tradition, but he remarked, "I think that there is a fundamental problem within the John Muir mythology, for all that it's contributed—and it's contributed a lot—and that is that somehow we can save nature by separating it from human activity."[5] Anthony later directed the Sustainable Metropolitan Communities Initiative of the Ford Foundation and continues to be active in several urban environmental organizations.

Blacks' distinctive history and religious traditions formed the crucible that molded African-American values regarding nature and the environment and made them of different stuff from Reformed Protestant–inflected environmentalism. Blacks as Southerners share with whites an individualist ethic, but as blacks also possessed a unique American communal experience under slavery and racial segregation. Well over 90 percent of American blacks descend from Southern slaves. As a predominantly rural people until the middle of the twentieth century, Southern blacks were intimately familiar with the natural world, which was at once home, workplace, space for recreation, food source, medical resource, place of magic, stories, and legends, and avenue for or barrier to travel or escape. White hunters and fishermen used slaves or hired black guides for their knowledge of woods and wildlife—most famously when President Theodore Roosevelt hunted with African-American guide Holt Collier and saved a bear from being shot, which inspired the craze for "teddy bears."[6]

Protestantism played a central role in the African-American experience. The black church was born of the plantation slave quarters, the one true community studding the Southern landscape of Jeffersonian yeoman farms, far more communal than Berry's voluntaristic communities. Quite in contrast with rural or poor Southern white churches of any denomination, slavery and segregation produced a sense of solidarity in the African-American community that offset individualism. Most Southern black churches were Baptist. Although Methodism appealed to blacks from the beginning, Methodist leadership in several slave conspiracies prompted whites to suppress African-American Methodism. The almost always illiterate preacher relied on his memory of Bible passages and stories, and on forceful, emotional preaching instead of educated exegesis. Worship services permitted blacks to express themselves and acquire a sense of self-worth and superiority over white oppressors. Emphasis on the Hebrew Bible, especially Exodus, lent blacks a sense of themselves as a chosen people whom a leader would bring out of oppression to the Promised Land. Vocal congregational responses to chanted sermons, the call-and-response style of song, and communal creation of songs and spirituals reinforced communal identity. African-American churches have long been noted for worshippers' intensity and emotion. In church, blacks experienced personal conviction of salvation, ecstatic communal worship, and assurance that God would care for blacks as a people and lead them to a better place and time.

Virtually the only black institution to survive slavery and segregation intact, the church was the one place where African Americans could organize themselves and choose their own leaders. From churches emerged black schools, banks, and insurance companies. After emancipation, the

Baptist preacher held a dual position as a religious leader to his congregation and a political leader respected by both blacks and whites who could negotiate relations between the black and white communities. Churches nurtured African-American culture, notably artistic and musical talent. Both then and now churches represent the communal hearts of black communities, especially in the South.[7] Churchgoers came away from worship with intense feelings of affirmation, empowerment, and divine protection. Activists for civil rights and environmental justice alike have taken this assurance and confidence with them into opposition to and confrontation with injustice.[8]

Religion affected the view of the land. In the absence of a natural theology, to believers nature was less the place where one found God than where he acted and spoke through natural events, as he did in the Bible. Wilderness held biblical meaning as a symbolic place of testing to cross or escape, as when Moses led his people from slavery to the Promised Land through forty years of wandering. Particularly under slavery, wilderness also signified a place of freedom for hunters and for runaways, a place of magic and spirits, a place for secret religious meetings, and a symbolic place in religion and sacred song. However, it lacked connotations that it developed among many whites as a place to escape overcivilized society and return to pure freedom and primal goodness. African Americans do not frequent the wild lands of state and national parks. Polls have repeatedly shown that African Americans prefer developed parks with clear human presence to unpeopled landscapes. As Twiggs's evocation of segregated recreation implies, they enjoy beaches and parks as much as whites but use them socially and not, like Ralph Waldo Emerson, as individuals alone in the woods with the currents of Universal Being flowing through them or, like John Muir, standing solitary on a mountaintop surveying the glorious works of God. Blacks were in a sense alienated from the land of their birth as a generally (but not always) landless race working on whites' land. The Promised Land did at times mean physical and not merely metaphorical places for African Americans: free states to slaves, cheap lands in Kansas and Oklahoma to post–Civil War "Exodusters," and Northern and Western cities to blacks oppressed by segregation. Yet nowhere in this country have African Americans felt the pride of full possession, of mythic origins tied to the soil, or of confidence in a divine destiny manifest in the land itself such as whites have felt for Plymouth Rock, Yosemite Valley, or Stone Mountain. The great monuments of black sacred history are human, not natural, and the dominant religious metaphor has been Moses in the wilderness, not Adam in Paradise.[9]

No other American churches would be as involved in environmental action as black Baptist churches. Baptist churches provided organizing experience, civic engagement, and racial consciousness in opposition to the dominant culture, which fostered an unusually strong tradition of political activism.[10] Congregational independence made Baptist pastors less vulnerable to civil and economic suppression and enabled their leadership in political activity and community advocacy. The civil rights movement drew strength and material support from networks of Southern churches. Black political organizations from the National Association for the Advancement of Colored People, to the National Urban League, to the Southern Christian Leadership Conference relied on churches for support and participation.[11] The Baptist church supplied an unusual number of civil rights leaders as well as the majority of membership in civil rights organizations. Booker T. Washington had been an unordained Baptist preacher. Martin Luther King Jr., King's father, and his maternal grandfather, all Baptist ministers, were also all social or political activists. Large urban Baptist churches provided social services, such as New York's Abyssinian Baptist under Reverend Adam Clayton Powell Sr. and his son, who served in the House of Representatives. The leadership of the leading Civil Rights organization, the Southern Christian Leadership Conference, was heavily Baptist, and Baptist ministers led the campaign against segregation in the civil rights era.[12]

Local black Baptist churches therefore often played essential roles in organizing resistance to Southern toxic waste dumps and toxic pollution, the cause that launched the black environmental justice movement. The environmental justice movement attracted the ecumenical alliance formed during the civil rights era with black clergy from United Church of Christ (UCC), the Congregational Church's successor. In 1982, in the first major African-American action for environmental justice, resistance to a toxic-waste dump in poor Warren County, North Carolina, coalesced around the Coley Springs Baptist Church. Its pastor asked the local UCC minister to help organize and apply tactics of civil disobedience. Sitting with protestors in front of trucks bringing loads of toxic waste to the dump, Methodist minister Joseph Lowery of the Southern Christian Leadership Conference, Baptist preacher Walter Fauntroy, UCC minister Benjamin Chavis, and UCC minister Leon White were arrested together. From this event, Chavis wrote the influential 1987 UCC study that claimed that "environmental racism" affected the siting of dumps and polluting industries. The UCC would sponsor the First and Second People of Color Environmental Leadership Summits in 1991 and 2002.[13]

Over the next decade or two, as the environmental justice movement reached its peak, black Baptist churches played a role in community after community in rallying and organizing against environmental dangers. In Halifax County, Virginia, community activist Cora Tucker, a devout member of Crystal Hills Baptist Church, organized the black community through local churches to fight a nuclear waste dump in 1986. The thoroughly Baptist environmental justice movement of Augusta, Georgia, fought in the 1990s to clean up toxic pollution in the black neighborhood of Hyde Park. Resistance to powerful polluting chemical companies came together in the late 1980s in Baptist churches of Diamond, Louisiana. Around the same time, local activists in Texarkana, Texas, used the Mount Zion Baptist Church to inform and organize the residents of Carver Terrace, a black neighborhood, to get action about the poisoned soil upon which it sat.[14] Examples could be multiplied.

In a symbol of the centrality of the black church to African-American environmentalism, in 1993 the interdenominational National Black Church Environmental and Economic Justice Summit met in Washington, DC. The summit asked Vice President Al Gore to name "a Black Church representative to the Sustainable Communities Task Force of the President's Council on Sustainable Development" and involve "local Black church congregations in major environmental decisions undertaken by the administration." The summit created a Black Church Environmental and Economic Justice Network. The delegates declared the unity of social and ecological justice that motivates African-American environmental thought and action: "We, African-American Church leaders, historically committed to justice issues, affirm the unitary nature of life and commit ourselves to the ministry of converging justice and environmental issues that are critical matters of life and death for our Church and for our community."[15]

Catholic Foundations for an Environmentalist Ethic

In the early 1860s, the war was raging that would finally end American slavery. While out in California Presbyterian Carleton Watkins was taking the photographs of Yosemite Valley that helped make it a park, Irish-born

Catholic Timothy H. O'Sullivan was tramping and camping with Union troops and making an invaluable photographic record of the conflict. When peace returned, O'Sullivan joined four government surveys between 1867 and 1874 that explored and mapped the resources of the little-known arid West. His pictures contrasted with those of Reformed Protestant photographers and painters of the dramatic landscape. Far more than they, O'Sullivan included people or their works. Sometimes he seems to have posed people for scale, but often they simply stand in the scene or gaze out at it along with the viewer (Figure 8.5). At times they are miniature figures nearly hidden in the large panoramic expanse, but clearly O'Sullivan asked them to stand in the frame, as if the landscape were empty without humans in it.[16]

O'Sullivan's fellow Catholics by and large have agreed that people belong in nature, a preference that Southerners and African Americans share. Catholics, too, have been important activists for environmental justice. However, Catholics arrived at those points by way of a completely different path. Catholicism is the oldest European religion in historically Protestant American society. Preceded in America by the Spanish and French, English Catholics arrived in 1634. Catholics remained a small minority until massive immigration from Ireland and Germany after 1830 swelled the denomination to the largest in the nation. Between the Civil War and World War I a larger wave added immigrants from Italy, Poland, and eastern Europe. A third wave, the largest of all, began in the 1980s and has brought multitudes of Catholics from Latin America. Today Catholics make up over a quarter of the American population and former Catholics about a tenth.[17] Catholics often felt ostracized and marginalized by the Protestant majority but since World War II have equaled other denominations in education, income, and influence.[18]

Catholicism has provided few national leaders in conservation or environmentalism. Some relatively minor figures, among them Thomas Berry, Matthew Fox, Rosemary Radford Ruether, and Lois Gibbs, all came to prominence after 1978 and aside from Gibbs, tended to be writers and thinkers rather than organizers and activists. In America and Europe alike, Catholics came later to environmental movements, disdained Deep Ecology, and emphasized nature's social utility or its role in furthering social justice.[19] Whereas for Protestants the Holy Spirit manifests itself in the words of the Bible as well as the ongoing creation of nature, for Catholics the Holy Spirit manifests itself primarily in the Bible and the Church, the body of Christians. God created nature, of course, but he

FIGURE 8.5 Timothy O'Sullivan, *Browns Park, Colorado*, 1872. Unlike Protestant landscape photographers Carleton Watkins, George Fiske, Eadweard Muybridge, and Ansel Adams, Catholic photographer O'Sullivan always posed people in the grand scenery of the American West.

also created society, in its organic unity with ranks and hierarchy. This worldview, historically coupled with mutual support of church and state in Catholic lands, encouraged conservatism about social and religious institutions.[20] Instructed to act with justice and compassion, religious Catholics dedicated themselves to service to the Church, the poor, or the unconverted. Protestants asserted individuals' right to read and understand the Bible and quite comfortably went alone into the woods for religious experience. Catholics, on the other hand, sought religious guidance from Church authorities and teachings and almost always experienced religion in sanctioned settings rather than alone among the works of creation.

At the time Congregationalists and Presbyterians were creating parks and forest reserves, nature preservation and conservation were far from a Catholic priority. The French Revolution and revolutions of 1848 shocked the Catholic Church into conservative reaction, but at the same time pushed it toward a greater emphasis on social justice and delayed attention to the environment crisis. Revolutions and secular states threatened the Church's monopoly. It grew defensive and withdrew into itself. European Church authorities preached against democracy, liberalism, and freedom of the press and of religion. To further shore up Church authority, in 1869 Pope Pius IX called a bishops' council, Vatican I, to confirm papal infallibility in matters of faith. By 1900 American Catholics had embarked on building a parallel society with its own schools, periodicals, charities, and social organizations.[21] Then Pope John XXIII called another council. Meeting from 1962 to 1965, Vatican II charted a decisively different direction. John set the tone with the encyclicals *Mater et Magistra* in 1961 and *Pacem in Terris* in 1963, which expressed special concern for the poor, peace, and world justice and development. Vatican II released *Gaudium et Spes* and *Lumen Gentium*, documents that envisioned a church actively engaged with society. Still organic but less monarchical, the Church had a divine role in the world to aid the poor, further peace, and bring social and economic justice for all peoples. Significantly, the Church was characterized by an old but little-used term, "the people of God," to connote equality and an active laity. The council emphasized the role of the Eucharist, rather than papal authority à la Pius IX, in uniting all believers and giving the Church its sacramental character. Finally, the bishops sanctioned action for social justice as a significant part of the Christian life.[22] Peace and social justice have dominated Church social teaching ever since.[23]

The Vatican did not specifically address ecological problems until after 1990, but in the 1980s a few Franciscan and quite a number of women's religious orders experimented locally with environmentally friendly practices. Nuns have had better success: three sisters founded an organization of religious women, Sisters of the Earth, in 1993, which holds biennial meetings and has grown continuously since its founding.[24] The first encyclical to mention ecology was Pope John Paul II's 1990 World Day of Peace message, "Peace with God the Creator; Peace with All of Creation." In his message the pope grounded his charge to respect the integrity of creation on the dual ideas that we otherwise reject God's plan for creation and perpetrate an injustice on society. The United States Conference of Catholic Bishops followed up with the pastoral letter *Renewing the Earth* in 1991. Two years later, the bishops' Office of Social Development & World Peace established the Environmental Justice Program, which has engaged in a variety of activities.[25] At all levels and in all activities, the American bishops linked the defense of the environment with economic, political, and especially social justice goals. To implement environmental goals locally, the bishops encouraged local parishes to work environmental issues into their social justice programs.[26]

Vatican II's new emphases on the church as community and on social justice have been points of identification for Catholics, both active and lapsed, of all generations. Studies show that although Catholics disagree about abortion, birth control, women in the church, clerical celibacy, and many other issues, they are unanimous on the centrality of the moral principle of social justice.[27] For William K. Reilly, director of the Environmental Protection Administration during the George H. W. Bush administration, these ideals were completely congruent with the goals of environmentalism. "Environmentalists are fundamentally groping in the same direction as Catholic social teaching," Reilly wrote, "because they are both looking for a system that values community more, one that involves an ethical extension of community that includes economy and nature as part of the same moral enterprise." Reilly blamed much of America's environmental problems on the nation's extreme individualism and the spiritual emptiness of people's lives that needed to be filled with material goods. "We have not," he said, "fostered a sufficient sense of community and interpersonal caring and responsibility." He believed that religious values, especially those contained in Catholic social teaching, would fill the void and create an ethical attitude of stewardship.[28]

Catholic Environmental Justice

Working-class Catholics often drew from the Church's revitalized tradition of social justice to build grassroots movements for environmental justice. Beginning in the 1970s, they created an environmentalism tailored to dangers they faced in their homes and workplaces, particularly from toxic environmental chemicals. Environmental justice movements emphasize the good of the community as the highest goal, often a specific ethnic community. Religion, language, culture, history, and perceived power relationships give communities self-conscious identities, which, strengthened by perception of common problems, can be used to organize against environmental threats. Activists knit environmental concerns together with issues of health, housing, fairness, and economics. They never speak in terms of the natural world apart from society. Quite strikingly for rather patriarchal and often macho Catholic cultures, women have almost always been prominent actors, organizers, and leaders, especially in urban areas. Throughout, the Catholic Church has been ever present, sometimes rather subtly, if rarely in leadership positions.

The environmental justice movement was born in 1978 when Lois Gibbs, a shy Irish-Catholic working-class housewife, was outraged to learn that her community and her son's elementary school in Love Canal, near Niagara Falls, New York, had been built over a buried toxic waste dump. Her son—and, as she soon learned, adults and especially children from all over the neighborhood—suffered serious unexplained illnesses. Learning community organizing by experience, Gibbs helped bring the scandal to national attention, forcing the administration of President Jimmy Carter to buy up the neighborhood and clean up the waste. People from across the country began to contact her with similar heart-wrenching concerns, so Gibbs founded the Citizens Clearinghouse for Hazardous Waste in 1981. It later expanded its goals beyond toxic wastes to a broader concern with protecting the health of communities and individuals from environmental threats and changed its name to Center for Health, Environment and Justice (CHEJ). This pioneering environmental justice network continues to inform and train local activists in pursuit of environmental equity between citizens and powerful interests.[29]

In the 1970s, deindustrialization began shutting down factories in the old industrial cities of the Northeast and Midwest where blue-collar Catholics had lived and worked amidst pollution and toxic waste. The Catholic environmental justice movement shifted to poor Hispanics on farms and in urban barrios and the Church began to assume a more active role.[30] Hispanics constitute a large and growing proportion of the population, now about 15 percent, but considerably greater in states bordering Mexico. The Catholicism of Mexican immigrants differs from that of northern and eastern Europeans, who sometimes barely recognize it as Catholicism at all.[31] Mexican Catholicism has special cultural force that shapes modes and forms of environmental activism. Latin American Catholicism in general and Mexican Catholicism in particular have a particular character reflecting their origins in Spain in the fifteenth century. The *reconquista,* the name for the centuries-long Christian reconquest of Iberia, as well as Spain's isolation, meant that the Church in Spain and its American colonies closely resembled the Catholicism of the Middle Ages or premodern Baroque. The core values and traits of Mexican Catholicism grew out of the *reconquista*-flavored goal of missionizing Indians and replacing native gods and rites with the conservative, rural Spanish Catholicism that missionaries knew.

The Roman Catholic hierarchy's close alliance with the ruling Spanish elite distanced it from the concerns of lower-class local churches. Generally of native or mixed-race ancestry, the lower classes resisted mixing religion and politics and remained suspicious of the church hierarchy, which they identified with the power that conquered and ruled them. Liturgy to them had less importance than such communal expressions of religion like processions and saints' days. Religion tended also to be very much a women's concern. Mothers and grandmothers offered blessings, arranged home altars, said the prayers, provided children and grandchildren with religious instruction, and led the family in religious song. Throughout Latin America, veneration of St. Mary was very strong. Women especially appealed to Mary for relief and comfort during the trials and tribulations of life. Accompanying the cult of Mary was a strong focus on the suffering of Christ crucified. Veneration of both Mary and the suffering Christ encouraged patient suffering of adversity.[32] In sum, traditional Mexican Catholicism gives important roles to women and is home-oriented, extraliturgical, communal, long-suffering, and often separated from the hierarchical powers of the institutional Church.

The Hispanic worldview subordinates nature to human needs and concerns. Hispanic landscape art manifests this and is frequently dreamlike, or gives bushes or animals anthropomorphic shapes, or makes landscape a backdrop or stage for human figures in the foreground. References to the land in literature and poetry often use the term *tierra,* which has many connotations of land, territory, and soil, and often recently has come to be associated with Aztlán, the mythical original land of the Aztecs that many now place in the American Southwest, or with a romanticized Indian past in which native cultures and civilizations lived in ecological harmony with *la tierra*. Hispanics integrate environmental issues with or subordinated them to a greater social agenda for the advancement of the whole community.[33]

The first Mexican American environmental action therefore appeared in a movement that was not primarily about the environment at all, César Chavez's United Farm Worker unionization work in the 1960s and 1970s. As the most famous Hispanic struggle, Chavez's crusade became the model for subsequent movements. His well-publicized battle to unionize migrant Mexican farmworkers faced numerous obstacles, including their status as migratory and unskilled labor easily replaceable by more Mexican immigrants as well as the sheer power of the growers and their control of law enforcement and courts. The movement acquired an environmental element when it placed the issue of pesticide exposure in the foreground. Rachel Carson's *Silent Spring* had made everyone aware of the dangers of pesticides in the environment. By 1970 consumers had become skittish about pesticides on produce. All farmworkers experienced and feared exposure to pesticides, which Chavez drew attention to as both a rallying point and an effective way to promote a boycott of grapes.[34]

Catholicism played a central role. With Vatican II fresh in mind, the Church lent important support to Chavez's movement, recognizing him as a committed and faithful Catholic. Deeply religious, Chavez had been active in the Catholic Cursillo movement. He often placed an image of the Virgin of Guadalupe at the head of marches. Chavez's 1968 challenge "Mexican Americans and the Church" stung the still conservative church hierarchy and inspired many priests and bishops to provide greater support and encouragement to the farmworker movement. Priests now joined farmworkers on picket lines and marches. Chavez frequently undertook religious fasts, which the more secular media or his more Marxist-oriented supporters interpreted as hunger strikes, but which led him to greater clarity of understanding and even visions.

Chavez's United Farm Worker movement and later similar groups like Farm Worker Network for Economic and Environmental Justice integrated environmental concerns into a framework of health and justice issues that included workplace democracy and workers' control of production, adequate housing, nutrition, and health care. The Farm Worker Network works to "improve farm worker safety, health, and economic well-being; strengthen and build farm worker organizations and communities as a means of self-representation for workers and families; [and] support the sustainability of . . . agriculture."[35] Despite the group's title, environmental issues are more implicit than explicit and secondary to communal and social goals.

A rather different Hispanic environmental movement arose to preserve traditional acequia agricultural practices of Hispanos, as they are called, in northern New Mexico and southern Colorado. In the seventeenth and eighteenth centuries, Spanish settlers built irrigation works known as acequias in Texas and New Mexico. Some survive in northern New Mexico and southern Colorado. Most of these Hispano communities were founded with communal land grants and depended on elaborate communally maintained networks of ditches. Troubles began when the Mexican war in 1845 brought the area under American jurisdiction, along with an unfamiliar legal system, sharp lawyers, rapacious speculators, and corrupt, ignorant, or racist government officials. In 1960, Taylor Ranch enclosed common lands in Colorado and sold the rights to Enron in the 1990s. Enron began clear-cutting the watershed despite lawsuits and the outcry of local Hispanos over the effect on the acequia water supply. Another controversy arose when former communal lands were incorporated into national forests in the early twentieth century. In the 1970s and 1980s, New Mexican Hispanos confronted government foresters and environmentalists regarding grazing of livestock and timber cutting in the Rio Arriba region, causing the rift between Carl Anthony and David Brower. By romanticizing their relationship to the land and representing themselves as endangered communities, they won increased influence on forest planning and management. In turn, contact and conflict with environmentalists raised their own ecological awareness. They now often emphasize their role in soil conservation, water quality, and wildlife habitat; their heirloom crop varieties adapted to local conditions; and their resistance to developers who threaten water rights. Other conflicts include the damage to watersheds and acequias by development of the Taos Ski Valley and battles against threats to local water quality from a Molycorp molybdenum strip mine in Questa, New Mexico, and a gold mine in San Luis, Colorado.

In the late 1990s various organizations arose out of these conflicts, including the Colorado Acequia Association, the Taos Valley Acequia Association, the New Mexico Acequia Association, and the Congreso de

Acequias. Here, too, Catholicism played an explicit role. Acequia communities revived the neglected tradition of honoring San Isidro Labrador, the patron saint of farmers, with a daylong procession blessing the acequias and beginning the annual communal work of cleaning and repairing the ditches.[36]

Almost always led by women, urban barrio and community activism has arisen in many places, primarily in response to toxic pollution of the air and water but also sometimes to the lack of local parkland. As in the farmworker movement, environmental concerns are frequently subsumed in such community goals as housing, community-based health care, locally oriented economic development, community gardens, and demands to reclaim or create community open space. One of the earliest and best-known organizations was Mothers of East Los Angeles, organized in 1985. Mothers of East L.A. scored some notable victories, including defeat of plans for a toxic waste incinerator, for a prison, and for a fuel pipeline. Around the same time, grassroots organizers led by Rose Marie Augustine in Tucson began to battle for cleanup of the Hughes Air Force Missile Plant No. 4, now owned by Raytheon, whose years of careless disposal of chemicals extensively contaminated groundwater, mainly under Hispanic South Tucson, and the Santa Cruz River as well. In small, poor, Kettleman City, California, Mary Lou Mares, Maricela Mares-Alatorre, and others founded El Pueblo para el Aire y Agua Limpio (People for Clean Air and Water) and fought successfully against the unlawful exclusion of local people by the Environmental Protection Agency and a large corporation in the decision to site a hazardous waste facility nearby. When in 1983 Albuquerque, New Mexico, was chosen as the site for an Intel plant, the Southwest Network for Environmental and Economic Justice campaigned against the company. Intel was responsible for three Superfund sites in California and for a huge drawdown of the aquifer to slake its thirsty industrial processes, which threatened local acequias and rural wells. Other victories include the large urban and environmental coalitions that achieved new parks in the Cornfield, Taylor Yard, and Baldwin Hills areas of Los Angeles, which previously almost completely lacked public open space. Notable Hispanic organizations have arisen in various regions and for various causes and include the Coalition for Justice in the Maquiladoras, People Organized to Demand Environmental and Economic Rights, Fuerza Unida, and the Labor/Community Strategy Center of Los Angeles.[37]

Varieties of Catholic Environmental Thought

In these actions for environmental justice, Catholic priests and church-men and -women often participated but the Church itself never initiated or sponsored them. The campaigns arose in an inherently bottom-up, local process from people desperate to protect the health and happiness of their families and communities. The Church's historical power and responsibility in Catholic countries to define, promote, and sometimes enforce the common good gave it a strong preference for top-down solutions. Where Puritans had established a sort of theocratic republic in New England in pursuit of a godly society, in Catholic societies the institutional Church provided moral authority and guidance for a just society. In the Catholic counterpart to the Puritan town's communal policing of farming and lumbering, farmers of Catholic parishes of Quebec adopted conservation practices under the watchful eye of the priests.[38] Consequently, priests and theologians have been leading Catholic environmental voices, in contrast with Protestant environmentalism, in which ministers like Ralph Waldo Emerson or Holmes Rolston III have been the exception. As Protestant environmentalists increasingly lapsed, Catholics along with Anglicans have fairly taken over the enterprise of environmental writing that is explicitly religious, as opposed to vaguely spiritual.

The best-known American Catholic environmental writers do not have names with origins in Latin America or southern or eastern Europe. Their environmental conversations have taken place in the language of Catholicism's rich intellectual heritage in the smaller, decorous northern-European rooms of the mansion of American Catholicism. Educated priests, bishops, brothers, and nuns arrived with northern-European Catholic immigrants or were sent by the Church. Bearing Catholicism's intellectual and theological traditions, they founded schools, seminaries, and universities from coast to coast. The open theological atmosphere after Vatican II fostered the first explicitly environmental elements in Catholic thought, in no small measure by encouraging experimentation with spiritual sources outside traditional Catholic theology.[39]

In the 1970s Dominican priest Matthew Fox of California popularized "creation spirituality," an ecstatic mysticism based on his reading of medieval mystics, particularly Hildegard of Bingen and Meister Eckhart, and drawn freely from Asian and native religions. In *Original Blessing* [in contrast to "Original Sin"]: *A Primer in Creation Spirituality* of 1983 and *The Coming of the Cosmic Christ: The Healing of Mother Earth and the Birth of a Global Renaissance* of 1988, Fox presented an exuberant, mystically informed antidote to the ills of modernity. Inspired by a Northern California–style therapeutic spiritualism, he believed mystical response to God's creation led to a reverent attitude toward the cosmos. Fox considered the universe a sacrament, which in Catholics theology signifies a channel of God's saving grace. His New-Age and neopagan borrowings alarmed the increasingly conservative Vatican. Cardinal Joseph Ratzinger, the future Pope Benedict XVI, enjoined a year of silence in 1989 and dismissed him from the Dominican order in 1993. Now an Episcopal priest, Fox founded and until 2005 led the University of Creation Spirituality (now Wisdom University) in Oakland, California.[40]

Other Catholic thinkers shared Fox's emphasis on individuals' spiritual state, urge to missionize with an environmentalist message, indifference to the social and political order, and sacramental view of nature. Thomas Berry, a priest in the Passionist order, forged a less-radical, widely praised ecological theology from the Catholic tradition. Berry called himself a "geologian," one who combines science and theology. Born in 1904, Berry was deeply impressed by Jesuit thinker Pierre Teilhard du Chardin's evolutionary theology. He believed humanity needed a "new story" of the earth, a new Genesis myth based on science and informed by theology, to help recreate the relationship between the divine, humans, and the earth. Berry's *The Dream of the Earth* of 1988 described the succession of ages on earth and our entry into an Ecozoic Era. In a rather Catholic way akin to seeking guidance from the Church, he spoke of going to the earth for guidance to learn again to live as a member of what he calls the "earth community." He wrote, "Only now have we begun to listen with some attention [to the earth] and with a willingness to respond to the earth's demands that we cease our industrial assault, that we abandon our inner rage against the conditions of our earthly existence, that we renew our human participation in the grand liturgy of the universe."[41] Berry's earth community recalled the conception of the Catholic Church as the people of God, a community united through liturgy.

Mathematician and physicist Brian Swimme teamed with Fox in 1983 to write *Manifesto for a Global Civilization*, then under the spell of Berry and Teilhard de Chardin published *The Universe Story* in 1992. Swimme produced a string of books and videos on the divine cosmological story. He resigned his academic position in mathematics to teach Philosophy, Cosmology, and Consciousness in the Ecology, Spirituality, and Religion program of California Institute of Integral Studies in San Francisco. In 2011, he and Mary Evelyn Tucker produced a public television video and companion book, *The Journey of the Universe*. With a joint appointment at the Forestry and Divinity Schools of Yale University, Tucker has been a zealous advocate for Berry and Swimme's holy scientifically inspired cosmological creation story. In the 1990s, she and John Grim of Yale organized a series of ten conferences on World Religions and Ecology at the Center for the Study of World Religions at Harvard Divinity School, which resulted in ten published volumes. Like Fox and Berry, Swimme, Tucker, and Grim advocate proselytizing for a universal spiritual transformation to redirect the destructive direction of global society, including environmental destruction. They often appeal to indigenous or Asian societies for examples of constructive ecological spirituality and ethics.

Other Catholics have developed related ideas. Jesuit priest and environmental ethicist Albert J. Fritsch believed that a liturgical people tend to adopt appropriate—that is, people-centered—technology. He also saw the Eucharist as a community-building sacrament that also could help humans heal the earth, which like Christ is crucified and will rise again. Appropriate technology, he wrote, was a "Eucharistic response" that would establish ecojustice. Fritsch here echoed German Catholic E.F. Schumacher's *Small Is Beautiful: Economics as if People Mattered*, a 1973 bestseller that also advocated appropriate technology to lift up the world's poor.[42]

The most hierarchical and liturgical Protestant church, the Episcopal (in America) or Anglican (in Britain) Church, has also fostered interest in this sort of cosmological divinity. Perhaps the common interest in cosmology of Episcopalians and Catholics is related to a disposition of hierarchical churches to emphasize the transcendent power and kingship of a deity who directs the development of the universe. In the 1920s mathematician Alfred North Whitehead, son of an Anglican priest, formulated the first modern cosmology. His "process philosophy" drew together elements from religion, development, and science. His chief disciple, Charles Hartshorne, another son of an Episcopal priest, transformed process philosophy into "process theology."[43] He coined "panentheism," to distinguish his theology from pantheism and describe a God who is not the world, but is not completely apart from it and participates in its evolution. His student John B. Cobb Jr., son of Georgian Methodist missionaries to Japan, carried on Hartshorne's work in light of ecology and social justice, Methodism being a hierarchical denomination with close historical ties to

Anglicanism. His most important book, *For the Common Good: Redirecting the Economy toward Community, Environment, and a Sustainable Future*, written with economist Herman Daly in 1989, veered in the Southern individualist direction to argue for a decentralized economy of small communities founded on recognition of human needs and environmental stewardship.[44]

Vatican II opened the door for laypeople, including women, to practice theology and thus break up the Church's long dominance of the field.[45] Outspoken Catholic women rebelled against patriarchal religious monopoly. They incorporated, revived, or emphasized feminist perspectives in the Catholic tradition and often reached back to a supposed past where women held priesthood and goddesses were venerated. Women pushed Catholic theology to its limits, or beyond. Mary Daly taught at a Jesuit school, Boston College, where she attacked the patriarchal influence on religion in a number of books, the most widely read of which was *Gyn/Ecology: The Metaethics of Radical Feminism* of 1978. Charlene Spretnak recovered prepatriarchal goddess worship in her popular 1978 *Lost Goddesses of Early Greece: A Collection of Pre-Hellenic Myths*. Dolores LaChapelle supported this approach and later combined it with advocacy of the philosophy of Deep Ecology.[46]

A Catholic environmental feminism emerged. "Ecofeminism" was coined in 1974 by French radical feminist Françoise d'Eaubonne and popularized in the United States by Ynestra King. Most influential has been Rosemary Radford Ruether's ecofeminist Christian theology. While she has been consistently critical of the Catholic Church, particularly regarding its views of gender, sexuality, and reproduction, she has remained Catholic. Her feminist analyses of social and environmental crises began to appear in the 1970s. In *New Woman, New Earth: Sexist Ideologies and Human Liberation* she linked the historical domination of nature and of woman and thus was one of the earliest expounders of ecofeminist ideology. Her *Sexism and God-Talk: Toward a Feminist Theology* of 1983 remains a standard work on women and Christianity. *Gaia & God: An Ecofeminist Theology of Earth Healing* of 1992 is a comprehensive discussion of ecofeminist theology.[47]

Episcopalians again have been active in the same areas. Theologian Sallie McFague operated in a theological tradition more influenced by Reformed theologian Karl Barth and other modern theologians and has had much greater influence on liberal Protestant theology. Influenced by ecofeminism and concerned with how language and metaphor shape understanding of God, McFague argued in such works as *Models of God* of 1987 and in *God's Body* of 1993 for recovering such neglected metaphors of God as "mother," "lover," and "friend" in place of "king," "ruler," and "lord," which are the metaphors that caused oppression of women and the earth. She advocated the panentheist position and argued the metaphor of the world and universe as God's body would lead toward greater respect for the environment. Carolyn Merchant's landmark 1980 *The Death of Nature: Women, Ecology, and the Scientific Revolution* made a major contribution to early development of ecofeminism from a nontheological point of view. She blamed the Enlightenment for laying the groundwork for both the ecological crisis and oppression of women. Also influential were two Presbyterians, Carol P. Christ, author of the influential 1978 essay "Why Women Need the Goddess," and Susan Griffin, author of *Woman and Nature: The Roaring Inside Her* of 1978, which influenced Merchant.[48]

Varieties of Jewish Social Environmentalism

Many Jewish women joined the ecofeminist movement as well. Traditionally, thoroughly patriarchal Judaism reserved all key rituals for men and restricted women to roles outside of the synagogue. Women were keepers of rituals of the home: lighting candles on Sabbaths and holy days, preparing special holiday meals, and keeping the dietary laws of *kashrut*. Beginning in the 1960s a generation of Jewish women rebelled against Judaism as a thoroughly masculine, patriarchal tradition that excluded and oppressed women. The vanguard of feminist thought and activism was heavily Jewish: Betty Friedan, Gloria Steinem (half Jewish), Bella Abzug, Gerda Lerner, Susan Brownmiller, Shulamith Firestone, and Andrea Dworkin.[49]

Taking ecofeminism far beyond the pagan flirtations of Fox and Spretnak, in the post–Earth Day era of the 1970s some embraced earth-based spirituality in reconstructed paganism, called Wicca, or in the traditions of indigenous peoples. Wicca was as ritual-filled as Judaism but worshipped a Mother Earth Goddess rather than a Father God. Many leaders and a large portion of believers have been Jewish in Goddess-worshipping circles both in America and Britain. Miriam Simos took the name Starhawk, formed a coven, and in 1979 published the bestselling *The Spiral Dance: A Rebirth of the Ancient Religion of the Great Goddess*, a "Judaism" for women, with rituals and a goddess. Wiccan priestess Margot Adler published *Drawing Down the Moon: Witches, Druids, Goddess-Worshippers, and Other Pagans in America Today* in the same year. Books like Merlin Stone's influential *When God Was a Woman* of 1976 purported to document widespread ancient goddesses worship suppressed by male Jewish and Christian authorities. Inspired by Biblical passages describing worship of both the Hebrew God and Near-Eastern goddesses, some Jewish neopagans sought to integrate those goddesses into existing Jewish traditions to counterbalance the starkly masculine God of the Torah.[50]

Wiccan advocates claimed that worship of the Earth Mother Goddess encouraged greater ecological consciousness than worship of the patriarchal God of Judaism, Christianity, and Islam. Prominent Jewish ecofeminists freely adopted pagan elements. In the 1990s Gloria Feman Orenstein, now of the University of Southern California, and Irene Diamond of the University of Oregon published *The Reflowering of the Goddess* and coedited the influential collection of essays *Reweaving The World: The Emergence of Ecofeminism.*[51] In the 1970s a number of Jews searched for an authentic religion that neither oppressed women nor exploited the earth and found it in indigenous or Eastern spirituality. Winona LaDuke, daughter of a Jewish mother and Ojibwe father, returned to her father's tribe to advocate for Native American rights as well as environmental causes and was the Green Party vice-presidential candidate in 2000. Other Jews have also felt the attraction of indigenous authenticity without entirely abandoning their heritage, among them David Abram, author of *The Spell of the Sensuous: Perception and Language in a More-than-Human World* of 1996, and Evan Eisenberg, author of *The Ecology of Eden* of 1998.

For most Jews, religious or secular, whether or not they followed the lure of pagan or native spiritual authenticity, Jewish heritage and culture oriented them toward an environmentalism that subordinated nature to social needs, similar to the ethic of blacks and Catholics. Pioneering photographer Alfred Stieglitz, for example, even when photographing nature invested his images with human meanings. Stieglitz discovered, nurtured, and promoted Reformed Modernist artists Arthur Dove, Marsden Hartley, John Marin, Georgia O'Keeffe, and Ansel Adams, and appreciated their spiritual, unpeopled landscapes, but he himself was no Emersonian and certainly no Puritan. Born in 1864 in Hoboken, New Jersey, to wealthy immigrant Jews from Germany, Stieglitz, like most German Americans, considered German culture far superior to American. As a teenager he repeatedly read Johann Wolfgang von Goethe's *Faust* rather than Milton's *Paradise Lost* or Emerson's essays. *Faust* gave him quiet in "despairing moments"[52] but lacked Milton's or Emerson's ecological implications.

FIGURE 8.6 Alfred Stieglitz, *Winter—Fifth Avenue*, 1892. Stieglitz made his reputation as a photographer for his striking urban compositions. Although he summered at Lake George, he took no Hudson-River-School-style pictures of the landscape without people.

Stieglitz achieved renown for innovative photographs of urban life (Figure 8.6). Nature or landscape subjects little interested him, even though the Stieglitz family vacationed on the shores of Lake George in the Adirondacks every year after 1868.

Then the Modernist revolution exposed Stieglitz to Emersonianism. Dove, Hartley, Marin, and O'Keeffe, the enduring core of his circle, spoke and wrote in a Transcendental-inflected idiom. Stieglitz picked up Emersonian phrases, such as his comment when he first saw

O'Keeffe's art in 1916: "Woman is, at last, on paper, expressing her relation to the Universe."[53] Hartley excitedly alerted him from Germany to Vasily Kandinsky's *Über das Geistige in der Kunst* (*On the Spiritual in Art*), which he reprinted and shared, and in the 1920s the vogue for Ouspensky and Gurdjieff engulfed him. Stieglitz began photographing in an Emersonian mode. At Lake George in the summer of 1922 and for the next dozen years, he aimed his camera at the cloud patterns in the sky, which technical advances had recently made possible. Still, nature to him had no meaning without human associations. He called his pictures *Equivalents* (Figure 8.7)—that is, symbolic equivalents to human emotions. The concept recalls Emerson's dictum "Nature always wears the colors of the spirit," that nature looks cheerful when one's mood is high and "is overspread with melancholy" when it is low.[54] The *Equivalents* photographs impressed Ansel Adams and struck a chord with his own Emersonian ideals.[55]

Stieglitz's preference in his own work for human presence or associations in nature reflected typical attitudes of Jews and future Jewish environmentalists. Jewish environmental attitudes had roots in ethical doctrines that share much with the social tenets of New England Puritans. Both groups developed social and environmental ethics designed for small communities—in the Puritan instance, for New England towns, and in the Jewish case, for the ghettos and *shtetlach* of Europe (Yiddish for "little towns"), where Jews were formerly legally confined under the oversight of their religious authorities. Jews were moreover inspired like Presbyterians by the Biblical prophets standing apart from government and religious institutions and preaching righteousness to the nation. Jews like Barry Commoner, Paul Ehrlich, and Michael Pollan have taken their places among the greats of environmentalism and are much more widely known than any black, Catholic, or Episcopal environmentalist.

However, Judaism and Christianity are rather different religious systems and has given rise to significantly different environmental ideals and goals. In contrast with Christianity's central attention to conversion and salvation, Judaism is a practical religion with relatively little interest in an afterlife. It emphasizes the ways in which Jews can conform daily life to God's will. In the Torah, the Talmud, and the latest interpretations of the rabbis, Jewish life centers on fulfilling God's commandments. Centuries of scholarly reasoning and debate produced elaborate rules for all aspects of living and as a byproduct left a strong cultural preference for reason, rationality, and argument. In this way Judaism contrasts with Christianity,

FIGURE 8.7 Alfred Stieglitz, *Equivalent,* 1926. The Emersonian spiritual seekers in his circle moved Stieglitz to take photographs of the sky in the 1920s. Just as Emerson thought that "Nature always wears the colors of the spirit," Stieglitz regarded the series as visual equivalents of human emotions.

which rejects the letter which killeth—obedience to religious law and formal rules—in favor of the spirit which giveth life—the inward state which only God can see (II Corinthians 3:6). Volumes of rabbinical commentary evince a fascination with the specifics of how to act morally in the world, in obedience to God's command. Despite the tendency of certain

Christian denominations to legalism, Christian behavior is bound by no comparably extensive, detailed advice. Instead, such general principles as "love thy neighbor" guide Christians, upon whose practical impossibility the Christian theology of salvation by grace rests. The Christian notion of charity, from Latin *caritas*, "love," reflects the inward state and morality of the individual giver, while the corresponding Jewish idea of *tzedakah*, charity, from the root *tzedek*, "justice" or "righteousness," implies social goals and duty.[56]

The attraction of socialism and socialistic solutions to twentieth-century Jewish radicals and some environmentalists echoes Jewish social modes of ethical thinking. Judaism is fundamentally communal. Central to Jewish identity is the concept of Jews as a people chosen by God. A Jew away from other Jews falls in danger of losing his identity. At least ten Jews are required for worship. All Jewish holy days, especially Passover, celebrate and reinforce collective identity. No holiday honors an individual, like Christmas and Catholic saints' days do for Christians. The laws and commandments reinforce this community identity and often restrict individual behavior for the common good. Special Jewish food, holidays, beliefs, practices, laws, identity, and in some cases clothing have reinforced a sense of alienation and outsiderness in Christian societies, away from the Promised Land of Israel.

Jews do not, like Reformed Protestants, seek solitude into the woods to communicate with the Spirit of God. Judaism downplays natural theology, the idea that God may be found through nature. Jews have authored no grand cosmologies like those of Berry or Whitehead. They historically rejected excessive religious interest in nature in itself or in attachment to the land. Rabbis believed that nature's beauty distracted students from study of God's Word in the Torah and attachment to any other land might weaken desire to return to the Promised Land of Israel.[57] All modern Jewish back-to-the-land movements have been weak or ephemeral except the *kibbutz* movement, with its strong socialist ideology and association with Zionism.[58] Almost no Jewish landscape artists have contributed significantly to the American tradition of landscape art.[59]

Jewish doctrines of nature are thoroughly practical. Despite the existence of a Jewish mystical tradition that focuses on nature's beauty as a path to union with God, for the most part Judaism contains little theological interest in nature in itself as mystical resource. While acknowledging the Genesis grant of dominion over the earth, Judaism emphasizes that humans are God's managers or stewards on his earth. Various Jewish laws dealing with nature discuss the problems of pollution, open space around settlements, rest for animals and land on the Sabbath and in Jubilee years, and prohibitions against pointless destruction of plants and animals. The governing principles are not to protect nature for itself but to limit detrimental social effects of individual action and acknowledge that all things on earth ultimately belong to God, not humans.[60] The yardstick for nature's value is its usefulness to society.

Stieglitz's parents arrived in America as part of a wave of German-Jewish immigration in the early and middle nineteenth century that counted a few important Jewish environmentalists among its descendants. Jews in Germany were less oppressed, less communal, less religious, and more assimilated than Jews in eastern Europe. Attracted to economic freedom in the United States as well as its Enlightenment ideals, German-Jewish immigrants tended far less than other Jews to preserve traditional values. They often immigrated as single men and lived away from established Jewish communities. Many started as peddlers, shopkeepers, and businessmen and often rose to the middle and upper classes.[61]

Robert ("Bob") Marshall was the first important Jewish environmental activist. Although Marshall typically kept to forestry circles or worked out of public view, he was an influential wilderness advocate in the 1920s and 1930s whose arguments for wilderness convinced his boss, Secretary of the Interior Harold Ickes, to protect undeveloped natural areas. His father, Louis Marshall, had grown up in a family of German-Jewish immigrant storekeepers in Rochester, New York, and came to be a national Jewish leader, prominent constitutional lawyer, and defender of minority rights. As was common with German Jews, Bob Marshall was raised in Reform Judaism, a "modernized" Judaism akin to liberal Protestantism. He attended the Ethical Culture School, which liberal German Jew Felix Adler founded to teach ethical principles without "anachronistic" religious ceremonies and beliefs. The Marshalls, like the Stieglitzes, spent summers in the Adirondacks, which Louis had been instrumental in preserving as a park and where Bob became an avid climber.

The social ethics of liberal Judaism left a clear mark on Marshall's activism for national forests and wilderness. Marshall chose a career in the Forest Service, where he could combine interests in ethics and conservation. Gifford Pinchot had imbued the service with the ideal of scientific restraint of private rapaciousness for the public good. This ethic complemented Marshall's advocacy of social control of selfish and avaricious actions that harmed the common good. Marshall's 1930 pamphlet

The Social Management of American Forests and his 1933 book *The People's Forests* called for increasing regulation of private lands and eventually elimination of private ownership altogether so that "social welfare is substituted for private gain as the major objective of management."[62] His arguments for preserving wilderness included such social purposes as transportation of poor youths to wilderness areas so that they could enjoy them as well as the middle class. He fought to end racial discrimination in private facilities within national forests.[63]

Beginning in the 1960s, biologist Paul R. Ehrlich warned of the dangers of overpopulation in books that have sold millions of copies and made population into an important environmental issue. With a liberal Jewish background, he has emphasized social solutions. Ehrlich's paternal grandparents emigrated from the Polish and Romanian parts of the Austrian empire, while his Reform-Jewish mother's German ancestors arrived in the 1840s. Born in 1932 in New Jersey, Ehrlich became a biologist and ecologist specializing in butterflies. At the urging of David Brower, in 1968 he published his ruminations on overpopulation in *The Population Bomb*, an apocalyptic blockbuster bestseller that set the terms of the debate on population control. Ehrlich stresses "how Americans could corporately make government more efficient and simultaneously save themselves by taking care of the environment and each other."[64] He believes that the root cause of global environmental and social problems is overpopulation and that the only effective solution is social and government action, indeed, "fundamental changes in the social and political institutions."[65] "Greed, myopia, prejudice, and denial" and naïve faith in "America, capitalism and technology" explain opposition to population control.[66] Although he is a biologist who has published several books on ecology and once approvingly discussed Deep Ecology, Ehrlich's population books treat nature as a limited, complex resource and seek out social sources of social and environmental problems in government and private policies that affect population growth, agriculture, technological fixes, urbanization, income distribution, and degradation of ecosystems. Solutions would require rational social, governmental, and concerted international action. In 1996 his faith in the power of reason led him to publish an attack on the irrationality of the antienvironmental movement in *Betrayal of Science and Reason: How Anti-Environmental Rhetoric Threatens Our Future*.[67]

The work of Peter Singer, son of Viennese Jews who fled to Australia in 1938, instigated the modern animal rights movement. In books like his 1975 *Animal Liberation: Towards an End to Man's Inhumanity to Animals*,

Singer took the moral arguments for extending equal rights to racial minorities, women, and homosexuals and applied them to treating sentient animals as if they also had rights. In 1972 Henry Spira, a civil-rights activist and grandson of a Hungarian rabbi, was inspired by Singer's work to start the movement for civil disobedience in defense of animals. He founded Animal Rights International in 1974, forerunner of People for the Ethical Treatment of Animals (PETA) and similar animal-rights groups.[68]

German Jewish liberals did not turn as far to the left as Jews from eastern Europe, whose deep ranks of political radicals supplied a number of prominent radical environmentalists. The hopeless desperation of Russian Jews between 1881 and 1920 encouraged radicalism and utopianism. Their opposition to established authority and sensitivity to class oppression were both natural responses to Russian persecution as well as secular versions of Biblical themes of deliverance from unjust, powerful oppressors. Universalist ideals of the Enlightenment drew great numbers away from traditional Judaism. Many gravitated to small socialist and communist parties. In the 1880s, movements arose to transform Jewish life with a return to the land in egalitarian agricultural communes in America or Palestine. Russian-born radical Raphael Zon, a leading figure in the Forest Service, argued for a socialism-inspired public ownership of the forests and possibly influenced Bob Marshall.[69]

The most radical American Jewish environmentalist, Murray Bookchin, was the son of immigrants fleeing Russian pogroms and failed revolution. "The values with which I was raised," he once remarked, "and which I still cherish above all else, are best summarized by the old communistic maxim: 'From each according to ability, to each according to need.' They include the key notions of complementarity, rationality, freedom, and self-consciousness."[70] In the 1950s, he took interest in the issue of uncontrolled pesticide use and published *Our Synthetic Environment* in 1962, the same year as *Silent Spring*. In the 1960s Bookchin's politics had moved past socialism to anarchism. Increasing ecological awareness led him in a series of books to theorize what he called "social ecology," notably *The Ecology of Freedom* of 1982. Bookchin attacked Earth First! and advocates of Deep Ecology for dangerous misanthropy, fuzzy mysticism, antihumanism, and especially, disregard for the origins of the ecological crisis in a society based on hierarchical domination and exploitation.[71] He countered with his vision of a society of equality and participatory democracy, based on reason and ecology: "An ecological society, structured around a confederal Commune of communes, each of which is shaped to conform with the ecosystem and bioregion in which it [is] located, would deploy [ecologically sustainable] technologies in an artistic way [and] make use of local resources."[72] Somewhat like Congregationalists extolling the model of the New England town, he was advocating egalitarian communities committed to ecological principles that recalled an idealized *shtetl*, the Jewish town of his eastern European ancestors. His proposals found an audience in the global radical-ecology movement.[73]

Barry Commoner moderated his youthful radicalism and achieved much broader environmental influence. Born in 1917 to Russian-Jewish immigrants, Commoner was drawn to radicalism as a student at Columbia University. During his career as a biologist at Washington University in St. Louis and Queens College in Brooklyn, his politics grew less radical but always leaned left. In the 1950s, the danger to humanity of nuclear testing and radioactive fallout alarmed Commoner and got him thinking about environmental issues. He organized the St. Louis Committee for Nuclear Information and founded the influential newsletter *Scientist and Citizen*. In a series of books, including the bestseller *The Closing Circle: Nature, Man, and Technology* of 1971, he called for fundamental changes in the political and economic systems of the world, which he saw as the source of the ecological crisis. Commoner drew attention to the limitations of science and insisted that moral values guide the implementation of scientific analysis and technological solutions to environmental problems. He hoped that a radical, decentralized democracy, a distant cousin to Bookchin's ecoanarchism, would replace centralized, technocratic planning. In 1970 *Time* magazine put him on its cover as the "Paul Revere of Ecology," and a decade later he ran for president as the candidate of the Citizens Party.[74]

Attraction to Marxism and socialism faded among succeeding generations of Jews, some of whom gravitated instead to the anarchistic, nonideological radical environmentalism of the 1980s and 1990s. Howard L. ("Howie") Wolke grew disenchanted with the commercial focus of the forestry program he enrolled in at the University of New Hampshire. In the 1970s he became a representative for David Brower's Friends of the Earth and in 1980 joined with Dave Foreman and three others to found Earth First! Six years later he served six months in a Wyoming county jail for pulling up survey stakes in a potential wilderness area. Like Foreman disillusioned with the direction Earth First! was taking, he left in 1990 and founded a nonprofit wilderness advocacy organization, Big Wild Advocates.[75] Judi Bari joined Earth First! just as Wolke was leaving it.

Daughter of two radical immigrants, a Jewish mother and Italian father, Bari had been an activist in antiwar, labor, and other leftwing social causes. In 1988 Bari moved to Oregon and got caught up in Earth First!'s attempts to organize resistance to the Pacific Lumber Company's plans to clear-cut redwoods to finance a junk-bond takeover by Houston financier Charles Hurwitz. She was the primary organizer of the Redwood Summer of 1990, modeled on the Freedom Summer of 1964 in Mississippi to attract sympathetic activists from across the country to participate in civil disobedience, in defense of old-growth redwoods. That May, Bari was severely wounded when a pipe bomb apparently planted by neo-Nazis exploded under her car seat. Redwood Summer successfully saved some forest and was instrumental in the eventual state-funded creation of Headwaters Forest Preserve in 1999. Bari's death from breast cancer in 1997 left Earth First! without a strong or charismatic leader.[76]

As the Progressive Presbyterian causes of parks and conservation have gradually faded from the headlines, the third leg of Congregational conservation, agriculture, has made a comeback, due in huge measure to Jews. Though largely an urban people, Jews since the 1920s have led the organic food movement in the United States, both as farmers and as prophets, and pushed this nonideological and once-marginal issue from the fringe to the mainstream. Unusually complicated religious dietary laws raise Jews' consciousness of food quality and purity. Keeping kosher requires constant mindfulness of what one is eating and how one is eating it. The social orientation of Judaism makes itself apparent in arguments which often emphasize human health prior to ecological health of the kind *Silent Spring* advocated.

The contemporary organic foods movement started with Ralph Borsodi. Borsodi advocated a back-to-the-land movement in the 1920s and 1930s to lead people away from unhealthy, crowded cities to healthier communities in tune with the land, similar to his contemporaries the Nearings but sans Baptist individualism. Son of Hungarian-Jewish immigrants, he published three widely read books, *The Distribution Age* in 1927, *This Ugly Civilization* in 1929, and *Flight from the City* in 1933, and moved to Long Island to found his School of Living in 1934. In 1950, Borsodi moved to Melbourne, Florida, a town founded on his principles.[77]

One visitor to Borsodi's School for Living was Jerome I. Cohen, born on New York City's Lower East Side in 1898 to orthodox Jewish immigrants from Poland. He studied to become a rabbi and although he dropped out after his father died, his biographer noted there forever remained something of a rabbi about him and his writings.[78] Changing his name to the invented, un-Jewish-sounding Rodale, he moved to Emmaus, Pennsylvania, and established an organic farm. To both Rodale and Borsodi, pure food was the foundation of good health and long life. Rodale popularized the word "organic" to describe food grown without harmful pesticides or chemical fertilizer. His Rodale Press published gardening books as well as the magazines *Organic Gardening* and *Prevention,* whose titles reflected his overarching concern for eating well to avoid ill health. No one was better poised to take advantage of rising worry over chemicals in food in the wake of *Silent Spring.* Long a movement of "food faddists," organic farming spread into the counterculture and from there into mainstream society. By 1970, Rodale's name appeared regularly in the popular press as the "prophet" or "guru" of organic food. After his death in 1972, his son and granddaughter carried on the family business and legacy.

Today the best-known advocate for organic food is Michael Pollan, author of a string of bestsellers on gardening and food: *Second Nature: A Gardener's Education* (1991); *The Botany of Desire: A Plant's Eye View of the World* (2001); *The Omnivore's Dilemma: A Natural History of Four Meals* (2006); *In Defense of Food: An Eater's Manifesto* (2008); *Food Rules: An Eater's Manual* (2009); and *Cooked: A Natural History of Transformation* (2013). Pollan acknowledges the influence on him of his grandfather and his Long-Island garden, rather than Borsodi or Rodale. The practical, rule-oriented Jewish dietary rules seem rather obviously echoed in the title and content of *Food Rules* with its sixty-four "simple" rules for healthy eating.[79] *The Omnivore's Dilemma,* the most original and influential of Pollan's books, and subsequent writings take on the processed-food industry. He argues for greater consciousness about the food we eat and for a diet of purer, healthier food.

One section of *Omnivore's Dilemma* describes the rise of organic agribusiness from small countercultural organic farms of the 1960s and 1970s. Perhaps Pollan did not notice it, but each of the large organic-foods companies he investigated was founded by Jews, which either illustrates the importance of Jewish organic farmers in spreading organic food to American tables, or is a remarkable coincidence. Drew and Myra Goodman founded Earthbound Farms and introduced the first packaged salads. Gene Kahn founded Cascadian Farms in 1971 as a hippie cooperative organic farm, made it a commercial success, and sold it to food giant General Mills in 2000.[80] Pollan also visited the large organic-chicken firm Petaluma Poultry, founded by Allen Shainsky. Shainsky descended from a member of a community of Yiddish-speaking leftist Russian-Jewish chicken farmers in Petaluma, California, whom agribusiness by and large drove out of business.[81]

An Environmentalism for Society's Needs

Presbyterian Rachel Carson wrote *Silent Spring* in 1962 to indict destructive human meddling in the wise workings of nature. The terrible stories Carson presented of the ways production and unwise use of dangerous chemicals affected people then opened the way for a new environmentalism oriented toward people as well as the natural world. The works of Alice Hamilton and Jane Jacobs, which never would have fit under the umbrella of "conservation," comfortably found space under the larger tent of "environmentalism." At the same time, blacks, Catholics, and Jews found or made increasing room in public life and engaged more frequently and prominently in environmental issues that had implications for the betterment of human society or human health. African Americans and Catholics organized the first environmental justice actions and remained its strongest advocates. Catholics and Episcopalians refashioned natural theology and made it grander if less personal. Reaction to patriarchal traditions brought attention to women, who had been relatively neglected in the rather masculine emphasis on outdoors activities and concerns. Jewish interest in food alerted a growing public to the quality and purity of food.

The transition in the 1960s and 1970s from Presbyterians to African-American Baptists, Catholics, and Jews was the second great denominational shift in American environmental history, following the earlier transition from Congregationalism to Presbyterianism six or seven decades earlier. Many environmentalists have celebrated the broadening of environmental concerns,[82] a trend which has brought greater inclusiveness to a once very Reformed-Protestant movement. This shift however also entailed a loss of the moral energy, urgency, and focus with which the children of Calvinism had infused the movement. The earlier concerns of the conservation and environmental movements have by no means disappeared. To the degree however that earlier achievements depend upon continued political support, the future is by no means assured, however. The Conclusion turns attention from surveying environmentalism's past to face its present and future.

Conclusion

Religion and American Environmentalism

A traveler passing along the Calvinist Crescent from Baltimore through Philadelphia and New York to Boston in the late eighteenth or nineteenth century would never long be out of sight of a Reformed Protestant church. In the interactions and conversations of Presbyterians, Huguenots, Dutch Reformed, and Congregationalists, especially in New York in the crescent's center where they all mingled, the dominant American scientific and aesthetic ideas about nature took shape. These people all saw God in his works, where man was a suspect intruder, but honored the conscientious farmer industriously sustaining his moral, well-ordered community. American landscape art, institutions of natural science and of agricultural education and research, conservation, and parks were all born along this arc.

When Huguenots and Puritans sought to reform people's relationship with God, with each other, and with nature, they laid the foundations for the conservation and environmental movements. Puritans very nearly achieved that totalistic Calvinism in the towns they built in Massachusetts and Connecticut. Congregationalists romanticized the New England town as the embodiment of taste, piety, democracy, useful industry, and careful husbandry. They saw these traits as necessary to a rapidly expanding nation, rife with disorder, immorality, shortsighted greed, rapacious destruction of natural resources, and crowded, polluted industrial cities. To forestall the threat of decline and make New England a model for the nation, they put forward the American program of conservation, with its three legs of agriculture, conservation, and parks. Congregationalists applied science to agriculture. They sparked a national conversation on the value of trees and forests. They founded and designed the first city, state, and national parks. They campaigned for humane, livable, tastefully built cities. But in the second half of the nineteenth century, the unstoppable decay of New England towns enervated Congregationalism and drained it of ardor to make America like New England.

Energetic Presbyterians, invigorated with freshness and vitality from immigration from Scotland and Ireland, forged from these beginnings a movement that became American environmentalism. In the Progressive Era between the 1880s and 1920, Presbyterian presidents, secretaries of the Interior and Agriculture, politicians, and journalists transformed Congregational conservation into a national crusade. They made conservation a cause and established the National Forests and National Parks systems. By the 1960s they transformed conservation into the broader, more popular (and more populist), more political, and deeply moralistic environmental movement. Yet, its Calvinism fading, postimmigration Presbyterianism was ceasing to produce nature's priesthood in the likes of John Muir, Gifford Pinchot, Rachel Carson, David Brower, and Edward Abbey. Although in the 1980s Catholics, Jews, and black Baptists broadened the environmental movements' concerns, notably environmental justice and organic foods, and local initiatives proliferated, they could not fill the place of the morally driven "preachers of righteousness" of Presbyterian upbringing. Environmental organizations are larger and less effective than ever. They lobby perpetually, yet Congress has passed no major environmental legislation since the 1990 Clean Air Act to combat acid rain. The inability to address the growing crisis of global warming more than anything else demonstrates environmentalism's apparent irrelevance. Presbyterianism wilts and environmentalism droops.

Wilderness and Wildlife

Many things fall neatly into place when the historical trajectory of American environmentalism is regarded as a sort of para-religious movement or an expression of Reformed Protestant belief and culture. Yet the post-Presbyterian environmentalism of Baptists, blacks, Catholics, and Jews did not come from nowhere. Presbyterianism had long supplied the preachers and evangelists for the cause, but such a relatively small denomination could never have provided the congregation. Presbyterian environmentalists preaching to the tiny numbers of converted could have accomplished little. Instead, in the tradition of John Knox, their church was the nation. Unlike the leadership of the environmental movement, denominational adherence correlates only weakly to popular support for environmentalism or environmental organizations.[1] Environmentalism did not spring from within any denomination and the churches themselves have never been the motors of the environmental movement. With the interesting exception of Catholics, the vast majority of major environmental figures headed for the exits of the religions of their parents and forebears and did not return. The influence has gone the opposite direction, as environmentalism stimulated churches and synagogues after 1970 to take up environmental causes. Opinion from the pews guided preaching from the pulpit.

Religion does not explain everything. The movements to preserve wilderness and protect wildlife run parallel to the mainstream of Reformed environmentalism. They have no connections to denominational history. Like tributaries that join the main stream but whose waters stay distinct, these movements swelled the environmental current and influenced its course but retained a separate identity. The wilderness movement began on October 19, 1934, during a convention of the American Forestry Association in Knoxville, Tennessee. Bob Marshall, Benton Mackaye, Harvey Broome, and Bernard and Miriam Frank climbed into the Franks' car for a field trip to a nearby camp of the Civilian Conservation Corps. During the drive, they talked over a proposal that Marshall had made in 1930 for an organization for the protection of wilderness. Someone had brought along a draft constitution. The conversation grew so enthusiastic that Frank stopped the car by the side of the road. The group piled out, clambered up an embankment, and then and there worked out the founding principles of the Wilderness Society. Soon afterward they invited four like-minded men to join them as the society's founding members: Aldo Leopold, Robert Sterling Yard, Ernest Oberholtzer, and Harold C. Anderson.

All eight men had witnessed with growing concern the rapid development of formerly remote natural areas. The advent of inexpensive automobiles democratized vacations, and camping, fishing, and hunting beckoned as recreation that almost anyone could afford. Roads were built and resorts constructed at mountain lakes and meadows that once could only be reached by foot or horseback. As Paul S. Sutter has shown, the eight fought to slow the juggernaut of development, separately at first and then in combination. According to a statement of January 21, 1935, they founded the Wilderness Society "for the purpose of fighting off invasion of the wilderness and of stimulating . . . an appreciation of its multiform emotional, intellectual, and scientific values."[2] The society's platform, published in its periodical, *The Living Wilderness,* asserted that "wilderness is a natural resource having the same basic relation to man's ultimate thought and culture as coal, timber and other physical resources have to his material needs."[3]

Nowhere in these foundational statements did Marshall, Leopold, Mackaye, Broome, and friends include the words "moral," "spiritual," "divine," or "community." The purpose of the national parks had from the beginning related to preservation of natural beauty for the benefit and enjoyment of the public. Not so wilderness. Wilderness was different. The Wilderness Society wanted to protect nature from machinery and from change. Parks were a Reformed Protestant spaces. Wilderness was not. None of the eight founders was Congregationalist or Presbyterian. All were religious outsiders of the early environmental movement. Marshall and Frank were Jewish. Leopold's ancestors were German Lutherans. Yard was son of a Methodist minister, and Broome was also Methodist. Mackaye was grandson of a Baptist minister. Oberholtzer was Unitarian. Anderson was Episcopalian.[4] The two most prominent of presidents of the Wilderness Society would be Howard Zahniser, son of a Free Methodist minister, who successfully lobbied for passage of the Wilderness Act in 1964, and Sigurd F. Olson, son of a Swedish Baptist minister, who authored a number of bestselling books of wilderness essays, notably *The Singing Wilderness* of 1956.[5] The cause of wilderness would be picked up by Presbyterians like David Brower and Edward Abbey, who turned it into a moral tale of avaricious developers against pristine creation, but its origins and core leaders came from denominations not otherwise strongly associated with environmentalism.

The surprising diversity of religious origins of founders and leaders of the wilderness movement points to the difference between wilderness defense and most other causes of American environmentalism. Moral, spiritual, or religious motives are missing or in the background. Wilderness, as Leopold famously put it, was a "blank spot on a map"[6]—a place of freedom and of no people and no civilization, where nature existed apart from humankind. The Wilderness Act of 1964 codified this definition: "A wilderness, in contrast with those areas where man and his own works dominate the landscape, is hereby recognized as an area where the earth and its community of life are untrammeled by man, where man himself is a visitor who does not remain."[7] Rapid development of natural places fed nostalgia for an America of plentiful wildlife and open spaces. Marshall envied nineteenth-century explorers like Lewis and Clark. While exploring the central Brooks Range of Alaska, he was mightily pleased to imagine he was the first white person to gaze upon the scene.[8] Leopold looked back on a boyhood when plentiful wildlife added to the pleasures of hunting and fishing. As a Forest Service supervisor he created the first formal wilderness area, the Gila Wilderness Area in New Mexico, and defined "wilderness area" as a region large enough for a two-week pack trip.[9]

The wilderness movement's independence from the Reformed-Protestant mainstream of environmentalism continued into its radical phase. In 1980 a group grew impatient and frustrated with the Wilderness Society's leadership, which had grown involved in political lobbying and compromise, and founded the radical, decentralized civil-disobedience group Earth First! to defend wilderness against development. The movement's three best-known founders and most effective leaders again came from the outsider denominations of environmental history. Dave Foreman grew up in the Churches of Christ. Howie Wolke was Jewish. Mike Roselle was Catholic. After the founders left Earth First! around 1990, Jewish-Catholic Judi Bari stepped forward as the movement's most charismatic and capable leader.[10]

Leopold's *A Sand County Almanac, and Sketches Here and There*, posthumously published in 1949, found a mass audience during the rise of the environmental movement in the 1960s and made its author the most famous founder of the Wilderness Society. Its influence has been felt from noisy rallies of Earth First! to quiet academic seminars on environmental ethics. The book also betrays hints of Leopold's German Lutheran heritage. Europe's historically Lutheran regions have produced some of the world's most active and successful Green movements, yet American Lutherans have been nearly absent in American environmentalist leadership. American Lutheranism, one of the larger Protestant denominations, remained far more conservative than in Europe. In addition, the denomination's founder, Martin Luther, resisted radical Protestants' demand to remake society according to Biblical precepts. His principle of the "two kingdoms" separated perfection in the next life from the compromised everyday world of this life. Lutherans consequently never thought to remake society the way Puritans did. In Leopold's more-secular family, steeped in German culture, Lutheranism was more a general cultural heritage than living belief. There seems more than a bit of the two kingdoms paradigm in his thought that emphasized the individual conscience but stopped short of social or political reform. *A Sand County Almanac* ignored the moral aspects of the human relationship with nature and focused on "the land ethic," Leopold's name for the individual's ethical responsibility toward what he called the "land community." The land ethic was a personal ethic that landowners ought to adopt—once again, conversion to right thinking (*orthodoxy* comes from the Greek for "right opinion"), akin Baptist or Catholic environmentalism—which would guarantee the ecological health of the land. The land ethic has few if any public policy implications, and seems anachronistic in an era of agribusiness and demands of the market on farmers to be efficient and profitable.

In his lifetime Leopold was best known for his pioneering work in wildlife management, which links him to an environmental cause, protection of wildlife, whose leading champions have also not been Reformed Protestants. William Temple Hornaday was raised Seventh-Day Adventist, a millennialist offshoot of the Baptist church, and like Leopold grew up in Iowa, where once-abundant wildlife was vanishing. This great Progressive-Era crusader for preservation of the bison and for protection of wildlife worked tirelessly for hunting restrictions to preserve wildlife species from destruction.[11] Another Iowan, editorial-cartoonist Jay Norwood ("Ding") Darling, was son of a Methodist preacher and an avid outdoorsman and conservationist. Darling succeeded Hornaday as the nation's leading advocate for wildlife conservation. In 1934 President Franklin Roosevelt appointed him to head the US Biological Survey, forerunner of the Fish and Wildlife Service, where he initiated the Duck Stamp program and a system of federal wildlife refuges. Darling cofounded the National Wildlife Federation, the largest hunters' conservation organization.[12] Although known for his advocacy of wilderness, Foreman often discusses it in terms of its undamaged ecosystem and full range of species and has proposed "rewilding" regions to allow species to rebound and ecosystems to regain health.[13] He has repeatedly cited the more ecological passages of Leopold's writings to bolster his point of view.

Yard, Broome, Zahniser, and Darling were all Methodists and three of them sons of ministers, a notable number from a denomination that has been remarkably and mysteriously relatively absent from the annals of environmentalism. At one time the nation's largest Protestant denomination, Methodism has contributed a mere handful of figures to environmental history, far fewer than the denomination's huge size would lead one to expect. As cosmologist John Cobb's concern for community suggests, Methodists generally have thought about nature primarily in relation to its usefulness to society. In 1878 John Wesley Powell, head of the US Geological Survey, who had led the first expedition down the Colorado River through the Grand Canyon in 1869, proposed a demo-cratic, small-scale system of control and development of the West's resources, especially its scarce water, but boosters and Western politicians fiercely resisted it. Yet Native Americans interested Powell more than Western landscape. He would be founding director in 1879 of Bureau of Ethnology of the Smithsonian Institution.[14] Author Mary Austin's beloved 1903 book on the arid Southwest, *The Land of Little Rain,* similarly focused on Southwestern Indians' relationship with the desert landscape.[15] David Brower's arch-nemesis, Floyd Dominy, commissioner of the US Bureau of Reclamation from 1959 to 1969, devoted his career to developing the water resources of the West for the benefit of people. Dominy left a legacy of enormous dams and vast reservoirs across the West, including the dam that Brower regretted most, Glen Canyon Dam, which inundated beau-tiful Glen Canyon under Lake Powell.[16] Wes Jackson founded the Land Institute in 1976 in his native Kansas, where he has focused on develop-ing a sustainable, perennial agriculture using domesticated or hybridized native plants that will produce yearly without plowing or planting.[17] Each of these Methodists was interested in issues having to do with the human relationship to the land and its resources.

A Post-Presbyterian Environmentalism?

In 2004, Michael Shellenberger and Ted Nordhaus published a contro-versial essay, "The Death of Environmentalism: Global Warming Politics in a Post-Environmental World," which they followed in 2007 with *Break Through: From the Death of Environmentalism to the Politics of Possibility.* Shellenberger and Nordhaus argued that people should come before nature and that the (small-p) progressive movement ought to absorb the causes of environmentalism. They decried what they saw as increasing bureaucratization of environmental organizations and their capture by Washington politics. They objected to what they called the "politics of limits," with its focus on regulation and government restraint, and advo-cated a "politics of possibility," with a more market-oriented "unleashing" of technology and business in partnership with government to "over-come" environmental problems.[18] Shellenberger and Nordhaus founded Breakthrough Institute to promote their faith, sometimes called "bright green environmentalism" or "ecopragmatism," that technology will make continued, ecologically sustainable prosperity possible.

Causality of course cannot be proven, but religious correlations are suggestive. Shellenberger, son of Mennonites, and Nordhaus, grandson of a Jewish lawyer and developer of ski resorts in New Mexico, met in the late 1990s as participants in the Earth First! campaign to stop Houston financier Charles Hurwitz's Pacific Lumber Company from clear-cutting old-growth redwoods in California. Mennonites belong to a pacifist branch of the Anabaptist movement, an old outsider group that baptizes adult believers and has endured persecution, which might help explain Shellenberger's preference for individualistic solutions. Like West Fraser a scion of a family of developers, Nordhaus seems to trust good-hearted capitalists to know best, or perhaps, like such prominent Jews of petty-bourgeois ancestry as Ayn Rand, Milton Friedman, and Alan Greenspan, he is attracted to the "reason" of libertarianism.

From a different perspective, the problems that Shellenberger and Nordhaus observe in environmentalism reflect the disappearance of charismatic leadership and the fading of moral urgency. Their free-market solutions buck against history and experience, which show that religious traditions that urge upon government the moral responsibility to restrain socially harmful behavior and promote the common good have left by far the more important and effective environmental legacy, from parks to safe food to clean air and water. Environmentalism owes much to American denominations with an ethic that balances individualism with the needs of the community: Congregationalism, African-American Baptism, Catholicism, and Judaism. Baptists and other individualistic denominations that have contributed more individualistic, laissez-faire versions of environmental responsibility have left a less clear legacy. Those who advocate converting everyone to the proper attitude toward the land community, or the earth, or the universe, in hopes of an environmental millennium, evince an optimism toward human possibility for which history supplies little supporting evidence.

Reformed Protestants, on the other hand, would fundamentally distrust neolibertarian market-oriented solutions as granting carte blanche to greed, which is so corrosive socially and so destructive environmentally. Calvinism imbued the Reformed Protestant tradition with a thoroughgoing pessimism about the possibility that everyone would behave well if just given the freedom to do so. The Progressives tried to put a leash on avarice for quite valid reasons over and above its questionable moral significance. The system of regulated capitalism for the common good was fundamentally a Reformed idea. Of the communally oriented denominations, Congregationalism alone offered a vision of democratic communities controlling their own resources and restraining the behavior of its members for the good of the community and future generations. The historical origins of environmentalism and conservation in this thoroughly human-centered vision of sustainable towns suggest a different model than that of Shellenberger and Nordhaus. For a time Congregationalists had the will and ambition to promote their vision as the basis for the nation. As they and their Reformed cousins the Presbyterians realized, self-interested capitalism could either benefit or threaten the community, but outright greed and so-called market pressures push businesses, willingly or not, toward exploitation of land and labor. Allowing individuals and economic interests a free hand, as Southern states did and do, leads inevitably to injustice and ecological degradation.

Jewish tradition and law evolved in and for small communities. Although without the conservation component in Congregationalism, they fostered both a social ethic and a concern for "pure food" that transitioned nicely into organic agriculture. Judaism also, like Reformed Protestantism, fostered prophetic figures who stood outside society and decried its sins. Isaiah provided a model of the prophet who demanded the state provide for the poor and restrain the greed of the rich. Congregationalism's system of independent churches, however, provided a model for self-organization and self-government that in effect trained organizers of early American reform societies, which Judaism did not do to any important extent. Consequently, Jews have often been "prophets" and social critics but less often have they created and led popular environmental organizations.

Black Baptists and Catholics could draw on traditions of social justice for their environmentalism. Yet although their churches nurtured and participated in the defense of communities against polluters, black and Hispanic environmental action has almost always been limited in scope and aims. Perhaps because the view from the lower rungs of society encourages resentment of those whom they regard as privileged elites, their movements have not produced an inclusive ideal of society that might address environmental problems more comprehensively. Underclasses and their political sympathizers have expressed suspicion that parks, national forests, wildlife conservation, and other causes championed by such "elite" figures as Gifford Pinchot and Theodore Roosevelt have been thinly veiled actions of self-interest.[19] Yet when environmental-justice leaders press for green space in poor communities, they carry forward the same principles that this elite championed in the nineteenth century. Moreover, the elite's wariness of the corrupting and destructive power of great wealth gave the nation the legacy of national forests and parks. Without the actions of the elite and the heirs of Connecticut river gods, these areas would have long ago passed into private hands, with consequences all too easily imagined.

What, then, is the future of environmentalism? Whether it is dead or not, the decay of Presbyterianism and Reformed Protestantism leave it a very different movement. Reformed societies wove religion and the social-political order together on the bases of morality and equity. Reformed environmentalism united a spiritual understanding of creation with an understanding of the environmental common good. Perhaps Reformed Protestantism's moment in history is simply coming to an end, or perhaps mightier forces have shoved it aside. Preachers formerly had little competition for the values that they thundered from the pulpit. Then came the yellow press, movies, mass magazines, radio, television, and the Internet, all vehicles of commerce. As French Reformed theologian Jacques Ellul noted, advertising at its core is propaganda for a self-indulgent, atomized, consumer society.[20] Thrifty, self-controlled, industrious, useful, sober, and modest citizens do not make anyone a lot of money. Mammon, one might say, has the bulliest pulpit of all. Then, in the last several decades, corporations and certain wealthy individuals upped the ante by funding foundations to puff small-government libertarian ideals and mounting campaigns of misinformation about acid rain, the ozone hole, and global warming.[21] Finally, in 1981, Ronald Reagan inaugurated a backlash against Progressivism that has pushed privatization and eroded public institutions.

The former "mainline" churches and other institutions that long taught the virtues of the Protestant ethic and gave environmentalism coherence and direction could not withstand such money-driven values delivered by such a seductive and ubiquitous messenger. No strong liberal or progressive political movement counterbalances and checks private enterprise, and it is difficult to see from which corner of society one might come forward. Much more at ease in a consumer society, Baptists, charismatics, and other denominations interested in reforming individuals—but not society—have flourished. Surely Baptists and Pentecostals, whether lapsed or believing, will never fill the places of Congregationalists or Presbyterians in the environmental movement. If it is not dead yet, environmentalism is certainly weak, divided, and wandering in the wilderness.

The Presbyterianness of the Progressive Era

CHILDHOOD RELIGIOUS AFFILIATION OF PRESIDENTS AND THEIR CABINETS

This chart shows graphically the dominance of Presbyterians in the Progressive Era, 1889–1921, and into the New Deal. Presbyterians show a signature attraction to Interior and Agriculture, the departments most closely connected to the natural world. The chart also shows a few other curious patterns. Presidents tended to appoint coreligionists to their cabinets. Presbyterians also disproportionately led State and War, whose implications for the Wilson administration Robert Morse Crunden discusses in *Ministers of Reform: The Progressives' Achievement in American Civilization, 1889–1920* (New York: Basic Books, 1982), chapter 8. On the right of the chart, Presbyterian presence diminishes dramatically. Clearly, the departments of "Mammon," Treasury and Commerce, held little attraction to them. Instead, the number of Methodists and Episcopalians is striking, as is the greater diversity of denominations.

	President	Interior	Agriculture	State	War	Atty. Gen.	Treasury	Commerce†	Labor
1885	P Cleveland	M Lamar		E Bayard	U Endicott	M Garland	E* Manning		
1886		C Vilas							
1887							M Fairchild		
1888			? Colman 89						
1889	P Harrison	P Noble	P Rusk	P Blaine	? Proctor	P Miller	Q Windom		
1890									
1891					P Elkins		? Foster		
1892				? Foster					
1893	P Cleveland	P Smith	E Morton	M Gresham	? Lamont	P Olney	? Carlisle		
1894						B Harmon			
1895		P Francis		P Olney					
1896									
1897	M McKinley	C Bliss	P Wilson	M Sherman	? Alger	RC McKenna	M Gage		
1898		P Hitchcock		L Day		P Griggs			
1899				P Hay	P Root				
1900									
1901	P TRoosevelt					M Knox			
1902							M Shaw		
1903								P Cortelyou	
1904					U Taft	E Moody		? Metcalf	

	President	Interior	Agriculture	State	War	Atty. Gen.	Treasury	Commerce†	Labor
1905				P Root					
1906		P Woodruff				RC Bonaparte	P Cortelyou	J Straus	
1907		D Garfield							
1908				P Bacon o9	M Wright				
1909	U Taft	C Ballinger		M Knox	P Dickinson	E Wickersham	M MacVeagh	L Nagel	
1910									
1911		P Fisher			P Stimson				
1912									
1913	P Wilson	P Lane	P* Houston	P Bryan	E Garrison	D McReynolds	E McAdoo	E Redfield	P Wilson
1914						P Gregory			
1915				P Lansing	E Baker				
1916									
1917									
1918							M Glass		
1919						Q Palmer	P* Houston	? Alexander	
1920		M Payne	M Meredith	B Colby					
1921	B Harding	D Fall	P HWallace	B Hughes	U Weeks	M Daugherty	E Mellon	Q Hoover	B* Davis
1922									
1923	C Coolidge	P Work		? Kellogg		Uv Sargent			
1924			B Gore						

(Continued)

	President	Interior	Agriculture	State	War	Atty. Gen.	Treasury	Commerce†	Labor
1925			C Jardine		? Davis				
1926									
1927		M West							
1928								? Whiting	
1929	Q Hoover	C Wilbur	M Hyde	P Stimson	? Hurley	P Mitchell		? Lamont	
1930									M Doak
1931									
1932							? Mills	? Chapin	
1933	E FDRoosevelt	P Ickes	P HAWallace	E Hull	C Dern	C Cummings	? Woodin	M Roper	C Perkins
1934							J Morganthau		
1935									
1936					D Woodring				
1937									
1938								M Hopkins	
1939						RC Murphy			
1940					P Stimson	B Jackson		B Jones	
1941			UB Wickard			E Biddle			

	1942	1943	1944	1945
			E Stettinius	
				P HAWallace

Note: I omitted the relatively minor positions of Secretary of the Navy and Postmaster General for simplicity and clarity.

Note: Until 1936, Presidents took office on March 4. Norman Jay Colman and Robert Bacon assumed their positions in previous administrations after January 1 and served only briefly.

† From its creation in 1903 until 1913, the Department of Commerce and Labor.

KEY

B	Baptist
C	Congregational
D	Disciples of Christ
E	Episcopalian
J	Jewish
L	Lutheran
M	Methodist
P	Presbyterian
Q	Quaker
RC	Catholic
U	Unitarian
UB	United Brethren
Uv	Universalist
?	No available information
*	Data lacking; inferred from affiliation of siblings, parents, and other close relations.

SOURCES FOR SECRETARIES OF THE INTERIOR AND
AGRICULTURE, WHERE NOT STATED IN THE TEXT

Edward Mayes, *Lucius Q. C. Lamar: His Life, Times, and Speeches* (Nashville, 1896).

Horace Samuel Merrill, *William Freeman Vilas: Doctrinaire Democrat* (State Historical Society of Wisconsin, 1954).

Harper Barnes, *Standing on a Volcano: The Life and Times of David Rowland Francis* (St. Louis: Missouri Historical Society Press, 2001).

"Cornelius N. Bliss," *Biographical History of Massachusetts*, vol. 2, ed. Samuel Atkins Eliot (Boston: Massachusetts Biographical Society, 1913), n.p.

"Hitchcock, Ethan Allen," *Biographical Directory of the United States Executive Branch: 1774–1989*, ed. Robert Sobel (Westport, CT.: Greenwood Press, 1990), 177.

"John Barton Payne," *Prominent Democrats of Illinois: A Brief History of the Rise and Progress of the Democratic Party of Illinois* (Chicago: Democrat Publishing Co., 1899), 300.

Ray L. Wilbur, *The Memoirs of Ray Lyman Wilbur: 1875–1949* (Stanford, CA: Stanford University Press, 1960).

Henry Casson, *Life of General Jeremiah M. Rusk* (Madison, WI: Hill, 1895).

[Edwin T. Meredith,] "Changes in the President's Cabinet," *The Continent*, February 5, 1900, 159.

Franklin D. Mitchell, "Arthur Mastick Hyde," in *Dictionary of Missouri Biography*, ed. Lawrence O Christensen, William E. Foley, Gary R. Kremer, and Kenneth H. Winn (Columbia: University of Missouri Press, 1999), 419.

SOURCES FOR SELECTED OTHERS

"Philander Chase Knox," *The Historical Register: A Record of People, Places and Events in American History*, ed. Edwin Charles Hill (New York: Hill, 1921).

[Charles Stebbins Fairchild,] "The New Secretary of the Treasury and His Assistant," *Bulletin of the American Iron and Steel Association*, April 6, 1887, 89.

"Manning," *Hudson-Mohawk Genealogical and Family Memoirs*, vol. 1, ed. Cuyler Reynolds (New York: Lewis Historical Publishing Co., 1911), 213–214. Daniel Manning's son was a member of St. Peter's Episcopal Church, Albany, N.Y.

Notes

INTRODUCTION

1. There are many histories of American religion, most following the standard narrative given here. For the evolution of a narrative in religious history, see Wilson, *Religion and the American Nation.*

2. See Huth; Nash; Runte; Marx; Pomeroy; Hyde; Sutter; Worster, *Dust Bowl*; Merchant, *Death of Nature*. See also Smith, *Virgin Land;* Callicott and Nelson.

CHAPTER 1

1. Thomas Cole's diary, May 22, 1836, quoted in Noble, *Life and Works,* 219.

2. Cole, letter to Luman Reed, September 18, 1833, quoted in Noble, *Life and Works,* 178.

3. Parry, *Art of Thomas Cole,* 30–31, 376; Cole, letter to Reed, undated (probably February 7, 1836), quoted in Parry, "Overlooking the Oxbow," 26.

4. Roque, 63–66.

5. Roque, 67–72; Wallach, "Making a Picture," 40.

6. Cole, letter to Luman Reed, March 2, 1836, Cole MSS, New York State Library (NYSL), Albany, New York, quoted in Roque, 66.

7. "Editors' Table."

8. Born, 80–86; Wallach, "Thomas Cole," 77.

9. Parry, "Overlooking the Oxbow," 7; Sweeney, 113.

10. Parry, "Overlooking the Oxbow," 50.

11. See Parry, "Overlooking the Oxbow." There are as many interpretations of *The Oxbow* as art historians. Wolfgang Born saw in it a peculiarly American sense of the openness of space against the narrow world of European landscapes. Born, 80–86. Barbara Novak saw the two halves of *The Oxbow* as representative of the contrast and tension between nature and culture. Novak, *American Painting,* 74–77; Novak, *Nature and Culture,* 161–162.

Angela Miller interpreted the view as transformation of wilderness to farmland, that is, as a conflation of the first two canvases of *The Course of Empire,*
from the savage to the Arcadian state. She also interpreted *The Oxbow* as a conservative political statement in the election year of 1836. Miller, "Thomas Cole
and Jacksonian America"; Miller, *Empire of the Eye,* 39–49. Miller missed evidence for the direction of the breeze from the right and asserted a nonexistent
ambiguity in the motion of the storm; 45–46.

Franklin Kelly, e-mail to author, March 20, 2009; and Parry, *Art of Thomas
Cole,* 50, also noted parallels between the first two panels of *Course of Empire* and
The Oxbow, possibly as a cautionary political tale to the United States about the
course of its own empire.

It seems to me that any but a general connection between *The Course of
Empire* and *The Oxbow* is unnecessarily speculative, although tempting due to
the creation of the latter during a pause in the creation of the former. It is true
that the first two paintings in the series correspond broadly with the left and
right halves of *The Oxbow:* they respectively illustrate the Salvatorian sublime
and the Claudean beautiful; and *The Savage State* shares a storm with the left
side and *The Arcadian or Pastoral State* shares "altar smoke," sailboats, and a
flock of sheep with the right. However, no primitive people appear on the left
of *The Oxbow* and the right side lacks tree stump, soldiers, arts, and other such
significant details. Furthermore, for symbolic reasons it is morning in spring or
early summer in the *Empire* pair and it is clearly late afternoon and harvesttime
in *The Oxbow.* If it is a warning, why is the right side so warm and beautiful, and
why does the painter turn his head to smile at us? The painting is surely entirely
too cheerful and optimistic to be a warning.

In a rather fanciful if creative interpretation, David Bjelajac attempted to turn
The Oxbow into a Christian allegory: see Bjelajac.

12. Gerdts, 41–54.
13. Cole, 2.
14. Cole, 3.
15. Cole, 5.
16. Cole, 11.
17. Cole, 11. Cole surely changed his mind after actually seeing Vaucluse for himself
    in 1841, declaring, "I have seldom felt the sublimity of nature more deeply." Cole,
    journal entry for Oct. 30, 1841, quoted in Noble, *The Life and Works,* 309.
18. Cole, 3.
19. Cole, letter to Reed, March 26, 1836, quoted in Noble, *Life and Works,* 217.
20. Noble, *Life and Works,* 290.
21. Cole, letter to Daniel Wadsworth, New York, November 10, 1828, in McNulty, 47, 49.
22. Cole, sketchbook of 1828, quoted in Wallach, "Thomas Cole," 90. See also Cole
    to Reed, September 18, 1833, quoted in Wallach, "Thomas Cole," 140; and Cole,
    sketchbook of 1827, reprinted in Powell, *Thomas Cole,* 132, 134.

23. Cole, letter to Wadsworth, early 1844, in McNulty, 71.
24. Bryant, 38.
25. Bryant, 35.
26. Cole, 2.
27. Cole, 12.
28. A popular poet, Lamb was schoolmate and lifelong friend of poet Samuel Taylor Coleridge. Cole also quotes Uvedale Price's influential *Essays on the Picturesque, as Compared with the Sublime and the Beautiful*, 2; and quotes very briefly: "The Prisoner of Chillon" by Byron, one of Cole's favorite poets, 3; "The Prairies" and "Autumn Woods" by his friend William Cullen Bryant, 4 and 5; John Bunyan's *Pilgrim's Progress*, 6; Shakespeare's *The Tempest*, 7; and John Dyer's "Ruins of Rome," 8.
29. Cole, 2–3. "Still small voice": 1 Kings 19:12; "Loving eye" alludes to Lord Byron's "The Prisoner of Chillon" and refers to the solace that the prisoner attempts to take from the view of nature he is granted from the window of his dungeon cell.
30. Cole, 5.
31. Cole, 12.
32. Baigell and Kaufman, 136–139. Baigell and Kaufman also argue that upside down (from God's point of view), the marks on the hills spell the Hebrew characters שדי, or "Shaddai" or "Almighty" in English. Given that Cole often called God "the Almighty" and that perhaps his first job in America was as an engraver for an edition of Bunyan's allegory *The Holy War Made by King Shaddai Upon Diabolus* (see Bjelajac, 81), this is a tempting theory. However, the markings only very vaguely resemble the Hebrew characters: shin is imperfect, dalet is reversed, and yod has an odd shape. Since the characters for "Noah" have no such difficulties and moreover are not mysteriously upside down, I think it is more likely the word Cole had in mind. The other markings on the hillside remain enigmatic.
33. Quoted in Parry, "Overlooking the Oxbow," 50. In light of Cole's deep religiosity, it is odd that Parry did not explore the religious associations of *The Oxbow*.
34. The scene is also reminiscent of Adam's vision from the high hill in *Paradise Lost*, in which he

> beheld a field,
> Part arable and tilth, whereon were Sheaves
> New reapt, the other part Sheep-walks and foulds;
> Ith' midst an Altar as the Land-mark stood
> Rustic, of grassie sord [i.e., sward]. . . . (11.429–433)

If such an association holds true, then the painter Cole is Adam seeing the future, but not a harmonious one. As Adam's vision continues he beholds in horror the fratricide between his sons Cain and Abel.
35. Martineau, 78. See also Hoppin, 231–244.
36. Trumbull and Pomeroy, ch. 1–3, 6, 16–17.

37. Bradstreet, "To my Dear Children," 217–218.
38. Bradstreet, "Contemplations," in Bradstreet, *Works*, 370–381. On Bradstreet, see Stanford; and Cowell and Stanford. See also Daly, *God's Altar*, ch. 3; Hammond, *Sinful Self*; Rosenmeier, *Anne Bradstreet Revisited*; Rosenmeier, "The Wounds Upon Bathsheba"; Scheick, 35–45; Schweitzer, ch. 4; and White, *Anne Bradstreet*.
39. Cottret, 111, 119.
40. Beza, 93. My description of Calvin's personality relies on this biography by Beza, Calvin's friend and successor in Geneva, 6–9, 111–115.
41. Calvin, *Institutes* 1.5.5; 1.5.8; 1.6.2; 1.14.20; 2.6.1; 3.9.2; and frequently throughout his other works.
42. Calvin, *Institutes* 1.5.9; 1.5.11–12.
43. Calvin, *Institutes* 1.5.9.
44. Calvin, *Institutes* 1.5.5.
45. Calvin, "Preface to Olivétan's New Testament," 59–60. On Calvin and nature, see Bouwsma, 33–34, 102–109; 163–166; Cottret, 312–313.
46. *The Humble Advice*, 1.
47. Clarke and Baxter, 175. What a fascinating traveling companion Staunton must have been.
48. Miller and Johnson, 66; Marsden, *Soul of the American University*, 39.
49. Ames, 103, 106. The italics are Ames's.
50. Stoddard, "Sermon III. That the Gospel is the Means of Conversion," in *Three Sermons*, 67.
51. Cotton Mather, *Winter Meditations*, 17.
52. Cotton Mather, *Magnalia Christi Americana*, 169.
53. Edwards, "Personal Narrative," 793–794.
54. Smith, "History of the Life," 2–3. The spellings are Smith's.
55. Noble, *The Course of Empire*, 81–82.
56. Calvin, *Institutes* 1.16; Schreiner, 7–38.
57. Ames, 101, 108.
58. Ames, 104.
59. Hoeveler, 43–45.
60. Willard, *A compleat body of divinity*, 140–141.
61. The reader might be reminded of Perry Miller's famous essay "From Edwards to Emerson," in which he describes "the incessant drive of the Puritan to learn how, and how most ecstatically, he can hold any sort of communion with the environing wilderness" (185).
62. Marsden, *Jonathan Edwards*, 72.
63. Edwards, *Dissertation I*, 432–433.
64. A number of works have explored this "green" side of Edwards's theology. See Holbrook, *Jonathan Edwards*; Lee, *Philosophical Theology*; Cooey.
65. Emerson, *Nature*, in Emerson, *Works*, vol. 1, 38–39.

66. Howe; Harrison, *Teachers of Emerson;* Hopkins. See also Stoll, *Protestantism, Capitalism, and Nature,* 15–17, 79–83.

67. On Talbot, see *In Memoriam, C. N. T.;* Bjelajac, 62, 65–66, 75.

68. Williams, *Genealogy and History,* 159–166; *Bulletin of Yale University,* 1156–1157; Tracy, 181–185.

69. Richardson, *Puritanism in North-West England,* 16–17; Davis, *Some Account,* 1–19; Middlekauff, 10–19.

70. Mostly Congregationalists with some Presbyterians (later Unitarians) and Baptists, residents later responded warmly to new religious movements like Methodism and even Swedenborgianism and Mormonism. Hardman, 8; Wadsworth and Mann, 42–43.

71. Didier, 25–28; *First Presbyterian Church, Baltimore,* 90; Wallach, "Thomas Cole," 35; Parry, *Art of Thomas Cole,* 38–44, 61–65, 92–94.

72. Wallach, "Thomas Cole," 38; Walker, prefatory note, 6; Buggeln, 434.

73. Wallach, "Thomas Cole," 38–39; Parry, *Art of Thomas Cole,* 131–187; Barrett, 50.

74. Wallach, "Thomas Cole," 39–42; Parry, *Art of Thomas Cole,* 227–228.

75. Durand, 235, 236.

76. Eire, 6–8; Dillenberger, part III; Michalski, esp. 191–194; Miles, 95–125; Aston, 92–121; Cottret, 335–338.

77. Calvin, *Institutes* 1.11.12.

78. Wencelius, esp. 97–126, 161–188; quotation, 186 (my translation). See also Dyrness, 62–83; Hardy; Stell; Guicharnaud; Koch; Mentzer. On architecture, see Kilde, ch.1; Loveland and Wheeler, ch. 1.

79. Quarles, A3.

80. Dyrness, 91–123.

81. Son of a portrait painter and godson of a landscape painter, Fuseli was also an amateur entomologist, and thus exemplified the connection between Reformed Protestantism, art, and natural history. His brother, Caspar Füssli, was also an entomologist and a painter of plants and insects. Tomory, 9–10, 22, 45, 211–213, 215.

82. For explorations of this theme, see Randall, *Building Codes;* Kamil.

83. Dyrness, 189–192; Bruyn, 84–103; de Jongh, *Question of Meaning,* 9–20. For a history of the iconographical debate, see de Jongh, "Iconological Approach," 200–223; Franits is the fullest study.

84. Du Bartas, 231–233; see "landscape," in Oxford English Dictionary.

85. Paulson, 3; see also Simon, *Hogarth.*

86. Dyrness, 104–105.

87. Powell, *Puritan Village,* 41.

88. Asfour and Williamson, 70–72; Armstrong, *Gainsborough,* 20, 23, 25.

89. Owen, "Early Influences," 16–17; and Kitson, 14.

90. Penny, 17–18; McTighe; Reynolds, *Discourses,* 53, 198.

91. Cole, journal entry for November 27, 1842, quoted in Noble, *Life and Works,* 335, 336.

92. Noble, *Life and Works*, 411, 413.

93. See, for example, Cole, quoted in Noble, *Life and Works*, 114–116.

94. Cole, 2.

95. Thomson, 20.

96. Sanford, 439. On Burke's religion, see Lock, ch.1.

97. Alison, 438.

98. Ringe, 315.

99. Tilley, 36–37; Braunrot, 11–13; Williams, *Common Expositor*, 27 ff. "Sepmaine" is the older spelling of "semaine." On the Huguenot development of the Bible epic, see Sayce.

100. Bradstreet, 85, 92, 100, 353, and passim.

101. For Milton's debt to du Bartas, see Taylor, *Milton's Use*.

102. For example, *Paradise Lost* 4.206; 5.330, 431; 7.328–331, 617. Scheifers, 42. Thanks to Donald Worster for bringing this essay to my attention.

103. Griffin, *Regaining Paradise*, 72–82.

104. See Scheifers, 43–44.

105. On Milton and Eden generally, see McColley, *Gust for Paradise*, ch. 4–6; Delumeau, ch. 10.

106. On the sources for his metaphor of light, see Madsen, *From Shadowy Types*, ch. 4; Daniel.

107. Stoddard, "Sermon IV. To Stir Up Young Men and Maidens to Praise the Name of the Lord," in *Three Sermons*, 93–118.

108. McColley, *Gust for Paradise*, ch. 6.

109. McColley, *Gust for Paradise*, ch. 6; McColley, "Beneficent Hierarchies"; McColley, "Milton's Environmental Epic"; Hiltner, *Milton and Ecology*; Hiltner, "Defense of Milton's Environmentalism." For a counterview, see Squires.

110. Edwards, *Milton and Natural World*; Madsen, *Idea of Nature*, ch. 2. See Lovejoy, 88–89, 160–162, 164–165. For Milton's scientific context, see Nicolson, ch. 3–6; Almond.

111. Willis, 10.

112. Hazard to Jeremy Belknap, 59–60. Congress appointed Hazard postmaster general in 1782.

113. Calvin, *Institutes* 1.14.20. Calvin's doctrines God the Creator and Providence: 1.5, 1.16–17. For a superb exposition of Calvin's thought, see Klaaren, 39–45.

114. Calvin, "Preface," 59.

115. Calvin, *Institutes* 2.1.4.

116. Calvin, *Institutes* 1.4.3. See also 1.11–12; 4.8.3, 4, 8, 9, 11, 13; 4.9.8; 4.10.8, 16–18.

117. Calvin, *Institutes* 2.1.5; 2.6.1.

118. Edwards, *Great Christian Doctrine*, 236.

119. Willard, *A compleat body of divinity*, 129.

120. Edwards, "Sinners in the Hands," 410.

121. Watts, *Improvement of the Mind,* 50–51.
122. Parker, "Of Conscious Religion," 154–155.
123. Increase Mather, *Practical Truths,* 75–95.
124. Cotton Mather, *Religion of the Closet,* 37.
125. Hambrick-Stowe, 156–194.
126. Clap, 49.
127. Edwards, *Life of David Brainerd,* 102–106; Bradstreet, verses 9, 24, 26, 27, 33, in *Works,* 370–381.
128. Jones, *Memoir,* 1, 10, 12–13.
129. Edwards, "Personal Narrative," 790–791.
130. Edwards, "Personal Narrative," 797.
131. Edwards, "Personal Narrative," 801.
132. Ola Elizabeth Winslow, quoted in Holbrook, 10.
133. Calvin did use a similar metaphor, comparing the Bible to "spectacles" that helped old people to read clearly, as it enabled humans to interpret nature correctly. Calvin, *Institutes* 1.6.1. Cp. 1.14.20–22. Instead of the "Book" of Nature, Calvin had preferred the popular medieval metaphor of the "mirror" of nature. Harrison, "'Book of Nature,'" 2–7. See, for example, Calvin, *Institutes* 1.5.1.
134. Authorized translation of the Reformed (Dutch) Church in America, reprinted in Cochrane, 189–190.
135. Nine earlier Reformed confessions from 1523 to 1560 collected in Cochrane do not mention the knowledge of God in creation.
136. In a nod to Calvin, Du Bartas added that "he that weares the spectacles of *Faith*" could easily read it. Du Bartas, 1.173–176, 193.
137. Milton, *Paradise Lost* 8.66–68. Milton lamented how his blindness rendered Nature's book to him a "Universal blanc" (3.47–49).
138. Cotton Mather, *Christian Philosopher,* 8.
139. Willard, *A compleat body of divinity,* 34; cp. 37–39.
140. Watts, *Psalms of David,* Psalm 19 (all parts), 111, 148. Today perhaps his most popular hymn, Psalm 98, Part2 ("Joy to the World") sings, "And heav'n and nature sing," "While fields and floods, rocks, hills, and plains / Repeat the sounding joy."
141. The metaphor jumped from theology to science with implications for how science was done. Protestant natural scientists made reference to nature's book over and over again throughout the seventeenth century. With the concept of the book of nature also came a method of interpretation. The Reformed method of interpreting the "facts" of the Bible affected their "reading" of the facts of nature's book. Protestant exegetes rejected medieval Biblical exegesis, in which every verse had four meanings, the literal, allegorical, moral, and analogical. They instead adopted a straightforward literal and historical reading and developed methods to "prove" theological assertions through the logical marshalling of passages of Scripture. Similarly,

Protestant scientists rejected medieval allegorical understanding of nature and applied comparable methods to prove scientific theories. Such an approach foreshadowed the scientific method, which Francis Bacon would articulate to great acclaim in the early seventeenth century. Harrison, *Bible, Protestantism, and Science.*

142. Parry, "Thomas Cole's Ideas," 37–38; Parry, "Acts of God," 53–74; Bedell, *Anatomy of Nature,* 17–45; and Bedell, "Thomas Cole."

143. Silliman, "Remarks," 210.

144. Smallwood and Smallwood, 57–86.

145. Smallwood and Smallwood, 86–100; Freemon.

146. On the history of science in Charleston before the Civil War, see Stephens, *Science, Race, and Religion.*

147. Smallwood and Smallwood, 102–129; Rowland, Moore, and Rogers, 398–400; Taylor, *South Carolina Naturalists,* 126.

148. See Underwood, 143; Cantor.

149. Barton's best biography is Ewan et al.

150. Glenn; Baatz, 117, 120, 124–134.

151. Wilson, *Life and Letters,* 4–5, 93–97.

152. Judd, *Common Lands, Common People,* 59–89.

153. Smallwood and Smallwood, 42–49.

154. Longfellow.

155. See Fitzmier.

156. Dwight, *Conquest of Canaan,* 9.1077–1080.

157. Greene, 11.

158. Guralnick, 1–17; Whitford and Whitford.

159. Wilson, "Benjamin Silliman," 1–10; Fisher, *Life of Silliman;* Fulton and Thomson; Brown, *Benjamin Silliman.*

160. Lawrence, "Edward Hitchcock"; Hitchcock, 281–297.

161. Derham, 3.

162. Hall, *Last American Puritan,* ch. 5; Winship, *Seers of God,* 64; Increase Mather, *Illustrious Providences,* n.p.

163. Middlekauff, 279–304; Silverman, 41–42, 167–168, 243–254, 406–410.

164. Cotton Mather, *Christian Philosopher,* 1–2, 3, 8, 13.

165. White, *Natural History of Selborne,* iv; Worster, *Nature's Economy,* 3–25. Armstrong, *English Parson-Naturalist.* See also Thomas, *Man and Natural World;* Gillispie, ch. 1.

166. Secord.

167. Baggerman.

168. Gallaudet, *Thomas Hopkins Gallaudet,* 1–44. See Smallwood and Smallwood, 217–228.

169. Jacob and Sturkenboom; Kohlstedt, "Parlors, Primers."

170. Lattin; Armitage, esp. 15–41; Kohlstedt, *Teaching Children Science.*

171. This is a complex subject with a huge literature. See Rupke; Walls, *Passage to Cosmos;* Sachs.

172. Georg Forster, "Ein Blick in das Ganze der Natur," in *Ausgewählte kleine Schriften von Georg Forster,* Albert Leitzmann, ed. (Stuttgart: G. J. Göschen'sche Verlargshandlung, 1894), 1–25.

173. Humboldt, *Cosmos,* 173.

174. Humboldt, *Cosmos,* 154, 201.

175. In his important book on Humboldt's influence in nineteenth-century America, Aaron Sachs argues the opposite, that Humboldt evinced a concern for humanity absent in the work of environmentalists like John Muir. That aspect of his argument is unconvincing. Sachs, ch. 10.

176. Humboldt, 24–25.

177. Kwa; Diener, 137–154. See also Novak, *Nature and Culture;* Bedell, *Anatomy of Nature.*

178. Noble, *Life and Works,* 85.

179. Parry, *Art of Thomas Cole,* 144.

180. A debate raged at the time about whether the earth was created by volcanic eruption or by settlement and crystallization in Noah's Flood. Parry believes that *Explusion* provides ambiguous evidence which side of the debate he favored. Parry, *Art of Thomas Cole,* 89–90.

181. Croker, 15; Cittadino, 532–533; Tabrum, 277.

CHAPTER 2

1. Frederic E. Church, letter to Thomas Cole, May 20, 1844, quoted in Howat, *Frederic Church,* 8.

2. Lanman, "Cole's Imaginative Paintings," 602–603; also in Lanman, *Letters,* 81–82, which was dedicated to George Perkins Marsh, a leading American art collector.

3. Trumbull, *Complete History,* 64–65.

4. Church changed the starting point from Cambridge to Plymouth, probably to associate them with the Pilgrims. By Church's day, Puritans were beginning to acquire a reputation as bigoted oppressors, hangers of witches and Quakers, in contrast to the pretty legend of Plymouth Separatists sitting down with Squanto at the first Thanksgiving. See Adams, *Specter of Salem,* 46–46, 72, 120, 135–148.

5. Tuckerman, 375.

6. Thanks to geologist Richard Thomas, Director of Exhibits, Connecticut Science Center, Hartford, Connecticut, for identifying the landmarks in this painting. Thomas, e-mail to the author, August 29, 2011. See also Kornhauser, 195–198.

7. Baigell.

8. Sellin, 25.

9. Cole, 9, 11–12.

10. See also Wilson, "Landscape of Democracy."

11. On Protestant hostility to the cross, see Smith, "The Cross."

12. Charles Dudley Warner, "An Unfinished Biography of the Artist," in Kelly, *Frederic Edwin Church*, 197.

13. Warner, in Kelly, *Frederic Edwin Church*, 185.

14. Howat, *Frederic Church*, 25.

15. Warner, in Kelly, *Frederic Edwin Church*, 197; Howat, *Frederic Church*, 27–29; *Home Book of Picturesque*, 137, 167–188.

16. In *Common Lands, Common People*, Richard W. Judd has argued that conservation ideals arose among the common people of New England. While this is true, the intellectual and political leadership of national conservationism did not come from northern but rather southwestern New England, and from the upper more than the lower classes. See also Judd, " 'Wonderfull Order and Ballance.' "

    Cumbler, *Reasonable Use*, traced the environmental history of the nineteenth-century Connecticut Valley, and Stoll, *Larding the Lean Earth*, 173–184, connected George Perkins Marsh and the agricultural improvement movement. Neither traced the deep history of conservationism to its source in a regional Puritan communal ethic or its embodiment in an idealized New England village.

17. Fischer, 13–206.

18. Perry Miller emphasized the ministers' commonalities. Miller, *Orthodoxy in Massachusetts*; Miller, *New England Mind: Seventeenth Century*; Miller, *The New England Mind: From Colony To Province*. Other historians tended to follow his lead. Recently historiographical emphasis has shifted toward recognition of diversity. See for example Knight; Breen; Winship, *Making Heretics*.

19. On the Great Migration, see Allen, *In English Ways*; Anderson, *New England's Generation*; Foster, 138–174.

20. "Steady habits" was a Jeffersonian term of rebuke for Connecticut's immovable Federalism, which Timothy Dwight reversed into a compliment in an Independence-Day oration that year. Dwight, *Oration*.

21. The essential study of this era is Corrigan.

22. See Biéler for the best and most thorough analysis.

23. Hooker, 188.

24. Hall, *Reforming People*, is excellent on the founding of New England towns and their dedication to social justice.

25. Bushman, *From Puritan to Yankee*, and Lucas describe the region's evolution.

26. Mary K. Talcott, "The Original Proprietors," in Trumbull, *Memorial History*, 237.

27. This was the argument of Miller, *Jonathan Edwards*. Tracy rejects it but not convincingly. McDermott supports Miller.

28. Buggeln, x–xi. For fuller accounts of the politics of Congregationalism, see Kuehne; Sassi; Roth; Scott, *From Office to Profession*. The first revivals of both the First and Second Great Awakenings broke out in the Connecticut Valley. On the unified culture of the Connecticut River Valley, see Ward and Hosley.

29. Census for 1820, 44–47.
30. Kemble, 146. Numerous English visitors declared Northampton and environs the most beautiful in America. Hoppin, 231–244.
31. Cole, 9.
32. For the development of the New England town, see Buggeln; Brodeur; Wood, "'Build, Therefore'"; Wood, "New England Village"; Jackson, *American Space*, 99–112; Donahue, 221–234.
33. Calvin, *Commentaries on Genesis*, 125. See, for example, Passmore, 29–30; Attfield.
34. Originally published in Hale, *Contemplations Moral and Divine*, vol. 1, irregularly paginated. The Hartford edition is Hale, *Great Audit*.
35. Whittelsey, 5.
36. Edwards, "The Duty of Charity to the Poor, explained and enforced," in *Practical Sermons*, 355.
37. Edwards again provides an excellent example in his sermon "The preciousness of Time," in *Practical Sermons*, 289.
38. Edwards, "Sinners in the Hands," 410.
39. Willard, *A compleat body of divinity*, 644.
40. Willard, *A compleat body of divinity*, 708.
41. See Heller, *Conquest of Poverty*; see also Heller, *Labour, Science, and Technology*.
42. Biéler, 195–233, 261–263, 282–286, 295–297, 309–315.
43. The title has been variously translated. "True Recipe" is another common rendering. Henry Morley makes it "Trustworthy Receipt" ("receipt" being in England a formerly common alternative to "recipe," both meaning "formula" before being confined to their current meanings).
44. Smith, "Giving Voice to Hands," 82; Heller, *Labour, Science and Technology*, 118; Duport, *Jardin et la nature*, 63–80. Duport offers a very convincing analysis of the purpose and design of *Recepte véritable*. See also Ceard, 139–147; Lestringant, 119–130. See Rivet, 167–180.
    "Stewardship" in the modern sense is a recent concept. Although Hale first articulated the notion of stewardship of the earth, the idea lay mostly dormant until the Progressives promoted it. Its contemporary currency dates only to the 1960s, when "earth stewardship" and related notions suddenly achieved widespread popularity.
45. Heller, *Labour, Science and Technology*, 98–99; Amico, 42.
46. Palissy, *Admirable Discourses*, 94, 148. The original passage is in Palissy, *Discours admirables*, 108–109, 148. On the Book of Nature among Protestants, see van Berkel and Vanderjagt, ix.
47. Estienne and Liébault, *L'agriculture*. This was a translation and expansion of Estienne's *Praedium rusticum* of 1554.
48. O'Malley, 408.
49. Serres; Gourdin; Boulaine; Duport, "'Science' d'Olivier de Serres,"; Dantec and Dantec, 64–74.

50. Heller, *Labour, Science and Technology*, 83–84. Besson's designs were more fan-ciful than labor-saving, but they represented the application of imagination to improvement of agricultural production.

51. See Debus.

52. Palissy, *Recepte véritable*, H.ii.r°. On the garden and its importance, see Amico, 158–159; Woodbridge, *Princely Gardens*, 84–87; Polizzi; Quenot; Duport, *Jardin et la nature*, 78–80; Amico, ch. 5.

53. Duport, *Jardin et la Nature*, 56, 86–91; Hazlehurst; Randall, *Building Codes*, ch. 3; Randall, "Structuring Protestant Scriptural Space." The literature on the rise of the English garden is vast; for a summary of its moral and religious aspects and their influence in the United States, see Stoll, "Milton in Yosemite."

54. Palissy, "The Naturalist Looking Out on Evil Days," in Morley, 249–250. The original passage is in Palissy, *Recepte véritable*, M.ii.r° and v°.

55. Heller, *Labour, Science, and Technology*, 94, 158–160; Toussaint-Samat, 547–551.

56. For a good account, see Cronon, 85–90.

57. Carroll; Willson, 12–17; Innes, 226–227, 280–306. On the self and Puritan soci-ety, the classic work is Bercovitch.

58. See Donahue, esp. ch. 7.

CHAPTER 3

1. Ruskin, xxxi–xxxii.

2. Kwa, 160; Diener, 137–154. See also Novak, *Nature and Culture*, 80–81; Bedell, *Anatomy of Nature*, ch. 3.

3. Ruskin, xxii–xxiii, xliii–xliv.

4. Amelia Sturges, letter to her mother, July 17, 1856, quoted in Howat, *Frederic Church*, 69.

5. See Howat, *Frederic Church*, 69–74; Kelly, "A Passion for Landscape," 50–54.

6. Winks, *Frederick Billings*, 303.

7. Winks, *Frederick Billings*, 303.

8. Howat, *Frederic Church*, 5; Warner, 177.

9. For Billings and Congregationalism (or Presbyterianism in San Francisco or New York), see Winks, *Frederick Billings*, 5, 86, 172, 223, 258, 306, 308, 310.

10. See, for example, Stoll, *Larding the Lean Earth*; Bidwell.

11. Grasso, 524; see Eliot, *Give Cesar His Due*.

12. Eliot, *Essays*, 138, 165.

13. True, *History of Agricultural Education*, 14.

14. Bjelajac, 66.

15. Jesse Buel, *The Farmer's Companion or, Essays on the Principles and Practice of American Husbandry* (Boston: Marsh, Capen, Lyon, and Webb, 1839), 21, quoted in Stoll, *Larding the Lean Earth*, 90. See also Buel.

16. Roper, 11.

17. Roper, 44; Olmsted, *Papers,* vol. 1, *The Formative Years: 1822–1852,* ed. Charles Capen McLaughlin, 75. On Tucker, see Bergen, 1001–1002.

18. True, *History of Agricultural Education,* 14; True, *History of Agricultural Experimentation,* 22–34, 41.

19. The Connecticut school was preceded by Maine's Gardiner Lyceum, established in 1821 by Congregational minister Benjamin Hale. True, *History of Agricultural Education,* 31–37.

20. Smith, "Reversing the Curse," 759–791.

21. White, *Life of Lyman Trumbull,* 2–3; True, *History of Agricultural Education,* 52, 56, 83–84, 91–94, 103.

22. Cross, 12–13, 77–87.

23. Introduction to Olmsted, *Papers,* vol. 6, *The Years of Olmsted, Vaux & Company, 1865–1874,* ed. David Schuyler and Jane Turner Censer, 10–16; Roper, 321.

24. Olmsted, *A Few Things to be Thought of before Proceeding to Plan Buildings for the National Agricultural Colleges,* in *Papers,* vol. 6, *Olmsted, Vaux & Company,* 142.

25. Williams, *Origins of Federal Support,* 57; Weeks.

26. Osborne, 205.

27. "Report of the President of Yale University for 1910," quoted in Osborne, 211.

28. Mangelsdorf, 142.

29. Roper, 321.

30. Bailey, 14.

31. See King, *Farmers of Forty Centuries;* Tanner and Simonson; Paull; Sligh and Cierpka, 31–32; and Stinner, 54–55. The founder of Anglophone organic agriculture, Sir Albert Howard, said in his own foundational text that King's book "should be prescribed as a textbook in every agricultural school and college in the world." Howard and Wad, 12. King's father was born in a town in the Connecticut Valley; his mother was a native of Nova Scotia, a descendant of New England Loyalists. I have found no reference to King's own religious affiliation.

32. Marsh, *Address,* 18–19.

33. Marsh, *Genealogy;* Lowenthal, 3–9, 42–43; Trumbull and Pomeroy, 107, 147; Judd and Boltwood, 19, 23, 32, 34, 211, 212.

34. Quoted in Lowenthal, 377. Compare Marsh, *Life and Letters,* 79.

35. Marsh, *Life and Letters,* 29.

36. See Marsh, *Address;* and Marsh, et al., *Report.*

37. On the New England origins of *Man and Nature,* see Lowenthal, 275–278. See also Stoll, "'Sagacious' Bernard Palissy," 19–22.

38. Marsh, *Man and Nature,* 8, 35.

39. Marsh, *Man and Nature,* 264.

40. Garvey, 111.

41. Haddock, 324–326; Hough; Steen, "Beginning of the National," 51–53; Ekirch.

42. Hollister, 21–23; Miller, "Amateur Hour"; Egleston, 12. On Hough and Egleston, see also Steen, *U.S. Forest Service,* 9–21.

43. See Rodgers, 17. No doubt a Lutheran, Fernow did have one connection to Congregationalism in that he was married to his American wife, daughter of English-born parents, in Brooklyn's Pilgrim Congregational Church by Henry Ward Beecher.

44. Olmsted, *A Few Things to be Thought of*, 139.

45. Olmsted, "Chicago in Distress," *Nation* (November 9, 1871), 302–305, in *Papers*, vol. 6, *Olmsted, Vaux & Company*, 483–484.

46. Olmsted, letter to Frederick J. Kingsbury, January 20, 1891, quoted in Roper, 416.

47. Miller, *Gifford Pinchot*, 102.

48. Carl A. Schenck, letter to Stella Obst, 24 August 1950, quoted in Roper, 467.

49. Pinchot, *Breaking New Ground*, 32.

50. Amos Enos House, Nomination Form; Miller, *Gifford Pinchot*, 69–70. Pinchot was raised Presbyterian.

51. Pinchot, *Breaking New Ground*, 1–2.

52. Miller, *Gifford Pinchot*, 55.

53. Hays, title.

54. Pinchot, *Fight for Conservation*, 133, 8, 5.

55. Pinchot, *Breaking New Ground*, 340–344.

56. Pinchot, "Problem," 7, 10–11. On Pinchot and the country life movement, see McGeary, 100–102, 243–244.

57. "Henry Solon Graves." For this reference, I am grateful to Carla Heister, Librarian, Yale School of Forestry and Environmental Studies. Graves's father graduated from Amherst College; his mother was from Mansfield, Massachusetts.

58. Carter, *History*, 261; "William B. Greeley," 77; Mason; Miller, *Gifford Pinchot*, 277–291.

59. Pinchot, *Breaking New Ground*, 322, 323, 326; Miller, *Gifford Pinchot*, 154–155.

60. Schuyler, 1–8.

61. Downing, *Treatise*, 21. See also 16, 73, 121, 388.

62. On Downing, see Schuyler, *Apostle of Taste*; Major; and McClelland, 17–36.

63. See, for example, Joseph Heely, *Letters on the Beauties of Hagley, Envil, and The Leasowes* (1777), in Hunt and Willis, 329; Heely, 12–13, 86, 102.

64. Walpole, 248–249; Newlyn, 20.

65. Shawcross, ch. 3; Nicolson, 273–276.

66. Downing, "A Short Chapter on Country Churches," in *Rural Essays*, 261.

67. Downing, "Moral Influence of Good Houses," in *Rural Essays*, 212.

68. Downing, "Moral Influence of Good Houses," in *Rural Essays*, 211–212.

69. Downing, "Our Country Villages," in *Rural Essays*, 237.

70. Downing, "Our Country Villages," in *Rural Essays*, 240n, 241.

71. Downing, "Trees in Towns and Villages," in *Rural Essays*, 305.

72. Olmsted, *Walks and Talks*, 79.

73. Rosenzweig and Blackmar, 26; Muller, 222.

74. Rosenzweig, and Blackmar, 20, 138.

75. Roper, 66–77.

76. Schuyler, 156–162.

77. Rosenzweig and Blackmar, 120.

78. "Park History."

79. Rosenzweig and Blackmar, ch. 5.

80. Downing, *Treatise*, 42.

81. Olmsted, letter to the Board of Commissioners of the Central Park, May 31, 1858, in *Papers*, vol. 3, *Creating Central Park 1857–1861*, ed. Charles E. Beveridge and David Schuyler, 196.

82. Eliot, *Charles Eliot*, 39–40.

83. Olmsted, "Mount Royal: Montreal," 1881, in *Papers*, suppl. ser., vol. 1, *Writings on Public Parks, Parkways, and Park Systems*, ed. Charles E. Beveridge and Carolyn R. Hoffman, 388. See also Scheper.

84. Eaton, 318.

85. Smith, *Sunshine and Shadow*, 361.

86. Richmond, 19. For Richmond's dominational affiliation, see "Religious Notices," *New York Times*, July 20, 1878, 7.

87. Olmsted, "Preliminary Report to the Commissioners for Laying Out a Park in Brooklyn, New York," in *Papers*, suppl. ser., vol. 1, *Writings*, 86.

88. Smith, *Sunshine and Shadow*, 369.

89. Olmsted, "Address to [the] Prospect Park Scientific Association [May 1868]," *Papers*, suppl. ser., vol. 1, *Writings*, 155.

90. Olmsted, letter to Charles Loring Brace, November 24, 1871, in Olmsted, *Papers*, vol. 6, *Olmsted, Vaux & Company*, 493.

91. Lloyd, 45–46.

92. Brewster, 1–27.

93. Davis, "Memorial of William Ashburner," 219–221.

94. See Sargent.

95. Holbrook, *Recollections*, ch. 17.

96. King, *Vacation Among the Sierras*.

97. Hammond and Adams, 58; Hickman and Pitts, viii.

98. Landow, ch. 4; Sears, *Sacred Places*, 140–142, and ch. 6. See Robertson, *West of Eden*; also Demars, 23–24, 33, 63.

99. Lippincott, 364, 305–306. On Lippinicott, see McHenry, 248.

100. Josiah Letchworth, Letter #13, May 22, 1880, in Letchworth and Letchworth, 84–85.

101. Ludlow, 412, 426.

102. Albert Bierstadt, letter to John Hay, quoted in Anderson and Ferber, 178.

103. Washburn.

104. Stoddard, *In the Footprints*, 256; Presbyterian, see 105.

105. Simpson, 385–86. I infer that he was not entirely serious.

106. Lamson, 151–52.

107. Minturn, 280.

108. Greenwood, 333–334.

109. Miller, "Yosemite," in *Poems*, 119. Sterling, 4. Sterling's mother was a staunch Presbyterian. Benediktsson, 14.

110. See for example Boston poet Proctor, "Yosemite," *Poems*, 47; Hazard, "The Yosemite," *The Yosemite*, 5; and Blande, 3, 5.

111. Bowles, 231.

112. Howat, *Frederic Church*, 5–6, 172–173.

113. Kent, 7–9, 51–70, 83; Nash, 175.

114. The two other cofounders were John C. Merriam, descended from Massachusetts Puritans on his father's side and from Scottish Presbyterians on his mother's, and raised Presbyterian; and Madison Grant, an Episcopalian with Puritan, Presbyterian, Huguenot, and Dutch Reformed but no Connecticut Congregationalist ancestors, and a graduate of Yale. Mark, 27–30; Spiro, 6, 8, 134.

115. Other offspring of New England (but not of the Connecticut Valley or Congregational Church) who led fights for creation of parks include George B. Dorr (Acadia), Virginia Donaghe McClurg (Mesa Verde), and Marjorie Stoneman Douglas (Everglades).

116. Mather, *Report of the Director*, 6.

117. Shankland, 12–14, 20, 287; quotation, 134. Mather's father switched to the Episcopal Church when he moved to New York City. Mather was named for an Episcopal clergyman in New York, but I have no information on the denomination of his childhood in California. Both Mather and his father returned to Connecticut from California and were buried there.

118. Quoted in McClelland, 10.

119. "Frank A. Waugh"; and "Dr. Frank A. Waugh"; and McClelland, 81–85. Thanks to Danielle Kovacs, Curator of Collections, Special Collections & University Archives, and her staff at the W.E.B. Du Bois Library, University of Massachusetts, for assistance with Waugh's background. (Wirth's ancestry was Swiss Reformed.)

120. Bushnell; Aron, 14–44; Putney, *Muscular Christianity*, 11–44.

121. Tucker, "Of Men and Mountains," 167.

122. Murray, 22, 24; Owen, "Art and the Artist"; Radford, 39–75; Cadbury, 10–75; Courtney, 132–139.

123. See Strauss; Nash, 108, 116–121; Terrie.

124. "Sumner F. Dudley," *New York Times*, March 15, 1897, 7.

125. Carlson, "Organized Camping," 83–84; Paris, *Children's Nature*, 30–60; Maynard.

126. Olmsted, quoted in Rybczynski, 293.

127. Jackson, *American Space*, 111.

128. Waugh, 90.

129. Moore, *Daniel H. Burnham*, 1–15.

130. Frank Lloyd Wright, quoted in Hines, 325.

131. On the history of the City Beautiful movement and the roles of Olmsted and Burnham, see Schuyler, *New Urban Landscape;* Wilson, *City Beautiful Movement;* Smith, *Plan of Chicago*.

132. Burgess, 102.

133. On Bates and "America the Beautiful," see Burgess; Sherr.

134. Olmsted, "Public Parks and the Enlargement of Towns," in *Papers,* suppl. ser. vi, *Writings,* 172.

135. This point is made in Danbom.

136. See Mayer.

137. Ifkovic, 197–205.

138. Annie Trumbull Slosson, "Riled," in *Among the Clouds* (July 17, 1893), quoted in Ifkovic, 260–261.

139. Ifkovic, 317–353.

140. Winks, *Laurance S. Rockefeller,* 106–112. On the Rockefeller women, see Stasz; Barbour, 271, 374; Kert, 46–47; 52–55; 68; 93–94; 134.

141. Maher, 196–208.

142. LeConte, 17.

143. See Gura.

CHAPTER 4

1. Reconstruction of the timing and circumstances of *Clearing Winter Storm* in Alinder, 144. On the MoMA show and the popularity of Adams's publications, Alinder, 313–16; Adams, *Yosemite,* cover. See also Adams, *Examples,* 102–106.

2. Adams, "Conversations with Ansel Adams," 4. His mother was raised in Nevada by natives of Ohio and Maryland. His paternal grandmother was raised Baptist in Thomaston, Maine, was married to his grandfather, William James Adams, by Thomaston's Unitarian minister, joined the Episcopal Church at age 35, and ended life as a Catholic. Unitarian influence must have been strong on Adams. His daughter would be an active Unitarian and married her minister. Helms, 32, 215.

3. See, for example, Huth, ch. 6; Nash, ch. 5; Novak, *American Painting,* esp. ch. 5–7; Worster, *Nature's Economy,* pt. 2; Dunlap, ch. 2.

4. On this topic, see Gillispie; Hovenkamp; Moore, *Post-Darwinian Controversies;* Carter, *Spiritual Crisis.*

5. This theme is explored in Noll, *Civil War;* and Rable.

6. Newhall, 36.

7. Adams and Alinder, 59, 18; Adams, "The Meaning of the National Parks," in *My Camera, in the National Parks: 30 Photographs With Interpretive Text and Informative Material on the Parks and Monuments, and Photographic Data* (Boston: Houghton Mifflin, 1950), reprinted in Adams, Turnage, and Stillman, 16, 18; Adams, letter to Harold Bradley, Richard Leonard, and David Brower, July 27, 1957, in Adams, Alinder, and Stillman, 248; "The Meaning of the National Parks," 17; Adams, letter to Cedric Wright, June 10, 1937, in Adams, Alinder, and Stillman, 95; Wallace Stegner, foreword to Adams, *Ansel Adams,* 15.

8. Alinder, 91.

9. Emerson, *Nature*, in *Collected Works*, vol. 1, *Nature, Addresses, and Lectures*, 38–39, 44.

10. Emerson, *Nature*, 7.

11. Emerson, *Nature*, 7.

12. Emerson, "The Over-Soul," in *Collected Works*, vol. 2, *Essays: First Series*, 174.

13. Emerson, "Art," in *Collected Works*, vol. 7, *Society and Solitude*, 47.

14. "Self-Reliance," in *Collected Works*, vol. 2, *Essays: First Series*, 29, 34.

15. See Rawson.

16. See Schmidt; Albanese, esp. 162–176.

17. Cayton; Teichgraeber, ch. 7–8; Teichgraeber, "'Our National Glory': Emerson in American Culture, 1865–1882," in Capper and Wright; Geselbracht; Wider, ch. 3–4.

18. Alinder, 17–22.

19. See Mitchell, ch. 1–2; Hoffman, 147–156.

20. Alinder, 10–11; Hammond and Adams, ch. 1; Peeler, ch. 15; Westerbeck; Cox.

21. Newhall, 60.

22. Quoted in Strand and Tompkins, 143.

23. Maddow; Strand, Busselle, and Stack; Phillips.

24. Adams, letter to Edwin Land, March 12, 1956, in Adams, Alinder, and Stillman, 244.

25. Fairfield Porter, letter, to Ted Leigh, October 26, 1973, in Porter, 320; Spring, 1–6.

26. Klee, 257–258.

27. Dyrness, 308.

28. Helm, 4.

29. Ward Lockwood, "The Marin I Knew: A Personal Reminiscence," in Strand, Busselle, and Stack, 93; Rosenfeld, 162.

30. Marin, *John Marin*, 35.

31. Helm, 96.

32. Marin, "Here It Is," *Selected Writings*, 76.

33. Pollitzer, 139–142.

34. Drohojowska-Philp and O'Keeffe, 303.

35. Quoted in Hogrefe, 3.

36. Hartley, 116.

37. Hogrefe, 11–20; Lisle, 4, 13, 46; Pollitzer, 56, 58, 59, 61, 62; Kandinsky, 8, 108, 9, 91.

38. Lisle, 55, 57–58.

39. Stieglitz and Dove, 319.

40. Haskell, 9–11; Wight, 19–28; Cohn, 1–18, 45–80.

41. Quoted in Haskell, 118.

42. Lisle, 329.

43. Morgan, 79–80.

44. Rosenfeld, 170; see also Crunden, 365–376.

45. American Federation of Arts, 53; Nancy E. Green, "Arthur Wesley Dow, Artist and Educator," in Green and Poesch, 55–86; Dow quoted, 57; Moffatt; Dow quoted, 340; Sharyn R. Udall, "Beholding the Epiphanies: Mysticism and the Art of Georgia O'Keeffe," in Merrill and Bradbury, 89–112; Schmidt, ch. 5. Fine et al., 28.

46. Quotations in Hartley, "Somehow a Past: Prologue to Imaginative Living," 67, and "Excerpts from 'Somehow a Past: A Sequence of Memories,'" 181, both in Hartley, *Somehow a Past;* and in Robertson, *Marsden Hartley,* 24. Ludington, *Marsden Hartley,* 15, 19–20; Ludington, *Seeking the Spiritual;* Nasgaard, ch. 10; Charles C. Eldredge, "Nature Symbolized: American Painting from Ryder to Hartley," in Tuchman, 112–129.

47. Quoted in Strand, Busselle, and Stack, 77.

48. For a rather different interpretation of O'Keeffe's development in her important work, see Peters. Peters infers a strong Symbolist influence on O'Keeffe (with little direct evidence) and focuses on the influence of photographers on her art: Strand, Charles Sheeler, Edward Steichen, and of course Stieglitz. She barely mentions Dove, whose art O'Keeffe consistently admired, and Hartley hardly at all.

49. Wilson, "Intimate Gallery." A thoughtful evaluation of Transcendental and other influences on O'Keeffe is in Castro, 157–171, 184 ch.7 n. 3. O'Keeffe's marriage to Alfred Stieglitz in 1924 also brought her into contact with such friends as Claude Bragdon, an architect-designer as well as theosophist, author, and translator of Ouspensky (and Yankee-bred Emersonian). Crunden, 377–392.

50. Udall, "Beholding the Epiphanies," 98, 99.

51. Sergeant, 200; O'Keeffe quoted in Eldredge, 27. On the Fellowship, see Friedland and Zellman.

52. Stoller, 7.

53. Owings, 15–19.

54. Wright, *Autobiography,* 37.

55. Wright, *Autobiography,* 30–31, 36–37. On religious radicalism of his mother's family, the Lloyd Joneses, see Secrest, ch. 1–2; on the influence of Ruskin, see 127–130. See also Hertz, esp. ch. 3 and 10.

56. Wright, *Autobiography,* 45.

57. Wright, *Autobiography,* 599.

58. Quoted in Wright, *Collected Writings,* 9.

59. Wright, "In the Cause of Architecture: V. The New World," *Architectural Record* (October 1927), in Wright, *In the Cause,* 151.

60. Wright, "The Architect and the Machine," in *Collected Writings,* 23.

61. Scully, 115.

62. Twombly, 372; Wright and Pfeiffer, 120.

63. Quinn, *Weaver of Dreams,* iii, 15, 17, 19, 20, 73–85; quotation, 79. See also Quinn, "Overcoming Obscurity"; Leavengood.

64. Pray; see also McClelland, 9.

65. Kaiser, 63–69.

66. No New Englander, Richardson hailed from a plantation near New Orleans, but note that his grandfather was the great Unitarian minister and scientist Joseph Priestly. He entered Harvard University in 1855 and never returned to the South. O'Gorman, 3–27, 91–111; McClelland, 43–45, 91–94. On Richardson's influence, see Scully.

67. Bosley, *Greene & Greene*, 8–21; quotation, 17. McClelland, 104–108, 110. The Greenes and Mather shared a common ancestor in Mather's great-grandfather, Rev. Moses Mather.

68. Wheaton, 15.

69. Cardwell, 13–19, 119, 185–186; quotations, 16; Bernard Maybeck, *San Francisco Call,* June 21, 1923, quoted in Woodbridge, *Bernard Maybeck,* 13. Daniel Hull, Park Service senior landscape engineer from 1920 to 1927, shared offices with Underwood after 1923. McClelland, 159, 171.

70. Keeler, 226.

71. Freudenheim, 1–20, 101–126.

72. Longstreth, 56–66, 111–117, 273–275, 308–309, 389 n28, 395 n30.

73. Keeler, 226.

74. Harris and Maybeck, 110–113; Bosley, *First Church.*

75. McClelland, 109–111; Zaitlin, 1–27, 53–81.

76. Alinder, 63; Newhall, 50.

77. Alinder, 128–130, 148.

78. McClelland, 226–228.

79. Adams and Alinder, 49–50.

CHAPTER 5

1. Badè, vol. 1, 365. Muir describes snow conditions in *Mountains of California,* 53. Biographers often mention only two visitors. Wolfe, citing Muir's manuscript "Walking," names three. Wolfe, 161.

2. Jeanne C. Carr, letter to John Muir, October 2, [1872,] Muir Correspondence.

3. Muir's manuscript "Walking," quoted in Wolfe, 162.

4. Muir, letter to [Jeanne C. Carr], [ca. October 15, 1872,] Muir Correspondence.

5. Muir, *Mountains of California,* 52.

6. Keith (first published in 1874 in the Boston *Advertiser*).

7. Muir, "Art Notes," San Francisco *Evening Bulletin,* June 20, 1874, 3.

8. Muir, "Art Notes," *Overland Monthly,* May 1875, 482.

9. Palmquist, 54; Watkins, *Carleton Watkins,* 26; Campbell, 35, 47. On Watkins and his photography, see Nickel; Naef; Naef and Hult-Lewis.

10. Knox, "A Sermon on Isaiah xxvi, 13–21, preached at St. Giles's Church, Edinburgh, 19th August 1565," in *Works,* vol. 6, 229–230, 230–231.

11. Knox, *The Reformation in Scotland,* in *Works,* vol. 2, 386–389; quotation, 362.

12. Benedict, *Christ's Churches,* 172.

13. The same principles animated Scottish Enlightenment philosophy. See Gordon Graham, "The Nineteenth-Century Aftermath," in Broadie, 342.

14. Knox, "The Confession of Faith, 1560," in *Works,* vol. 2, 108.

15. Benedict, 152–172, 392–395, 405–408, 412–415, 418–421; Roger Emerson, "The Contexts of the Scottish Enlightenment," in Broadie, 11–15; Stewart J. Brown,

"The Ten Years' Conflict and the Disruption of 1843," in Brown and Fry. On the Scottish Reformation, see Cowan.

16. David W. Miller, "Religious Commotions in the Scottish Diaspora: A Transatlantic Perspective on 'Evangelicalism' in a Mainline Denomination," in Wilson and Spencer, 25.

17. On the movement of peoples and culture from Ulster to America, see Griffin, *People With No Name*.

18. On the history of American Seceders and Covenanters, see Fisk.

19. Wilson, 69–102, 171–200; Mark G. Spencer, "'Stupid Irish Teagues' and the Encouragement of Enlightenment: Ulster Presbyterian Students of Moral Philosophy in Glasgow University, 1730–1795," in Wilson and Spencer, 50–61.

20. Gaustad and Barlow, 136.

21. Unless otherwise noted, all biographical information for Keith is drawn from Cornelius. On Craigdam's church, see Mackelvie, 59–60.

22. [Campbell], *Declaration and Address*, 4.

23. Muir, *Boyhood, and Youth*, 121, 212. Dates are from the historical marker at the Wee White Kirk, Marquette County, Wisconsin.

24. Muir, *Boyhood and Youth*, 263.

25. Muir, *Our National Parks*, 1, 132.

26. Baker, 367–368.

27. Muir, *Boyhood and Youth*, 245.

28. Muir once gave *Paradise Lost* as a birthday gift to the son of a favorite professor in Madison. See Osborn, 30; Daryl Morrison, "John Muir and the Bairns: Muir and His Relationship with Children," in Miller and Morrison, 54. Muir's life has been chronicled by numerous biographers, but for the facts of his life I have primarily relied on Wolfe and Worster, *Passion for Nature*.

29. Muir, "Art Notes," *Overland Monthly*, 481.

30. Paul Wood, "Science in the Scottish Enlightenment," in Broadie, 94–116; Andrew S. Skinner, "Economic Theory," in Broadie, 178–204; Broadie, "Art and Aesthetic Theory," in Broadie, 280–297; M. A. Stewart, "Religion and Rational Theology," in Broadie, 31–59.

31. Astore discusses Dick's biography and influence in the United States.

32. Badè, vol. 1, 143, 306.

33. On Muir and Carr, see Muir and Carr; and Bonnie Johanna Gisel, "'Those Who Walk Apart but Ever Together Are True Companions': Jeanne Carr and John Muir in the High Sierra," in Miller and Morrison, 215–234.

34. Muir, *Boyhood and Youth*, 225.

35. Walls, *Passage to Cosmos*, 290–295; Sachs, 305–337.

36. Wolfe, 104.

37. Muir, autobiographical manuscript, in Badè, vol. 1, 155.

38. Muir, "Explorations," 143.

39. Huxley and Hooker, 1–37. See Gisel; Worster, *Passion for Nature*, 202–208.

40. Colby, Introduction.

41. Muir to Emily Pelton, May 23, 1865, quoted in Wolfe, 95.
42. Muir, *Our National Parks*, 74.
43. Muir, *My First Summer*, 49.
44. Muir, *Travels in Alaska*, 70.
45. Quoted in Wolfe, 154.
46. Joanna Brown to Muir, December 8(?), 1889, quoted in Worster, *Passion for Nature*, 303–304.
47. Terry Gifford, "Muir's Ruskin: John Muir's Reservations about Ruskin Reviewed," in Miller; Gifford, 75–85; Worster, *Passion for Nature*, 208–215.
48. Ogden, 94, 104–106.
49. Stegner, 289.
50. Muir, *Yosemite*, 257, 261–262.
51. The ill-favored conservative Republican Douglas McKay during Dwight D. Eisenhower's first term.
52. Swett, 38–53, 231–233.
53. Worster, *Passion for Nature*, 236.
54. Muir, "God's First Temples," 8.
55. See Socolofsky and Spetter.
56. Gourley, 14; Hannum. His brother Henry, a Columbus lawyer, taught Sunday School. "Henry C. Noble," 248–253.
57. Dilsaver, and Tweed, ch. 4; "Savior of Sequoias Heeds Call: Col. Stewart, Visalian Who Obtained Two Parks for Nation," *Los Angeles Times*, Sep. 8, 1931, 6. On Vandever's religious beliefs, see Anderson, "More Conscience Than Force," 168.
58. Johnson, *Remembered Yesterdays*, 3–27.
59. Dilsaver and Tweed, ch. 4; Worster, *Passion for Nature*, 310–316.
60. Colby, *Reminiscences*, 7–8; LeConte, 42–42. Founder David Starr Jordan was raised Universalist in western New York; Jordan, 46.
61. See a list of forest-related bills introduced into Congress and their sponsors in "Forestry Legislation." See "Thomas Chipman McRae, 1921–1925," in Donavan, Gatewood, and Whayne, 157–164; Grant.
62. Bowers was a Hartford native, Episcopalian, and Yale graduate. "Edward August Bowers."
63. Socolofsky and Spetter, 70–73; Steen, *U.S. Forest Service*, 26–28.
64. Johnson, *Remembered Yesterdays*, 292–296; quotations, 296. For the Muir-Johnson campaign, see Worster, *Passion for Nature*, 319–328.
65. John W. Noble to John Muir, November 20, 1907, Muir Correspondence.
66. Brodsky, 296; Grantham, 3–13.
67. Barnes, 21, 32, 99–101.
68. Steen, *U.S. Forest Service*, 34–37; Grantham, 88–91, 117.
69. Roosevelt, *Autobiography*, 379.
70. See Brinkley, whose book shows signs of haste but is the most thorough retelling of Roosevelt's astonishing activity and legacy.

71. Hawley, 1–19.
72. All quotations in Reisner, *Roosevelt's Religion*, 204–205.
73. Abbott, 430.
74. Roosevelt, "New Nationalism," 21, 22, 20–21.
75. Roosevelt, *Autobiography*, 441–442; Miller, *Gifford Pinchot*, 159–160; Hays, 44–45, 78–79, 118, 130–131; Bates, 35; Balogh, 205–206; "George Washington Woodruff"; Woodruff, "Disposal of Public Lands"; Woodruff, "Classification of Public Lands."
76. Roosevelt, *Outdoor Pastimes*, 316.
77. Muir to Johnson, July 16, 1906, quoted in Johnson, *Remembered Yesterdays*, 292. There are many accounts of the meeting of Muir and Roosevelt. See Johnson, 387–388; Roosevelt, "John Muir: An Appreciation"; Worster, *Passion for Nature*, 366–371; Brinkley, 536–547.
78. Johnson, *Remembered Yesterdays*, 300–304.
79. These events have been retold many times, most recently in Righter. There have also been many accounts of Muir's friendship and split with Pinchot, probably best told in Miller, *Gifford Pinchot*, 123–136, 119–124, 138–144. On Pinchot as Presbyterian, see Pinchot and Steen, 14, 16, 17.
80. Lane, Lane, and Wall, 1–16, quotations on 8.
81. Albright and Albright, 3–7, 118.
82. "To Scatter Lane's Ashes: They Will Be Thrown From Peak—Body Cremated in Chicago," *New York Times*, May 20, 1921, 12.
83. Turner, 37.
84. Morris, *Rise of Theodore Roosevelt*, 383–385, 465–466; Brinkley, 201–207; Nash, 145–147.
85. See Seton, "King Of Currumpaw"; Seton, *Wild Animals*.
86. Seton, *Lives of Game Animals*, vol. 3, *Hoofed Animals*, 502, 533, 535, 571; Seton, "Sage of the Sierra," vol. 4, *Rodents, Etc.*, 156; Anderson, *The Chief*, 90; Seton, *Animal Tracks*, 90; physical description, Witt, 18, 45, 50. Biographical information is drawn from Anderson and Witt.
87. Burroughs, "Real and Sham Natural History." See Lutts.
88. See Seton, *Natural History*; Seton, *Gospel of Red Man*.
89. Scott and Murphy; quotation, "West Says Seton Is Not a Patriot," *New York Times*, December 7, 1915, 4.

   The other major forerunner of the Boy Scouts was the Sons of Daniel Boone, which however never achieved the success of Seton's Woodcraft movement. Its founder and leader was Daniel Carter Beard, of Connecticut Yankee origin on his father's side and Quaker–Huguenot–Ulster Scot origin on his mother's. Beard was raised Swedenborgian in Cincinnati, Ohio. The Sons of Daniel Boone lacked the spiritual aspect of Seton's Woodcraft Indians and instead presented a romanticized pioneering frontiersman for youthful emulation. See Beard.
90. Anderson, *The Chief*, 166–169; Buckler, 3–49.
91. Putney, "Legacy of the Gulicks," quotation, 29.

92. Putney, *Muscular Christianity*, 113.

93. Young, *Alaska Days*, 13. See Muir, *Travels in Alaska*, 50–55; Young, *Hall Young of Alaska;* Worster, *Passion for Nature*, 246–254, although Worster mistakenly puts the ship captain's words in Muir's mouth.

94. See Maclean.

95. Van Dyke, 168, 298–312.

96. I am not making this up, you know. Ninde, 373.

97. Babcock, 180. See Ninde, 373–377; Stone, *Footsteps in a Parish;* Robinson, *Maltbie Davenport Babcock;* Verrill, 369–371.

98. Boy Scouts of America, *Eagles Soaring High.*

99. See Penick. For Ballinger's religious affiliation, see Bagley, 619–621.

100. Roosevelt, *Confession of Faith*, 32.

101. Ickes, 217.

102. Trani; Goldman, 302.

103. For the record, Albert B. Fall was raised Disciples of Christ and Ray Lyman Wilbur Congregationalist. Stratton, 11–13; Wilbur, 21.

104. Ickes, 1–27. The Ickes family belonged to the Second Presbyterian Church, which was organized in 1870 by the Huntingdon Presbytery of the United Presbyterian Church. See Hall, *Hall's Index.*

105. Watkins, *Righteous Pilgrim* is my source for Ickes's biographical information. On Watkins, see Bruce Weber, "T. H. Watkins, 63, Environmental Writer and Historian," *New York Times*, February 26, 2000, B10.

106. Walter Lippman, "Today and Tomorrow," *New York Herald Tribune*, February 7, 1952, quoted in Mackintosh, 78.

107. "Ickes Asks Church to Aid New Deal," *New York Times*, May 24, 1934, 7.

108. See Glover, 166–167, 171, 177, 182, 185–186, 200–201, 206–209.

109. "Ickes on the Parks," *New York Times*, May 14, 1933, E4.

110. Watkins, *Righteous Pilgrim*, 549–579; Mackintosh, 78–84; Dilsaver and Tweed, ch. 7.

111. Watkins, *Righteous Pilgrim*, 484–494.

112. Only one Presbyterian, the justly forgotten Clinton P. Anderson, has been Secretary of Agriculture since.

113. I infer David F. Houston's Presbyterian affiliation from his Presbyterian marriage ceremony. I also infer that he changed to Episcopalian, as his affiliation is listed as such in 1913 and he had an Episcopal funeral. Payne; "Editorial Briefs," *The Protestant Magazine*, May 1913, 237.

114. Ferleger, 215–219; Wilcox and Wilson, quotation on 188.

115. Schapsmeier and Schapsmeier, 2–17; Lord, 1–258.

116. Schapsmeier and Schapsmeier, 184–195, 266–274.

117. Wallace, 20.

118. Standard biographies are Simon, *Independent Journey;* Murphy.

119. Reich, xi.

120. Douglas, *Of Men and Mountains*, 18, x.

121. See Douglas, *My Wilderness: Pacific West*; Douglas, *My Wilderness: East to Katahdin*; Douglas and Stein.

122. See Douglas, *Wilderness Bill of Rights*; Douglas, *Farewell to Texas*; Douglas, *Three Hundred Year War*, 199–200.

123. Carson, *Silent Spring*, 67, 68, 72, 158–159.

124. Douglas, *Sierra Club* v. *Morton*, 405 US 727 (1972), in *Nature's Justice*.

125. Sowards, 121.

CHAPTER 6

1. Fraser, memo.

2. Fraser, e-mail to the author, August 18, 2013.

3. Clements, 6–15; Danielson, 12–95; Fraser, e-mail to the author, January 12, 2015.

4. Fraser, e-mail to the author, June 12, 2013.

5. Coyle, 65.

6. "The Confession of 1967" 9.53, in Presbyterian Church, 262. Many scholars have explored the topics that are summarized here. See Balmer and Fitzmier; Smith, *Presbyterian Ministry*; Szasz; White and Hopkins; Cauthen; Carter, *Decline and Revival*; Hutchison; Meyer; Porterfield; Wuthnow. Oh, and of course Carroll, "The Hunting of the Snark," Fit the Eighth.

7. McHarg, 11, 241.

8. Zelov and Cousineau, 67.

9. See Fábos.

10. For Simonds's biographical information, I have relied on Slade; Nemmers.

11. McPhee, *Encounters with the Archdruid*, 79–150, quotation, 95.

12. Fraser, e-mail to the author, August 18, 2013.

13. Sully, 60–62.

14. Poesch, esp. 282–290.

15. Averitt, 329; for a history of Sea Pines Plantation, see Fraser and Greer.

16. This is the theme of Holifield; and Stephens, *Science, Race, and Religion*.

17. Breen, *Puritans and Adventurers*, 106–198; Breen, *Tobacco Culture*; Fischer, 207–418, 605–782; see Einhorn for the connection between slavery and tax policy.

18. On the religious transformation of the South, see Hill, *South and the North*; Isaac; Ragosta; Bruce. On religion's adaptation to a slave society, see Wigger, 122–125, 148–155, 292–299, 308, 334; Butler, 129–163; Heyrman, ch. 5.

19. See Carr, *Handbook of Turtles*; Carr, *Windward Road*; Carr, *So Excellent A Fishe*.

20. For biographical details I have relied on Davis, *Man Who Saved Sea Turtles*.

21. Marjorie Harris Carr's parents, Charles E. Harris and Clara L. Haynes, were married on April 5, 1909, by Unitarian minister Edward B. Maglathlin. "Massachusetts, Marriages, 1841–1915," index and images, *FamilySearch*, https://

familysearch.org/pal:/MM9.1.1/N4D8-K5R, Charles E Harris and Clara L Haynes, 1909. Maglathlin was Unitarian minister of Bridgewater, Massachusetts. No other evidence of their religious affiliation can be found.

22. Marjorie Harris Carr, interview with Leslie Kemp Poole, October 18, 1990, quoted in MacDonald, 49; for the Carrs' continued Presbyterian adherence, 4.

23. Herrmann, 159.

24. Robinson, "Nature, Value, Duty," 477.

25. For evaluations of Rolston's philosophy, see Preston and Ouderkirk; Weir, 260–267. See also Preston; Rolston, 184–187.

26. On Templeton, see Herrmann; Aitken; "John Marks Templeton," *New York Times*, July 11, 2008, C11.

27. Brower, *For Earth's Sake*, 251.

28. Brower and Schrepfer, 13–14.

29. McPhee, *Encounters with the Archdruid*, 83.

30. Brower, *Wildness Within*, 7.

31. Brower and Schrepfer, 12–14, 305. See also Brower, *For Earth's Sake*, 3, 19–20.

32. Harold Gilliam, in Brower, *Wildness Within*, 51.

33. Cohen titled his chapter over the controversy "The Brawl"; *History of the Sierra Club*, 395–433.

34. Brower, *Wildness Within*, 9.

35. Rorty, 1–2.

36. Deutsch, 45.

37. "A rare moment of peace," 38.

38. Biographical information is drawn from Bennett and Powell. For a portrait of his father, see Kelso, 50.

39. Jeffers, "Preface to 'Judas,'" X3.

40. Adams and Alinder, 69–70.

41. Brower, Adams, and Jeffers, 23, 27.

42. Jeffers, "New Year's Dawn, 1947," in *Collected Poetry*, vol. 3, *1938–1962*, 213.

43. Jeffers, "The Double Axe, II. The Inhumanist," in *Collected Poetry*, vol. 3, *1938–1962*, 257.

44. Everson, vii, ix; Jeffers to Frederic I. Carpenter, quoted in Everson, ix.

45. Jeffers and Mallette Dean, *Themes in My Poems* (San Francisco: Book Club of California, 1956), quoted in Bennett and Powell, 182.

46. Jeffers, *Themes*, quoted in Bennett and Powell, 185.

47. Jeffers, "Hurt Hawks," in *Collected Poetry*, vol. 1, *1920–1928*, 378.

48. McPhee, *Encounters with the Archdruid*, 95.

49. Parton, 21.

50. White, "Historical Roots"; on White's Presbyterianism, "Lynn (Townsend) White, Jr."

51. Abbey, *Desert Solitaire*, 52, 169.

52. For Abbey's biography, see Cahalan; McCann. For criticism of his works, see Ronald; Pozza, especially for its attention to the Pennsylvania novels.

53. Abbey, *Desert Solitaire,* 167.
54. Abbey, "A Writer's Credo," *One Life at a Time,* 161, 165.
55. Abbey, "A Writer's Credo," *One Life at a Time,* 177–178.
56. Seaman, 1173.
57. Zakin, 9.
58. Foreman, *Confessions,* 4.
59. *Earth First! Newsletter,* June 21, 1983, 9. For Wildlands Project, see Foreman and Wolke; Foreman, *Rewilding North America.*
60. Denver and Tobier, 102, 15, 88; Denver and Tobier is my source for biographical details and lyrics.
61. Denver, 96.
62. Biographical information comes from "Obituaries," Princeton *Town Topics,* November 21, 1984, 32; McPhee, "The Patch," 32–35; Pearson.
63. Brower and Chapple, 144.
64. Hamilton, 38.
65. Hamilton to Agnes Hamilton, March 20, 1892, in Sicherman, 39; see also 33.
66. For Hamilton's biography, see Hamilton; Sicherman.
67. Jacobs and Keeley, 20; "Widow of City Physician, Bess Butzner, Ex-Teacher-Nurse, Celebrates 90th Birthday Saturday," *The Scrantonian* (June 15, 1969), in Allen, *Ideas That Matter,* 133; *Historical and Biographical Annals,* 568; Presbyterian Church in the U.S.A., 37; Jacobs, "Autobiography," in Allen, *Ideas That Matter,* 3.
68. Carson, *Edge of the Sea,* 2, 7, 250.
69. Carson, *Lost Woods,* 160, 162; for Carson's biography, see Lear. For an introduction to the sizable literature on Carson and her work, see Stoll, *Rachel Carson's "Silent Spring."*
70. Dillard, *Pilgrim at Tinker Creek,* 159–181.
71. Dillard, *American Childhood,* 227.
72. For Dillard's biography, see Dillard, *American Childhood;* Richardson, "Biography of Annie Dillard." See Dillard, *Holy the Firm;* Dillard, *For the Time Being.* There is a large body of criticism of Dillard. For an example of comparison with Thoreau, see James A. Papa Jr., "Water-Signs: Place and Metaphor in Dillard and Thoreau," in Schneider, 70–79.
73. See Flippen.
74. Worster, *Passion for Nature,* 281–283, 285–286.
75. Jacobs and Keeley, 17–18.
76. See Garb.

CHAPTER 7

1. Address by W. Whittredge, *Gifford Memorial Meeting of the Century: Friday Evening, Nov. 19, 1880* (New York: Century Association, 1880), 33–34, quoted in Avery, "Gifford and the Catskills," 25.
2. For the classic analysis of American outsider religion, see Moore, *Religious Outsiders.*

3. See Stradling, ch. 1.

4. For genesis of the painting, see Avery and Kelly, 175–178; Weiss, 105, 257–260. Weiss insightfully reads significant Civil War symbolism into the painting, 95–97. On the symbolism of stumps, see Cikovsky. Cole and most Hudson-River School artists painted similar scenes, although significance varied. See Cikovsky and Wallach.

5. Miller, "All in the Family," 122.

6. Miller, *Gifford Pinchot*, 23, 108–110.

7. Johnson, "From a Woodland Elegy," B1.

8. Avery, "Sanford R. Gifford," 229–231.

9. Burroughs and Burroughs, 108–109.

10. McLoughlin, *New England Dissent*, 122, 165–199; Brooke, 30–58.

11. On the early history of Baptists in New England, see McLoughlin, *New England Dissent;* Goen; McLoughlin, *Isaac Backus.*

12. Branham and Hartnett, 55–59.

13. For on the mentality, culture, and history of Baptists and Southern Baptists, and evangelicals in general, see Eighmy; Glass; Hankins; Harper; Harrell; Harvey, *Redeeming the South;* Hill, *Southern Churches in Crisis;* Hill, *South and the North;* Hill, *Varieties;* Krapohl and Lippy, ch. 1–11; Leonard; Noll, *American Evangelical Christianity;* Noll, *America's God;* Wills.

14. For example, Tolles.

15. Weiss, 54, 13–45.

16. Caruthers; Kelly, "Nature Distilled," 6, 10, 11; Avery, "Gifford and the Catskills," 26–29; Harvey, "Tastes in Transition," 81–82.

17. Renehan, 12–13.

18. Renehan, 45–46. Quotations from Burroughs's journals.

19. Burroughs and Johnson, 176–177; Barrus, *Our Friend*, 129–130; compare Barrus, *Our Friend*, 105, 125–130; Barrus, *Life and Letters*, vol. 1, 41.

20. Renehan, 64–65; Westbrook, 77.

21. Burroughs, "Before Genius," *Birds and Poets*, 168.

22. Renehan, 11, 14, 97.

23. Renehan, 19–20.

24. Renehan, 23–27, 271–276.

25. Barrus, *Our Friend*, 132, 133.

26. Burroughs, "In the Hemlocks," *Wake-Robin*, 43.

27. Burroughs, "Birch Browsings," *Wake-Robin*, 171.

28. Burroughs, "A Bird Medley," *Birds and Poets*, 92; "Birds and Poets," *Birds and Poets*, 27–28.

29. Burroughs, "Birch Browsings," *Wake-Robin*,174.

30. Burroughs, "The Invitation," *Wake-Robin*, 227–228.

31. Burroughs, "John Muir's 'Yosemite,'" 1165.

32. Worster, *Passion for Nature*, 432.

33. See Mercier.
34. See, for example, "Miss Cather in Lincoln," *Lincoln Journal* (Nov. 2, 1921), in Bohlke, 40–41; and Eleanor Hinman, "Willa Cather," *Lincoln Star* (Nov. 6, 1921), in Bohlke, 47.
35. Willa Cather, "Seton-Thomson at Tea," *Nebraska State Journal* (Feb. 6, 1901), 9, in Cather, *World and the Parish,* vol. 2, 824.
36. Cather, "Utterly Irrelevant," *Nebraska State Journal* (Oct. 7, 1894), 13, in Cather, *World and the Parish,* vol. 1, 117.
37. Woodress, 23, 51.
38. Acocella, 26.
39. Ryder, 75–84. My sources for biographical details are Gerber; Lee, *Willa Cather.* Some readers may find more value that I did in Rosowski.
40. Burroughs, "Thoreau's Wildness," 74–75; Burroughs, "Henry D. Thoreau," 368–379; Burroughs, "Henry David Thoreau," 530–533.
41. *Nation* 22 (January 27, 1876):66; quoted in Warren, 34. Warren discusses the Burroughs's competition with Thoreau, 19–22, 33–41.
42. Kennedy, 152–153.
43. Sharp, 58.
44. McLoughlin, "Massive Civil Disobedience."
45. Compare Robinson, "'Unchronicled Nations.'"
46. Emerson, *Journals and Miscellaneous Notebooks,* 96.
47. See Sattelmeyer, *Thoreau's Reading;* Richardson, *Henry Thoreau.* Walls, *Seeing New Worlds* is especially good on Humboldt. See also Worster, *Nature's Economy,* 57–111.
48. Sattelmeyer, *"Walden:* Climbing the Canon," 11–27.
49. Nearing and Nearing, 46, 71, 98, 108, 149, 156, 162–163, 180. See also Nearing, 29, where Thoreau is listed among his life's influences.
50. Nearing and Nearing, ix.
51. Nearing, 34.
52. Saltmarsh, 4. Saltmarsh likens the conversion experience to Transcendental transformation, but Baptist conversion makes a good deal more sense in Nearing's case.
53. Saltmarsh, 3.
54. Nearing and Nearing, 48.
55. Saltmarsh, 254–263.
56. Portola Institute, 47.
57. On the Nearings, see Saltmarsh; Nearing; Whitfield, *Scott Nearing;* Killinger.
58. Wright, "Extension of the Work," 131.
59. Wright, "The Disappearing City," 77.
60. Marty and Marty, 87.
61. Wright, "Extension of the Work," 130.
62. See Marty and Marty, esp. 1–14.
63. Wright, *Autobiography,* 560.

64. Twombly, 236.

65. Wright, "The Disappearing City," 71.

66. Wright, "New Frontier," 47.

67. Wright, "New Frontier," 55, 56.

68. Blassingame; Genovese.

69. Cowdrey, 65–126; Silver, ch. 4–6; Kirby, ch. 2–4.

70. Bennett, *Our American Land;* Bennett, *Thomas Jefferson.* Bennett's standard biography is unfortunately silent on religion: Brink. Among Bennett's ancestors were two preachers, Nevel Bennett and Archibald Harris. His father and his first wife were married by a Methodist minister, L. A. Johnson.

71. Berry, *Long-Legged House,* 140.

72. Olson, 65.

73. For Berry's biography, see Angyal.

74. Berry, *Sex, Economy, Freedom & Community,* 117–173.

75. Berry, *Sex, Economy, Freedom & Community,* 119–120.

76. Berry, *Unsettling of America,* 23.

77. Berry, *Unforeseen Wilderness,* 28.

78. Wilson, *Naturalist,* 139.

79. Klinkenborg, C23.

80. Wilson, *Consilience,* 4, 6; *Naturalist,* 45.

81. Wilson, afterword, 1482.

82. See Blackwell; Ruse, "The Faith of an Evolutionist"; Ruse, *Mystery of Mysteries,* 172–193.

83. Wilson, e-mail to the author, July 27, 2005.

84. Wilson, *Diversity of Life,* 348–351; see Wilson, Pope, and Hefner.

85. Wilson, *Consilience,* 289.

86. Sociologist Segerstråle, who knew and interviewed Wilson, believed that he deliberately aimed at religion in *Sociobiology.* Segerstråle, 38–39.

87. Wilson, *Sociobiology,* 560.

88. Wilson, *Sociobiology,* 243.

89. Wilson, *Consilience,* 263.

90. Wilson, *Creation,* ch. 17.

91. Gore, 14, 16, 368. See Maraniss and Nakashima, 157.

92. Dr. George Easterbrook, DDS, obituary, *Lockport Union-Sun & Journal.* October 12, 2012, http://lockportjournal.com/obituaries/x1400167534/George-Easterbrook.

93. Easterbrook, xvii.

94. Quoted in Guzzo, 7. Guzzo's campaign biography is the only full biography of Ray; for her family and religion; see 17–27.

95. Ray and Guzzo, *Trashing the Planet,* 70; Ray and Guzzo, *Environmental Overkill,* 189.

96. "Resolution on Environmentalism."

97. See Mohler.

98. Merritt, 2.
99. Ronald Henri[e] Arnold was born in 1937. His young mother married his father right before he was born and divorced right after. Arnold was adopted and raised by maternal grandparents and took their name. For his Methodism, see his grandfather's obituary, *San Antonio Express,* April 13, 1970, 23.
100. For the charismatic tradition, see Stephens, *Fire Spreads;* Synan; Wacker. For James G. Watt, see Arnold; and Short.
101. N. C. Meeker, "A Western Colony," in Willard, *Union Colony at Greeley,* 2. Boyd, 15; Sprague, 3.
102. Davis, "New England Origins"; Brooke, 59–88.
103. Bushman, *Joseph Smith,* 8–29.
104. Arrington, *Brigham Young,* 7–18.
105. See Ricks; Nelson; Arrington, *Great Basin Kingdom,* 24; Hansen, 123–130; Hill, *Quest for Refuge,* xii–xiii, 31–54; Reps, 286–343; Alexander, "Mormon Prophets and Environment," 85–103.
106. Arrington, *Great Basin Kingdom,* 323; Peterson; Leone, 86–110.
107. Flake, ch. 5; Moore, 25–47.
108. See Petersen; Nibley.
109. Udall, viii.
110. Ure, 65–75.
111. Williams, *Refuge.*

CHAPTER 8

1. Twiggs, 213. Biographical information is drawn from Twiggs; Twiggs, telephone interview with the author, August 19, 2014; Laufer.
2. Twiggs, 231.
3. See Fisher, "African Americans"; Bush; Kahrl.
4. Anthony, 8–10.
5. Roszak, 265, 273; Anthony, 59–63; quotation on 63. For an analysis of the differences between the mainstream environmental and environmental justice movements, see Taylor, "Women of Color," 38–58.
6. See Stewart; Giltner, "Slave Hunting and Fishing"; Giltner, *Hunting and Fishing;* Brinkley, 431–444.
7. Long, 24–25; Blassingame, 131; Creel, ch. 2, and see also Part IV. See also Raboteau, *Fire in the Bones;* Sobel.
8. Paris, *Spirituality of African Peoples,* 44–45, 57, 101, 111, 120–24; Raboteau, "African Americans, Exodus"; Raboteau, "Black Experience in American Evangelicalism"; Long, 29–30; Levine, 33, 50–51, 187–89; Blassingame, 33–34, 147–48; Pitts, ch. 1–2; Harris, 75–81, 86–87.
9. Long, 26; Sernett, ch. 3; Painter, 195–196.
10. Robert Booth Fowler, quoted in Baer and Singer, x.

11. See Harris, *Something Within;* Lincoln and Mamiya; Baer and Singer; Lawrence, *Reviving the Spirit;* Brown, "Negotiating and Transforming."

12. Paris, *Social Teaching,* xi; George; Lincoln and Mamiya, 43–58, 121, 202–03, 210–11, 231; Baer and Singer, 30, 58–64; Carson, "Martin Luther King, Jr."; Harris, 66. Even an apparent exception, Reverend Al Sharpton, precociously ordained a Pentecostal minister at age ten, as a teenager attended Bethany Baptist Church, a politically active congregation in Bedford-Stuyvesant in New York City whose pastor, Reverend William A. Jones Jr., mentored the boy and set him on the path of politics and protest. Michael Powell, "Outspoken Activist Takes the National Stage," *Washington Post,* June 29, 2003, A1.

13. See McGurty; Swift; Harris, 182; "Benjamin F. Chavis."

14. Garland, 128; Checker, esp. 167–171; Lerner, 61–71; Oliver; Bullard, 109. A sociological study suggests that membership and activity in churches positively correlate with black environmentalism, but not with white environmentalism: Arp and Boeckelman.

15. Pinn, 86–88.

16. See O'Sullivan. Others have also noted O'Sullivan's preference for figures in the landscape. See Sachs, 23.

17. Pew Forum on Religion & Public Life, 10.

18. For general histories of the American Catholic experience, see McGreevy; O'Toole.

19. Stoll, "Les influences religieuses"; Stoll, "Protestant, Catholic, Green," paper delivered at the European Society for Environmental History meeting, St. Andrews, Scotland, September 7, 2001.

20. Klaaren, 51.

21. Morris, *American Catholic,* 69. See also Hennesey, 160, 167ff., 217.

22. See Hastings; Gremillion, 58, 188; Dorr, 49.

23. Morris, 327–330; Hastings; Gremillion; Dorr, 49–61.

24. See "Sisters of the Earth"; Jones, "Eco-spirituality"; Ruether, "Sisters of Earth."

25. The program produced three parish resources in succeeding years: United States Catholic Conference, *Renewing the Face of the Earth;* United States Catholic Conference, *Peace with God the Creator;* United States Catholic Conference, *Let the Earth Bless the Lord.*

26. Grazer, 578–587.

27. Davidson, *Search for Common Ground,* 54, 185. See also Tropman, pt. 4.

28. Reilly, esp. 22–30; quotations on 28.

29. See Blum; Gibbs, 106–110. Both of Lois Marie Conn Gibbs's parents, Joseph P. and Patricia A. Conn, are buried in Assumption Roman Catholic Cemetery in Grand Island, New York.

30. The terms "Latino/Latina" and "Hispanic" are contested. "Latino/Latina" includes all Western-Hemisphere speakers of Spanish or Portuguese. "Hispanic" refers to Americans who speak Spanish or are from Spanish-speaking nations. Regionally, Westerners prefer "Latino/Latina" and Easterners "Hispanic." Where

I live the preferred term is "Hispanic," which I will use since I write it most naturally and because it is gender-neutral.

31. The same is said of the Catholicism of southern Italians. See Orsi, ch. 8.

32. Lane, *Landscapes of the Sacred*, 100–123.

33. The description here and below of Mexican, Latin American, and Hispanic Catholicism and politics relies on the following accounts: De La Torre and Espinosa; Medina; Kane, "American Catholic Culture"; Arroyo and Cadena; García; Casarella and Gómez; Díaz-Stevens and Arroyo; Badillo; Matovina, and Riebe-Estrella; Dolan and Deck; and Dolan and Hinojosa.

   Robert Wright, professor of systematic theology at Oblate School of Theology in San Antonio, Texas, acknowledges that I have correctly summarized the literature on Hispanic popular Catholicism but draws somewhat different conclusions from his own research: "I would assert that traditional Mexican Catholicism is pervasively present (home, church, street, business), typically assigns different roles to men and women, is expressed liturgically and through devotional practices, hopes against hope, and is not always in line with the hierarchical authorities of the Church." Robert Wright, e-mail to the author, January 13, 2009.

   For Mexican-American environmental justice, see Peña, *Mexican Americans and Environment;* Fairbank, Maslin, Maullin & Associates, and California League of Conservation Voters.

34. See Pulido, 57–124.

35. Farm Worker Network mission statement, quoted in Peña, "Tierra y Vida," 191.

36. On the acequias, see DeBuys; DeBuys and Harris; Pulido, 125–190.

37. Arce, 79–83; Ostertag, 49–50; Di Chiro; "Battling Toxic Racism: El Pueblo Para El Aire y Agua Limpio," in Street and Orozco, 20–32; SouthWest Organizing Project editors.

38. See Barriault.

39. Hebblethwaite, 242.

40. See Fox, *On Becoming;* Fox, *Whee! We, Wee;* Fox, *Spirituality Named Compassion;* Fox, *Original Blessing;* Fox, *Coming of Cosmic Christ.* On Fox, see "About Matthew Fox," Matthew Fox Website, www.matthewfox.org/about-matthew-fox.

41. Berry, *Dream of the Earth,* esp. ch. 15; quotation on 215. For biographical information, see Tucker; Berry, "Thomas Berry." See also Berry, "Ecological Geography"; Berry, "Earth Systems . . . Human Systems"; Berry, "Christianity's Role in the Earth Project"; Dalton, introduction and ch. 1–4.

42. Fritsch, "Appropriate Technology"; see Schumacher. See also Fritsch, "Catholic Approach."

43. Hartshorne, 45–55.

44. See Cobb and Daly. It is not my purpose here to give a thorough history of process theology. Many figures, most from other denominations than the Episcopal or Methodist Churches, have contributed to its development, but I mention only the most influential and best-known. For a fuller account, see Dorrien, 58–132, 190–268.

45. Morris, *American Catholic,* 334ff. discusses this trend.

46. See Daly; Spretnak; LaChapelle.

47. See Ruether, *New Woman New Earth;* Ruether, *Sexism and God-Talk;* Ruether, *Gaia & God.* See also Ruether, "Ecofeminism." See Grant D. Miller Francisco, "Rosemary Radford Ruether (1936–)," http://people.bu.edu/wwildman/ WeirdWildWeb/courses/mwt/dictionary/mwt_themes_908_ruether.htm.

48. See McFague, *Models of God;* McFague, *Body of God.* For biographical information, see McFague, *Life Abundant,* 3–24; Dorrien, 358–372. See Merchant, *Death of Nature;* see also Merchant, *Earthcare.* On Merchant's Episcopalianism, see Bryson. See Christ; Griffin, *Woman and Nature.*

49. Antler, 259–284.

50. Eller, 22–23; Raphael, 25n9. See Stone, *When God Was a Woman.* For documents relating to the goddess restoration movement in Judaism, see essays and poems in Pirani.

51. See also Merchant, *Earthcare,* 139–166.

52. Fine et al., 34.

53. Alfred Stieglitz to Georgia O'Keeffe, quoted in Pollitzer, 164.

54. Emerson, *Nature,* in *Collected Works,* vol. 1, *Nature, Addresses, and Lectures,* ed. Robert Ernest Spiller and Alfred Riggs Ferguson, 10.

55. Whelan, 35–41, 49; Lisle, 160, 167; on his O'Keeffe-inspired photography at Lake George, see Stieglitz and Szarkowski. Following his death in 1946, O'Keeffe took Stieglitz's ashes to the family summer home and mixed them with the soil at the root of a tree at the edge of Lake George. Lowe, 377–378.

56. Sorin, 3.

57. See, for example, Benstein.

58. See Herscher, especially ch. 4; Near, ch. 1. Exceptions, such as the long-lived Jewish farms of New Jersey, owe their success to proximity to New York or other urban areas, allowing for part-time truck farming and industrial employment. See also Eisenberg; Jewish Agricultural Society; Lavender and Steinberg; Davidson; Norman; Brandes and Douglas.

59. Landscape painter Alan Gussow (1931–1997) is an exception. With the assistance of David Brower, he published *A Sense of Place: The Artist and the American Land* (San Francisco: Friends of the Earth, 1972), an album of American landscape art, including his own. Born in New York to Lithuanian Conservative-Jewish immigrants, he grew up on Long Island, spent summer vacations in New Jersey and Monhegan, Maine, and went to Middlebury College in Vermont. The vacations and college in the mountains of Vermont got him interested in landscape. He married a lapsed Presbyterian and settled in the Hudson River Valley, where the family raised organic food. Gussow was an active environmentalist. His landscape art was intended to promote a connection to the land through sense of place. Joan Gussow, e-mail to author, November 9, 1998.

60. Among the different explications of Jewish ecological thought, an accessible and concise account is in Katz. See also Rose, introduction and "Introduction to the Jewish Faith," in Rose; and Schwartz.

61. See Cohen, *Encounter with Emancipation*, esp. ch. 1.

62. Marshall, *People's Forests*, 123.

63. For biographical information on Louis Marshall and his parents, see Adler; Rosenstock; and Glover, 7–14. On the Ethical Culture movement, see Friess; Kraut. For Marshall, see Glover. For one of the rare discussions of Marshall's Jewishness, see Cohen, "The Bob." See also Marshall, *Alaska Wilderness*.

64. Ehrlich, Ehrlich, and Daily, xiii.

65. Ehrlich, Ehrlich, and Holden, 259.

66. Ehrlich, Ehrlich, and Daily, xv.

67. Ehrlich and Ehrlich. On Ehrlich, see "Paul Ehrlich," in DeLeon; Ehrlich, telephone interview with the author, April 13, 1999. Ehrlich's primary books for the nonspecialist on overpopulation are *Population Bomb*; with Anne Ehrlich: *Population, Resources, Environment*; *Population Explosion*; Ehrlich, Ehrlich, and Daily, *The Stork and the Plow*; and Ehrlich, Ehrlich, and Holden, *Human Ecology*.

68. See Singer, *Animal Liberation*; Singer, *Ethics into Action*.

69. On Russian Jewish radicalism, see Frankel. On the survival of radicalism among Jews in the United States, see especially Whitfield, *Voices of Jacob*, ch. 5, and, on the persistence of liberalism among succeeding generations of American Jews, ch. 6. Sorin discusses religious sources and aspects of Russian Jewish radicalism, especially ch. 2. See also Haberer, ch. 8. On Zon, see Schmaltz.

70. Murray Bookchin, e-mail to the author, February 13, 2001.

71. See Steve Chase, "Introduction: Whither the Radical Ecology Movement?," in Bookchin, Foreman, and Chase. See Bookchin, "Crisis in the Ecology Movement"; Bookchin, *Remaking Society*, 7–18.

72. Bookchin, *Remaking Society*, 193.

73. See Bookchin, *Ecology of Freedom*. Other major works include *Our Synthetic Environment*; *Post-Scarcity Anarchism*; *Rise of Urbanization*; *Re-Enchanting Humanity*. See also White, *Bookchin*; Bookchin, *Murray Bookchin Reader*; Bookchin, *Philosophy of Social Ecology*. Bookchin discusses his background in Bookchin, *Anarchism, Marxism, and the Future of the Left*, pt. 1.

74. See Commoner, *Closing Circle*. Other major works include *Poverty of Power*; *Politics of Energy*; *Making Peace with the Planet*. On Commoner, see Egan; and Kriebel.

75. Kane, "One Man's Wilderness."

76. See Coleman. Coleman's biography is controversial.

77. Carlson, *New Agrarian Mind*, 55–74. See Crepeau.

78. Jackson, *J. I. Rodale*, 39. Details of Rodale's life come from Jackson.

79. See Pollan, *Second Nature*; Pollan, *Botany of Desire*; Pollan, *Omnivore's Dilemma*; Pollan, *In Defense of Food*; Pollan, *Cooked*; Pollan, *Food Rules*.

80. Pollan, *Omnivore's Dilemma*, 144–156; Fishman; Glassner, 71–74.

81. Lowry, 203–209. See also Kann.

82. For example, Gottlieb.

CONCLUSION

1. The social science literature on religion and environmental attitudes is fairly large. For a thorough review, see Djupe and Hunt; Sherkat and Ellison. I know of no study of denominational differences. All social science research with which I am familiar focuses on rather general Christian tenets like "dominion," under the influence of White, "Historical Roots of Our Ecologic Crisis." Hence they tend to control for the very denominational differences that might yield more informative results.

2. Harold C. Anderson, et al., *The Wilderness Society* (Washington, DC: 1935), 4, quoted in Nash, 207.

3. "The Wilderness Society Platform," *Living Wilderness* 1 (1935): 2, quoted in Nash, 207–208. For the origins of the Wilderness Society, see Sutter, 3–7.

4. For Bob Marshall see chapter 8 in this volume. Bernard Frank's parents, Isaac Frank and Rachel (Rabinowitz, a name that implies Frank's ancestors included rabbis) Bernard, were Russian-Jewish immigrants; folder on Bernard Frank, alumnus, Rare and Manuscript Collections, Cornell University, Ithaca, NY. I am grateful to Hilary Dorsch Wong for this reference. For Aldo Leopold, see Meine, 15. For Robert Sterling Yard, see the obituary of his mother, Mrs. Sarah Purdue Yard, Methodist Episcopal Church, Newark Conference, *Minutes of the Newark Conference of the Methodist Episcopal Church* (1916): 93–94. For Benton Mackaye, see Anderson, *Benton MacKaye*, 10. For Ernest Oberholtzer, see Paddock, 10–11. For Harvey Broome, see Cotham, 55. Harold C. Anderson's father and grandfather were vestrymen in their Episcopal Church; see "Parochial Reports," 165. On the founding of the Wilderness Society, see Fox, *John Muir and His Legacy*, 210–212.

5. See Harvey, *Wilderness Forever*, 9; Backes, 2–15.

6. Leopold, 149.

7. Public Law 88-577 (16 USC 1131–1136), 88th Congress, Second Session, September 3, 1964.

8. Glover, 17, 19–20, 74, 82, 104–107.

9. Meine, 18–20; Meine, "Aldo Leopold's Early Years," in Callicott.

10. For Dave Foreman, see chapter 6 in this volume; for Howie Wolke and Judi Bari, see chapter 8. For Mike Roselle, see Roselle, 7–14. Roselle also came to radical environmentalism via political activism. I can find no background information about the other two of the original five founders of Earth First!, Bart Koehler and Ron Kezar, who appear in any case to have played lesser roles in the organization.

11. Dehler, 127–28.

12. Lendt, ch. 1.

13. See, for example, Foreman, *Man Swarm*.

14. For Powell's definitive biography, see Worster, *River Running West*.

15. See Austin. For a biography, see Fink.

16. McPhee, *Encounters with the Archdruid*, 151–245; Reisner, *Cadillac Desert*, 214–254.

17. See Jackson, *Altars of Unhewn Stone*; Jackson, *New Roots for Agriculture*; The Land Institute Website, www.landinstitute.org.

18. Nordhaus and Shellenberger; quotations, 18. On the essay and the controversy it sparked, see Barringer; Horowitz; Tobias, 10.

19. For examples of this sort of perspective among scholars of American environmental history, see Jacoby; Steinberg, 136–154; Germic.

20. Ellul, 405–407. Religion itself has become a commodity, as Moore provocatively explores in *Selling God*.

21. See Oreskes and Conway.

Bibliography

NEWSPAPERS

Lockport (New York) *Union-Sun & Journal*
Los Angeles *Times*
New York *Times*
Princeton *Town Topics*
San Antonio *Express*
Washington *Post*

PRIMARY SOURCES

Abbey, Edward. *Desert Solitaire: A Season in the Wilderness.* New York: McGraw-Hill, 1968.

Abbey, Edward. *One Life at a Time, Please.* New York: Holt, 1988.

Adams, Ansel. *Ansel Adams—Images, 1923–1974.* Boston: New York Graphic Society, 1974.

Adams, Ansel. "Conversations with Ansel Adams." An oral history conducted 1972, 1974, 1975 by Ruth Teiser and Catherine Harroun. Regional Oral History Office, Bancroft Library, University of California, Berkeley, 1978.

Adams, Ansel. *Examples: The Making of 40 Photographs.* Boston: Little, Brown, 1983.

Adams, Ansel. *Yosemite and the Range of Light.* Boston: New York Graphic Society, 1979.

Adams, Ansel, and Mary Street Alinder. *Ansel Adams, an Autobiography.* Boston: Little, Brown, 1985.

Adams, Ansel, Mary Street Alinder, and Andrea Gray Stillman. *Ansel Adams: Letters and Images, 1916–1984.* Boston: Little, Brown, 1988.

Adams, Ansel, William A. Turnage, and Andrea Gray Stillman. *Ansel Adams: Our National Parks.* Boston: Little, Brown, 1992.

Albright, Horace M., and Marian Albright Schenck. *Creating the National Park Service: The Missing Years.* Norman: University of Oklahoma Press, 1999.

Alison, Archibald. *Essays on the Nature and Principles of Taste.* 5th ed. Vol. 2. Edinburgh: Willison, 1817.

Ames, William. *The Marrow of Theology.* Translated by John D. Eusden. Durham, NC: Labyrinth, 1968.

Anthony, Carl. "The Civil Rights Movement, and Expanding the Boundaries of Environmental Justice in the San Francisco Bay Area, 1960–1999." Oral history by Carl Wilmsen, 1999, Regional Oral History Office, Bancroft Library, University of California, Berkeley, 2003.

Austin, Mary. *The Land of Little Rain.* Boston: Houghton, Mifflin, 1903.

Babcock, Maltbie D. *Thoughts for Every-Day Living: From the Spoken and Written Words.* New York: Scribner, 1902.

Badè, William Frederic. *The Life and Letters of John Muir.* 2 vols. Boston: Houghton Mifflin, 1923.

Bailey, L. H. *The Holy Earth.* New York: C. Scribner's Sons, 1915.

Beard, Daniel Carter. *Hardly a Man Is Now Alive: The Autobiography of Dan Beard.* New York: Doubleday, Doran, 1939.

Bennett, Hugh H. *Our American Land: The Story of Its Abuse and Its Conservation.* Washington, DC: US Dept. of Agriculture, 1946.

Bennett, Hugh H. *Thomas Jefferson, Soil Conservationist.* Washington, DC: United States Dept. of Agriculture, Soil Conservation Service, 1944.

Berry, Thomas. "Christianity's Role in the Earth Project." In *Christianity and Ecology: Seeking the Well-Being of Earth and Humans.* Edited by Dieter T. Hessel and Rosemary Radford Ruether. Cambridge, MA: Harvard University Press, 2000.

Berry, Thomas. *The Dream of the Earth.* San Francisco: Sierra Club Books, 1988.

Berry, Thomas. "Earth Systems . . . Human Systems." In *Fugitive Faith: Conversations on Spiritual, Environmental, and Community Renewal.* Benjamin Webb, interviewer. Maryknoll, NY: Orbis Books, 1998.

Berry, Thomas. "Ecological Geography." In *Christianity and Ecology: Seeking the Well-Being of Earth and Humans.* Edited by Dieter T. Hessel and Rosemary Radford Ruether. Cambridge, MA: Harvard University Press, 2000.

Berry, Thomas. "Ecological Geography." In *Worldviews and Ecology.* Edited by Mary Evelyn Tucker and John A. Grim. Lewisburg, PA: Bucknell University Press, 1993.

Berry, Thomas. "Thomas Berry: A Spirit in the Smokies Interview." *Spirit in the Smokies: Magazine of New Paradigm Living.* http://spiritinthesmokies.com/interviews/thomasb.html.

Berry, Wendell. *The Long-Legged House.* New York: Harcourt, Brace & World, 1969.

Berry, Wendell. *Sex, Economy, Freedom & Community: Eight Essays.* New York: Pantheon Books, 1993.

Berry, Wendell. *The Unsettling of America: Culture & Agriculture.* San Francisco: Sierra Club Books, 1977.

Berry, Wendell, and Ralph Eugene Meatyard. *The Unforeseen Wilderness: An Essay on Kentucky's Red River Gorge.* Lexington: University Press of Kentucky, 1971.

Blande, Henry Meade. "In Yosemite." In *Yosemite and Other Poems,* in *Short Story Quarterly* (Summer 1920): 1–6.

Bookchin, Murray. *Anarchism, Marxism, and the Future of the Left: Interviews and Essays, 1993–1998.* Edinburgh: A.K. Press, 1999.

Bookchin, Murray. "Crisis in the Ecology Movement." *Z Magazine,* July–August 1988, 121–123.

Bookchin, Murray. *The Ecology of Freedom: The Emergence and Dissolution of Hierarchy.* Palo Alto, CA: Cheshire Books, 1982.

Bookchin, Murray. *The Murray Bookchin Reader.* Edited by Janet Biehl. London: Cassell, 1997.

Bookchin, Murray. *Our Synthetic Environment.* New York: Knopf, 1962.

Bookchin, Murray. *The Philosophy of Social Ecology: Essays on Dialectical Naturalism.* 2nd ed. Montréal: Black Rose Books, 1995.

Bookchin, Murray. *Re-Enchanting Humanity: A Defense of the Human Spirit against Antihumanism, Misanthropy, Mysticism, and Primitivism.* London: Cassell, 1995.

Bookchin, Murray. *Remaking Society.* Montréal: Black Rose Books, 1989.

Bookchin, Murray. *The Rise of Urbanization and the Decline of Citizenship.* San Francisco: Sierra Club Books, 1987.

Bookchin, Murray, Dave Foreman, and Steve Chase. *Defending the Earth: A Dialogue between Murray Bookchin and Dave Foreman.* Boston: South End Press, 1991.

Bowles, Samuel. *Across the Continent: A Summer's Journey to the Rocky Mountains, the Mormons, and the Pacific States, with Speaker Colfax.* New York: Hurd & Holton, 1865.

Boy Scouts of America. *Eagles Soaring High: Trail Worship for Christians, Muslims and Jews.* Cimarron, NM: Philmont Scout Ranch, 2008.

Bradstreet, Anne. "To my Dear Children." In *The Complete Works of Anne Bradstreet.* Edited by Joseph R. McElrath Jr. and Allan P. Robb. Boston: Twayne, 1981.

Bradstreet, Anne. *The Works of Anne Bradstreet, In Prose and Verse.* Edited by John Harvard Ellis. 1867. Reprint, New York: Smith, 1932.

Brower, David, Ansel Adams, and Robinson Jeffers. *Not Man Apart: Lines from Robinson Jeffers.* San Francisco: Sierra Club, 1965.

Brower, David, and Susan R. Schrepfer. *David R. Brower, Environmental Activist, Publicist and Prophet.* Berkeley: Regional Oral History Office, the Bancroft Library, University of California, 1980.

Brower, David Ross. *For Earth's Sake: The Life and Times of David Brower.* Salt Lake City, UT: Peregrine Smith Books, 1990.

Brower, David Ross, and Steve Chapple. *Let the Mountains Talk, Let the Rivers Run: A Call to Those Who Would Save the Earth.* San Francisco: HarperCollins West, 1995.

Bryant, William Cullen. *A Funeral Oration, Occasioned by the Death of Thomas Cole, Delivered Before the National Academy of Design, New-York, May 4, 1848.* New York: Appleton, 1848.

Buel, Jesse. *The Cultivator* 4, December 1837, 159–162.

Burroughs, John. *Birds and Poets.* New York: Houghton Mifflin, 1877.

Burroughs, John. "Henry D. Thoreau." *Century Magazine,* July 1882.

Burroughs, John. "Henry David Thoreau." *Chautauquan,* July 1889.

Burroughs, John. "John Muir's 'Yosemite.'" *Literary Digest,* June 1, 1912.

Burroughs, John. "Real and Sham Natural History." *Atlantic Monthly,* March 1903.

Burroughs, John. "Thoreau's Wildness." *Critic,* March 26, 1881.

Burroughs, John. *Wake-Robin.* New York: Hurd and Houghton, 1871.

Burroughs, John, and Julian Burroughs. *My Boyhood.* Garden City, NY: Doubleday, Page, 1922.

Burroughs, John, and Clifton Johnson. *John Burroughs Talks: His Reminiscences and Comments.* Boston: Houghton Mifflin, 1922.

Bushnell, Horace. *An Oration Delivered Before the Society of Phi Beta Kappa, at Cambridge, August 24, 1848.* Cambridge, MA: Nichols, 1848.

Calvin, John. *Commentaries on the First Book of Moses Called Genesis.* Vol. 1. Translated by John King. Edinburgh: Calvin Translation Society, 1847.

Calvin, John. *Institutes of the Christian Religion.* 2 vols. Translated by Ford Lewis Battles. Edited by John T. McNeill. London: S.C.M. Press, 1960.

Calvin, John. "Preface to Olivétan's New Testament." In *Calvin: Commentaries.* Translated by Joseph Haroutunian. Philadelphia: Westminster Press, 1958.

[Campbell, Thomas.] *Declaration and Address of the Christian Association of Washington.* Washington, PA: Brown & Sample, 1809.

Carr, Archie. *Handbook of Turtles: The Turtles of the United States, Canada, and Baja California.* Ithaca, NY: Comstock, 1952.

Carr, Archie. *So Excellent a Fishe: A Natural History of Sea Turtles.* Garden City, NY: Natural History Press, 1967.

Carr, Archie. *The Windward Road: Adventures of a Naturalist on Remote Caribbean Shores.* New York: Knopf, 1956.

Carson, Rachel. *The Edge of the Sea.* Boston: Houghton Mifflin, 1955.

Carson, Rachel. *Lost Woods: The Discovered Writing of Rachel Carson.* Edited by Linda J. Lear. Boston: Beacon Press, 1998.

Carson, Rachel. *Silent Spring.* Boston: Houghton Mifflin, 1962.

Cather, Willa. *The World and the Parish: Willa Cather's Articles and Reviews, 1893–1902.* Edited by William Martin Curtin. Lincoln: University of Nebraska Press, 1970.

Census for 1820. Washington, DC: Gales & Seaton, 1820.

Christ, Carol P. "Why Women Need the Goddess." *Heresies: The Great Goddess Issue* (Spring 1978): 8–13.

Clap, Roger. *Memoirs of Capt. Roger Clap.* 1731. Reprint, Boston: Clap, 1844.

Cobb, John B., Jr., and Herman E. Daly. *For the Common Good: Redirecting the Economy Toward Community, the Environment, and a Sustainable Future.* Boston: Beacon Press, 1989.

Colby, William E. *Reminiscences, an Interview Conducted by Corinne L. Gilb.* Regional Cultural History Project. Bancroft Library, University of California General Library, Berkeley, Berkeley, CA, 1954.

Cole, Thomas. "Essay on American Scenery." *American Monthly Magazine,* January 1836, 1–12.

Commoner, Barry. *Making Peace with the Planet.* New York: Pantheon, 1990.

Commoner, Barry. *The Closing Circle: Nature, Man, and Technology.* New York: Knopf, 1971.

Commoner, Barry. *The Poverty of Power: Energy and the Economic Crisis.* New York: Knopf, 1976.

Daly, Mary. *Gyn/Ecology: The Metaethics of Radical Feminism.* Boston: Beacon Press, 1978.

Denver, John, and Arthur Tobier. *Take Me Home: An Autobiography.* New York: Harmony Books, 1994.

Derham, William. *Physico-Theology, or, a Demonstration of the Being and Attributes of God from this Works of Creation.* 2nd ed. London: Innys, 1714.

Dillard, Annie. *An American Childhood.* New York: Harper & Row, 1987.

Dillard, Annie. *For the Time Being.* New York: Knopf, 1999.

Dillard, Annie. *Holy the Firm.* New York: Harper & Row, 1977.

Dillard, Annie. *Pilgrim at Tinker Creek.* New York: Harper's Magazine Press, 1974.

Douglas, William O. *Farewell to Texas: A Vanishing Wilderness.* New York: McGraw-Hill, 1967.

Douglas, William O. *My Wilderness: East to Katahdin.* Garden City, NY: Doubleday, 1961.

Douglas, William O. *My Wilderness: The Pacific West.* Garden City, NY: Doubleday, 1960.

Douglas, William O. *Nature's Justice: Writings of William O. Douglas.* Edited by James O'Fallon. Corvallis: Oregon State University Press, 2000.

Douglas, William O. *Of Men and Mountains.* New York: Harper, 1950.

Douglas, William O. *The Three Hundred Year War: A Chronicle of Ecological Disaster.* New York: Random House, 1972.

Douglas, William O. *A Wilderness Bill of Rights.* Boston: Little, Brown, 1965.

Douglas, William O., and Harvé Stein. *Muir of the Mountains.* Boston: Houghton Mifflin, 1961.

Downing, A. J. *Rural Essays.* New York: G.P. Putnam, 1853.

Downing, A. J. *A Treatise on the Theory and Practice of Landscape Gardening, Adapted to North America: With a View to the Improvement of Country Residences.* 2nd ed., rev. and enl. New York: Wiley and Putnam, 1844.

Du Bartas, Guillaume Salluste. *The Divine Weeks and Works of Guillaume de Saluste Sieur du Bartas.* Vol. 1. Translated by Joshua Sylvester. Edited by Susan Snyder. Oxford: Clarendon Press, 1979.

Durand, A. B. "Letter II." *Crayon*, January 17, 1855, and "Letter III," *Crayon*, January 31, 1855. In *Kindred Spirits: Asher B. Durand and the American Landscape*. Edited by Linda S. Ferber. London: Giles, 2007.

Dwight, Timothy. *The Conquest of Canaan: A Poem, in Eleven Books*. Hartford, CT: Babcock, 1785.

Dwight, Timothy. *Oration, delivered at New-Haven on the 7th of July, A.D. 1801, before the Society of the Cincinnati, for the State of Connecticut, Assembled to Celebrate the Anniversary of American Independence*. Hartford, CT: Hudson and Goodwin, 1801.

Easterbrook, Gregg. *A Moment on the Earth: The Coming Age of Environmental Optimism*. New York: Viking, 1995.

Eaton, Rev. Horace. "Sermon XXIX: Moral Analogies of Central Park." *National Preacher*, December 1864.

Edwards, Jonathan. *Dissertation I, Concerning the End for which God Created the World*. In *The Works of Jonathan Edwards*. Edited by John E. Smith. Vol. 8, *Ethical Writings*. Edited by Paul Ramsey. New Haven, CT: Yale University Press, 1989.

Edwards, Jonathan. *The Great Christian Doctrine of Original Sin Defended*. In *The Works of Jonathan Edwards*. Edited by John E. Smith. Vol. 3, *Original Sin*. Edited by Clyde A. Holbrook. New Haven, CT: Yale University Press, 1970.

Edwards, Jonathan. "Personal Narrative." In *The Works of Jonathan Edwards*. Edited by Harry S. Stout. Vol. 16, *Letters and Personal Writings*. Edited by George S. Claghorn. New Haven, CT: Yale University Press, 1998.

Edwards, Jonathan. *Practical Sermons, never before published*. Edinburgh: Gray, 1788.

Edwards, Jonathan. "Sinners in the Hands of an Angry God." In *The Works of Jonathan Edwards*, Edited by Harry S. Stout. Vol. 22, *Sermons and Discourses, 1739–1742*. Edited by Harry S. Stout. New Haven, CT: Yale University Press, 2003.

Edwards, Jonathan. *The Works of Jonathan Edwards*. Vol. 7, *The Life of David Brainerd*. Edited by Norman Pettit. New Haven, CT: Yale University Press, 1985.

Egleston, Nathaniel Hillyer. *Villages and Village Life, With Hints for Their Improvement*. New York: Harper, 1878.

Ehrlich, Paul R. *The Population Bomb*. New York: Ballantine Books, 1968.

Ehrlich, Paul R., and Anne H. Ehrlich. *Betrayal of Science and Reason: How Anti-Environmental Rhetoric Threatens Our Future*. Washington, DC: Island Press, 1996.

Ehrlich, Paul R., and Anne H. Ehrlich. *Population Resources Environment: Issues in Human Ecology*. San Francisco: Freeman, 1970.

Ehrlich, Paul R., Anne H. Ehrlich, and Gretchen C. Daily. *The Stork and the Plow: The Equity Answer to the Human Dilemma*. New York: Putnam's, 1995.

Ehrlich, Paul R., Anne H. Ehrlich, and John P. Holdren. *Human Ecology: Problems and Solutions*. San Francisco: Freeman, 1973.

Eliot, Jared. *Essays upon field husbandry in New England, and other papers, 1748–1762*. Edited by Harry J. Carman and Rexford G. Tugwell. New York, Columbia University Press, 1934.

Eliot, Jared. *Give Cesar His Due: Or, The Obligation That Subjects Are Under to Their Civil Rulers. . . .* New London, CT: Green, 1738.

Emerson, Ralph Waldo. *The Collected Works of Ralph Waldo Emerson.* 10 vols. Cambridge, MA: Harvard University Press, 1971–2013.

Emerson, Ralph Waldo. *The Journals and Miscellaneous Notebooks.* Vol. 8, *1841–1843.* Edited by William Henry Gilman. Cambridge, MA: Harvard University Press, 1960.

Estienne, Charles, and Jean Liébault. *L'agriculture, et maison rustique; plus un Bref recueil des chasses . . . et de la fauconnerie.* Lyon: Jaques du Puys, 1583. Bibliothèque nationale de France, http://gallica.bnf.fr/ark:/12148/bpt6k52175n.

Foreman, Dave. *Confessions of an Eco-Warrior.* New York: Harmony Books, 1991.

Foreman, Dave. *Man Swarm and the Killing of Wildlife.* Durango, CO: Raven's Eye, 2011.

Foreman, Dave. *Rewilding North America: A Vision for Conservation in the 21st Century.* Washington, DC: Island Press, 2004.

Foreman, Dave, and Howie Wolke. *The Big Outside: A Descriptive Inventory of the Big Wilderness Areas of the United States.* New York: Harmony Books, 1992.

Fox, Matthew. *The Coming of the Cosmic Christ: The Healing of Mother Earth and the Birth of a Global Renaissance.* San Francisco: Harper & Row, 1988.

Fox, Matthew. *On Becoming a Musical, Mystical Bear: Spirituality American Style.* New York: Harper & Row, 1972.

Fox, Matthew. *Original Blessing: A Primer in Creation Spirituality Presented in Four Paths, Twenty-Six Themes, and Two Questions.* Santa Fe, NM: Bear & Co, 1983.

Fox, Matthew. *A Spirituality Named Compassion and the Healing of the Global Village, Humpty Dumpty and Us.* Minneapolis: Winston Press, 1979.

Fox, Matthew. *Whee! We, Wee All the Way Home: A Guide to a Sensual, Prophetic Spirituality.* 1976. Reprint, Santa Fe, NM: Bear & Co., 1981.

Fox, Stephen. *John Muir and His Legacy: The American Conservation Movement.* Boston: Little Brown, 1981.

Fraser, Joseph B., and Margaret Greer. "The Sea Pines Story." Part I, *Hilton Head Monthly,* April 2005, 37–41; Part II, May 2005, 52–38; Part III, June 2005, 50–56.

Fraser, West. Memo to Mark Mussari, "On Paintings," for *Southwest Art,* December 2010. In "Journal." www.westfraserstudio.com/journal/.

Fritsch, Albert. "A Catholic Approach." In *The Greening of Faith: God, the Environment, and the Good Life.* Edited by John E. Carroll, Paul T. Brockelman, and Mary Westfall. Hanover, NH: University Press of New England, 1997.

Fritsch, Albert. "Appropriate Technology and Healing the Earth." In *Embracing Earth: Catholic Approaches to Ecology.* Edited by Albert J. LaChance and John E. Carroll. Maryknoll, NY: Orbis Books, 1994.

Gallaudet, T. H. *The Youth's Book on Natural Theology Illustrated in Familiar Dialogues, with Numerous Engravings.* Hartford, CT: Cooke, 1832.

Gibbs, Lois. "Lois Gibbs." In *Environmental Activists.* Edited by John F. Mongillo and Bibi Booth. Westport, CT: Greenwood Press, 2001.

Gore, Albert. *Earth in the Balance: Ecology and the Human Spirit.* Boston: Houghton Mifflin, 1992.

Hale, Sir Matthew. *Contemplations Moral and Divine.* 2 vols. London: Godbid, 1676.

Hale, Sir Matthew. *The Great Audit, or, Good Steward Being Some Necessary and Important Considerations to Be Considered of by All Sorts of People.* Hartford, CT: Babcock, 1802.

Hamilton, Alice. *Exploring the Dangerous Trades: The Autobiography of Alice Hamilton, M.D.* Boston: Little, Brown and Company, 1943.

Hartley, Marsden. *Adventures in the Arts: Informal Chapters on Painters, Vaudeville and Poets.* New York: Boni and Liveright, 1921.

Hartley, Marsden. *Somehow a Past: The Autobiography of Marsden Hartley.* Edited by Susan Elizabeth Ryan. Cambridge, MA: MIT Press, 1997.

Hartshorne, Charles. *The Darkness and the Light: A Philosopher Reflects Upon His Fortunate Career and Those Who Made It Possible.* Albany: State University of New York Press, 1990.

Hazard, Caroline. *The Yosemite, And Other Verse.* Boston: Houghton Mifflin, 1917.

Hazard, Ebenezer, letter to Jeremy Belknap, June 27, 1780. *Collections of the Massachusetts Historical Society,* fifth series. Vol. 2 Boston: Massachusetts Historical Society, 1877.

Heely, Joseph. *A Description of Hagley, Envil and the Leasowes. . . .* Birmingham: Swinney, 1775.

Hitchcock, Edward. *Reminiscences of Amherst College, Historical, Scientific, Biographical and Autobiographical.* Northampton, MA: Bridgman & Childs, 1863.

Holbrook, John C. *Recollections of a Nonagenarian: Life in New England, the Middle West, and New York, Including a Mission to Great Britain.* Boston: Pilgrim, 1897.

Home Book of the Picturesque: or American Scenery, Art, and Literature. New York: Putnam, 1852.

Hooker, Thomas. *A Survey of the Summe of Church-Discipline: Wherein the Way of the Churches of New-England is warranted out of the Word, and all Exceptions of weight, which are made against it, answered . . .* London: A. M., 1648.

Hough, Franklin B. "On the Duty of Governments in the Preservation of Forests." *Proceedings of the American Association for the Advancement of Science, Twenty-Second Meeting, Held at Portland, Maine, August, 1873* (Salem, MA: Salem Press, 1874), 1–10.

The Humble Advice of the Assembly of Divines, Now by Authority of Parliament sitting at Westminster, Concerning a Confession of Faith. London: E. Tyler, 1647.

Humboldt, Alexander von. *Cosmos: A Sketch of a Physical Description of the Universe.* Vol. 1. Translated by E. C. Otté. New York: Harper & Brothers, 1850.

Ickes, Harold L. *The Autobiography of a Curmudgeon.* New York: Reynal & Hitchcock, 1943.

Jackson, Wes. *Altars of Unhewn Stone: Science and the Earth.* San Francisco: North Point Press, 1987.

Jackson, Wes. *New Roots for Agriculture.* San Francisco: Friends of the Earth, 1980.

Jacobs, Jane, and Richard Carroll Keeley. "An Interview with Jane Jacobs." In *Ethics in Making a Living: The Jane Jacobs Conference.* Edited by Fred Lawrence. Atlanta: Scholars Press, 1989.

Jeffers, Robinson. *The Collected Poetry of Robinson Jeffers.* Edited by Tim Hunt. Stanford, CA: Stanford University Press, 1988.

Jeffers, Robinson. "Preface to 'Judas': Writer Explains the Inspiration for His Poem Now Set for the Stage." *New York Times,* October 5, 1947, X3.

Jeffers, Robinson, and Mallette Dean. *Themes in My Poems.* San Francisco: Book Club of California, 1956.

Johnson, Robert Underwood. *Remembered Yesterdays.* Boston: Little, Brown, 1923.

Jones, Abner Dumont. *Memoir of Elder Abner Jones.* Boston: Crosby, 1842.

Jordan, David Starr. *The Days of a Man: Being Memories of a Naturalist, Teacher, and Minor Prophet of Democracy.* Vol. 1. Yonkers-on-Hudson, NY: World Book, 1922.

Kandinsky, Wassily. *Concerning the Spiritual in Art.* Translated by Michael Sadleir. New York: Dover Publications, 1977.

Keeler, Charles. "Bernard Maybeck: A Gothic Man in the 20th Century." *Friends Bearing Torches.* Charles Keeler Family Papers, University of California, Berkeley.

Keith, William. "Sketching with Wm. Keith." *The Wasp,* February 9, 1907, 92.

Kemble, Fanny, writing as Frances Anne Butler. *Journal.* Vol. 2. Philadelphia: Carey, Lea & Blanchard, 1835.

King, F. H. *Farmers of Forty Centuries: or, Permanent Agriculture in China, Korea and Japan.* Madison, WI: Mrs. F. H. King, 1911.

King, Thomas Starr. *A Vacation Among the Sierras: Yosemite in 1860.* Edited by John A. Hussey. San Francisco: Book Club of California, 1962.

Klee, Paul. "Creative Credo." In *Manifesto: A Century of Isms.* Edited by Mary Ann Caws. Lincoln: University of Nebraska Press, 2001.

Knox, John. *The Works of John Knox.* Edited by David Laing. Edinburgh: Wordow Society, 1864.

LaChapelle, Dolores. *Sacred Land, Sacred Sex: Rapture of the Deep: Concerning Deep Ecology and Celebrating Life.* Durango, CO: Kivakí Press, 1988.

Lamson, J. *Round Cape Horn: Voyage of the Passenger-Ship James W. Paige, from Maine to California in the Year 1852.* Bangor, ME: O. F. & W. H. Knowles, 1878.

Lane, Franklin K., Anne Wintermute Lane, and Louise Herrick Wall. *The Letters of Franklin K. Lane, Personal and Political.* Boston: Houghton Mifflin, 1922.

LeConte, Joseph. *The Autobiography of Joseph Le Conte.* Edited by William Dallam Armes. New York: Appleton, 1903.

Leopold, Aldo. *A Sand County Almanac and Sketches Here and There.* New York: Oxford University Press, 1949.

Letchworth, Josiah, and P. E. Letchworth. *Letters from Josiah Letchworth, 1880.* Compiled by P. E. Letchworth. Genesee Valley Historical Collection. SUNY Geneseo, 1966.

Lippincott, Sara Jane Clarke, writing as Grace Greenwood. *New Life in New Lands: Notes of Travel.* New York: Ford, 1873.

Longfellow, Henry Wadsworth. "The Fiftieth Birthday of Agassiz, May 28, 1857." *The Courtship of Miles Standish, and Other Poems.* Boston: Ticknor and Fields, 1858.

Ludlow, Fitz Hugh. *The Heart of the Continent: A Record of Travel Across the Plains and in Oregon, with an Examination of the Mormon Principle.* New York: Hurd and Houghton, 1870.

Marin, John. *John Marin.* Edited by Cleve Gray. New York: Holt, Rinehart and Winston, 1970.

Marin, John. *The Selected Writings of John Marin.* Edited by Dorothy Norman. New York: Pellegrini & Cudahy, 1949.

Marsh, George P. *Address Delivered Before the Agricultural Society of Rutland County, Sept. 30, 1847.* Rutland, VT: Herald, 1848.

Marsh, George P. *Man and Nature, or, Physical Geography As Modified by Human Action.* New York: Scribner, 1864.

Marsh, George P., Karl Christoph Vogt, Jules Haime, and Elijah Chapman Kellogg. *Report Made Under Authority of the Legislature of Vermont: On the Artificial Propagation of Fish.* Burlington, VT: Free Press, 1857.

Marshall, Robert. *Alaska Wilderness: Exploring the Central Brooks Range.* 3rd ed. Edited by George Marshall. Berkeley: University of California Press, 2005.

Marshall, Robert. *The People's Forests.* New York: Smith and Haas, 1933.

Martineau, Harriet. *Retrospect of Western Travel.* 2 vols. London: Saunders and Otley, 1838.

Mather, Cotton. *The Christian Philosopher.* London: Matthews, 1721.

Mather, Cotton. *Magnalia Christi Americana.* Vol. 2. Hartford, CT: Andrus, 1953.

Mather, Cotton. *The Religion of the Closet.* 2nd ed. Boston: Green, 1706.

Mather, Cotton. *Winter Meditations: Directions How to Employ the Leisure of the Winter for the Glory of God: accompanied with reflections as well historical as theological, not only upon the circumstances of winter, but also upon the notable works of God, both in creation and Providence.* Boston: Harris, 1693.

Mather, Increase. *An Essay for the Recording of Illustrious Providences.* Boston: Green, 1684.

Mather, Increase. *Practical Truths Tending to Promote the Power of Godliness.* Boston: Green, 1682.

Mather, Stephen T. *Report of the Director of the National Park Service to the Secretary of the Interior for 1926.* Washington, DC: US Government Printing Office, 1926.

McFague, Sallie. *The Body of God: An Ecological Theology.* Minneapolis: Fortress Press, 1993.

McFague, Sallie. *Life Abundant: Rethinking Theology and Economy for a Planet in Peril.* Minneapolis: Fortress Press, 2001.

McFague, Sallie. *Models of God: Theology for an Ecological, Nuclear Age.* Philadelphia: Fortress Press, 1987.

McHarg, Ian L. *A Quest for Life: An Autobiography*. New York: Wiley, 1996.

McPhee, John. "The Patch." *New Yorker*, February 8, 2010.

Merchant, Carolyn. *Earthcare: Women and the Environment*. New York: Routledge, 1996.

Merritt, Jonathan. *Green Like God: Unlocking the Divine Plan for Our Planet*. New York: FaithWords, 2010.

Miller, Joaquin. *Poems*. Vol. 2. San Francisco: Whitaker, 1909.

Minturn, William. *Travels West*. London: Tinsley, 1877.

Mohler, Albert. Website. www.albertmohler.com.

Muir, John. "Art Notes." *Overland Monthly*, May 1875, 482.

Muir, John. "Art Notes." San Francisco *Evening Bulletin*, June 20, 1874, 3.

Muir, John. Correspondence. University of the Pacific Library Holt-Atherton Special Collections, Stockton, California.

Muir, John. "Explorations in the Great Tuolumne Cañon." *Overland Monthly*, August 1873, 139–147.

Muir, John. "God's First Temples: How Shall We Preserve Our Forests?" Sacramento *Daily Record-Union*, February 5, 1876, 8.

Muir, John. *The Mountains of California*. New York: Century, 1894.

Muir, John. *My First Summer in the Sierra*. Boston: Houghton Mifflin, 1911.

Muir, John. *Our National Parks*. Boston: Houghton, Mifflin, 1901.

Muir, John. *The Story of My Boyhood and Youth*. Boston: Houghton Mifflin, 1913.

Muir, John. *Travels in Alaska*. Boston: Houghton Mifflin, 1915.

Muir, John. *The Yosemite*. New York: Century, 1912.

Muir, John, and Jeanne C. Smith Carr. *Kindred & Related Spirits: The Letters of John Muir and Jeanne C. Carr*. Edited by Bonnie Johanna Gisel. Salt Lake City: University of Utah Press, 2001.

Murray, W. H. H. *Adventures in the Wilderness, or, Camp-Life in the Adirondacks*. Boston: Fields, Osgood, 1869.

Nearing, Helen, and Scott Nearing. *Living the Good Life: How to Live Sanely and Simply in a Troubled World*. Reprint. New York: Schocken Books, 1970.

Nearing, Scott. *The Making of a Radical: A Political Autobiography*. New York: Harper & Row, 1972.

Nibley, Hugh W. "Brigham Young on the Environment." In *To the Glory of God: Mormon Essays on Great Issues—Environment—Commitment—Love—Peace—Youth—Man*. Edited by Hugh Nibley. Salt Lake City, UT: Deseret, 1972.

Nordhaus, Ted, and Michael Shellenberger. *Break Through: From the Death of Environmentalism to the Politics of Possibility*. Boston: Houghton Mifflin, 2007.

O'Sullivan, Timothy H. *Framing the West: The Survey Photographs of Timothy H. O'Sullivan*. Edited by Toby Jurovics. Washington, DC: Library of Congress, 2010.

Olmsted, Frederick Law. *The Papers of Frederick Law Olmsted*. 5 vols. Baltimore, MD: Johns Hopkins University Press, 1977–2013.

Olmsted, Frederick Law. *Walks and Talks of an American Farmer in England*. Vol. 1. New York: G. P. Putnam, 1852.

Palissy, Bernard. *The Admirable Discourses of Bernard Palissy.* Translated by Aurèle la Rocque. Urbana: University of Illinois Press, 1957.

Palissy, Bernard. Discours admirables de la nature des eaux et fontaines, tant naturelles qu'artificielles, des métaux, des sels et salines, des pierres, des terres, du feu et des émaux. Paris: Martin le jeune, 1580. Bibliothèque nationale de France, http://gallica.bnf.fr/ark:/12148/bpt6k1050822.

Parker, Theodore. "Of Conscious Religion and the Soul." *Ten Sermons of Religion.* Boston: Crosby, Nichols, 1853.

Pinchot, Gifford. *Breaking New Ground.* New York: Harcourt, Brace, 1947.

Pinchot, Gifford. *The Fight for Conservation.* New York: Doubleday, Page, 1910.

Pinchot, Gifford. "The Problem." In Paul Leroy Vogt, ed. *The Church and Country Life.* New York: Missionary Education Movement of the United States and Canada, 1916.

Pinchot, Gifford, and Harold K. Steen. *The Conservation Diaries of Gifford Pinchot.* Durham, NC: Forest History Society, 2001.

Pollan, Michael. *The Botany of Desire: A Plant's Eye View of the World.* New York: Random House, 2001.

Pollan, Michael. *Cooked: A Natural History of Transformation.* New York: Penguin, 2013.

Pollan, Michael. *Food Rules: An Eater's Manual.* New York: Penguin, 2009.

Pollan, Michael. *In Defense of Food: An Eater's Manifesto.* New York: Penguin, 2008.

Pollan, Michael. *The Omnivore's Dilemma: A Natural History of Four Meals.* New York: Penguin, 2006.

Pollan, Michael. *Second Nature: A Gardener's Education.* New York: Atlantic Monthly, 1991.

Porter, Fairfield. *Material Witness: The Selected Letters of Fairfield Porter.* Edited by Ted Leigh. Ann Arbor: University of Michigan Press, 2005.

Presbyterian Church (U.S.A.). *The Constitution of the Presbyterian Church (U.S.A.).* Vol. 1. *The Book of Confessions.* Louisville, KY: Office of the General Assembly, 1999.

Proctor, Edna Dean. *Poems.* Boston: Houghton Mifflin, 1890.

Quarles, Francis. *Emblemes.* London: G[eorge] M[iller], 1635.

Ray, Dixy Lee, and Louis R. Guzzo. *Environmental Overkill: Whatever Happened to Common Sense?* Washington, DC: Regnery Gateway, 1993.

Ray, Dixy Lee, and Louis R. Guzzo. *Trashing the Planet: How Science Can Help Us Deal with Acid Rain, Depletion of the Ozone, and Nuclear Waste (Among Other Things).* Washington, DC: Regnery Gateway, 1990.

Reilly, William K. "Prospects for Enduring Economies and Cultures." In *Fugitive Faith: Conversations on Spiritual, Environmental, and Community Renewal.* Benjamin Webb, interviewer. Maryknoll, NY: Orbis Books, 1998.

"Resolution on Environmentalism and Evangelicals." Southern Baptist Convention, June 2006, Greensboro, North Carolina. www.sbc.net/resolutions/amResolution.asp?ID=1159.

Reynolds, Sir Joshua. *Discourses*. In *The Works of Sir Joshua Reynolds, Knt.* Vol. 1. London: Cadell and Davies, 1797.

Richmond, John Francis. *New York and Its Institutions, 1609–1871*. New York: Treat, 1872.

Rolston, III, Holmes. "A Philosopher Gone Wild." In *Falling in Love with Wisdom: American Philosophers Talk About Their Calling*. Edited by David D. Karnos and Robert G. Shoemaker. New York: Oxford University Press, 1993.

Roosevelt, Theodore. *An Autobiography*. New York: Macmillan, 1913.

Roosevelt, Theodore. "The New Nationalism." In *The New Nationalism*. New York: Outlook, 1910.

Roosevelt, Theodore. *Outdoor Pastimes of an American Hunter*. 2nd ed. New York: Scribner, 1908.

Roosevelt, Theodore. *Theodore Roosevelt's Confession of Faith before the Progressive National Convention, August 6, 1912*. [New York: Progressive Party, 1912.]

Roselle, Mike. *Tree Spiker: From Earth First! to Lowbagging: My Struggles in Radical Environmental Action*. New York: St. Martin's Press, 2009.

Ruether, Rosemary Radford. "Ecofeminism: The Challenge to Theology." In *Christianity and Ecology: Seeking the Well-Being of Earth and Humans*. Edited by Dieter T. Hessel and Rosemary Radford Ruether. Cambridge, MA: Harvard University Press, 2000.

Ruether, Rosemary Radford. *Gaia & God: An Ecofeminist Theology of Earth Healing*. San Francisco: HarperSanFrancisco, 1992.

Ruether, Rosemary Radford. *New Woman, New Earth: Sexist Ideologies and Human Liberation*. New York: Seabury Press, 1975.

Ruether, Rosemary Radford. *Sexism and God-Talk: Toward a Feminist Theology*. Boston: Beacon Press, 1983.

[Ruskin, John]. *Modern Painters*. Vol. 1. 1st American from the 3rd London ed. New York: J. Wiley, 1848.

Schumacher, E. F. *Small Is Beautiful: Economics As If People Mattered*. New York: Harper & Row, 1973.

Serres, Olivier de. Theatre d'agriculture et mesnage des champs. Paris: J. Métayer, 1600. Bibliothèque nationale de France, http://gallica.bnf.fr/ark:/12148/bpt6k52175n.

Seton, Ernest Thompson. *Animal Tracks and Hunter Signs*. Garden City, NY: Doubleday, 1958.

Seton, Ernest Thompson. *The Gospel of the Red Man: An Indian Bible*. Garden City, NY: Doubleday, Doran, 1936.

Seton, Ernest Thompson. "The King Of Currumpaw: A Wolf Story." *Scribner's Magazine*, November 1894.

Seton, Ernest Thompson. *Lives of Game Animals*. 4 vols. Garden City, NY: Doubleday, Page, 1925–1928.

Seton, Ernest Thompson. *The Natural History of the Ten Commandments.* New York: Scribner, 1907.

Seton, Ernest Thompson. *Wild Animals I Have Known.* New York: Scribner, 1898.

Silliman, Benjamin. "Remarks upon a letter from Daniel Wadsworth." *American Journal of Science and Arts* 18(2) (July 1830): 210.

Simpson, William. *Meeting the Sun: A Journey All Round the World Through Egypt, China, Japan and California.* London: Longmans, Green, Reader, and Dyer, 1874.

Singer, Peter. *Animal Liberation: A New Ethics for Our Treatment of Animals.* New York: New York Review, 1975.

Smith, Joseph, Jr. "A History of the Life of Joseph Smith." In *Personal Writings of Joseph Smith.* Edited by Dean Jessee. Salt Lake City, UT: Deseret, 1984.

Smith, Matthew Hale. *Sunshine and Shadow in New York.* Hartford, CT: Burr, 1869.

Spretnak, Charlene. *Lost Goddesses of Early Greece: A Collection of Pre-Hellenic Mythology.* Berkeley, CA: Moon, 1978.

Stegner, Wallace. *Wolf Willow: A History, a Story, and a Memory of the Last Plains Frontier.* New York: Viking Press, 1962.

Sterling, George. *Yosemite, An Ode.* San Francisco: Robertson, 1916.

Stieglitz, Alfred, and Arthur Garfield Dove. *Dear Stieglitz, Dear Dove.* Edited by Ann Lee Morgan. Newark: University of Delaware Press, 1988.

Stoddard, Charles Warren. *In the Footprints of the Padres.* San Francisco: Robertson, 1902.

Stoddard, Solomon. *Three Sermons Lately Preached at Boston.* Boston: Green, 1717.

Stone, Merlin. *When God Was a Woman.* New York: Dial Press, 1976.

Strand, Paul, Rebecca Busselle, and Trudy Wilner Stack. *Paul Strand, Southwest.* New York: Aperture, 2004.

Strand, Paul, and Calvin Tomkins. *Paul Strand: Sixty Years of Photographs.* Millerton, NY: Aperture, 1976.

Swett, John. *Public Education in California: Its Origin and Development, with Personal Reminiscences of Half a Century.* New York: American, 1911.

Thomson, James. *The Castle of Indolence: An Allegorical Poem written in Imitation of Spenser.* London: Millar, 1748.

Turner, Frederick Jackson. "The Significance of the Frontier in American History." *The Frontier in American History.* New York: Holt, 1920.

Twiggs, Leo. *Messages from Home: The Art of Leo Twiggs.* [Orangeburg, SC]: Claflin University Press, 2011.

Udall, Stewart L. *The Quiet Crisis.* New York: Holt, Rinehart and Winston, 1963.

United States Catholic Conference. *Let the Earth Bless the Lord: God's Creation and Our Responsibility: a Catholic Approach to the Environment.* Washington, DC: United States Catholic Conference, 1996.

United States Catholic Conference. *Peace with God the Creator, Peace with All Creation.* Washington, DC: United States Catholic Conference, 1995.

United States Catholic Conference. *Renewing the Face of the Earth: A Resource for Parishes.* Washington, DC: United States Catholic Conference, 1994.

Wallace, Henry A. "Practical Religion in the World of Tomorrow." In *Christian Bases of World Order*. New York: Abingdon-Cokesbury Press, [1943].

Walpole, Horace. "John Milton." In "On Modern Gardening." *Anecdotes of Painting in England*. Vol. 4. London: Shakspeare Press, 1828.

Washburn, Jean Bruce. *Yo Semite. A Poem*. San Francisco: Roman, 1871.

Watkins, Carleton E. *Carleton Watkins: Photographs from the J. Paul Getty Museum*. Los Angeles: J. Paul Getty Museum, 1997.

Watts, Isaac. *The Improvement of the Mind: or, a Supplement to the Art of Logick*. London: Brackstone, 1741.

Watts, Isaac. *The Psalms of David, imitated in the language of the New Testament*. 12th ed. London: Hett and Brackston, 1740.

Waugh, Frank Albert. *Rural Improvement: The Principles of Civic Art Applied to Rural Conditions, Including Village Improvement and the Betterment of the Open Country*. New York: Orange Judd, 1914.

White, Gilbert. *The Natural History and Antiquities of Selborne, in the County of Southampton*. London: Bensley, 1789.

White, Lynn Townsend, Jr. "The Historical Roots of Our Ecologic Crisis." *Science* 155(3767) (March 10, 1967): 1203–1207.

Whittelsey, Chauncey. *A sermon preach'd at New-Haven on the Sabbath preceeding the Publick Commencement, Sept. 9th, anno Dom, 1744. Wherein is considered the true Notion of a Faithful Improvement of our Talents, and the Wisdom of being Early & in Earnest therein*. New London, CT: Green, 1744.

Wilbur, Ray Lyman. *The Memoirs of Ray Lyman Wilbur: 1875–1949*. Edited by Edgar Eugene Robinson, and Paul Carroll Edwards. Stanford, CA: Stanford University Press, 1960.

Willard, Samuel. *A compleat body of divinity in two hundred and fifty expository lectures on the Assembly's Shorter catechism wherein the doctrines of the Christian religion are unfolded, their truth confirm'd, their excellence display'd, their usefulness improv'd; contrary errors & vice refuted & expos'd, objections answer'd, controversies settled, cases of conscience resolv'd; and a great light thereby reflected on the present age*. Boston: Green and Kneeland, 1726.

Williams, Terry Tempest. *Refuge: An Unnatural History of Family and Place*. New York: Pantheon Books, 1991.

Willis, Nathaniel Parker. *American Scenery; or, Land, Lake, and River: Illustrations of Transatlantic Nature*. Vol. 1. London: Virtue, 1840.

Wilson, Alexander. *The Life and Letters of Alexander Wilson*. Edited by Clark Hunter. Philadelphia: American Philosophical Society, 1983.

Wilson, Edward O. Afterword to *From so Simple a Beginning: The Four Great Books of Charles Darwin* by Charles Darwin. Edited by Edward O. Wilson. New York: Norton, 2006.

Wilson, Edward O. *Consilience: The Unity of Knowledge*. New York: Knopf, 1998.

Wilson, Edward O. *The Creation: An Appeal to Save Life on Earth*. New York: Norton, 2006.

Wilson, Edward O. *The Diversity of Life.* Cambridge, MA: Harvard University Press, 1992.

Wilson, Edward O. *Naturalist.* Washington, DC: Island Press, 1994.

Wilson, Edward O. *Sociobiology: The New Synthesis.* Cambridge, MA: Harvard University Press, 1975.

Wilson, Edward O., Stephen Pope, and Philip Hefner. "E. O. Wilson, Stephen Pope, and Philip Hefner: A Conversation." *Zygon* 36(2) (2001): 250–251.

Woodruff, George W. "Classification of the Public Lands." *Annals of the American Academy of Political and Social Science* 33(3) (May, 1909): 121–126.

Woodruff, George W. "The Disposal of Public Lands." *Proceedings of the Society of American Foresters* 1 (November 1905): 53–61.

Wright, Frank Lloyd. *An Autobiography.* New York: Horizon Press, 1977.

Wright, Frank Lloyd. *Collected Writings.* Vol. 1, *1894–1930.* Edited by Bruce Brooks Pfeiffer. New York: Rizzoli, 1992.

Wright, Frank Lloyd. "The Disappearing City." In *Frank Lloyd Wright Collected Writings.* Edited by Bruce Brooks Pfeiffer. Vol. 3. New York: Rizzoli, 1993.

Wright, Frank Lloyd. "An Extension of the Work in Architecture at Talieson to Include Apprentices in Residence." In *Frank Lloyd Wright Collected Writings.* Edited by Bruce Brooks Pfeiffer. Vol. 4. New York: Rizzoli, 1994.

Wright, Frank Lloyd. *In the Cause of Architecture.* New York: McGraw-Hill, 1975.

Wright, Frank Lloyd. "The New Frontier: Broadacre City." In *Frank Lloyd Wright Collected Writings.* Edited by Bruce Brooks Pfeiffer. Vol. 4. New York: Rizzoli, 1994.

Wright, Frank Lloyd, and Bruce Brooks Pfeiffer. *Treasures of Taliesin: Seventy-Seven Unbuilt Designs.* 2nd ed. San Francisco: Pomegranate, 1999.

Young, Samuel Hall. *Alaska Days with John Muir.* New York: Revell, 1915.

Young, Samuel Hall. *Hall Young of Alaska, "The Mushing Parson": The Autobiography of S. Hall Young.* New York: Revell, 1927.

SECONDARY SOURCES

Abbott, Lyman. "A Review of President Roosevelt's Administration: IV—Its Influence on Patriotism and Public Service." *The Outlook,* February 27, 1909.

Acocella, Joan Ross. *Willa Cather and the Politics of Criticism.* Lincoln: University of Nebraska Press, 2000.

Adams, Gretchen A. *The Specter of Salem: Remembering the Witch Trials in Nineteenth-Century America.* Chicago: University of Chicago Press, 2008.

Adler, Cyrus. *Louis Marshall: A Biographical Sketch.* New York: American Jewish Committee, 1931.

Aitken, Jonathan. "From Winchester to Westminster." *American Spectator* 42 (July/August 2009): 68–69.

Albanese, Catherine L. *A Republic of Mind and Spirit: A Cultural History of American Metaphysical Religion.* New Haven, CT: Yale University Press, 2007.

Alexander, Thomas G. "Mormon Prophets and the Environment: Creation, Sin, the Fall, Redemption, and the Millennium." In *Dreams, Myths, & Reality: Utah and the American West*. Edited by William Thomas Allison and Susan J. Matt. Salt Lake City, UT: Signature, 2008.

Alinder, Mary Street. *Ansel Adams: A Biography*. New York: Holt, 1996.

Allen, David Grayson. *In English Ways: The Movement of Societies and the Transferal of English Local Law and Custom to Massachusetts Bay in the Seventeenth Century*. Chapel Hill: University of North Carolina Press, 1981.

Allen, Max, ed. *Ideas That Matter: The Worlds of Jane Jacobs*. Owen Sound, Ont.: Ginger, 1997.

Almond, Philip C. *Adam and Eve in Seventeenth-Century Thought*. Cambridge: Cambridge University Press, 1999.

American Federation of Arts. *Who's Who in American Art*. 1940. New York: Bowker, 1981.

Amico, Leonard N. *Bernard Palissy: In Search of Earthly Paradise*. Paris: Flammarion, 1996.

Amos Enos House, Nomination Form, National Park Service, National Register Information System no. 75001935. http://pdfhost.focus.nps.gov/docs/NRHP/Text/75001935.pdf.

Anderson, Douglas Firth. "'More Conscience Than Force': U.S. Indian Inspector William Vandever, Grant's Peace Policy, and Protestant Whiteness." *Journal of the Gilded Age and Progressive Era* 9(2) (April 2010): 167–196.

Anderson, H. Allen. *The Chief: Ernest Thompson Seton and the Changing West*. College Station: Texas A&M University Press, 1986.

Anderson, Larry. *Benton MacKaye: Conservationist, Planner, and Creator of the Appalachian Trail*. Baltimore, MD: Johns Hopkins University Press, 2002.

Anderson, Virginia DeJohn. *New England's Generation: The Great Migration and the Formation of Society and Culture in the Seventeenth Century*. Cambridge: Cambridge University Press, 1991.

Angyal, Andrew J. *Wendell Berry*. New York: Twayne, 1995.

Antler, Joyce. *The Journey Home: Jewish Women and the American Century*. New York: Free Press, 1997.

Arce, José Manuel Valenzuela. "Mexican Cultural Identity in a U.S. City: The Roots of Collective Action in Los Angeles." In *Common Border, Uncommon Paths: Race, Culture, and National Identity in U.S.-Mexican Relations*. Edited by Jaime E. Rodríguez O. and Kathryn Vincent Lepp. Wilmington, DE: Scholarly Resources, 1997.

Armitage, Kevin C. *The Nature Study Movement: The Forgotten Popularizer of America's Conservation Ethic*. Lawrence: University Press of Kansas, 2009.

Armstrong, Patrick. *The English Parson-Naturalist: A Companionship Between Science and Religion*. Leominster, UK: Gracewing, 2000.

Armstrong, Walter. *Thomas Gainsborough.* New York: Dutton, 1906.

Arnold, Ron. *At the Eye of the Storm: James Watt and the Environmentalists.* Chicago: Regnery Gateway, 1982.

Aron, Cindy Sondik. *Working at Play: A History of Vacations in the United States.* New York: Oxford University Press, 1999.

Arp, William, III, and Keith Boeckelman. "Religiosity: A Source of Black Environmentalism and Empowerment?" *Journal of Black Studies* 28(2) (1997): 255–267.

Arrington, Leonard J. *Brigham Young: American Moses.* New York: Knopf, 1985.

Arrington, Leonard J. *Great Basin Kingdom: An Economic History of the Latter-Day Saints, 1830–1900.* Cambridge, MA: Harvard University Press, 1958.

Asfour, Amal, and Paul Williamson. *Gainsborough's Vision.* Liverpool: Liverpool University Press, 1999.

Aston, Margaret. "Puritans and Iconoclasm, 1560–1660." In *The Culture of English Puritanism, 1560–1700.* Edited by Christopher Durston and Jacqueline Eales. New York: St. Martin's, 1996.

Astore, William J. *Observing God: Thomas Dick, Evangelicalism, and Popular Science in Victorian Britain and America.* Aldershot, Hants, UK: Ashgate, 2001.

Attfield, Robin. "Christian Attitudes to Nature." *Journal of the History of Ideas* 44(3) (July–Sep. 1983): 369–386.

Averitt, Jack N. "Joseph Bacon Fraser." In *Georgia's Coastal Plain: Family and Personal History.* Vol. 3. New York: Lewis, 1964.

Avery, Kevin J. "Gifford and the Catskills." In *Hudson River School Visions: The Landscapes of Sanford R. Gifford.* Edited by Kevin J. Avery and Franklin Kelly. New York: Metropolitan Museum of Art, 2003.

Avery, Kevin J. "Sanford R. Gifford." In *American Paradise: The World of the Hudson River School.* Edited by John K. Howat. New York: Metropolitan Museum of Art, 1987.

Avery, Kevin J., and Franklin Kelly. "Catalogue." In *Hudson River School Visions: The Landscapes of Sanford R. Gifford.* Edited by Kevin J. Avery and Franklin Kelly. New York: Metropolitan Museum of Art, 2003.

Baatz, Simon. "Philadelphia Patronage: The Institutional Structure of Natural History in the New Republic, 1800–1833." *Journal of the Early Republic* 8(2) (1988): 111–138.

Backes, David. *A Wilderness Within: The Life of Sigurd F. Olson.* Minneapolis: University of Minnesota Press, 1997.

Badillo, David A. *Latinos and the New Immigrant Church.* Baltimore, MD: Johns Hopkins University Press, 2006.

Baer, Hans A., and Merrill Singer. *African-American Religion in the Twentieth Century: Varieties of Protest and Accommodation.* Knoxville: University of Tennessee Press, 1992.

Baggerman, Arianne. "Children's Walks in the Book of Nature: The Reception of J.F. Martinet's *Katechismus der Natuur* around 1800." In *The Book of Nature in Early Modern and Modern History*. Edited by Klaas van Berkel and Arjo Vanderjagt. Leuven: Peeters, 2006.

Bagley, Clarence. *History of Seattle from the Earliest Settlement to the Present Time*. 3 vols. Chicago: Clarke, 1916.

Baigell, Matthew. "Frederic Church's 'Hooker and Company': Some Historic Considerations." *Arts Magazine* 56 (January 1982): 124–125.

Baigell, Matthew, and Allen Kaufman. "Thomas Cole's 'The Oxbow': A Critique of American Civilization." *Arts Magazine* 55 (1981): 136–139.

Baker, Ray Stannard. "John Muir." *The Outlook*, June 6, 1903.

Balmer, Randall Herbert, and John R. Fitzmier. *The Presbyterians*. Westport, CT: Greenwood, 1993.

Balogh, Brian. "Scientific Forestry and the Roots of the Modern American State: Gifford Pinchot's Path to Progressive Reform." *Environmental History* 7(2) (Apr. 2002): 198–225.

Barbour, Fannie Cooley Williams. *Spelman Genealogy: The English Ancestry and American Descendants of Richard Spelman of Middletown, Connecticut, 1700*. New York: Allaben, 1910.

Barnes, Harper. *Standing on a Volcano: The Life and Times of David Rowland Francis*. St. Louis, MO: Francis, 2001.

Barrett, Walter. *The Old Merchants of New York City.* 4th series. New York: Carleton, 1866.

Barriault, Frédéric. "Religion, culture et nature dans le Québec catholique du XIXe siècle, 1850–1900." PhD diss., Université Laval, Quebec City, Quebec, 2006.

Barringer, Felicity. "Paper Sets Off a Debate on Environmentalism's Future." *New York Times*, February 6, 2005.

Barrus, Clara. *The Life and Letters of John Burroughs*. 2 vols. Boston: Houghton Mifflin, 1925.

Barrus, Clara. *Our Friend John Burroughs*. Boston: Houghton Mifflin, 1914.

Bates, J. Leonard. "Fulfilling American Democracy: The Conservation Movement, 1907 to 1921." *Mississippi Valley Historical Review* 44(1) (June 1957): 29–57.

Bedell, Rebecca Bailey. *The Anatomy of Nature: Geology & American Landscape Painting, 1825–1875*. Princeton, NJ: Princeton University Press, 2001.

Bedell, Rebecca. "Thomas Cole and the Fashionable Science." *Huntington Library Quarterly* 59(2/3) (1996): 349–378.

Benedict, Philip. "Calvinism as a Culture? Preliminary Remarks of Calvinism and the Visual Arts." In *Seeing Beyond the Word: Visual Arts and the Calvinist Tradition*. Edited by Paul Corby Finney. Grand Rapids, MI: Eerdmans, 1999.

Benedict, Philip. *Christ's Churches Purely Reformed: A Social History of Calvinism*. New Haven, CT: Yale University Press, 2002.

Benediktsson, Thomas E. *George Sterling*. Boston: Twayne, 1980.

"Benjamin F. Chavis." *Current Biography Yearbook, 1994.* Edited by Judith Graham. New York: Wilson, 1994.

Bennett, Melba Berry, and Lawrence Clark Powell. *The Stone Mason of Tor House: The Life and Work of Robinson Jeffers.* Los Angeles: Ritchie, 1966.

Benstein, Jeremy. "'One, walking and studying. . .': Nature vs. Torah." *Judaism* 44 (Spring 1995): 146–168.

Bercovitch, Sacvan. *The Puritan Origins of the American Self.* New Haven, CT: Yale University Press, 1975.

Bergen, Tunis G., ed. *Genealogies of the State of New York: A Record of the Achievements of Her People in the Making of a Commonwealth and the Founding of a Nation.* New York: Lewis, 1915.

Beza, Theodore. *The Life of John Calvin.* Translated by Henry Beveridge. Philadelphia: Westminster Press, 1909.

Bidwell, Percy W. "The Agricultural Revolution in New England." *American Historical Review* 26 (July 1921): 683–702.

Biéler, André. *Calvin's Economic and Social Thought.* Edited by Edward Dommen. Translated by James Greig. Geneva: World Alliance of Reformed Churches, World Council of Churches, 2006.

Bjelajac, David. "Thomas Cole's Oxbow and the American Zion Divided." *American Art* 20(1) (2006): 60–83.

Blackwell, Richard J. "Sociobiology: The New Religion." Institute for Theological Encounter with Science and Technology. 1997. http://itestfaithscience.org/Articles/Articles_Pdfs/BLACK001.pdf.

Blassingame, John W. *The Slave Community: Plantation Life in the Antebellum South.* New York: Oxford University Press, 1972.

Blum, Elizabeth D. *Love Canal Revisited: Race, Class, and Gender in Environmental Activism.* Lawrence: University Press of Kansas, 2008.

Bohlke, L. Brent. *Willa Cather in Person: Interviews, Speeches, and Letters.* Lincoln: University of Nebraska Press, 1986.

Born, Wolfgang. *American Landscape Painting: An Interpretation.* New Haven, CT: Yale University Press, 1948.

Bosley, Edward R. *First Church of Christ, Scientist, Berkeley: Bernard Maybeck.* London: Phaidon, 1994.

Bosley, Edward R. *Greene & Greene.* London: Phaidon, 2000.

Boulaine, Jean. "Innovations agronomiques d'Olivier de Serres." *Bulletin de l'Association d'étude sur l'humanisme, la réforme et la renaissance* 50 (June 2000): 11–19.

Bouwsma, William. *John Calvin: A Sixteenth-Century Portrait.* New York: Oxford University Press, 1988.

Boyd, David. *A History: Greeley and the Union Colony of Colorado.* Greeley, CO: Greeley Tribune Press, 1890.

Brandes, Joseph, and Martin Douglas. *Immigrants to Freedom: Jewish Communities in Rural New Jersey Since 1882.* Philadelphia: University of Pennsylvania Press, 1971.

Branham, Robert J., and Stephen J. Hartnett. *Sweet Freedom's Song: "My Country 'Tis of Thee" and Democracy in America*. Oxford: Oxford University Press, 2002.

Braunrot, Bruno. *L'Imagination Poétique Chez Du Bartas: Éléments de Sensibilité Baroque dans la Création Du Monde*. Chapel Hill, NC: UNC Dept. of Romance Languages, 1973.

Breen, Louise A. *Transgressing the Bounds: Subversive Enterprises among the Puritan Elite in Massachusetts, 1630–1692*. New York: Oxford University Press, 2001.

Breen, T. H. *Puritans and Adventurers: Change and Persistence in Early America*. New York: Oxford University Press, 1980.

Breen, T. H. *Tobacco Culture: The Mentality of the Great Tidewater Planters on the Eve of Revolution*. Princeton, NJ: Princeton University Press, 1985.

Brewster, Edwin Tenney. *Life and Letters of Josiah Dwight Whitney*. Boston: Houghton Mifflin, 1909.

Brink, Wellington. *Big Hugh: The Father of Soil Conservation*. New York: Macmillan, 1951.

Brinkley, Douglas. *The Wilderness Warrior: Theodore Roosevelt and the Crusade for America*. New York: HarperCollins, 2009.

Broadie, Alexander, ed. *The Cambridge Companion to the Scottish Enlightenment*. Cambridge: Cambridge University Press, 2003.

Brodeur, David D. "Evolution of the New England Town Common: 1630–1966." *Professional Geographer* 19 (November 1967): 313–318.

Brodsky, Alyn. *Grover Cleveland: A Study in Character*. New York: St. Martin's, 2000.

Brooke, John L. *The Refiner's Fire: The Making of Mormon Cosmology, 1644–1844*. Cambridge: Cambridge University Press, 1994.

Brower, Kenneth. *The Wildness Within: Remembering David Brower*. Berkeley, CA: Heyday, 2012.

Brown, Chandos Michael. *Benjamin Silliman: A Life in the Young Republic*. Princeton, NJ: Princeton University Press, 1989.

Brown, Elsa Barkley. "Negotiating and Transforming the Public Sphere: African American Political Life in the Transition from Slavery to Freedom." In *Time Longer Than Rope: A Century of African American Activism, 1850–1950*. Edited by Charles M. Payne and Adam Green. New York: New York University Press, 2003.

Brown, Stewart J., and Michael Fry. *Scotland in the Age of the Disruption*. Edinburgh: Edinburgh University Press, 1993.

Bruce, Dickson D. *And They All Sang Hallelujah: Plain-Folk Camp-Meeting Religion, 1800–1845*. Knoxville: University of Tennessee Press, 1974.

Bruyn, Josua. "Toward a Scriptural Reading of Seventeenth-Century Dutch Landscape Painting." In *Masters of Seventeenth-Century Dutch Landscape Painting*. Edited by Peter C. Sutton. Boston: Museum of Fine Arts, 1987.

Bryson, J. Scott. "Partnership, Narrative, and Environmental Justice: An Interview with Carolyn Merchant." *Interdisciplinary Literary Studies: A Journal of Criticism and Theory* 3(1) (Fall 2001): 124–125.

Buckler, Helen. *Wo-He-Lo: The Story of Camp Fire Girls, 1910–1960*. New York: Holt, Rinehart and Winston, 1961.

Buggeln, Gretchen Townsend. "Elegance and Sensibility in the Calvinist Tradition: The First Congregational Church of Hartford, Connecticut." In *Seeing Beyond the Word: Visual Arts and the Calvinist Tradition*. Edited by Paul Corby Finney. Grand Rapids, MI: Eerdmans, 1999.

Bullard, Robert D. *Dumping in Dixie: Race, Class, and Environmental Quality*. Boulder, CO: Westview Press, 2000.

Bulletin of Yale University, First Series, No. 5, July 1905, *Obituary Record of Graduates, 1904–1905* (New Haven, CT: Yale University, 1905).

Burgess, Dorothy Whittemore Bates. *Dream and Deed: The Story of Katharine Lee Bates*. Norman: University of Oklahoma Press, 1952.

Bush, Gregory. "Politicized Memories in the Struggle for Miami's Virginia Key Beach." In *"To Love the Wind and the Rain": African Americans and Environmental History*. Edited by Dianne D. Glave and Mark Stoll. Pittsburgh, PA: University of Pittsburgh Press, 2006.

Bushman, Richard L. *From Puritan to Yankee: Character and the Social Order in Connecticut, 1690–1765*. Cambridge, MA: Harvard University Press, 1967.

Bushman, Richard L. *Joseph Smith: Rough Stone Rolling*. New York: Knopf, 2005.

Butler, Jon. *Awash in a Sea of Faith: Christianizing the American People*. Cambridge, MA: Harvard University Press, 1990.

Cadbury, Warder H. Introduction to William H. H. Murray. *Adventures in the Wilderness*. Edited by William K. Verner. Syracuse, NY: Syracuse University Press, 1970.

Cahalan, James M. *Edward Abbey: A Life*. Tucson: University of Arizona Press, 2001.

Callicott, J. Baird, ed. *Companion to a Sand County Almanac: Interpretive and Critical Essays*. Madison: University of Wisconsin Press, 1987.

Callicott, J. Baird, and Michael P. Nelson, eds. *The Great New Wilderness Debate: An Expansive Collection of Writings Defining Wilderness from John Muir to Gary Snyder*. Athens: University of Georgia Press, 1998.

Campbell, Dudley M. *A History of Oneonta from Its Earliest Settlement to the Present Time*. Oneonta, NY: Fairchild, 1906.

Cantor, Geoffrey. "Quakers in the Royal Society, 1660–1750." *Notes and Records of the Royal Society of London* 51(2) (1997): 175–193.

Capper, Charles, and Conrad Edick Wright, eds. *Transient and Permanent: The Transcendentalist Movement and Its Contexts*. Boston: Massachusetts Historical Society, 1999.

Cardwell, Kenneth H. *Bernard Maybeck: Artisan, Architect, Artist*. Santa Barbara, CA: Peregrine Smith, 1977.

Carlson, Allan C. *The New Agrarian Mind: The Movement Toward Decentralist Thought in Twentieth-Century America*. New Brunswick, NJ: Transaction, 2000.

Carlson, Reynold E. "Organized Camping." *Annals of the American Academy of Political and Social Science* 313 (Sep. 1957): 83–86.

Carroll, Charles F. *The Timber Economy of Puritan New England.* Providence, RI: Brown University Press, 1973.

Carson, Clayborne. "Martin Luther King, Jr., and the African-American Social Gospel." In *African-American Christianity: Essays in History.* Edited by Paul E. Johnson, Berkeley: University of California Press, 1994.

Carter, Charles S. *History of the Class of '70: Department of Literature and Science and the Arts, University of Michigan.* Milwaukee, WI: Burdick & Allen, 1903.

Carter, Paul A. *The Decline and Revival of the Social Gospel: Social and Political Liberalism in American Protestant Churches, 1920–1940.* Hamden, CT: Archon, 1971.

Carter, Paul A. *The Spiritual Crisis of the Gilded Age.* DeKalb: Northern Illinois University Press, 1971.

Caruthers, J. Wade. "Who Was Octavius Brooks Frothingham?" *New England Quarterly* 43(4) (1970): 631–637.

Casarella, Peter J., and Raúl Gómez. *El Cuerpo De Cristo: The Hispanic Presence in the U.S. Catholic Church.* New York: Crossroad, 1998.

Castro, Jan Garden. *The Art & Life of Georgia O'Keeffe.* New York: Crown, 1985.

Cauthen, Kenneth. *The Impact of American Religious Liberalism.* 2nd ed. Washington, DC: University Press of America, 1983.

Cayton, Mary Kupiec. "The Making of an American Prophet: Emerson, His Audiences, and the Rise of the Culture Industry in Nineteenth-Century America." *American Historical Review* 92 (June 1987): 597–620.

Ceard, Jean. "Les talents de Bernard Palissy." In *L'Intelligence du passé: les faits, l'écriture et le sens: mélanges offerts à Jean Lafond.* Edited by Pierre Aquilon, François Weil, and Jean Lafond. Tours: Université de Tours, 1988.

Checker, Melissa. *Polluted Promises: Environmental Racism and the Search for Justice in a Southern Town.* New York: New York University Press, 2005.

Cikovsky, Nicolai, Jr. "'The Ravages of the Axe': The Meaning of the Tree Stump in Nineteenth-Century American Art." *Art Bulletin* 61(4) (Dec. 1979): 611–626.

Cikovsky, Nicolai, Jr., and Alan Wallach. "Thomas Cole's 'River in the Catskills' as Antipastoral." *Art Bulletin* 84 (2) (June 2002): 334–350.

Cittadino, Eugene. "A 'Marvelous Cosmopolitan Preserve': The Dunes, Chicago, and the Dynamic Ecology of Henry Cowles." *Perspectives on Science* 1(3) (1993): 520–559.

Clarke, Samuel, and Richard Baxter. "The Life and Death of Dr. Edmund Staunton." *The Lives of Sundry Eminent Persons in This Later Age.* London: T. Simmons, 1683.

Clements, Emily. "Daws Island: Rich in History, Rich in Art." *South Carolina Wildlife,* January–February 2002, 6–15.

Cochrane, Arthur C., ed. *Reformed Confessions of the 16th Century.* Philadelphia: Westminster Press, 1966.

Cohen, Michael P. *The History of the Sierra Club, 1892–1970.* San Francisco: Sierra Club Books, 1988.

Cohen, Michael. "The Bob: Confessions of a Fast-Talking Urban Wilderness Advocate." In *Wilderness Tapestry: An Eclectic Approach to Preservation.* Edited by Samuel I. Zeveloff, L. Mikel Vause, and William H. McVaugh. Reno: University of Nevada Press, 1992.

Cohen, Naomi Wiener. *Encounter with Emancipation: The German Jews in the United States, 1830–1914.* Philadelphia: Jewish Publication Society, 1984.

Cohn, Sherrye. *Arthur Dove: Nature As Symbol.* Ann Arbor: UMI Research Press, 1985.

Colby, William E. Introduction to *Studies in the Sierra* by John Muir. San Francisco: Sierra Club, 1950.

Coleman, Kate. *The Secret Wars of Judi Bari: A Car Bomb, the Fight for the Redwoods, and the End of Earth First!* San Francisco: Encounter Books, 2005.

Cooey, Paula M. *Jonathan Edwards on Nature and Destiny: A Systematic Analysis.* Lewiston, NY: Mellen, 1985.

Cornelius. *Keith, Old Master of California.* New York: Putnam, 1942.

Corrigan, John. *The Prism of Piety: Catholick Congregational Clergy at the Beginning of the Enlightenment.* New York: Oxford University Press, 1991.

Cotham, Steve. *The Great Smoky Mountains National Park.* Charleston, SC: Arcadia, 2006.

Cottret, Bernard. *Calvin: A Biography.* Translated by M. Wallace McDonald. Grand Rapids, MI: Eerdmans, 2000.

Courtney, Steve. *Joseph Hopkins Twichell: The Life and Times of Mark Twain's Closest Friend.* Athens: University of Georgia Press, 2008.

Cowan, Ian Borthwick. *The Scottish Reformation: Church and Society in Sixteenth Century Scotland.* New York: St. Martin's, 1982.

Cowdrey, Albert E. *This Land, This South: An Environmental History.* Lexington: University Press of Kentucky, 1983.

Cowell, Pattie, and Ann Stanford, eds. *Critical Essays on Anne Bradstreet.* Boston: Hall, 1983.

Cox, F. Brett. " 'What Need, Then, for Poetry?': The Genteel Tradition and the Continuity of American Literature." *New England Quarterly* 67 (June 1994): 212–233.

Coyle, Daniel. "The High Cost of Being David Brower." *Outside,* December 1995, 60–66.

Creel, Margaret Washington. *A Peculiar People: Slave Religion and Community-Culture Among the Gullahs.* New York: New York University Press, 1988.

Crepeau, Richard C. *Melbourne Village: The First Twenty-Five Years, 1946–1971.* Orlando: University of Central Florida Press, 1988.

Croker, Robert A. *Stephen Forbes and the Rise of American Ecology.* Washington, DC: Smithsonian Institution Press, 2001.

Cronon, William. *Changes in the Land: Indians, Colonists, and the Ecology of New England.* New York: Hill and Wang, 1983.

Cross, Coy F. *Justin Smith Morrill: Father of the Land-Grant Colleges.* East Lansing: Michigan State University Press, 1999.

Crunden, Robert M. *Body & Soul: The Making of American Modernism*. New York: Basic Books, 2000.

Cumbler, John T. *Reasonable Use: The People, the Environment, and the State, New England, 1790–1930*. Oxford: Oxford University Press, 2001.

Dalton, Anne Marie. *A Theology for the Earth: The Contributions of Thomas Berry and Bernard Lonergan*. Ottawa: University of Ottawa Press, 1999.

Daly, Robert. *God's Altar: The World and the Flesh in Puritan Poetry*. Berkeley: University of California Press, 1978.

Danbom, David B. "Romantic Agrarianism in Twentieth-Century America." *Agricultural History* 65(4) (Autumn 1991): 1–12.

Daniel, Clay. "Milton's Neo-Platonic Angel?" *SEL Studies in English Literature 1500–1900* 44(1) (2004): 173–188.

Danielson, Michael N., and Patricia R. F. Danielson. *Profits and Politics in Paradise: The Development of Hilton Head Island*. Columbia: University of South Carolina Press, 1995.

Dantec, Denise le, and Jean-Pierre le Dantec. *Reading the French Garden: Story and History*. Translated by Jessica Levine. Cambridge, MA: MIT Press, 1990.

Davidson, Gabriel. *Our Jewish Farmers and the Story of the Jewish Agricultural Society*. New York: Fischer, 1943.

Davidson, James D. *The Search for Common Ground: What Unites and Divides Catholic Americans*. Huntington, IN: Our Sunday Visitor, 1997.

Davis, David Brion. "The New England Origins of Mormonism." In *Mormonism and American Culture*. Edited by James B. Allen and Marvin S. Hill. New York: Harper & Row, 1972.

Davis, Frederick Rowe. *The Man Who Saved Sea Turtles: Archie Carr and the Origins of Conservation Biology*. Oxford: Oxford University Press, 2007.

Davis, Horace. "Memorial of William Ashburner." *Overland Monthly*, August 1887.

Davis, Valentine D. *Some Account of the Ancient Chapel of Toxteth Park, Liverpool, from the Year 1618 to 1883, and of its Ministers, Especially of Richard Mather, the First Minister*. Liverpool: Young, 1884.

Debus, Allen G. "Palissy, Plat, and English Agricultural Chemistry in the 16th and 17th Centuries." *Archives internationals d'histoire des sciences* 21(82–83) (1968): 67–88.

DeBuys, William Eno. *Enchantment and Exploitation: The Life and Hard Times of a New Mexico Mountain Range*. Albuquerque: University of New Mexico Press, 1985.

DeBuys, William Eno, and Alex Harris. *River of Traps: A Village Life*. Albuquerque: University of New Mexico Press, 1990.

Dehler, Gregory John. "An American Crusader: William Temple Hornaday and Wildlife Protection in America, 1840–1940." PhD diss., Lehigh University, 2001.

De Jongh, E. "The Iconological Approach to Seventeenth-Century Dutch Painting." In *The Golden Age of Dutch Painting in Historical Perspective*. Edited by Frans Grijzenhout and Henk van Veen. Cambridge: Cambridge University Press, 1999.

De Jongh, E. *Question of Meaning: Theme and Motif in Dutch Seventeenth-Century Painting*. Translated by Michael Hoyle. Leiden: Primavera Pers, 2000.

De La Torre, Miguel A., and Gastón Espinosa. *Rethinking Latino(a) Religion and Identity*. Cleveland, OH: Pilgrim Press, 2006.

De Leon, David. *Leaders from the 1960s: A Biographical Sourcebook of American Activism*. Westport, CT: Greenwood Press, 1994.

Delumeau, Jean. *History of Paradise: The Garden of Eden in Myth and Tradition*. Translated by Matthew O'Connell. New York: Continuum, 1995.

Demars, Stanford E. *The Tourist in Yosemite, 1855–1985*. Salt Lake City: University of Utah Press, 1991.

Deutsch, Babette. "Brains and Lyrics." *New Republic* 43 (27 May 1925): 23–24. In *Critical Essays on Robinson Jeffers*. Edited by James Karman (Boston: Hall, 1990), 45.

Díaz-Stevens, Ana María, and Antonio M. Stevens Arroyo. *Recognizing the Latino Resurgence in U.S. Religion: The Emmaus Paradigm*. Boulder, CO: Westview Press, 1997.

Di Chiro, Giovanna. "Steps to an Ecology of Justice: Women's Environmental Networks Across The Santa Cruz River Watershed." In *Seeing Nature Through Gender*. Edited by Virginia Scharff. Lawrence: University Press of Kansas, 2003.

Didier, Eugene L. "The Social Athens of America." *Harper's New Monthly Magazine* 65, June 1882, 25–28.

Diener, Pablo. "Humboldt und die Kunst." In *Alexander von Humboldt: Netzwerke des Wissens*. Edited by Frank Holl. Ostfildern, Ger.: Hatje Cantz, 1999.

Dillenberger, John. *Images and Relics: Theological Perceptions and Visual Images in Sixteenth-Century Europe*. New York: Oxford University Press, 1999.

Dilsaver, Lary M., and William C. Tweed. *Challenge of the Big Trees: A Resource History of Sequoia and Kings Canyon National Parks*. Three Rivers, CA: Sequoia Natural History Association, 1990.

Djupe, Paul A., and Patrick Kieran Hunt. "Beyond the Lynn White Thesis: Congregational Effects on Environmental Concern." *Journal for the Scientific Study of Religion* 48 (December 2009): 670–686.

"Dr. Frank A. Waugh, State College Faculty Member 40 Years, Dies." Unidentified newspaper clipping, March 24, 1943. Special Collections and University Archives. University of Massachusetts Amherst.

Dolan, Jay P., and Allan Figueroa Deck. *Hispanic Catholic Culture in the U.S.: Issues and Concerns*. Notre Dame, IN: University of Notre Dame Press, 1994.

Dolan, Jay P., and Gilberto Miguel Hinojosa. *Mexican Americans and the Catholic Church, 1900–1965*. Notre Dame, IN: University of Notre Dame Press, 1994.

Donahue, Brian. *The Great Meadow: Farmers and the Land in Colonial Concord*. New Haven, CT: Yale University Press, 2004.

Donovan, Timothy Paul, Willard B. Gatewood, and Jeannie M. Whayne, eds. *The Governors of Arkansas: Essays in Political Biography*. Fayetteville: University of Arkansas Press, 1995.

Dorr, Donal. *The Social Justice Agenda: Justice, Ecology, Power, and the Church.* Maryknoll, NY: Orbis Books, 1991.

Dorrien, Gary J. *The Making of American Liberal Theology.* Vol 3, *Crisis, Irony, and Postmodernity 1950–2005.* Louisville, KY: Westminster John Knox Press, 2006.

Drohojowska-Philp, Hunter, and Georgia O'Keeffe. *Full Bloom: The Art and Life of Georgia O'Keeffe.* New York: Norton, 2004.

Dunlap, Thomas R. *Faith in Nature: Environmentalism As Religious Quest.* Seattle: University of Washington Press, 2004.

Duport, Danièle. *Le jardin et la nature: Ordre et variété dans la littérature de la Renaissance.* Geneva: Droz, 2002.

Duport, Danièle. "La 'science' d'Olivier de Serres et la connaissance du 'naturel.'" *Bulletin de l'Association d'étude sur l'humanisme, la réforme et la renaissance* 50 (June 2000): 185–95.

Dyrness, William A. *Reformed Theology and Visual Culture: The Protestant Imagination from Calvin to Edwards.* Cambridge: Cambridge University Press, 2004.

Earth First! Newsletter, June 21, 1983.

"Editorial Briefs." *The Protestant Magazine* 5(5) (May 1913): 237.

"Editors' Table," *The Knickerbocker; or New York Monthly Magazine,* July 1836.

"Edward August Bowers, B.A. 1879." *Bulletin of Yale University,* Twenty-first Series, No. 22, August 1, 1925, *Obituary Record of Graduates of Yale College, 1924–1925* (New Haven, CT: Yale University, 1925), 1343–1345.

Edwards, Karen L. *Milton and the Natural World: Science and Poetry in "Paradise Lost."* Cambridge: Cambridge University Press, 1999.

Egan, Michael. *Barry Commoner and the Science of Survival: The Remaking of American Environmentalism.* Cambridge, MA: MIT Press, 2007.

Eighmy, John Lee. *Churches in Cultural Captivity: A History of the Social Attitudes of Southern Baptists.* Knoxville: University of Tennessee Press, 1972.

Einhorn, Robin L. *American Taxation, American Slavery.* Chicago: University of Chicago Press, 2006.

Eire, Carlos M. N. *War Against the Idols: The Reformation of Worship from Erasmus to Calvin.* Cambridge: Cambridge University Press, 1986.

Eisenberg, Ellen. *Jewish Agricultural Colonies in New Jersey, 1882–1920.* Syracuse, NY: Syracuse University Press, 1995.

Ekirch, Arthur A., Jr. "Franklin B. Hough: First Citizen of the Adirondacks." *Environmental Review* 7(3) (Autumn 1983): 270–274.

Eldredge, Charles C. *Georgia O'Keeffe: American and Modern.* New Haven, CT: Yale University Press, 1993.

Eliot, Charles William. *Charles Eliot, Landscape Architect, a Lover of Nature and of His Kind, Who Trained Himself for a New Profession, Practised It Happily and Through It Wrought Much Good.* Boston: Houghton Mifflin, 1903.

Eller, Cynthia. *Living in the Lap of the Goddess: The Feminist Spirituality Movement in America.* New York: Crossroad, 1993.

Ellul, Jacques. *The Technological Society*. Translated by John Wilkinson. New York: Knopf, 1964.

Everson, William. "Introduction." In *Cawdor: A Long Poem, and Medea: After Euripides*. By Robinson Jeffers. New York: New Directions, 1970.

Ewan, Joseph, Nesta Ewan, Victoria C. Hollowell, Eileen P. Duggan, and Marshall R. Crosby. *Benjamin Smith Barton: Naturalist and Physician in Jeffersonian America*. St. Louis: Missouri Botanical Garden Press, 2007.

Fábos, J. G. "Greenway Planning in the United States: Its Origins and Recent Case Studies." *Landscape and Urban Planning* 68(2–3) (May 30, 2004): 321–342.

Fairbank, Maslin, Maullin & Associates, and California League of Conservation Voters. *Environmental Attitudes Among California Voters: With a Special Analysis of Environmental Attitudes Among Latino Voters and Voters of Color: Report of Survey Results*. Santa Monica, CA: Fairbank, Maslin, Maullin & Associates, 2001.

Ferber, Linda S., and Nancy K. Anderson. *Albert Bierstadt: Art & Enterprise*. New York: Brooklyn Museum, 1991.

Ferleger, Louis. "Arming American Agriculture for the Twentieth Century: How the USDA's Top Managers Promoted Agricultural Development." *Agricultural History* 74(2) (Spring 2000): 211–226.

Fine, Ruth E., Elizabeth Glassman, Juan Hamilton, Sarah L. Burt, and Georgia O'Keeffe. *The Book Room: Georgia O'Keeffe's Library in Abiquiu*. New York: Grolier Club, 1997.

Fink, Augusta. *I-Mary: A Biography of Mary Austin*. Tucson: University of Arizona Press, 1983.

First Presbyterian Church, Baltimore, Md.: 1761–1895. Baltimore, MD: Stanley Stirling, 1895.

Fischer, David Hackett. *Albion's Seed: Four British Folkways in America*. New York: Oxford University Press, 1989.

Fisher, Colin. "African Americans, Outdoor Recreation, and the 1919 Chicago Race Riot." In *"To Love the Wind and the Rain": African Americans and Environmental History*. Edited by Dianne D. Glave and Mark Stoll. Pittsburgh, PA: University of Pittsburgh Press, 2006.

Fisher, George P. *Life of Benjamin Silliman, M.D., LL.D.* 2 vols. New York: Scribner, 1866.

Fishman, Charles. "A Farming Fairy Tale." *Fast Company*, May 2006. www.fastcompany.com/magazine/105/food-organic.html.

Fisk, William L. *The Scottish High Church Tradition in America: An Essay in Scotch-Irish Ethnoreligious History*. Lanham, MD: University Press of America, 1995.

Fitzmier, John R. *New England's Moral Legislator: Timothy Dwight, 1752–1817*. Bloomington: Indiana University Press, 1998.

Flake, Kathleen. *The Politics of American Religious Identity: The Seating of Senator Reed Smoot, Mormon Apostle*. Chapel Hill: University of North Carolina Press, 2004.

Flippen, J. Brooks. *Nixon and the Environment*. Albuquerque: University of New Mexico Press, 2000.

"Forestry Legislation." *Proceedings of the American Forestry Association.* Vol. 12. Washington, DC: American Forestry Association, 1897, 41–68.

Foster, Stephen. *The Long Argument: English Puritanism and the Shaping of New England Culture, 1570–1700.* Chapel Hill: University of North Carolina Press, 1991.

Fowler, Robert Booth. *The Greening of Protestant Thought.* Chapel Hill: University of North Carolina Press, 1995.

Franits, Wayne. *Looking at Seventeenth-Century Dutch Art: Realism Reconsidered.* Cambridge: Cambridge University Press, 1997.

"Frank A. Waugh: A Biographical Sketch." In the program for "A Dinner in Observance of the Retirement of Dr. Frank A. Waugh from Active Teaching, Massachusetts State College, June 9, 1939." Special Collections and University Archives. University of Massachusetts Amherst.

Frankel, Jonathan. *Prophecy and Politics: Socialism, Nationalism, and the Russian Jews, 1862–1917.* Cambridge: Cambridge University Press, 1981.

Freemon, Frank R. "American Colonial Scientists Who Published in the *Philosophical Transactions* of the Royal Society." *Notes and Records of the Royal Society of London* 39(2) (1985): 191–206.

Freudenheim, Leslie Mandelson. *Building with Nature: Inspiration for the Arts & Crafts Home.* Salt Lake City, UT: Gibbs Smith, 2005.

Friedland, Roger, and Harold Zellman. *The Fellowship: The Untold Story of Frank Lloyd Wright & the Taliesin Fellowship.* New York: Regan, 2006.

Friess, Horace L., and Fannia Weingartner. *Felix Adler and Ethical Culture: Memories and Studies.* New York: Columbia University Press, 1981.

Fulton, John F., and Elizabeth H. Thomson. *Benjamin Silliman, 1779–1864: Pathfinder in American Science.* New York: Schuman, 1947.

Garb, Yaakov. "Change and Continuity in Environmental World-View: The Politics of Nature in Rachel Carson's *Silent Spring.*" In *Minding Nature: The Philosophers of Ecology.* Edited by David Macauley. New York: Guilford Press, 1996.

García, Ismael. *Dignidad: Ethics Through Hispanic Eyes.* Nashville, TN: Abingdon Press, 1997.

Garland, Anne Witte. *Women Activists: Challenging the Abuse of Power.* New York: Feminist Press at the City University of New York, 1988.

Garvey, T. Gregory. "The Civic Intent of George Perkins Marsh's Anthrocentric Environmentalism." *New England Quarterly* 82(1) (March 2009): 80–111.

Gallaudet, Edward Miner. *Life of Thomas Hopkins Gallaudet.* New York: Holt, 1888.

Gaustad, Edwin S., and Philip L. Barlow. *New Historical Atlas of Religion in America.* Oxford: Oxford University Press, 2001.

Genovese, Eugene D. *Roll, Jordan, Roll: The World the Slaves Made.* New York: Pantheon Books, 1974.

George, Carol V. R. "Widening the Circle: The Black Church and the Abolitionist Crusade, 1830–1860." In *African-American Religion: Interpretive Essays in*

History and Culture. Edited by Timothy Earl Fulop and Albert J. Raboteau. New York: Routledge, 1997.

"George Washington Woodruff." *Yale University Obituary Record of Graduates Deceased during the Year Ending July 1, 1934*. New Haven, CT: Yale University, 1934, 65–66.

Gerber, Philip L. *Willa Cather*. Boston: Twayne, 1975.

Gerdts, William H. "American Landscape Painting: Critical Judgments, 1730–1845." *American Art Journal* 17(1) (Winter 1985): 39–55.

Germic, Stephen. *American Green: Class, Crisis, and the Deployment of Nature in Central Park, Yosemite, and Yellowstone*. Lanham, MD: Lexington Books, 2001.

Geselbracht, Raymond H. "Transcendental Renaissance in the Arts, 1890–1920." *New England Quarterly* 48 (Dec. 1975): 463–486.

Gifford, Terry. *Reconnecting with John Muir: Essays in Post-Pastoral Practice*. Athens: University of Georgia Press, 2006.

Gillispie, Charles Coulston. *Genesis and Geology: A Study in the Relations of Scientific Thought, Natural Theology, and Social Opinion in Great Britain, 1790–1850*. Cambridge, MA: Harvard University Press, 1951.

Giltner, Scott E. *Hunting and Fishing in the New South: Black Labor and White Leisure After the Civil War*. Baltimore, MD: Johns Hopkins University Press, 2008.

Giltner, Scott. "Slave Hunting and Fishing in the Old South." In *"To Love the Wind and the Rain": African Americans and Environmental History*. Edited by Dianne D. Glave and Mark Stoll. Pittsburgh, PA: University of Pittsburgh Press, 2006.

Gisel, Bonnie Johanna. *Nature's Beloved Son: Rediscovering John Muir's Botanical Legacy*. Berkeley, CA: Heyday Books, 2008.

Glass, William R. *Strangers in Zion: Fundamentalists in the South, 1900–1950*. Macon, GA: Mercer University Press, 2001.

Glassner, Barry. *The Gospel of Food: Everything You Think You Know about Food Is Wrong*. New York: Ecco, 2007.

Glenn, L. C. "Gerard Troost." *American Geologist* 35 (February 1905): 72–94.

Glover, James M. *A Wilderness Original: The Life of Bob Marshall*. Seattle, WA: Mountaineers, 1986.

Goen, C. C. *Revivalism and Separatism in New England, 1740–1800: Strict Congregationalist and Separate Baptists in the Great Awakening*. New Haven, CT: Yale University Press, 1962.

Goldman, Ralph Morris. *The National Party Chairmen and Committees: Factionalism at the Top*. Armonk, NY: Sharpe, 1990.

Gottlieb, Robert. *Forcing the Spring: The Transformation of the American Environmental Movement*. Washington, DC: Island Press, 1993.

Gourdin, Henri. *Olivier de Serres: "Science, expérience, diligence" en agriculture au temps de Henri IV*. Arles, France: Actes Sud, 2001.

Gourley, John. "General History." *Proceedings of the Centennial Celebration of the First Presbyterian Church of Lancaster, Ohio, Held October 20th, 21st and 22nd, 1905*. N.p., 1905.

Grant, James Richard. *The Life of Thomas C. McRae: Arkansas' Educational Governor, 1921–1925*. Russellville, AR: Russellville, 1932.

Grantham, Dewey W. *Hoke Smith and the Politics of the New South*. Baton Rouge: Louisiana State University Press, 1958.

Grasso, Christopher. "The Experimental Philosophy of Farming: Jared Eliot and the Cultivation of Connecticut." *William and Mary Quarterly* 50 (July 1993): 502–528.

Grazer, Walter E. "Strategy for Environmental Engagement: Building a Catholic Constituency." In *Christianity and Ecology: Seeking the Well-Being of Earth and Humans*. Edited by Dieter T. Hessel and Rosemary Radford Ruether. Cambridge, MA: Harvard University Press, 2000.

Green, Nancy E., and Jessie J. Poesch, eds. *Arthur Wesley Dow and American Arts & Crafts*. New York: Abrams, 2000.

Greene, John C. "Protestantism, Science, and American Enterprise: Benjamin Silliman's Moral Universe." In *Benjamin Silliman and his Circle: Studies on the Influence of Benjamin Silliman on Science in America: Prepared in Honor of Elizabeth H. Thomson*. Edited by Leonard G. Wilson. New York: Science History Publications, 1979.

Gremillion, Joseph. "Justice and Peace." In *Modern Catholicism: Vatican II and After*. Edited by Adrian Hastings. London: SPCK, 1991.

Greven, Philip J. *The Protestant Temperament: Patterns of Child-Rearing, Religious Experience, and the Self in Early America*. New York: Knopf, 1977.

Griffin, Dustin. *Regaining Paradise: Milton and the Eighteenth Century*. Cambridge: Cambridge University Press, 1986.

Griffin, Patrick. *The People with No Name: Ireland's Ulster Scots, America's Scots Irish, and the Creation of a British Atlantic World, 1689–1764*. Princeton, NJ: Princeton University Press, 2001.

Griffin, Susan. *Woman and Nature: The Roaring Inside Her*. New York: Harper & Row, 1978.

Guicharnaud, Hélène. "An Introduction to the Architecture of Protestant Temples Constructed in France before the Revocation of the Edict of Nantes." In *Seeing Beyond the Word: Visual Arts and the Calvinist Tradition*. Edited by Paul Corby Finney. Grand Rapids, MI: Eerdmans, 1999.

Gura, Philip F. *American Transcendentalism: A History*. New York: Hill and Wang, 2007.

Guralnick, Stanley M. *Science and the Ante-Bellum American College*. Philadelphia: American Philosophical Society, 1975.

Guzzo, Louis R. *Is It True What They Say About Dixy? A Biography of Dixy Lee Ray*. Mercer Island, WA: Writing Works, 1980.

Haberer, Erich. *Jews and Revolution in Nineteenth-Century Russia*. Cambridge: Cambridge University Press, 1995.

Haddock, John A. "Dr. Franklin B. Hough." In *Growth of a Century: As Illustrated in the History of Jefferson County, New York, from 1793 to 1894*. Philadelphia: Sherman, 1894.

Hall, David D. *A Reforming People: Puritanism and the Transformation of Public Life in New England.* New York: Knopf, 2011.

Hall, Michael G. *The Last American Puritan: The Life of Increase Mather, 1639–1723.* Middletown, CT: Wesleyan University Press, 1988.

Hall, Russell. *Hall's Index of American Presbyterian Congregations.* www.history.pcusa.org/collections/hiapc.cfm.

Hambrick-Stowe, Charles E. *The Practice of Piety: Puritan Devotional Disciplines in Seventeenth-Century New England.* Chapel Hill: University of North Carolina Press, 1982.

Hammond, Anne, and Ansel Adams. *Ansel Adams: Divine Performance.* New Haven, CT: Yale University Press, 2002.

Hammond, Jeffrey A. *Sinful Self, Saintly Self: The Puritan Experience of Poetry.* Athens: University of Georgia Press, 1993.

Hankins, Barry. *Uneasy in Babylon: Southern Baptist Conservatives and American Culture.* Tuscaloosa: University of Alabama Press, 2002.

Hannum, William Hamilton. *Subscriptions for the Meeting-House at Tarlton, Ohio, in 1830.* Columbus, Ohio: the author, 1900.

Hansen, Klaus J. *Mormonism and the American Experience.* Chicago: University of Chicago Press, 1981.

Hardman, Malcolm. *Classic Soil: Community, Aspiration, and Debate in the Bolton Region of Lancashire, 1819–1845.* Cranbury, NJ: Associated University Presses, 2003.

Hardy, Daniel W. "Calvinism and the Visual Arts: A Theological Introduction." In *Seeing Beyond the Word: Visual Arts and the Calvinist Tradition.* Edited by Paul Corby Finney. Grand Rapids, MI: Eerdmans, 1999.

Harper, Keith. *The Quality of Mercy: Southern Baptists and Social Christianity, 1890–1920.* Tuscaloosa: University of Alabama Press, 1996.

Harrell, David Edwin, ed. *Varieties of Southern Evangelicalism.* Macon, GA: Mercer University Press, 1981.

Harris, Dianne Suzette, and Bernard R. Maybeck. *Maybeck's Landscapes: Drawing in Nature.* San Francisco: Stout, 2004.

Harris, Fredrick C. *Something Within: Religion in African-American Political Activism.* New York: Oxford University Press, 1999.

Harrison, John S. *The Teachers of Emerson.* New York: Sturgis, 1910.

Harrison, Peter. *The Bible, Protestantism, and the Rise of Natural Science.* Cambridge: Cambridge University Press, 1998.

Harrison, Peter. "The 'Book of Nature' and Early Modern Science." In *The Book of Nature in Early Modern and Modern History.* Edited by Klaas van Berkel and Arjo Vanderjagt. Leuven: Peeters, 2006.

Harvey, Eleanor Jones. "Tastes in Transition: Gifford's Patrons." In *Hudson River School Visions: The Landscapes of Sanford R. Gifford.* Edited by Kevin J. Avery and Franklin Kelly. New York: Metropolitan Museum of Art, 2003.

Harvey, Mark. *Wilderness Forever: Howard Zahniser and the Path to the Wilderness Act.* Seattle: University of Washington Press, 2005.

Harvey, Paul. *Redeeming the South: Religious Cultures and Racial Identities Among Southern Baptists, 1865–1925.* Chapel Hill: University of North Carolina Press, 1997.

Haskell, Barbara. *Arthur Dove.* San Francisco: San Francisco Museum of Art, 1974.

Hastings, Adrian. "The Key Texts." In *Modern Catholicism: Vatican II and After.* Edited by Adrian Hastings. London: SPCK, 1991.

Hawley, Joshua David. *Theodore Roosevelt: Preacher of Righteousness.* New Haven, CT: Yale University Press, 2008.

Hays, Samuel P. *Conservation and the Gospel of Efficiency: The Progressive Conservation Movement, 1890–1920.* Cambridge, MA: Harvard University Press, 1959.

Hazlehurst, Franklin Hamilton. *Jacques Boyceau and the French Formal Garden.* Athens: University of Georgia Press, 1966.

Hebblethwaite, Margaret. "Devotion." In *Modern Catholicism: Vatican II and After.* Edited by Adrian Hastings. London: SPCK, 1991.

Heller, Henry. *The Conquest of Poverty: The Calvinist Revolt in Sixteenth Century France.* Leiden: Brill, 1986.

Heller, Henry. *Labour, Science, and Technology in France, 1500–1620.* Cambridge: Cambridge University Press, 1996.

Helm, MacKinley. *John Marin.* Boston: Pellegrini & Cudahy, 1948.

Helms, Anne Adams. *The Descendants of William James Adams and Cassandra Hills Adams.* Salinas, CA: Helms, 1999.

Hennesey, James J. *American Catholics: A History of the Roman Catholic Community in the United States.* Oxford: Oxford University Press, 1981.

"Henry C. Noble." *Bench and Bar of Ohio: A Compendium of History and Biography.* Vol. 1. Chicago: Century, 1897.

"Henry Solon Graves, 1871–1951." *Yale Forest School News* 39(2) (1951): 22–24.

Herrmann, Robert L. *Sir John Templeton: Supporting Scientific Research for Spiritual Discoveries.* Philadelphia: Templeton Foundation Press, 2004.

Herscher, Uri D. *Jewish Agricultural Utopias in America, 1880–1910.* Detroit, MI: Wayne State University Press, 1981.

Hertz, David Michael. *Angels of Reality: Emersonian Unfoldings in Wright, Stevens, and Ives.* Carbondale: Southern Illinois University Press, 1993.

Heyrman, Christine Leigh. *Southern Cross: The Beginnings of the Bible Belt.* New York: Knopf, 1997.

Hickman, Paul, and Terence Pitts. *George Fiske, Yosemite Photographer.* Flagstaff, AZ: Northland, 1980.

Hill, Marvin S. *Quest for Refuge: The Mormon Flight from American Pluralism.* Salt Lake City, UT: Signature, 1989.

Hill, Samuel S. *The South and the North in American Religion.* Athens: University of Georgia Press, 1980.

Hill, Samuel S. *Southern Churches in Crisis.* New York: Holt, Rinehart and Winston, 1967.

Hill, Samuel S. *Varieties of Southern Religious Experience.* Baton Rouge: Louisiana State University Press, 1988.

Hiltner, Ken. "A Defense of Milton's Environmentalism." *English Language Notes* (June 2003): 11–24.

Hiltner, Ken. *Milton and Ecology.* Cambridge: Cambridge University Press, 2003.

Hines, Thomas S. *Burnham of Chicago: Architect and Planner.* New York: Oxford University Press, 1974.

Historical and Biographical Annals of Columbia and Montour Counties, Pennsylvania. Vol. 1. Chicago: Beers, 1915.

Hoeveler, J. David. *Creating the American Mind: Intellect and Politics in the Colonial Colleges.* Lanham, MD: Rowman & Littlefield, 2002.

Hoffman, Frederick John. *The Twenties: American Writing in the Postwar Decade.* Rev. ed. New York: Free Press, 1965.

Hogrefe, Jeffrey. *O'Keeffe: The Life of an American Legend.* New York: Bantam, 1992.

Holbrook, Clyde A. *Jonathan Edwards, the Valley and Nature.* Lewisburg, PA: Bucknell University Press, 1987.

Holifield, E. Brooks. *The Gentlemen Theologians: American Theology in Southern Culture, 1795–1860.* Durham, NC: Duke University Press, 1978.

Hollister, John C. *Historical Record of the Class of 1840, Yale College.* New Haven, CT: Tuttle, Morehouse & Taylor, 1897.

The Home Book of the Picturesque: or, American Scenery, Art, and Literature. New York: Putnam, 1852.

Hopkins, Vivian C. "Emerson and Cudworth: Plastic Nature and Transcendental Art." *American Literature* 23 (March 1951): 80–98.

Hoppin, Martha J. "Arcadian Vales: The Connecticut Valley in Art." In *A Place Called Paradise: Culture and Community in Northampton, Massachusetts, 1654–2004.* Edited by Kerry Wayne Buckley. Amherst: University of Massachusetts Press, 2004.

Horowitz, Mark. "Burning Down the House." *Wired,* October 2007. http://archive.wired.com/science/planetearth/magazine/15-10/mf_burning.

Hovenkamp, Herbert. *Science and Religion in America, 1800–1860.* Philadelphia: University of Pennsylvania Press, 1978.

Howard, Albert, and Yeshwant D. Wad. *The Waste Products of Agriculture: Their Utilization As Humus.* London: Humphrey Milford, Oxford University Press, 1931.

Howat, John K. *American Paradise: The World of the Hudson River School.* New York: Metropolitan Museum of Art, 1987.

Howat, John K. *Frederic Church.* New Haven, CT: Yale University Press, 2005.

Howe, Daniel Walker. "The Cambridge Platonists of Old England and the Cambridge Platonists of New England." *Church History* 57 (Dec. 1988): 470–485.

Hunt, John Dixon, and Peter Willis. *The Genius of the Place: The English Landscape Garden, 1620–1820.* Cambridge, MA: MIT Press, 1988.

Hutchison, William R. *The Modernist Impulse in American Protestantism.* Cambridge, MA: Harvard University Press, 1976.

Huth, Hans. *Nature and the American: Three Centuries of Changing Attitudes.* Berkeley: University of California Press, 1957.

Huxley, Leonard, and Joseph Dalton Hooker. *Life and Letters of Sir Joseph Dalton Hooker, O.M., G.C.S.I.: Based on Materials Collected and Arranged by Lady Hooker.* Vol. 1. London: Murray, 1918.

Hyde, Anne Farrar. *An American Vision: Far Western Landscape and National Culture, 1820–1920.* New York: New York University Press, 1990.

Ifkovic, Edward. *The Life and Work of Writer Annie Trumbull Slosson: A Connecticut Local Colorist.* Lewiston, NY: Mellen, 2004.

In Memoriam, C. N. T, November 29, 1874. New York: Printed for the family circle, 1874.

Innes, Stephen. *Creating the Commonwealth: The Economic Culture of Puritan New England.* New York: Norton, 1995.

Isaac, Rhys. *The Transformation of Virginia, 1740–1790.* Chapel Hill: University of North Carolina Press, 1982.

Jackson, Carlton. *J. I. Rodale: Apostle of Nonconformity.* New York: Pyramid Books, 1974.

Jackson, John Brinckerhoff. *American Space: The Centennial Years, 1865–1876.* New York: Norton, 1972.

Jacob, Margaret C., and Dorothée Sturkenboom. "A Women's Scientific Society in the West: The Late Eighteenth-Century Assimilation of Science." *Isis* 94 (June 2003): 217–252.

Jacoby, Karl. *Crimes Against Nature: Squatters, Poachers, Thieves, and the Hidden History of American Conservation.* Berkeley: University of California Press, 2001.

Jewish Agricultural Society. *Jews in American Agriculture: The History of Farming by Jews in the United States.* New York: Jewish Agricultural Society, 1954.

Johnson, Kirk. "From a Woodland Elegy, A Rhapsody in Green: Hunter Mountain Paintings Spurred Recovery." *New York Times,* June 7, 2001.

Jones, Arthur. "Eco-spirituality." *National Catholic Reporter,* July 30, 1999. http://nat-cath.org/NCR_Online/archives2/1999c/073099/073099a.htm.

Judd, Richard W. *Common Lands, Common People: The Origins of Conservation in Northern New England.* Cambridge, MA: Harvard University Press, 1997.

Judd, Richard W. "A 'Wonderfull Order and Ballance': Natural History and the Beginnings of Forest Conservation in America, 1730–1830." *Environmental History* 11 (January 2006): 8–36.

Judd, Sylvester, and Lucius M. Boltwood. *History of Hadley, Including the Early History of Hatfield, South Hadley, Amherst and Granby, Massachusetts.* Northampton, MA: Metcalf, 1863.

Kahrl, Andrew W. *The Land Was Ours: African American Beaches from Jim Crow to the Sunbelt South.* Cambridge, MA: Harvard University Press, 2012.

Kaiser, Harvey H. *Great Camps of the Adirondacks.* Boston: Godine, 1982.

Kamil, Neil. *Fortress of the Soul: Violence, Metaphysics, and Material Life in the Huguenots' New World, 1517–1751.* Baltimore, MD: Johns Hopkins University Press, 2005.

Kane, Joe. "One Man's Wilderness." *Sierra,* March/April 2000, 46.

Kane, Paula M. "American Catholic Culture in the Twentieth Century." In *Perspectives on American Religion and Culture.* Edited by Peter W. Williams. Malden, MA: Blackwell, 1999.

Kann, Kenneth. *Comrades and Chicken Ranchers: The Story of a California Jewish Community.* Ithaca, NY: Cornell University Press, 1993.

Katz, Eric. "Judaism and the Ecological Crisis." In *Worldviews and Ecology.* Edited by Mary Evelyn Tucker and John A. Grim. Lewisburg, PA: Bucknell University Press, 1993.

Kelly, Franklin, ed. *Frederic Edwin Church.* Washington, DC: National Gallery of Art, 1989.

Kelly, Franklin. "Nature Distilled: Gifford's Vision of Landscape." In *Hudson River School Visions: The Landscapes of Sanford R. Gifford.* Edited by Kevin J. Avery and Franklin Kelly. New York: Metropolitan Museum of Art, 2003.

Kelly, Franklin. "A Passion for Landscape: The Paintings of Frederic Edwin Church." In *Frederic Edwin Church.* Edited by Franklin Kelly. Washington, DC: National Gallery of Art, 1989.

Kelso, James A. "The Rev. William Hamilton Jeffers, D.D., L.L.D." *Bulletin of the Western Theological Seminary* 7(4) (April 1915): 50.

Kennedy, William Sloane. *In Portia's Gardens.* Boston: Whidden, 1897.

Kent, Elizabeth Thacher. *William Kent, Independent: A Biography.* N.p., 1950.

Kert, Bernice. *Abby Aldrich Rockefeller: The Woman in the Family.* New York: Random House, 1993.

Kilde, Jeanne Halgren. *When Church Became Theatre: The Transformation of Evangelical Architecture and Worship in Nineteenth-Century America.* New York: Oxford University Press, 2002.

Killinger, Margaret O. *The Good Life of Helen K. Nearing.* Burlington, VT: University of Vermont Press, 2007.

Kirby, Jack Temple. *Mockingbird Song: Ecological Landscapes of the South.* Chapel Hill: University of North Carolina Press, 2006.

Kitson, Michael. "A Context for Constable's Naturalism." In Gainsborough's House and Leger Galleries. *From Gainsborough to Constable: The Emergence of Naturalism in British Landscape Painting 1750–1810.* Sudbury, UK: Gainsborough's House Society, 1991.

Klaaren, Eugene M. *Religious Origins of Modern Science: Belief in Creation in Seventeenth-Century Thought.* Grand Rapids, MI: Eerdmans, 1977.

Klinkenborg, Verlyn. "Life Lessons, Taught by Insects." *New York Times,* April 9, 2010.

Knight, Janice. *Orthodoxies in Massachusetts: Rereading American Puritanism.* Cambridge, MA: Harvard University Press, 1994.

Koch, Matthew. "Calvinism and the Visual Arts in Southern France, 1561 to 1685." In *Seeing Beyond the Word: Visual Arts and the Calvinist Tradition.* Edited by Paul Corby Finney. Grand Rapids, MI: Eerdmans, 1999.

Kohlstedt, Sally Gregory. "Parlors, Primers, and Public Schooling: Education for Science in Nineteenth-Century America." *Isis* 81 (Sep. 1990): 424–445.

Kohlstedt, Sally Gregory. *Teaching Children Science: Hands-on Nature Study in North America, 1890–1930.* Chicago: University of Chicago Press, 2010.

Kornhauser, Elizabeth Mankin. *American Paintings Before 1945 in the Wadsworth Atheneum.* Vol. 1. New Haven, CT: Yale University Press, 1996.

Krapohl, Robert H., and Charles H. Lippy. *The Evangelicals: A Historical, Thematic, and Biographical Guide.* Westport, CT: Greenwood Press, 1999.

Kraut, Benny. *From Reform Judaism to Ethical Culture: The Religious Evolution of Felix Adler.* Cincinnati, OH: Hebrew Union College Press, 1979.

Kriebel, David L., ed. *Barry Commoner's Contribution to the Environmental Movement: Science and Social Action.* Amityville, NY: Baywood, 2002.

Kuehne, Dale S. *Massachusetts Congregationalist Political Thought 1760–1790: The Design of Heaven.* Columbia: University of Missouri Press, 1996.

Kwa, Chunglin. "Alexander von Humboldt's Invention of the Natural Landscape." *European Legacy* 10(2) (2005): 149–162.

Landow, George P. *Ruskin.* Oxford: Oxford University Press, 1985.

Lane, Belden C. *Landscapes of the Sacred: Geography and Narrative in American Spirituality.* Baltimore, MD: Johns Hopkins University Press, 2002.

Lanman, Charles. "Cole's Imaginative Paintings." *United States Democratic Review* 12(60) (June 1843): 602–603.

Lanman, Charles. *Letters from a Landscape Painter.* Boston: Munroe, 1845.

Lattin, Frank H. *Penikese: A Reminiscence.* Albion, NY: Lattin, 1895.

Laufer, Marilyn. "Myths and Metaphors: The Life of Leo Twiggs." In *Myths and Metaphors: The Art of Leo Twiggs.* Edited by Marilyn Laufer. Athens, GA: Georgia Museum of Art, 2004.

Lavender, Abraham D., and Clarence B. Steinberg. *Jewish Farmers of the Catskills: A Century of Survival.* Gainesville: University Press of Florida, 1995.

Lawrence, Beverly Hall. *Reviving the Spirit: A Generation of African Americans Goes Home to Church.* New York: Grove Press, 1996.

Lawrence, Philip J. "Edward Hitchcock: The Christian Geologist." *Proceedings of the American Philosophical Society* 116 (Feb. 15, 1972): 21–34.

Lear, Linda. *Rachel Carson: Witness for Nature.* London: Allen Lane, 1998.

Leavengood, David. "A Sense of Shelter: Robert C. Reamer in Yellowstone National Park." *Pacific Historical Review* 54(4) (November 1985): 495–513.

Lee, Hermione. *Willa Cather: Double Lives.* New York: Pantheon, 1989.

Lee, Sang Hyun. *The Philosophical Theology of Jonathan Edwards.* Princeton, NJ: Princeton University Press, 1988.

Lendt, David L. *Ding: The Life of Jay Norwood Darling.* Ames: Iowa State University Press, 1979.

Leonard, Bill. *God's Last and Only Hope: The Fragmentation of the Southern Baptist Convention.* Grand Rapids, MI: Eerdmans, 1990.

Leone, Mark P. *Roots of Modern Mormonism.* Cambridge, MA: Harvard University Press, 1979.

Lerner, Steve. *Diamond: A Struggle for Environmental Justice in Louisiana's Chemical Corridor.* Cambridge, MA: MIT Press, 2005.

Lestringant, Frank. "L'Éden et les ténèbres extérieures: de la *Recepte véritable* aux *Discours admirables."* In *Bernard Palissy, 1510–1590: l'écrivain, le réformé, le céramiste: journées d'études 29 et 30 juin 1990, Saintes, Abbaye-aux-dames: actes du colloque.* Edited by Frank Lestringant. Paris: Editions interuniversitaires, 1992.

Levine, Lawrence W. *Black Culture and Black Consciousness: Afro-American Folk Thought from Slavery to Freedom.* New York: Oxford University Press, 1977.

Lincoln, C. Eric, and Lawrence H. Mamiya. *The Black Church in the African-American Experience.* Durham, NC: Duke University Press, 1990.

Lisle, Laurie. *Portrait of an Artist: A Biography of Georgia O'Keeffe.* New York: Seaview, 1980.

Lloyd, Harriet Raymond. *Life and Letters of John Howard Raymond.* New York: Fords, Howard, & Hulbert, 1881.

Lock, F. P. *Edmund Burke.* Vol. 1, *1730–1784.* Oxford: Oxford University Press, 2007.

Long, Charles J. "Perspectives for a Study of African-American Religion in the United States." In *African-American Religion: Interpretive Essays in History and Culture.* Edited by Timothy Earl Fulop and Albert J. Raboteau. New York: Routledge, 1997.

Longstreth, Richard W. *On the Edge of the World: Four Architects in San Francisco at the Turn of the Century.* New York: Architectural History Foundation, 1983.

Lord, Russell. *The Wallaces of Iowa.* Boston: Houghton Mifflin, 1947.

Lovejoy, Arthur O. *The Great Chain of Being: A Study of the History of an Idea.* Cambridge, MA: Harvard University Press, 1936.

Loveland, Anne C., and Otis B. Wheeler. *From Meetinghouse to Megachurch: A Material and Cultural History.* Columbia: University of Missouri Press, 2003.

Lowe, Sue Davidson. *Stieglitz: A Memoir/Biography.* New York: Farrar Straus Giroux, 1983.

Lowenthal, David. *George Perkins Marsh, Prophet of Conservation.* Seattle: University of Washington Press, 2000.

Lowry, Thea Snyder. *Empty Shells: The Story of Petaluma, America's Chicken City.* Novato, CA: Manifold Press, 2000.

Lucas, Paul Robert. *Valley of Discord: Church and Society Along the Connecticut River, 1636–1725.* Hanover, NH: University Press of New England, 1976.

Ludington, Townsend. *Marsden Hartley: The Biography of an American Artist.* Boston: Little, Brown, 1992.

Ludington, Townsend. *Seeking the Spiritual: The Paintings of Marsden Hartley*. Ithaca, NY: Cornell University Press, 1998.

Lutts, Ralph H. *The Nature Fakers: Wildlife, Science & Sentiment*. Charlottesville: University Press of Virginia, 2001.

"Lynn (Townsend) White, Jr." *Contemporary Authors Online*. Gale, 2002.

MacDonald, Margaret F. "'Our Lady of the Rivers': Marjorie Harris Carr, Science, Gender, and Environmental Activism." PhD diss., University of Florida, 2010. http://purl.fcla.edu/fcla/etd/UFE0024406.

Mackelvie, William. *Annals and Statistics of the United Presbyterian Church*. Edinburgh: Oliphant and Elliot, 1873.

Mackintosh, Barry. "Harold L. Ickes and the National Park Service." *Journal of Forest History* 29(2) (Apr. 1985): 78–84.

Maclean, Norman. *A River Runs Through It, and Other Stories*. Chicago: University of Chicago Press, 1976.

Maddow, Ben. "A View from Below: Paul Strand's Monumental Presence." *American Art* 5(3) (Summer 1991): 48–67.

Madsen, William G. *From Shadowy Types to Truth: Studies in Milton's Symbolism*. New Haven, CT: Yale University Press, 1968.

Madsen, William G. *The Idea of Nature in Milton's Poetry*. In *Three Studies in the Renaissance: Sidney, Jonson, Milton*. New Haven, CT: Yale University Press, 1958.

Maher, Neil M. *Nature's New Deal: The Civilian Conservation Corps and the Roots of the American Environmental Movement*. Oxford: Oxford University Press, 2008.

Major, Judith K. *To Live in the New World: A.J. Downing and American Landscape Gardening*. Cambridge, MA: MIT Press, 1997.

Mangelsdorf, Paul C. *Donald Forsha Jones: April 16, 1890–June 19, 1963*. Washington, DC: National Academy of Sciences, 1975.

Maraniss, David, and Ellen Nakashima. *The Prince of Tennessee: The Rise of Al Gore*. New York: Simon & Schuster, 2000.

Mark, Stephen R. *Preserving the Living Past: John C. Merriam's Legacy in the State and National Parks*. Berkeley: University of California Press, 2005.

Marsden, George M. *Jonathan Edwards: A Life*. New Haven, CT: Yale University Press, 2003.

Marsden, George M. *The Soul of the American University: From Protestant Establishment to Established Nonbelief*. New York: Oxford University Press, 1994.

Marsh, Caroline Crane. *Life and Letters of George Perkins Marsh*. Vol. 1. New York: Scribner, 1888.

Marsh, Dwight Whitney. *Genealogy of the Marsh Family*. Amherst, MA: Williams, 1886.

Marty, Myron A., and Shirley L. Marty. *Frank Lloyd Wright's Taliesin Fellowship*. Kirksville, MO: Truman State University Press, 1999.

Marx, Leo. *The Machine in the Garden: Technology and the Pastoral Ideal in America*. New York: Oxford University Press, 1964.

Mason, David T. "In Summary from a Forester's Point of View: Pinchot, Cary, Greeley: Architects of American Forestry." *Forest History* 5 (Summer 1961): 6–8.

Matovina, Timothy M., and Gary Riebe-Estrella. *Horizons of the Sacred: Mexican Traditions in U.S. Catholicism.* Ithaca, NY: Cornell University Press, 2002.

Mayer, Sylvia. *Naturethik und Neuengland-Regionalliteratur: Harriet Beecher Stowe, Rose Terry Cooke, Sarah Orne Jewett, Mary E. Wilkins Freeman.* Heidelberg, Ger.: Universitätsverlag Winter, 2004.

Maynard, W. Barksdale. "'An Ideal Life in the Woods for Boys': Architecture and Culture in the Earliest Summer Camps." *Winterthur Portfolio* 34 (Spring 1999): 3–29.

McCann, Garth. *Edward Abbey.* Boise, Idaho: Boise State University, 1977.

McClelland, Linda Flint. *Building the National Parks: Historic Landscape Design and Construction.* Baltimore, MD: Johns Hopkins University Press, 1998.

McColley, Diane Kelsey. "Beneficent Hierarchies: Reading Milton Greenly." In *Spokesperson Milton: Voices in Contemporary Criticism.* Edited by Charles W. Durham and Kristin Pruitt McColgan. Selinsgrove, PA: Susquehanna University Press, 1994.

McColley, Diane Kelsey. *A Gust for Paradise: Milton's Eden and the Visual Arts.* Urbana: University of Illinois Press, 1993.

McColley, Diane Kelsey. "Milton's Environmental Epic: Creature Kinship and the Language of *Paradise Lost.*" In *Beyond Nature Writing: Expanding the Boundaries of Ecocriticism.* Edited by Karla Armbruster and Kathleen R. Wallace. Charlottesville: University Press of Virginia, 2001.

McDermott, Gerald R. *One Holy and Happy Society: The Public Theology of Jonathan Edwards.* University Park: Pennsylvania State University Press, 1992.

McGeary, M. Nelson. *Gifford Pinchot, Forester-Politician.* Princeton, NJ: Princeton University Press, 1960.

McGreevy, John T. *Catholicism and American Freedom: A History.* New York: Norton, 2003.

McGurty, Eileen Maura. *Transforming Environmentalism: Warren County, PCBS, and the Origins of Environmental Justice.* New Brunswick, NJ: Rutgers University Press, 2007.

McHenry, Robert. *Famous American Women: A Biographical Dictionary from Colonial Times to the Present.* New York: Dover, 1983.

McLoughlin, William G. "Massive Civil Disobedience as a Baptist Tactic in 1773." *American Quarterly* 21(4) (Winter 1969): 710–727.

McLoughlin, William Gerald. *Isaac Backus and the American Pietistic Tradition.* Boston: Little, Brown, 1967.

McLoughlin, William Gerald. *New England Dissent, 1630–1833: The Baptists and the Separation of Church and State.* Vol. 1. Cambridge, MA: Harvard University Press, 1971.

McNulty, J. Bard, ed. *The Correspondence of Thomas Cole and Daniel Wadsworth* Hartford, CT: Connecticut Historical Society, 1983.

McPhee, John. *Encounters with the Archdruid.* New York: Farrar, Straus and Giroux, 1971.

McTighe, Shella. "Abraham Bosse and the Language of Artisans: Genre and Perspective in the Academie royale de peinture et de sculpture, 1648–1670." *Oxford Art Journal* 21(1) (1998): 3–26.

Medina, Lara. *Las Hermanas: Chicana/Latina religious-political activism in the U.S. Catholic Church.* Philadelphia: Temple University Press, 2004.

Meine, Curt D. *Aldo Leopold: His Life and Work.* 2nd ed. Madison: University of Wisconsin Press, 2010.

Mentzer, Raymond A., Jr. "The Reformed Churches of France and the Visual Arts." In *Seeing Beyond the Word: Visual Arts and the Calvinist Tradition.* Edited by Paul Corby Finney. Grand Rapids, MI: Eerdmans, 1999.

Merchant, Carolyn. *The Death of Nature: Women, Ecology, and the Scientific Revolution.* New York: Harper & Row, 1980.

Mercier, Stephen M. "When Congress Debated Migration: John Burroughs, Henry Ford, Ernest Thompson Seton, and the Debate over the Weeks-McLean Law." *Wake-Robin: Newsletter of the John Burroughs Association at the Museum of Natural History* 39(2) (2007): 6–10.

Merrill, Christopher, and Ellen Bradbury, eds. *From the Faraway Nearby: Georgia O'Keeffe As Icon.* Reading, MA: Addison-Wesley, 1992.

Meyer, Donald B. *The Protestant Search for Political Realism, 1919–1941.* Middletown, CT: Wesleyan University Press, 1988.

Michalski, Sergiusz. *The Reformation and the Visual Arts: The Protestant Image Question in Western and Eastern Europe.* London: Routledge, 1993.

Middlekauff, Robert. *The Mathers: Three Generations of Puritan Intellectuals 1596–1728.* New York: Oxford University Press, 1971.

Miles, Margaret R. *Image as Insight: Visual Understanding in Western Christianity and Secular Culture.* Boston: Beacon Press, 1985.

Miller, Angela. *Empire of the Eye: Landscape Representation and American Cultural Politics, 1825–1875.* Ithaca, NY: Cornell University Press, 1993.

Miller, Angela. "Thomas Cole and Jacksonian America: 'The Course of Empire' as Political Allegory." *Prospects* 14 (October 1989): 65–92.

Miller, Char. "All in the Family: The Pinchots of Milford." *Pennsylvania History* 66 (Spring 1999): 117–142.

Miller, Char. "Amateur Hour: Nathaniel H. Egleston and Professional Forestry in Post-Civil War America." *Forest History Today* (Spring/Fall 2005): 20–26.

Miller, Char. *Gifford Pinchot and the Making of Modern Environmentalism.* Washington, DC: Island Press, 2001.

Miller, Perry. "From Edwards to Emerson." In *Errand into the Wilderness.* Cambridge, MA: Harvard University Press, 1956.

Miller, Perry. *Jonathan Edwards.* [New York]: Sloane, 1949.

Miller, Perry. *The New England Mind: From Colony To Province*. Cambridge, MA: Harvard University Press, 1953.

Miller, Perry. *The New England Mind: The Seventeenth Century*. Cambridge, MA: Harvard University Press, 1954.

Miller, Perry. *Orthodoxy in Massachusetts, 1630–1650: A Genetic Study*. Cambridge, MA: Harvard University Press, 1933.

Miller, Perry, and Thomas Herbert Johnson, eds. *The Puritans*. New York: American Book Co., 1938.

Miller, Sally M., ed. *John Muir in Historical Perspective*. New York: Peter Lang, 1999.

Miller, Sally M., and Daryl Morrison, eds. *John Muir: Family, Friends, and Adventures*. Albuquerque: University of New Mexico Press, 2005.

Mitchell, Charles E. *Individualism and Its Discontents: Appropriations of Emerson, 1880–1950*. Amherst: University of Massachusetts Press, 1997.

Moffatt, Frederick C. "Arthur Wesley Dow and the Ipswich School of Art." *New England Quarterly* 49(3) (Sept. 1976): 339–355.

Moore, Charles. *Daniel H. Burnham: Architect, Planner of Cities*. Vol. 1. Boston: Houghton Mifflin, 1921.

Moore, James R. *The Post-Darwinian Controversies: A Study of the Protestant Struggle to Come to Terms with Darwin in Great Britain and America, 1870–1900*. Cambridge: Cambridge University Press, 1979.

Moore, R. Laurence. *Religious Outsiders and the Making of Americans*. New York: Oxford University Press, 1986.

Moore, R. Laurence. *Selling God: American Religion in the Marketplace of Culture*. New York: Oxford University Press, 1994.

Morgan, Ann Lee. *Arthur Dove: Life and Work, with a Catalogue Raisonné*. Newark: University of Delaware Press, 1984.

Morley, Henry. *Palissy the Potter: The Life of Bernard Palissy, of Saintes, His Labours and Discoveries in Art and Science; with an Outline of His Philosophical Doctrines, and a Translation of Illustrative Selections from His Works*. London: Chapman and Hall, 1852.

Morris, Charles R. *American Catholic: The Saints and Sinners Who Built America's Most Powerful Church*. New York: Times Books, 1997.

Morris, Edmund. *The Rise of Theodore Roosevelt*. New York: Coward, McCann & Geoghegan, 1979.

Muller, Gilbert H. *William Cullen Bryant: Author of America*. Albany: State University of New York Press, 2008.

Murphy, Bruce Allen. *Wild Bill: The Legend and Life of William O. Douglas*. New York: Random House, 2003.

Naef, Weston J. *Carleton Watkins in Yosemite*. Los Angeles: J. Paul Getty Museum, 2008.

Naef, Weston J., and Christine Hult-Lewis. *Carleton Watkins: The Complete Mammoth Photographs*. Los Angeles: J. Paul Getty Museum, 2011.

Nasgaard, Roald. *The Mystic North: Symbolist Landscape Painting in Northern Europe and North America, 1890–1940*. Toronto: University of Toronto Press, 1984.

Nash, Roderick. *Wilderness and the American Mind*. 5th ed. New Haven, CT: Yale University Press, 2012.

Near, Henry. *The Kibbutz Movement: A History*. Vol. 1, *Origins and Growth, 1909–1939*. Oxford: Oxford University Press, 1992.

Nelson, Lowry. *The Mormon Village: A Pattern and Technique of Land Settlement*. Salt Lake City: University of Utah Press, 1952.

Nemmers, John R. "A Guide to the John Ormsbee Simonds Collection." University of Florida Smathers Libraries—Special and Area Studies Collections, January 2006. www.uflib.ufl.edu/spec/manuscript/guides/Simonds.htm.

Newhall, Nancy Wynne. *Ansel Adams: The Eloquent Light*. Rev. ed. Millerton, NY: Aperture, 1980.

Newlyn, Lucy. *"Paradise Lost," and the Romantic Reader*. Oxford: Clarendon Press, 1993.

Nickel, Douglas R. *Carleton Watkins: The Art of Perception*. San Francisco: San Francisco Museum of Modern Art, 1999.

Nicolson, Marjorie Hope. *Mountain Gloom and Mountain Glory: The Development of the Aesthetics of the Infinite*. Ithaca, NY: Cornell University Press, 1959.

Ninde, Edward S. *The Story of the American Hymn*. New York: Abingdon Press, 1921.

Noble, Louis L. *The Life and Works of Thomas Cole*. 3rd ed. New York: Sheldon, Blakeman, 1856.

Noble, Louis Legrand. *The Course of Empire, Voyage of Life, and Other Pictures of Thomas Cole, N.A.: With Selections from his Letters and Miscellaneous Writings Illustrative of His Life, Character, and Genius*. New York: Lamport, Blakeman & Law, 1853.

Noll, Mark A. *America's God: From Jonathan Edwards to Abraham Lincoln*. Oxford: Oxford University Press, 2002.

Noll, Mark A. *American Evangelical Christianity: An Introduction*. Oxford: Blackwell, 2001.

Noll, Mark A. *The Civil War As a Theological Crisis*. Chapel Hill: University of North Carolina Press, 2006.

Norman, Theodore. *An Outstretched Arm: A History of the Jewish Colonization Association*. London: Routledge & Kegan Paul, 1985.

Novak, Barbara. *American Painting of the Nineteenth Century: Realism, Idealism, and the American Experience*. New York: Praeger, 1969.

Novak, Barbara. *Nature and Culture: American Landscape and Painting, 1825–1875*. 3rd ed. New York: Oxford University Press, 2007.

Ogden, Kate Nearpass. "God's Great Plow and the Scripture of Nature: Art and Geology at Yosemite." *California History* 71 (Spring 1992): 88–109.

O'Gorman, James F. *H. H. Richardson: Architectural Forms for an American Society*. Chicago: University of Chicago Press, 1987.

Oliver, Patsy Ruth. "Living on a Superfund Site in Texarkana." In *The Quest for Environmental Justice: Human Rights and the Politics of Pollution*. Edited by Robert D. Bullard. San Francisco: Sierra Club Books, 2005.

Olson, Ted. "Wendell Berry's Revision of Thoreau's Experiment." In *Thoreau's Sense of Place: Essays in American Environmental Writing*. Edited by Richard J. Schneider. Iowa City: University of Iowa Press, 2000.

O'Malley, Therese. "Appropriation and Adaptation: Early Gardening Literature in America." *Huntington Library Quarterly* 55 (Summer 1992): 401–431.

Oreskes, Naomi, and Erik M. Conway. *Merchants of Doubt: How a Handful of Scientists Obscured the Truth on Issues from Tobacco Smoke to Global Warming*. New York: Bloomsbury Press, 2010.

Orsi, Robert A. *The Madonna of 115th Street: Faith and Community in Italian Harlem, 1880–1950*. New Haven, CT: Yale University Press, 1985.

Osborn, Henry Fairfield. "John Muir." *Sierra Club Bulletin*, January 1916.

Osborne, Thomas B. *Biographical Memoir of Samuel William Johnson, 1830–1909*. Washington, DC: National Academy of Sciences, 1911.

Ostertag, Bob. "School of Hard Toxics." *Mother Jones*, January/February 1991, 49.

O'Toole, James M. *The Faithful: A History of Catholics in America*. Cambridge, MA: Harvard University Press, 2008.

Owen, Charles Hunter. "Art and the Artist—An Appreciation of John Lee Fitch." *Connecticut Magazine* 10(2) (April–June 1906): 332–335.

Owen, Felicity. "Early Influences on John Constable." In Gainsborough's House and Leger Galleries. *From Gainsborough to Constable: The Emergence of Naturalism in British Landscape Painting 1750–1810*. Sudbury, UK: Gainsborough's House Society, 1991.

Owings, Frank N., Jr. "Taliesin: A Magnet for Legendary Visitors." *Frank Lloyd Wright Quarterly* 14(3) (2003): 15–19.

Paddock, Joe. *Keeper of the Wild: The Life of Ernest Oberholtzer*. St. Paul: Minnesota Historical Society Press, 2001.

Painter, Nell Irvin. *Exodusters: Black Migration to Kansas After Reconstruction*. New York: Knopf, 1977.

Palmquist, Peter E. *Carleton E. Watkins, Photographer of the American West*. Albuquerque: University of New Mexico Press, 1983.

Paris, Leslie. *Children's Nature: The Rise of the American Summer Camp*. New York: New York University Press, 2008.

Paris, Peter J. *The Social Teaching of the Black Churches*. Philadelphia: Fortress Press, 1985.

Paris, Peter J. *The Spirituality of African Peoples: The Search for a Common Moral Discourse*. Minneapolis, MN: Fortress Press, 1995.

"Park History." *Bushnell Park Foundation*. www.bushnellpark.org/Content/Park_History.asp.

"Parochial Reports." *Journal of the Proceedings of the Fourteenth Annual Convention of the Protestant Episcopal Church in the Diocese of Albany*. Albany, NY: Weed, Parsons, 1882, 119–208.

Parry, Ellwood C., III. "Acts of God, Acts of Man: Geological Ideas and the Imaginary Landscapes of Thomas Cole." In *Two Hundred Years of Geology in America: Proceedings of the New Hampshire Bicentennial Conference on the History of Geology.* Edited by Cecil J. Schneer. Hanover, NH: University Press of New England, 1979.

Parry, Ellwood C., III. *The Art of Thomas Cole: Ambition and Imagination* Newark: University of Delaware Press, 1988.

Parry, Ellwood C., III. "Overlooking the Oxbow: Thomas Cole's 'View from Mount Holyoke' Revisited." *Art Journal* 34 (2003–2004): 6–61.

Parry, Ellwood C., III. "Thomas Cole's Ideas for Mr. Reed's Doors." *American Art Journal* 12 (Summer 1980): 33–45.

Parton, James. "Pittsburg." *Atlantic Monthly,* January 1868.

Passmore, John. *Man's Responsibility for Nature.* New York: Scribner, 1974.

Paull, John. "The Making of an Agricultural Classic: *Farmers of Forty Centuries or Permanent Agriculture in China, Korea and Japan,* 1911–2011." *Agricultural Sciences* 2(3) (2011): 175–180.

Paulson, Ronald. *Hogarth: His Life, Art, and Times.* Abridged by Anne Wilde. New Haven, CT: Yale University Press, 1974.

Payne, John W., Jr. "Houston, David Franklin." *Handbook of Texas Online.* www.tsha-online.org/handbook/online/articles/fho70.

Pearson, Michael. *John McPhee.* New York: Twayne, 1997.

Peeler, David P. *The Illuminating Mind in American Photography: Stieglitz, Strand, Weston, Adams.* Rochester, NY: University of Rochester Press, 2001.

Peña, Devon G. "Tierra y Vida: Chicano Environmental Justice Struggles in the Southwest." In *The Quest for Environmental Justice: Human Rights and the Politics of Pollution.* Edited by Robert D. Bullard. San Francisco: Sierra Club Books, 2005.

Peña, Devon Gerardo. *Mexican Americans and the Environment: Tierra Y Vida.* Tucson: University of Arizona Press, 2005.

Penick, James L. *Progressive Politics and Conservation: The Ballinger-Pinchot Affair.* Chicago: University of Chicago Press, 1968.

Penny, Nicolas. "An Ambitious Man: The Career and the Achievement of Sir Joshua Reynolds." In *Reynolds.* Edited by Nicolas Penny. New York: Abrams, 1986.

Peters, Sarah Whitaker. *Becoming O'Keeffe: The Early Years.* 2nd ed. New York: Abbeville, 2001.

Petersen, Boyd. *Hugh Nibley: A Consecrated Life.* Salt Lake City, UT: Kofford, 2002.

Peterson, Charles S. "Imprint of Agricultural Systems on the Utah Landscape." In *The Mormon Role in the Settlement of the West.* Edited by Richard H. Jackson. Provo, UT: Brigham Young University Press, 1978.

Pew Forum on Religion & Public Life. *U.S. Religious Landscape Survey.* Washington, DC: Pew Forum on Religion & Public Life, 2008. http://religions.pewforum.org.

Phillips, Sandra S. "Photography II: Adams and Stieglitz: A Friendship." *Art in America* 93(1) (2005): 62–71.

Pinn, Anthony B. *The Black Church in the Post-Civil Rights Era*. Maryknoll, NY: Orbis Books, 2002.

Pirani, Alix, ed. *The Absent Mother: Restoring the Goddess to Judaism and Christianity*. London: Mandala, 1991.

Pitts, Walter F. *Old Ship of Zion: The Afro-Baptist Ritual in the African Diaspora*. New York: Oxford University Press, 1993.

Poesch, Jessie J. *The Art of the Old South: Painting, Sculpture, Architecture & the Products of Craftsmen, 1560–1860*. New York: Knopf, 1983.

Polizzi, Gilles. "L'intégration du modèle: le *Poliphile* et le discours du jardin dans *La recepte veritable*." In *Bernard Palissy, 1510–1590: l'écrivain, le réformé, le céramiste: journées d'études 29 et 30 juin 1990, Saintes, Abbaye-aux-dames: actes du colloque*. Edited by Frank Lestringant. Paris: Editions interuniversitaires, 1992.

Pollitzer, Anita. *A Woman on Paper: Georgia O'Keeffe*. New York: Simon & Schuster, 1988.

Pomeroy, Earl S. *In Search of the Golden West: The Tourist in Western America*. New York: Knopf, 1957.

Porterfield, Amanda. *The Transformation of American Religion: The Story of a Late-Twentieth-Century Awakening*. Oxford: Oxford University Press, 2001.

Portola Institute. *The Last Whole Earth Catalog: Access to Tools*. Menlo Park, CA: Portola Institute, 1971.

Powell, Earl A. *Thomas Cole*. New York: Abrams, 1990.

Powell, Sumner Chilton. *Puritan Village: The Formation of a New England Town*. Middletown, CT: Wesleyan University Press, 1963.

Pozza, David M. *Bedrock and Paradox: The Literary Landscape of Edward Abbey*. New York: Peter Lang, 2006.

Pray, James Sturgis. "Minute on the Life and Service of Charles Pierpont Punchard, Jr." *Landscape Architecture* 11(3) (April 1921): 105–110.

Presbyterian Church in the U.S.A., *Minutes of the Winter and Spring [1956] Meetings of East Hanover Presbytery*. N.p., n.d.

Preston, Christopher J. *Saving Creation: Nature and Faith in the Life of Holmes Rolston III*. San Antonio, TX: Trinity University Press, 2009.

Preston, Christopher J., and Wayne Ouderkirk. *Nature, Value, Duty: Life on Earth with Holmes Rolston, III*. Dordrecht, Neth.: Springer, 2007.

Pulido, Laura. *Environmentalism and Economic Justice: Two Chicano Struggles in the Southwest*. Tucson: University of Arizona Press, 1996.

Putney, Clifford. "The Legacy of the Gulicks, 1827–1964." *International Bulletin of Missionary Research* 25(1) (2001): 28–35.

Putney, Clifford. *Muscular Christianity: Manhood and Sports in Protestant America, 1880–1920*. Cambridge, MA: Harvard University Press, 2001.

Quenot, Yvette. "Du jardin de Bernard Palissy au jardin d'Olivier de Serres." In *Bernard Palissy, 1510–1590: l'écrivain, le réformé, le céramiste: journées d'études 29 et 30 juin 1990, Saintes, Abbaye-aux-dames: actes du colloque*. Edited by Frank Lestringant. Paris: Editions interuniversitaires, 1992.

Quinn, Ruth. "Overcoming Obscurity: The Yellowstone Architecture of Robert C. Reamer." *Yellowstone Science* 12(2) (Spring 2004): 23–38.

Quinn, Ruth. *Weaver of Dreams: The Life and Architecture of Robert C. Reamer.* Gardiner, MT: Quinn, 2004.

Rable, George C. *God's Almost Chosen Peoples: A Religious History of the American Civil War.* Chapel Hill: University of North Carolina Press, 2010.

Raboteau, Albert J. "African Americans, Exodus, and the American Israel." In *African-American Christianity: Essays in History.* Edited by Paul E. Johnson. Berkeley: University of California Press, 1994.

Raboteau, Albert J. "The Black Experience in American Evangelicalism: The Meaning of Slavery." In *African-American Religion: Interpretive Essays in History and Culture.* Edited by Timothy Earl Fulop and Albert J. Raboteau. New York: Routledge, 1997.

Raboteau, Albert J. *A Fire in the Bones: Reflections on African-American Religious History.* Boston: Beacon Press, 1995.

Radford, Harry V. *Adirondack Murray: A Biographical Appreciation.* New York: Broadway, 1905.

Ragosta, John A. *Wellspring of Liberty: How Virginia's Religious Dissenters Helped Win the American Revolution and Secured Religious Liberty.* Oxford: Oxford University Press, 2010.

Randall, Catharine. *Building Codes: The Aesthetics of Calvinism in Early Modern Europe.* Philadelphia: University of Pennsylvania Press, 1999.

Randall, Catharine. "Structuring Protestant Scriptural Space in Sixteenth-Century Catholic France." *Sixteenth Century Journal* 25(2) (1994): 341–352.

Raphael, Melissa. *Introducing Thealogy: Discourse on the Goddess.* Cleveland, OH: Pilgrim Press, 2000.

"A rare moment of peace for Robinson Jeffers." *Life,* February 2, 1962.

Rawson, Michael. *Eden on the Charles: The Making of Boston.* Cambridge, MA: Harvard University Press, 2010.

Reich, Charles A. "Forward: 'He Shall Not Pass This Way Again.'" In *"He Shall Not Pass This Way Again": The Legacy of Justice William O. Douglas.* Edited by Stephen L. Wasby. Pittsburgh, PA: University of Pittsburgh Press, 1990.

Reisner, Christian F. *Roosevelt's Religion.* New York: Abingdon Press, 1922.

Reisner, Marc. *Cadillac Desert: The American West and Its Disappearing Water.* New York: Viking, 1986.

Renehan, Edward. *John Burroughs: An American Naturalist.* Post Mills, VT: Chelsea Green, 1992.

Reps, John William. *Cities of the American West: A History of Frontier Urban Planning.* Princeton, NJ: Princeton University Press, 1979.

Richardson, Bob. "A Biography of Annie Dillard." *Annie Dillard—Official Website.* 2010, www.anniedillard.com/biography-by-bob-richardson.html.

Richardson, R. C. *Puritanism in North-West England: a regional study of the Diocese of Chester to 1642.* Manchester, UK: University of Manchester Press, 1972.

Richardson, Robert D. *Henry Thoreau: A Life of the Mind.* Berkeley: University of California Press, 1986.

Ricks, Joel. *Forms and Methods of Early Mormon Settlement in Utah and the Surrounding Region, 1847 to 1877.* Logan: Utah State University Press, 1964.

Righter, Robert W. *The Battle Over Hetch Hetchy: America's Most Controversial Dam and the Birth of Modern Environmentalism.* New York: Oxford University Press, 2005.

Ringe, Donald A. "Horatio Greenough, Archibald Alison and the Functionalist Theory of Art." *College Art Journal* 19 (Summer 1960): 314–321.

Rivet, Bernard. "Réflexions sur quelques aspects économiques de l'œuvre de Bernard Palissy." In *Bernard Palissy, 1510–1590: l'écrivain, le réformé, le céramiste: journées d'études 29 et 30 juin 1990, Saintes, Abbaye-aux-dames: actes du colloque.* Edited by Frank Lestringant. Paris: Editions interuniversitaires, 1992.

Robertson, Bruce. *Marsden Hartley.* New York: Abrams, 1995.

Robertson, David. *West of Eden: A History of the Art and Literature of Yosemite.* Yosemite National Park, CA: Yosemite Natural History Association, 1984.

Robinson, Charles E. *Maltbie Davenport Babcock, A Reminiscent Sketch and Memorial.* New York: Revell, 1904.

Robinson, Christopher C. "Nature, Value, Duty: Life on Earth with Holmes Rolston, III." *Journal of Agricultural and Environmental Ethics* 21 (2008): 477–484.

Robinson, David M. "'Unchronicled Nations': Agrarian Purpose and Thoreau's Ecological Knowing." *Nineteenth-Century Literature* 48(3) (Dec. 1993): 326–340.

Robinson, Phyllis C. *Willa: the Life of Willa Cather.* Garden City, NY: Doubleday, 1983.

Rodgers, Andrew Denny, III. *Bernhard Eduard Fernow: A Story of North American Forestry.* Princeton, NJ: Princeton University Press, 1951.

Ronald, Ann. *The New West of Edward Abbey.* Albuquerque: University of New Mexico Press, 1982.

Roosevelt, Theodore. "John Muir: An Appreciation." *The Outlook,* January 6, 1915.

Roper, Laura Wood. *FLO: A Biography of Frederick Law Olmsted.* Baltimore, MD: Johns Hopkins University Press, 1973.

Roque, Oswaldo Rodriguez. "'The Oxbow' by Thomas Cole: Iconography of an American Landscape Painting." *Metropolitan Museum Journal* 17 (1982): 63–73.

Rorty, James. "In Major Mold." *New York Herald and Tribune Books,* March 1, 1925.

Rose, Aubrey, ed. *Judaism and Ecology.* London: Cassell, 1992.

Rosenfeld, Paul. *Port of New York: Essays on Fourteen American Moderns.* Urbana: University of Illinois Press, 1961.

Rosenmeier, Rosamond R. *Anne Bradstreet Revisited.* Boston: Twayne, 1991.

Rosenmeier, Rosamond R. "The Wounds Upon Bathsheba: Anne Bradstreet's Prophetic Art." In *Puritan Poets and Poetics: Seventeenth-Century American Poetry in Theory and Practice.* Edited by Peter White. University Park: Pennsylvania State University Press, 1985.

Rosenstock, Morton. *Louis Marshall, Defender of Jewish Rights*. Detroit, MI: Wayne State University Press, 1965.

Rosenzweig, Roy, and Elizabeth Blackmar. *The Park and the People: A History of Central Park*. Ithaca, NY: Cornell University Press, 1992.

Rosowski, Susan J. *Willa Cather's Ecological Imagination*. Lincoln: University of Nebraska Press, 2003.

Roszak, Theodore. "Ecopsychology and the Deconstruction of Whiteness: An Interview with Carl Anthony." In *Ecopsychology: Restoring the Earth, Healing the Mind*. Edited by Theodore Roszak, Mary E. Gomes, and Allen D. Kanner. San Francisco: Sierra Club Books, 1995.

Roth, Randolph A. *The Democratic Dilemma: Religion, Reform, and the Social Order in the Connecticut River Valley of Vermont, 1791–1850*. Cambridge: Cambridge University Press, 1987.

Rowland, Lawrence Sanders, Alexander Moore, and George C. Rogers. *The History of Beaufort County, South Carolina*. Vol. 1. Columbia: University of South Carolina Press, 1996.

Ruether, Rosemary Radford. "Sisters of Earth: Religious Women and Ecological Spirituality." Witness, May 2000. http://thewitness.org/archive/may2000/may.ruether.html.

Runte, Alfred. *National Parks: The American Experience*. Lincoln: University of Nebraska Press, 1979.

Rupke, Nicolaas A. *Alexander von Humboldt. A Metabiography*. Corrected ed. Chicago: University of Chicago Press, 2008.

Ruse, Michael. "The Faith of an Evolutionist." *Politics and Life Sciences* 18(2) (1999): 347–349.

Ruse, Michael. *Mystery of Mysteries: Is Evolution a Social Construction?* Cambridge, MA: Harvard University Press, 1999.

Rybczynski, Witold. *A Clearing in the Distance: Frederick Law Olmsted and America in the Nineteenth Century*. New York: Scribner, 1999.

Ryder, Mary R. "Willa Cather as Nature Writer: A Cry in the Wilderness." In *Such News of the Land: U.S. Women Nature Writers*. Edited by Thomas S. Edwards and Elizabeth A. De Wolfe. Hanover, NH: University Press of New England, 2001.

Sachs, Aaron. *The Humboldt Current: Nineteenth-Century Exploration and the Roots of American Environmentalism*. New York: Viking, 2006.

Saltmarsh, John A. *Scott Nearing: An Intellectual Biography*. Philadelphia: Temple University Press, 1991.

Sanford, Charles L. "The Concept of the Sublime in the Works of Thomas Cole and William Cullen Bryant." *American Literature* 28(4) (January 1957): 434–448.

Sargent, Shirley. *Galen Clark, Yosemite Guardian*. San Francisco: Sierra Club, 1964.

Sassi, Jonathan D. *A Republic of Righteousness: The Public Christianity of the Post-Revolutionary New England Clergy*. Oxford: Oxford University Press, 2001.

Sattelmeyer, Robert. *Thoreau's Reading: A Study in Intellectual History with Bibliographical Catalogue*. Princeton, NJ: Princeton University Press, 1988.

Sattelmeyer, Robert. "*Walden:* Climbing the Canon." In *More Day to Dawn: Thoreau's Walden for the Twenty-First Century*. Edited by Sandra Harbert Petrulionis and Laura Dassow Walls. Amherst: University of Massachusetts Press, 2007.

Sayce, R. A. *The French Biblical Epic in the Seventeenth Century*. Oxford: Oxford University Press, 1955.

Schaffer, Kristen, and Paul Rocheleau. *Daniel H. Burnham: Visionary Architect and Planner*. New York: Rizzoli, 2003.

Schapsmeier, Edward L., and Frederick H. Schapsmeier. *Henry A. Wallace of Iowa: The Agrarian Years, 1910–1940*. Ames: Iowa State University Press, 1968.

Scheick, William J. *Design in Puritan American Literature*. Lexington: University Press of Kentucky, 1992.

Scheifers, Bernhard. *On the "Sentiment for Nature" in Milton's Poetical Works*. Eisleben, Ger.: Ernst Schneider, 1901.

Scheper, George L. "The Reformist Vision of Frederick Law Olmsted and the Poetics of Park Design." *New England Quarterly* 62 (September 1989): 369–402.

Schmaltz, Norman J. "Raphael Zon: Forest Researcher." Part 1, *Journal of Forest History* 24 (January 1980): 24–39. Part 2, *Journal of Forest History* 24 (April 1980): 86–97.

Schmidt, Leigh Eric. *Restless Souls: The Making of American Spirituality*. San Francisco: HarperSanFrancisco, 2005.

Schneider, Richard J. *Thoreau's Sense of Place: Essays in American Environmental Writing*. Iowa City: University of Iowa Press, 2000.

Schreiner, Susan Elizabeth. *The Theater of His Glory: Nature and the Natural Order in the Thought of John Calvin*. Durham, NC: Labyrinth Press, 1991.

Schuyler, David. *Apostle of Taste: Andrew Jackson Downing, 1815–1852*. Baltimore, MD: Johns Hopkins University Press, 1996.

Schuyler, David. *The New Urban Landscape: The Redefinition of City Form in Nineteenth-Century America*. Baltimore, MD: Johns Hopkins University Press, 1986.

Schwartz, Eilon. "*Bal Tashchit:* A Jewish Environmental Precept." *Environmental Ethics* 18 (Winter 1997): 355–374.

Schweitzer, Ivy. *The Work of Self-Representation: Lyric Poetry in Colonial New England*. Chapel Hill: University of North Carolina Press, 1991.

Scott, David C., and Brendan Murphy. *The Scouting Party: Pioneering and Preservation, Progressivism and Preparedness in the Making of the Boy Scouts of America*. Irving, TX: Red Honor Press, 2010.

Scott, Donald M. *From Office to Profession: The New England Ministry, 1750–1850*. Philadelphia: University of Pennsylvania Press, 1978.

Scully, Vincent, Jr. *The Shingle Style and the Stick Style: Architectural Theory and Design from Downing to the Origins of Wright*. Rev. ed. New Haven, CT: Yale University Press, 1971.

Seaman, Donna. "Adult Books: Nonfiction: *The Serpents of Paradise.*" *Booklist* 91(13) (March 1995): 1173.

Sears, John F. *Sacred Places: American Tourist Attractions in the Nineteenth Century.* New York: Oxford University Press, 1989.

Secord, James A. "Newton in the Nursery: Tom Telescope and the Philosophy of Tops and Balls." *History of Science* 23 (1985): 127–151.

Secrest, Meryle. *Frank Lloyd Wright.* New York: Knopf, 1992.

Segerstråle, Ullica Christina Olofsdotter. *Defenders of the Truth: The Battle for Science in the Sociobiology Debate and Beyond.* Oxford: Oxford University Press, 2000.

Sellin, David. *American Art in the Making: Preparatory Studies for Masterpieces of American Painting, 1800–1900.* Washington, DC: Smithsonian Institution Press, 1976.

Sergeant, John. *Frank Lloyd Wright's Usonian Houses: The Case for Organic Architecture.* New York: Whitney Library of Design, 1976.

Sernett, Milton C. *Bound for the Promised Land: African American Religion and the Great Migration.* Durham, NC: Duke University Press, 1997.

Shankland, Robert. *Steve Mather of the National Parks.* 3rd ed. New York: Knopf, 1970.

Sharp, Dallas Lore. *The Seer of Slabsides.* Boston: Houghton Mifflin, 1921.

Shawcross, John T. *John Milton and Influence: Presence in Literature, History, and Culture.* Pittsburgh, PA: Duquesne University Press, 1991.

Sherkat, Darren E., and Christopher G. Ellison. "Structuring the Religion-Environment Connection: Identifying Religious Influences on Environmental Concern and Activism." *Journal for the Scientific Study of Religion* 46(1) (March 2007): 71–85.

Sherr, Lynn. *America the Beautiful: The Stirring True Story Behind Our Nation's Favorite Song.* New York: Public Affairs, 2001.

Short, C. Brant. *Ronald Reagan and the Public Lands: America's Conservation Debate, 1979–1984.* College Station: Texas A & M University Press, 1989.

Sicherman, Barbara. *Alice Hamilton: A Life in Letters.* Urbana: University of Illinois Press, 2003.

Silver, Timothy. *A New Face on the Countryside: Indians, Colonists, and Slaves in South Atlantic Forests, 1500–1800.* Cambridge: Cambridge University Press, 1990.

Silverman, Kenneth. *The Life and Times of Cotton Mather.* New York: Harper & Row, 1984.

Simon, James F. *Independent Journey: The Life of William O. Douglas.* New York: Harper & Row, 1980.

Simon, Robin. *Hogarth, France and British Art: The Rise of the Arts in 18th-Century Britain.* London: Hogarth Arts, 2007.

Singer, Peter. *Ethics into Action: Henry Spira and the Animal Rights Movement.* Lanham, MD: Rowman & Littlefield, 1998.

"Sisters of the Earth." *Earthkeeping News: A Newsletter of the North American Coalition for Christianity and Ecology* 8(6) (September/October 1999). www.nacce.org/1999/Earthsibs.html.

Slade, Nancy. "Biography of John Ormsbee Simonds, 1913–2005." The Cultural Landscape Foundation Website. www.tclf.org/pioneer/john-ormsbee-simonds/biography-john-ormsbee-simonds.

Sligh, Michael and Thomas Cierpka. "Organic Values." In *Organic Farming: An International History.* Edited by William Lockeretz. Wallingford, UK: CAB International, 2007.

Smallwood, William Martin, and Mabel Sarah Coon Smallwood. *Natural History and the American Mind.* New York: Columbia University Press, 1941.

Smith, Brett H. "Reversing the Curse: Agricultural Millennialism at the Illinois Industrial University." *Church History* 73(4) (December 2004): 759–791.

Smith, Carl S. *The Plan of Chicago: Daniel Burnham and the Remaking of the American City.* Chicago: University of Chicago Press, 2006.

Smith, Elwyn A. *The Presbyterian Ministry in American Culture, A Study in Changing Concepts, 1700–1900.* Philadelphia: Westminster Press, 1962.

Smith, Henry Nash. *Virgin Land: The American West as Symbol and Myth.* Cambridge, MA: Harvard University Press, 1950.

Smith, Pamela H. "Giving Voice to Hands: The Articulation of Material Literacy in the Sixteenth Century." In *Popular Literacy: Studies in Cultural Practices and Poetics.* Edited by John Trimbur. Pittsburgh, PA: University of Pittsburgh Press, 2001.

Smith, Ryan K. "The Cross: Church Symbol and Contest in Nineteenth-Century America." *Church History* 70 (Dec. 2001): 705–734.

Sobel, Mechal. *Trabelin' on: The Slave Journey to an Afro-Baptist Faith.* Westport, CT: Greenwood Press, 1979.

Socolofsky, Homer Edward, and Allan B. Spetter. *The Presidency of Benjamin Harrison.* Lawrence: University Press of Kansas, 1987.

Sorin, Gerald. *The Prophetic Minority: American Jewish Immigrant Radicals, 1880–1920.* Bloomington: Indiana University Press, 1985.

SouthWest Organizing Project editors. *Intel Inside New Mexico: A Case Study of Environmental and Economic Injustice.* Albuquerque, NM: SouthWest Organizing Project, 1995.

Sowards, Adam M. *The Environmental Justice: William O. Douglas and American Conservation.* Corvallis: Oregon State University Press, 2009.

Spiro, Jonathan Peter. *Defending the Master Race: Conservation, Eugenics, and the Legacy of Madison Grant.* Burlington: University of Vermont Press, 2009.

Sprague, Marshall. *Massacre: the Tragedy at White River.* Boston: Little, Brown, 1957.

Spring, Justin. *Fairfield Porter: A Life in Art.* New Haven, CT: Yale University Press, 2000.

Squires, Vernon Purinton. "Milton's Treatment of Nature." *Modern Language Notes* 9 (Dec. 1894): 227–327.

Stanford, Ann. *Ann Bradstreet: The Worldly Puritan.* New York: Franklin, 1974.

Stasz, Clarice. *The Rockefeller Women: Dynasty of Piety, Privacy, and Service.* New York: St. Martin's, 1995.

Steen, Harold K. "The Beginning of the National Forest System." In *American Forests: Nature, Culture, and Politics.* Edited by Char Miller. Lawrence: University Press of Kansas, 1997.

Steen, Harold K. *The U.S. Forest Service: A History.* Durham, NC: Forest History Society in association with University of Washington Press, 2004.

Steinberg, Theodore. *Down to Earth: Nature's Role in American History.* New York: Oxford University Press, 2013.

Stell, Christopher. "Puritan and Nonconformist Meetinghouses in England." In *Seeing Beyond the Word: Visual Arts and the Calvinist Tradition.* Edited by Paul Corby Finney. Grand Rapids, MI: Eerdmans, 1999.

Stephens, Lester D. *Science, Race, and Religion in the American South: John Bachman and the Charleston Circle of Naturalists, 1815–1895.* Chapel Hill: University of North Carolina Press, 2000.

Stephens, Randall J. *The Fire Spreads: Holiness and Pentecostalism in the American South.* Cambridge, MA: Harvard University Press, 2008.

Stevens Arroyo, Antonio M., and Gilbert Cadena, eds. *Old Masks, New Faces: Religion and Latino Identities.* New York: Bildner Center for Western Hemisphere Studies, 1995.

Stewart, Mart. "Slavery and the Origins of African American Environmentalism." In *"To Love the Wind and the Rain": African Americans and Environmental History.* Edited by Dianne D. Glave and Mark Stoll. Pittsburgh, PA: University of Pittsburgh Press, 2006.

Stieglitz, Alfred, and John Szarkowski. *Alfred Stieglitz at Lake George.* New York: Museum of Modern Art, 1995.

Stinner. Deborah H. "The Science of Organic Farming." In *Organic Farming: An International History.* Edited by William Lockeretz. Wallingford, UK: CAB International, 2007.

Stoll, Mark. "Les influences religieuses sur le mouvement écologiste français." In *Une protection de l'environnement à la française?: (XIXe–XXe siècles).* Edited by Charles-François Mathis and Jean-François Mouhot. Seyssel, France: Champ Vallon, 2013.

Stoll, Mark. "Milton in Yosemite: *Paradise Lost* and the National Parks Idea." *Environmental History* 13 (April 2008): 237–274.

Stoll, Mark. *Protestantism, Capitalism, and Nature in America.* Albuquerque: University of New Mexico Press, 1997.

Stoll, Mark. *Rachel Carson's "Silent Spring," A Book That Changed the World.* Online exhibition. Environment & Society Portal. www.environmentandsociety.org/exhibitions/silent-spring/overview.

Stoll, Mark. "'Sagacious' Bernard Palissy: Pinchot, Marsh, and the Connecticut Origins of Conservation." *Environmental History* 16 (January 2011): 4–37.

Stoll, Steven. *Larding the Lean Earth: Soil and Society in Nineteenth-Century America.* New York: Hill and Wang, 2002.

Stoller, Ezra. *Frank Lloyd Wright's Taliesin West*. New York: Princeton Architectural Press, 1999.

Stone, John Timothy. *Footsteps in a Parish: An Appreciation of Maltbie Davenport Babcock As a Pastor*. New York: Scribner, 1908.

Stradling, David. *Making Mountains: New York City and the Catskills*. Seattle: University of Washington Press, 2007.

Stratton, David H. *Tempest Over Teapot Dome: The Story of Albert B. Fall*. Norman: University of Oklahoma Press, 1998.

Strauss, David. "Toward a Consumer Culture: 'Adirondack Murray' and the Wilderness Vacation." *American Quarterly* 39 (Summer 1987): 270–286.

Street, Richard Steven, and Samuel Orozco. *Organizing for Our Lives: New Voices from Rural Communities*. Portland, OR: NewSage Press and California Rural Legal Assistance, 1992.

Sully, Susan. "Points of View." *Art & Antiques* 28(5) (May 2005): 60–62.

Sutter, Paul. *Driven Wild: How the Fight against Automobiles Launched the Modern Wilderness Movement*. Seattle: University of Washington Press, 2002.

Sweeney, Gray. "The Advantages of Genius and Virtue: Thomas Cole's Influence, 1848–58." In *Thomas Cole: Landscape into History*. Edited by William H. Truettner and Alan Wallach. New Haven, CT: Yale University Press, 1994.

Swift, David Everett. *Black Prophets of Justice: Activist Clergy Before the Civil War*. Baton Rouge: Louisiana State University Press, 1989.

Synan, Vinson. *The Holiness-Pentecostal Tradition: Charismatic Movements in the Twentieth Century*. Grand Rapids, MI: Eerdmans, 1997.

Szasz, Ferenc Morton. *The Divided Mind of Protestant America, 1880–1930*. Tuscaloosa: University of Alabama Press, 1982.

Tabrum, Arthur H. *Religious Beliefs of Scientists*. New and enl. ed. London: Hunter & Longhurst, 1913.

Tanner, C.B. and R.W. Simonson. "Franklin Hiram King—Pioneer Scientist." *Soil Science Society of America Journal* 57(1) (January–February 1993): 286–292.

Taylor, David. *South Carolina Naturalists: An Anthology, 1700–1860*. Columbia: University of South Carolina Press, 1998.

Taylor, Dorceta. "Women of Color, Environmental Justice, and Ecofeminism." In *Ecofeminism: Women, Culture, Nature*. Edited by Karen Warren. Bloomington: Indiana University Press, 1997.

Taylor, George Coffin. *Milton's Use of Du Bartas*. Cambridge, MA: Harvard University Press, 1934.

Teichgraeber, Richard F. *Sublime Thoughts/Penny Wisdom: Situating Emerson and Thoreau in the American Market*. Baltimore, MD: Johns Hopkins University Press, 1995.

Terrie, Philip G. "'Imperishable Freshness': Culture, Conservation, and the Adirondack Park." *Forest & Conservation History* 37 (July 1993): 132–141.

Thomas, Keith. *Man and the Natural World: A History of the Modern Sensibility.* New York: Pantheon Books, 1983.

Tilley, Arthur. *The Literature of the French Renaissance.* Vol. 2. Cambridge: Cambridge University Press, 1904.

Tobias, Henry. "Robert J. Nordhaus." *Legacy: Newsletter of the New Mexico Jewish Historical Society,* March 2007, 10.

Tolles, Frederick B. "Emerson and Quakerism." *American Literature* 10 (May 1938): 142–165.

Tomory, Peter. *The Life and Art of Henry Fuseli.* New York: Praeger, 1972.

Toussaint-Samat, Maguelonne. *A History of Food.* Expanded edition. Translated by Anthea Bell. Chichester, UK: Wiley-Blackwell, 2009.

Tracy, Patricia J. *Jonathan Edwards, Pastor: Religion and Society in Eighteenth-Century Northampton.* New York: Hill and Wang, 1980.

Trani, Eugene P. "Hubert Work and the Department of the Interior, 1923–28." *Pacific Northwest Quarterly* 61(1) (Jan. 1970): 31–40.

Tropman, John E. *The Catholic Ethic in American Society: An Exploration of Values.* San Francisco: Jossey-Bass, 1995.

True, Alfred Charles. *A History of Agricultural Education in the United States 1785–1925.* Reprint. New York: Arno, 1969.

True, Alfred Charles. *A History of Agricultural Experimentation and Research in the United States, 1607–1925: Including a History of the United States Department of Agriculture.* Washington, DC: US Department of Agriculture, 1937.

Trumbull, Benjamin. *A Complete History of Connecticut, Civil and Ecclesiastical, from the Emigration of its First Planters from England, in the Year 1630, to the Year 1764; and to the Close of the Indian Wars.* Vol. 1. New Haven, CT: Maltby, Goldsmith, and Samuel Wadsworth, 1818.

Trumbull, J. Hammond, ed. *The Memorial History of Hartford County, Connecticut, 1633–1884.* Boston: Osgood, 1886.

Trumbull, James Russell, and Seth Pomeroy. *History of Northampton, Massachusetts, From Its Settlement in 1654.* Vol. 1. Northampton, MA: Gazette, 1898.

Tuchman, Maurice, ed. *The Spiritual in Art: Abstract Painting 1890–1985.* New York: Abbeville Press, 1986.

Tucker, Mary Evelyn. "Thomas Berry and The New Story: An Introduction to the Work of Thomas Berry." In *The Intellectual Journey of Thomas Berry: Imagining the Earth Community.* Edited by Heather Eaton. Lanham, MD: Lexington Books, 2014.

Tucker, Mark. "Of Men and Mountains: Ives in the Adirondacks." In *Charles Ives and His World.* Edited by J. Peter Burkholder. Princeton: Princeton University Press, 1996.

Tuckerman, Henry T. *Book of the Artists: American Artist Life.* New York: Putnam, 1867.

Twombly, Robert C. *Frank Lloyd Wright, His Life and His Architecture.* New York: Wiley, 1979.

Udall, Sharyn R. "Beholding the Epiphanies: Mysticism and the Art of Georgia O'Keeffe." In *From the Faraway Nearby: Georgia O'Keeffe as Icon.* Edited by Christopher Merrill and Ellen Bradbury. Reading, MA: Addison-Wesley, 1992.

Underwood, T. L. "Quakers and the Royal Society of London in the Seventeenth Century." *Notes and Records of the Royal Society of London* 31(1) (1976): 133–150.

Ure, James W. *Leaving the Fold: Candid Conversations with Inactive Mormons.* Salt Lake City, UT: Signature Books, 1999.

Van Berkel, Klaas, and Arjo Vanderjagt. Introduction to *The Book of Nature in Early Modern and Modern History.* Edited by Klaas van Berkel and Arjo Vanderjagt. Leuven: Peeters, 2006.

Van Dyke, Tertius. *Henry Van Dyke: A Biography.* New York: Harper, 1935.

Verrill, Dorothy Lord. *Maltby-Maltbie Family History.* Newark, NJ: Maltbie, 1916.

Wacker, Grant. *Heaven Below: Early Pentecostals and American Culture.* Cambridge, MA: Harvard University Press, 2001.

Wadsworth, Alfred P., and Julia De Lacy Mann. *The Cotton Trade and Industrial Lancashire, 1600–1780.* [Manchester, UK]: Manchester University Press, 1931.

Walker, George Leon. Prefatory note to Daniel Wadsworth, *Diary of the Rev. Daniel Wadsworth, Seventh Pastor of the First Church of Christ in Hartford.* Hartford, CT: Case, Lockwood & Brainard, 1894.

Wallach, Alan. "Making a Picture of the View from Mount Holyoke." *Bulletin of the Detroit Institute of Arts* 66(1) (1990): 35–46.

Wallach, Alan. "Thomas Cole: Landscape and the Course of American Empire." In *Thomas Cole: Landscape into History.* Edited by William H. Truettner and Alan Wallach. New Haven, CT: Yale University Press, 1994.

Walls, Laura Dassow. *Seeing New Worlds: Henry David Thoreau and Nineteenth-Century Natural Science.* Madison: University of Wisconsin Press, 1995.

Walls, Laura Dassow. *The Passage to Cosmos: Alexander Von Humboldt and the Shaping of America.* Chicago: University of Chicago Press, 2009.

Ward, Gerald W. R., and William N. Hosley Jr., eds. *The Great River: Art & Society of the Connecticut Valley, 1635–1820.* Hartford, CT: Wadsworth Atheneum, 1985.

Warner, Charles Dudley. "An Unfinished Biography of the Artist." In *Frederic Edwin Church.* Edited by Franklin Kelly. Washington, DC: National Gallery of Art, 1989.

Warren, James Perrin. *John Burroughs and the Place of Nature.* Athens: University of Georgia Press, 2006.

Watkins, T. H. *Righteous Pilgrim: The Life and Times of Harold L. Ickes, 1874–1952.* New York: Holt, 1990.

Weeks, James Powell. "George Washington Atherton and the Creation of the Hatch Act." *Pennsylvania History* 56 (October 1989): 299–317.

Weir, Jack. "Holmes Rolston III, 1932–." In *Fifty Key Thinkers on the Environment.* Edited by Joy A. Palmer. London: Routledge, 2001.

Weiss, Ila. *Poetic Landscape: The Art and Experience of Sanford R. Gifford.* Newark: University of Delaware Press, 1987.

Wencelius, Léon. *L'Esthétique de Calvin*. Paris: Société d'Edition "Les Belles Lettres," 1937.

Westbrook, Perry D. *John Burroughs*. New York: Twayne, 1974.

Westerbeck, Colin. "Ansel Adams: the Man and the Myth." In *Ansel Adams: New Light: Essays on His Legacy and Legend*. Edited by Michael Read. San Francisco: The Friends of Photography, 1993.

Wheaton, Rodd L. "Architecture of Yellowstone: A Microcosm of American Design." *Yellowstone Science* 8(4) (Fall 2000): 14–19.

Whelan, Richard. *Alfred Stieglitz: A Biography*. Boston: Little, Brown, 1995.

White, Damian F. *Bookchin: A Critical Appraisal*. London: Pluto Press, 2008.

White, Elizabeth Wade. *Anne Bradstreet: "The Tenth Muse."* New York: Oxford University Press, 1971.

White, Horace. *The Life of Lyman Trumbull*. Boston: Houghton Mifflin, 1913.

White, Ronald C., and Charles Howard Hopkins. *The Social Gospel: Religion and Reform in Changing America*. Philadelphia: Temple University Press, 1976.

Whitfield, Stephen J. *Scott Nearing: Apostle of American Radicalism*. New York: Columbia University Press, 1974.

Whitfield, Stephen J. *Voices of Jacob, Hands of Esau: Jews in American Life and Thought*. Hamden, CT: Archon Books, 1984.

Whitford, Kathryn, and Philip Whitford. "Timothy Dwight's Place in Eighteenth-Century American Science." *Proceedings of the American Philosophical Society* 114 (Feb. 16, 1970): 60–71.

Wider, Sarah Ann. *The Critical Reception of Emerson: Unsettling All Things*. Rochester, NY: Camden House, 2000.

Wigger, John H. *American Saint: Francis Asbury and the Methodists*. Oxford: Oxford University Press, 2009.

Wight, Frederick Stallknecht. *Arthur G. Dove*. Berkeley: University of California Press, 1958.

Wilcox, Earley Vernon, and Flora H. Wilson. *Tama Jim*. Boston: Stratford, 1930.

Willard, James F., ed. *The Union Colony at Greeley, Colorado, 1869–1871*. Boulder, CO: Robinson, 1918.

"William B. Greeley." *Biographical Record of the Graduates and Former Students of the Yale Forest School*. New Haven, CT: Yale Forest School, 1913.

Williams, Arnold. *The Common Expositor: An Account of the Commentaries on Genesis 1527–1633*. Chapel Hill: University of North Carolina Press, 1948.

Williams, Roger L. *The Origins of Federal Support for Higher Education: George W. Atherton and the Land-Grant College Movement*. University Park: Pennsylvania State University Press, 1991.

Williams, Stephen W. *The Genealogy and History of the Family of Williams in America, More Particularly of the Descendants of Robert Williams of Roxbury*. Greenfield, CT: Merriam & Mirick, 1847.

Wills, Gregory A. *Democratic Religion: Freedom, Authority, and Church Discipline in the Baptist South, 1785–1900*. New York: Oxford University Press, 1997.

Willson, Lillian M. *Forest Conservation in Colonial Times*. St. Paul: Forest Products History Foundation, 1948.

Wilson, Christopher Kent. "The Landscape of Democracy: Frederic Church's *West Rock, New Haven*." *American Art Journal* 18 (Summer, 1986): 20–39.

Wilson, David A., and Mark G. Spencer. *Ulster Presbyterians in the Atlantic World: Religion, Politics and Identity*. Dublin: Four Courts, 2006.

Wilson, David B. *Seeking Nature's Logic: Natural Philosophy in the Scottish Enlightenment*. University Park: Pennsylvania State University Press, 2009.

Wilson, John Frederick. *Religion and the American Nation: Historiography and History*. Athens: University of Georgia Press, 2003.

Wilson, Kristina. "The Intimate Gallery and the 'Equivalents': Spirituality in the 1920s Work of Stieglitz." *Art Bulletin*, 85(4) (December 2003): 746–768.

Wilson, Leonard G. "Benjamin Silliman: A Biographical Sketch." In *Benjamin Silliman and his Circle: Studies on the Influence of Benjamin Silliman on Science in America: Prepared in Honor of Elizabeth H. Thomson*. Edited by Leonard G. Wilson. New York: Science History Publications, 1979.

Wilson, William H. *The City Beautiful Movement*. Baltimore, MD: Johns Hopkins University Press, 1989.

Winks, Robin W. *Frederick Billings: A Life*. New York: Oxford University Press, 1991.

Winks, Robin W. *Laurance S. Rockefeller: Catalyst for Conservation*. Washington, DC: Island Press, 1997.

Winship, Michael P. *Making Heretics: Militant Protestantism and Free Grace in Massachusetts, 1636–1641*. Princeton, NJ: Princeton University Press, 2002.

Winship, Michael. *Seers of God: Puritan Providentialism in the Restoration and Early Enlightenment*. Baltimore, MD: Johns Hopkins University Press, 1996.

Witt, David L. *Ernest Thompson Seton: The Life and Legacy of an Artist and Conservationist*. Layton, UT: Gibbs Smith, 2010.

Wolfe, Linnie Marsh. *Son of the Wilderness: The Life of John Muir*. New York: Knopf, 1945.

Wood, Joseph S. "'Build, Therefore, Your Own World': The New England Village as Settlement Ideal." *Annals of the Association of American Geographers* 81 (March 1991): 32–50.

Wood, Joseph S. "The New England Village as an American Vernacular Form." *Perspectives in Vernacular Architecture* 2 (1986): 54–63.

Woodbridge, Kenneth. *Princely Gardens: The Origins and Development of the French Formal Style*. New York: Rizzoli, 1986.

Woodbridge, Sally Byrne. *Bernard Maybeck: Visionary Architect*. New York: Abbeville, 1992.

Woodress, James Leslie. *Willa Cather: A Literary Life*. Lincoln: University of Nebraska Press, 1987.

Worster, Donald. *Dust Bowl: The Southern Plains in the 1930s*. New York: Oxford University Press, 1979.

Worster, Donald. *Nature's Economy: A History of Ecological Ideas.* 2nd ed. Cambridge: Cambridge University Press, 1994.

Worster, Donald. *A Passion for Nature: The Life of John Muir.* Oxford: Oxford University Press, 2008.

Worster, Donald. *A River Running West: The Life of John Wesley Powell.* New York: Oxford University Press, 2001.

Wuthnow, Robert. *After Heaven: Spirituality in America Since the 1950s.* Berkeley: University of California Press, 1998.

Zaitlin, Joyce. *Gilbert Stanley Underwood: His Rustic, Art Deco, and Federal Architecture.* Malibu, CA: Pangloss Press, 1989.

Zakin, Susan. *Coyotes and Town Dogs: Earth First! and the Environmental Movement.* New York: Viking, 1993.

Zelov, Chris, and Phil Cousineau. *Design Outlaws on the Ecological Frontier.* Philadelphia: Knossus, 1997.

Picture Credits

FIGURE 1.1. Oil on canvas. 51½" × 76" (130.8 × 193 cm). Metropolitan Museum of Art, gift of Mrs. Russell Sage, 1908 (08.228). Image © The Metropolitan Museum of Art.

FIGURE 1.2. Oil on canvas. 52⅞" × 79¾" (134.3 × 202.6 cm). National Gallery of Art, Ailsa Mellon Bruce Fund, 1971.16.3.

FIGURE 1.3. Oil on canvas. Amon Carter Museum of American Art, Fort Worth, Texas.

FIGURE 1.4. Oil on canvas. 39¾" × 54½" (100.96 × 138.43 cm). © Museum of Fine Arts, Boston, gift of Martha C. Karolik for the M. and M. Karolik Collection of American Paintings, 1815–1865, 47.1188.

FIGURE 1.5. Oil on canvas. 35¾" × 47¾" (90.8 × 121.4 cm). Smithsonian American Art Museum, gift of Mrs. Katie Dean in memory of Minnibel S. and James Wallace Dean and museum purchase through the Smithsonian Institution Collections Acquisition Program 1983.40.

FIGURE 2.1. Oil on canvas. New Britain Museum of American Art, John Butler Talcott Fund, 1950.10.

FIGURE 2.2. Oil on canvas, 40¼" × 60 3/16". Wadsworth Atheneum Museum of Art, Hartford, Connecticut, museum purchase.

FIGURE 2.3. Connecticut Historical Society, Hartford, Connecticut, Maps box 81. Detail.

FIGURE 2.4. Connecticut Historical Society, Hartford, Connecticut. 1956.84.23.

FIGURE 2.5. Connecticut Historical Society, Hartford, Connecticut. 1954.5.96.

FIGURE 2.6. Houghton Library, Harvard University. FC5.P1764.563ra.

FIGURE 3.1. Connecticut Historical Society, Hartford, Connecticut, x.1992.137.7.

FIGURE 3.2. Oil on canvas. 40" × 90½" (106.5 × 229.9 cm). Scala/White Images/ Art Resource, New York. Corcoran Gallery, Museum Purchase, Gallery Fund. 76.15.

FIGURE 4.1. Gelatin silver print. 15⅝" × 19 3/16". © The Ansel Adams Publishing Rights Trust. Philadelphia Museum of Art: Gift of Mr. and Mrs. Robert A. Hauslohner, 1976.

FIGURE 4.2. Watercolor and black chalk on off-white watercolor paper. 15½" × 22". Acquired 1937. Phillips Collection, Washington, DC. © 2014 Estate of John Marin / Artists Rights Society (ARS), New York.

FIGURE 4.3. Oil on canvas mounted to board. 24¼" × 36¼" (61.6 × 92.1 cm). Georgia O'Keeffe Museum. Gift of The Burnett Foundation (1997.06.15). © 2014 Georgia O'Keeffe Museum /Artists Rights Society (ARS), New York.

FIGURE 4.4. Pastel on paper. 458 × 550 mm. The Art Institute of Chicago, Alfred Stieglitz Collection, 1949.533.

FIGURE 4.5. Brooklyn Museum, Dick S. Ramsay Fund, 58.75.

FIGURE 4.6. Oil on canvas. 30" × 36" (76.2 × 91.4 cm). Philadelphia Museum of Art, The Alfred Stieglitz Collection, 1949.

FIGURE 4.7. Coro. Licensed under Creative Commons Attribution-Share Alike 3.0 via Wikimedia Commons.

FIGURE 4.8. Bernard Maybeck Collection, Environmental Design Archives, University of California, Berkeley.

FIGURE 4.9. Records of the National Park Service, Ansel Adams Photographs, 79-G-27C-1.

FIGURE 5.1. Oil on canvas, 16¼" × 25¼". Collection of Saint Mary's College Museum of Art, college purchase, 0-12.

FIGURE 5.2. Oil on canvas. 40½" × 72½". Los Angeles County Museum of Art, A. T. Jergins Bequest, M.71.115.

FIGURE 5.3. Oil on canvas. 24" × 36". Collection of Saint Mary's College Museum of Art, gift of Adrienne Williams, 1973, 0-168.

FIGURE. 5.4. Oil on wood. 23¾" × 28¼". Collection of Saint Mary's College Museum of Art, gift of Celia Tobin Clark, 1949, 0-1.

FIGURE 6.1. Oil on linen, 30" × 36". Courtesy of the artist.

FIGURE 7.1. Oil on canvas, 30⅝" × 54⅛" (77.8 × 137.5 cm). Daniel J. Terra Collection, 1999.57. Terra Foundation for American Art, Chicago/Art Resource, New York.

FIGURE 7.2. Pencil on tracing paper. 27" × 36". © 2014 Frank Lloyd Wright Foundation, Scottsdale, AZ/Artists Rights Society (ARS), New York.

FIGURE 8.1. 40" × 35". Courtesy of the artist.

FIGURE 8.2. 40" × 34". Collection of Jack and Jane Shaw. Courtesy of the artist.

FIGURE 8.3. 33½" × 30". Collection of the artist. Courtesy of the artist.

FIGURE 8.4. 21½" × 27". Collection of Keven Lewis. Courtesy of the artist.

FIGURE **8.5.** Photogravure. Library of Congress. Lot 7096, no. 58 [P&P], LC-DIG-ppmsca-11844.

FIGURE **8.6.** Photogravure published in *Camera Work,* No. 12, October 1905. Library of Congress. LC-USZ62-96557.

FIGURE **8.7.** Gelatin silver print. 4⅝" × 3⅝". Alfred Stieglitz Collection, 1949 (49.55.29). Metropolitan Museum of Art. © 2014 Georgia O'Keeffe Museum /Artists Rights Society (ARS), New York.

Index